PENGUIN BOOKS

THE PENGUIN FOOD GUIDE TO INDIA

Charmaine O'Brien is an independent culinary writer, historian and educator. She is the author of *Flavours of Delhi: A Food Lover's Guide*, *Recipes from an Urban Village: A Cookbook from Basti Hazrat Nizamuddin* and *Flavours of Melbourne: A Culinary Biography*. She also teaches Indian cookery; designs and caters special-occasion meals; works with individuals to reconnect them to psychosocial and physical wellness through eating and cookery practices; and writes the blog www.eatingindia.com.

She writes to unravel the world and put it all back together so that all roads lead to food. It is her way of channelling her constant thought of 'what shall I eat next' into something more interesting than excess kilos.

Charmaine is currently working on a book about food in colonial Australia.

THE PENGUIN

FOOD
GUIDE TO
INDIA

CHARMAINE
O'BRIEN

PENGUIN BOOKS

An imprint of Penguin Random House

PENGUIN BOOKS

USA | Canada | UK | Ireland | Australia
New Zealand | India | South Africa | China | Singapore

Penguin Books is part of the Penguin Random House group of companies
whose addresses can be found at global.penguinrandomhouse.com

Published by Penguin Random House India Pvt. Ltd
4th Floor, Capital Tower 1, MG Road,
Gurugram 122 002, Haryana, India

Penguin
Random House
India

First published by Penguin Books India 2013

10 9 8 7 6 5 4 3 2

ISBN 9780143414568

Typeset in Adobe Garamond Pro by Eleven Arts, New Delhi

Printed at Manipal Technologies Limited, India

www.penguin.co.in

MIX
Paper | Supporting
responsible forestry
FSC
www.fsc.org   FSC® C043100

CONTENTS

SOUTH-WESTERN INDIA

SOUTH INDIA

ACKNOWLEDGEMENTS

Atithi devo bhava is an age-old dictum in India. It means that 'the guest is an incarnation of god'. I would like to thank all the people throughout India who have treated me as such in both the personal and professional spheres.

My special thanks to: Kavita Chesetty, Christopher Moore, Kamini Prakash, Kiran and Sunil Chainani, Kinny and Gogi Sandhu, Bhuvan Kumari, Bharti Kumari, Vishu Vardhan Singh, Amrita and Ranjeet Batra, Bunny Gupta, Indira Basu, Rashmi Sawant, Mrs and Mr D. Majithia, Jaiwardhan and Neelu of Sukhdham Koti, Maharani of Wankaner, Vijayan Kannampilly, Maria Teresa Menezes, Chef Parveen Anand, Chef Debashis, Chef Raj Sekhar, Chef Ashwin Shenoy, Chef Shiva, Chef Mohan, Steven Dominic, Jugnal (Jodhpur), Luis Antonio Francisco Novais de Souza, Jack Ajit Sukhija, A. Chandramouli, Johnny Peter, Anand Gopinath, Chef Ajeeth Janardanan, Parveen Sikkander, Malvika, Claire Prest, Diya Kar Hazra, Daleep Akoi, Sunil Chauhan, Meenakshi Meyyappam, Thressi John, Kaumudi Marathe, Mohsina Mukadam, Mini Chandran, Mohammed Hamid and family, Deborah Blah, Atsei Kire, B.K. Singh (Hotel Maurya, Patna), Ajai and Nalani Singh, Divya Singh of Komakhan, Manjali Singh, Mudita Chauhan-Mubayi and Richa Burman.

INTRODUCTION

MY JOURNEY INTO INDIAN FOOD

It seems unbelievable to me now but when I first visited India, back in 1995, I expected that the food I would find here would be exactly the same as I had eaten in Indian restaurants in Australia. After all, each one of those I had dined in had served the same dishes and these tasted much the same in each place—surely this was evidence of the existence of a national Indian cuisine. When I arrived on the subcontinent, I was confident that I was in the land of curry and tandoori chicken; in fact, my initial experiences proved me right. The eateries that a popular guidebook recommended to me, in places such as Delhi, Agra, Jaipur, Jodhpur and Varanasi, served up much the same dishes I had eaten in Indian restaurants back home—only, these were tastier and freshly baked naan cost a pittance compared to what is charged for it outside India.

It was only in the final weeks of this trip that I began to eat from street stalls and eateries not included in my guidebook. I recall entering a restaurant in Hospet (Karnataka) where the signage and menu were in the local language. I had been attracted to it by the sight of its crowded dining room although I had no particular insight into what these patrons might have been eating. I took a seat and almost immediately a plate of rice was placed in front of me, along with bowls of what I took as assorted sauces. I looked around for cutlery; there was none. I observed the people around me and saw that they poured small amounts of the 'sauces' over the rice, mashed it a little with their right hand, rolled it into balls and deftly flicked these into their mouths: I followed suit. I was nowhere near as elegant as the locals but I got the knack and felt quite pleased with myself. Not only was I chuffed with my tangible cultural achievement, the food was a revelation. I had no idea what most of it was yet I had never tasted anything as zingy, as complex, as zesty.

As I traversed India by train—from north to south and back again—I noticed that whenever we pulled into a major station, the food items sold on the platform or hawked by vendors through the train carriages would be quite different from those available at the previous halt. This intrigued me. Added to my other experiences, such as the one in Hospet, this inspired me to want to know more and thus began my exploration into Indian food history, culture and practice. I can still recall what I thought 'Indian food' tasted like before 1995: a singular flavour shared by almost all dishes—no matter what flashy name was given to them—served in a typical Indian restaurant in Australia. It is my memory of this, and of my complicity in accepting it, that made me determined to encourage others to explore India's culinary bounty and use their palates to discover this ancient, complex, multifaceted, fascinating—and sometimes frustrating—land.

To the unknowing, such as my younger self, the homogeneity of menus in Indian restaurants around the world does suggest the existence of a homogeneous 'Indian' cuisine. Such a thing does not exist, however: what does is a culinary landscape so expansive and so finely nuanced that to capture it properly would require an encyclopaedic work. This book is a rather more humble offering.

If we take the time to examine food in a broader context, it can connect us to history, to culture, to the material world. What people eat and how they cook can be a code to a society. Each chapter of this book begins with a condensed history of a particular state and historical detail is interwoven throughout. When I write of regional cuisine, I am concerned with the traditional food of a distinct area, and the history of that area is important because it will have significantly affected the development of that region's cuisine. I have learnt so much about India's history, culture, politics and social idiosyncrasies through my study of Indian food. I have also gained an education in global history as India has long been connected to much of the rest of the world, including my native Australia to which it was physically conjoined many millions of years ago, and to which it became socially reconnected in the eighteenth century as part of the British Empire.

My aim in writing this book was to create a historical and cultural guide to India's regional cuisine, and to recommend places where you—domestic tourist or international visitor—can find distinct regional food and season your travel experiences with some genuine local flavour. In doing so, I hope to inspire you to think more about the food you see and taste because it offers an easily navigated route into a more profound understanding of the diverse cultures that make up India. If you are an armchair traveller or a scholar with an interest in Indian culture and food, you will find this book equally rewarding as it is densely packed with stories and information: I hope that reading it might encourage you to take a trip to taste India.

HOW TO USE THIS BOOK

To research this book I visited every state of India (with the exception of Tripura, Manipur and Mizoram). It was not possible, though, for me to visit every part of each state or to uncover and visit every place that might have been suitable for inclusion in this book. I wanted to create a work that would inspire you to plan your own unique gastronomic explorations. By guiding you through the flavours and foods peculiar to a particular region, I am arming you with the practical tools to become your own culinary archaeologist. I want to encourage you to look around, to ask questions, to taste new foods, to sample dishes you have never heard of and to gather gustatory memories that might just render the culinary clichés of what I call *Menu indicus typicus* unpalatable to you ever after. (As a remedy to this, I have provided a list of regional cookbooks that you could cook from. You can also visit my website at www.eatingindia.com for recipes for many of the dishes mentioned in this book.)

I have eaten at most of the restaurants, cafes, dhabas, guest houses, hotels, etc., which I have recommended in this book but I have also included a handful of recommendations for places that were advocated to me by knowledgeable people, which I could not get to. I do not expect that you will be limited to my recommendations though and will make your own discoveries inspired by what you learn here.

My basic criterion for recommending a place to you was that it served good regional food. There are referrals to exclusive hotels as well as the simplest of eateries, and some of the best regional food can be enjoyed at street stalls. Not all of you will feel comfortable eating from these rudimentary open-air kitchens and will exercise your own discretion in choosing street eats but here are a few points in their favour. The street vendor does not have the option of storing food; he—or she, although street stalls are largely run by men—buys only the food needed for that day; he knows exactly how many serves he will sell and therefore exactly how much food to purchase; he prepares only as many items as are duly sold out . . . and then, the next day, he starts afresh.

I have not experienced any adverse health consequences from eating at street stalls in India but I have after eating in tourist restaurants—during my earlier travels—with menus designed to appeal to people of any nationality or regional identity. As for details of the recommended places, I have provided as much information as possible to help you find them but some don't have phone numbers, some have vague street addresses and, at times, it was challenging to confirm the exact opening hours. If a place does prove a bit hard to locate I hope you will see that as part of your food adventure.

I have not included a price guide as such in the book. As a rule, if I write that a place is 'luxurious', you can expect a meal to cost upwards of 2000 rupees for two people (and probably double that if you have wine or alcoholic drinks other than beer with your meal). If I have described a place as 'simple' or 'homely', it could be anything from 200 to 500 rupees a meal. At a 'basic' place you can expect to pay 50 to 200 rupees. You would have to knock yourself out to spend more than 100 rupees at a street-side stall (unless you are buying for a small group). Some of the guest houses and resorts I recommend include meals in their tariff. Prices do change though and if you want a more accurate estimate you should contact the places directly using the contact information provided.

I recommend that you read this book in its entirety. This seems an obvious directive for an author to make yet I make it for your benefit not for my ego. There are so many cultural connections across the subcontinent that seeing the bigger picture will enhance your culinary explorations no matter where in India you find yourself. I understand though that you might want to focus only on the states you plan to visit; in that case, I recommend you read the chapter on Punjab, in addition to those that are of more immediate interest to you, for it covers India's earliest food history and gives you a basis to work up from. Using the food and general index will help you fill in any gaps.

As a singular national entity, 'India' is only a relatively recent development. For most of its 5000 years of civilization, the subcontinental land mass has been occupied by a patchwork of kingdoms, principalities and chieftainships, each essentially functioning as an independent country. The borders of these varied realms constantly shifted. During the reign of the famed Ashoka in the second century BC, his Mauryan Empire stretched from Afghanistan to Mysore but fell short of capturing the southernmost parts of the Indian peninsula. In the Middle Ages, the Mughal dynasty ruled over similar territory; the far south eluded them too. In the wake of the demise of such epic empires, the previously cohesive territory would splinter into smaller dominions until the next time these were subsumed into the larger realm of another ruler aiming for universal subcontinental dominance. It was the British who came closest to drawing all of India under their imperial diktat after 1857. In 1947, upon granting India freedom from their rule, the British partitioned off the western and eastern flanks of the country to create Pakistan and Bangladesh (East Pakistan until 1971).

I have structured this book around the modern Indian states, most of which did not come into being until after 1950; to do otherwise would have necessitated writing a far more complex historical background for each region than was warranted for this work. The borders of seventeen of the current twenty-eight states were drawn up around a discrete language spoken by the majority of the population of that particular area, and when you have a unique language, you have a unique culture, including a distinct food culture. I acknowledge that there are shortcomings in my presenting India's regional food to you by state, but the configuration of these generally captures a particular traditional culinary culture within its administrative boundaries. *

This book is concerned with exploring what differentiates the various regional cuisines of India, and these differences are addressed in each chapter. There are, however, some universal themes in the development of Indian cuisine and important commonalities in the types of food eaten, cooking techniques deployed and equipment used. To avoid repetition in explaining these, I am going to devote the remainder of this introduction to exploring these themes and describing some of the most important of these shared features before we get under way with our focused explorations.

THE LAND

Before there was history, there was geography. The topography, climate, soil and water—whether available or lacking—determined the types of food that could be gathered, hunted and cultivated in a particular area. It is these indigenous foods—and those that took root so long ago that they qualify as such—that are the foundation on which each distinct regional

* I have taken what looks like an inconsistent naming approach in the text to states with double-barrelled names but I have done this to reflect my experience of how these are named by their inhabitants. For example, Uttar Pradesh is UP but Arunachal Pradesh is Arunachal.

cuisine in India has risen. This raises another point about my use of modern administrative boundaries to delineate provincial food ways: the differences that distinguish a cuisine do not discontinue at state borders but flow contiguously across India and alter incrementally with changes in the natural environment. It was largely geography that determined where people settled and subsequently affected food sources in cultural and social ways to create local food culture.

THE GODS

Hinduism is a complex philosophy and a way of life though it is commonly referred to as a religion. It is one of the world's oldest living spiritual creeds (pre-dating Christianity and Islam by thousands of years) and is the predominant faith in India. There is no prescribed set of common beliefs in Hinduism, but there is an accepted set of 'rules' about food and these have played a fundamental role in shaping Indian cuisine.

In Hindu philosophy, food is divided into three categories:
1. *Sattvic* food is light, bland, almost always vegetarian and white and gold in colour such as milk, rice, honey, grains, nuts and most fruit and vegetables.
2. *Rajasic* food is gold and red in colour and includes heavily spiced and rich dishes, fish, eggs and alcohol.
3. *Tamasic* food is red and black in colour and includes pork, mutton, beef, fish without scales, onion and garlic; it is considered heavy and appealing to the base nature of man.

Intersecting with this is the Hindu social construct of caste. There are four major castes among Hindus:
1. Brahmins: priests, teachers, intellectuals, administrators
2. Kshatriyas: warriors, defenders, rulers
3. Vaishyas: cultivators, traders
4. Shudras: artisans, menial workers

Outside of these castes is a class of people called Dalits—historically, the untouchables—who are meant to perform the so-called 'dirty' work such as tanning and working with leather, cleaning the streets and rubbish removal and sorting.

Brahmins, who act as religious/cultural leaders in this system, were meant to eat sattvic foods, considered most conducive to a spiritual life.

Rajasic foods are believed to arouse passion and were considered best for kings and warriors of the Kshatriya caste. Traders of the Vaishya caste often adopted the dietary habits of Brahmins because they could afford them and wanted to enjoy the spiritual benefits—and social prestige—associated with these. Tamasic foods were avoided by those who could. These food 'rules' were not always strictly adhered to: many coast-dwelling Brahmins enjoyed fish and ingeniously anointed it 'fruit of the sea' to make it fit for them to eat. Kshatriya women were often strict vegetarians, as atonement for and counter to the spiritual weight their men took on by slaying their enemies.

In Hindu philosophy, food has the potential to be spiritually 'polluting'. Brahmins claimed to be at the highest risk of becoming sullied so the rules governing the preparation and serving of their food were complex, and ultimately supported their elevated social position. Since such effort was expended in feeding them, it demonstrated how important they were. A person at the bottom of the social pile, a Shudra, was not considered to warrant such care in his or her cuisine and was expected to be satisfied with whatever they got. But spiritual cleanliness and merit were important to them too, and many in this caste were as careful about what they ate as Brahmins, albeit simpler food.

Two key principles in the Hindu dietetic discourse are those of *kaccha* and *pukka* foods. Kaccha foods are those that cannot be safely eaten outside the home, such as rice, dal and flatbread cooked on an iron plate. Pukka foods are those that can be eaten outside the home without the risk of 'pollution', such as items fried in ghee or prepared from parched grains. The impact of these ancient rules is still evident in India today. Most street foods are fried or prepared from items such as puffed rice to ensure acceptability to the widest number of consumers, and it is a regular practice to pack deep-fried breads called puris for eating outside the home, for example on long journeys or picnics (technically, puris also hold up better over a longer time). On one occasion, some friends in Madhya Pradesh were provisioning me for a long rail journey and they were taken aback by my request for plain-cooked rotis rather than puris to eat on the train as they said this was just not 'done'. Pragmatically, it could be said that Hindu food rules around pollution might have been an early form of food hygiene practice, prescribed to avoid physical food poisoning. In *Curry: A Tale of Cooks and Conquerors*, author Lizzie Collingham succinctly summed up the effect of Hindu food philosophy when she wrote: 'when he [a Hindu man] ate, what he ate, and who he ate with was thus a significant statement of . . . [his] position in the natural, familial and social order'.

THE LOTUS-EATERS

Indian food is widely perceived to be predominantly vegetarian yet less than half of the population is vegetarian, and some estimates put the number as low as 20 per cent. Vegetarianism has been a major influence in the evolution of Indian cuisine, which inarguably contains the world's most diverse and sophisticated selection of vegetarian dishes. However, the abstinence from meat eating has been influenced as much by economics as by spirituality; many Indians simply could not afford to eat meat. As India grows economically, consumption of meat is increasing; what's more, Indian Muslims, the country's second biggest religious population, have always been very fond of meat. Vegetarians, upon discovering these facts, need not feel concerned that the choices available to them will soon be limited. Hindus observe a multitude of spiritual fasts and festival days throughout the year, and the food eaten on these occasions is almost always vegetarian. Even the most committed carnivore will observe this practice, at least in his own domicile: the dark, windowless bars of India are renowned as places where men seek refuge in chicken tikka and chilli chicken from the meat-free regimes enforced by their wives. Because of its association with spirituality, vegetarian food is highly valued and given as much attention as meat-based food. In fact, meat preparations are referred to as 'non-vegetarian'.

THE BUYERS, THE SELLERS

Indian cuisine was 'global' long time before this term was used to describe the food of modern multicultural societies such as the United States and Australia. India's history of trading brought many external influences into its varied cuisines. It would be a rare person who did not associate Indian food with the use of spices yet many of these now used daily by Indian cooks are not indigenous to the country, and came into India via ancient sea and land trade routes to South East Asia, the Middle East, Africa and China. When Europeans finally found their way to India in the late fifteenth century, they were actually the last people to get there despite the way Western history often credits them with the 'discovery of India'. Despite being latecomers the Portuguese and British did bring a multitude of new foods into India, including the chilli.

THE RICH

Socio-economic class structure has also had a considerable effect on the development of Indian cuisine. In hierarchical societies, the food enjoyed by the upper classes is always desirable to the lower. As soon as circumstances permit, the larger populace enthusiastically adopts the foods, dishes and cooking techniques over which the aristocratic class has had exclusive provenance; these become modified in form as they trickle down through the classes and eventually become commonplace. The overtly rich, costly and exotic food that was exclusively enjoyed by the Mughal emperors and their court in the Middle Ages has now become the fodder of millions at the wedding buffets of all Indians but the very poorest. Until a decade ago, it was only the wealthiest Indians who were able to afford to eat 'Western-style' food. Now, with India's rapidly rising collective wealth, the middle classes have the means to eagerly devour pizza, pasta, hamburgers, cheese, chocolate and espresso coffee. This has knocked some of the gloss off imported foods for the elites and they have begun to focus their attention on traditional regional cuisines—in part because of the 'health benefits' reported to be associated with eating these (the strong international trend for eating seasonally and locally is another possible influence in this). This is good news for the culinary explorer because more regional-style dishes and local foods are finding their way into restaurant menus in response to this revived interest.

THE NEO-INDUSTRIAL REVOLUTION

Over the past eighteen years, I have watched as India has undergone a kind of 'industrial revolution' that is altering the country in ways similar to that experienced in Britain in the nineteenth century. There is mass movement away from rural areas, where economic opportunities are limited, into cities (turning places such as Delhi and Mumbai into 'mega cities'). This is pertinent to this book as it was the Industrial Revolution that caused Britain to lose its distinct regional food traditions as people moved away from their native areas into places where they had to make do with whatever food they could find. At the same time, many industrialized 'convenience' foods were introduced and these homogenized generic items were taken up across Britain; not only was this detrimental to a diverse food culture but it often had negative health consequences. I see something similar happening in India now. I do not think there is any immediate danger of India's distinctive food culture homogenizing into one that might end up looking like that found on an 'Indian' restaurant menu but the diversity is slowly being eroded. Many global food corporations are expending large marketing budgets on trying to entice Indians to swap dal and roti for pizza; lassi for fizzy drinks; gulab jamun for chocolate; and local bazaars for supermarkets. My experience has been that by taking an interest in traditional foods in India I have caused some people to look at them afresh and given support to others trying to preserve their unique culinary heritage. Your interest and the application of your tourist dollars—or rupees—in patronizing and preferring places that serve regional foods will do the same.

MYTH BUSTERS

When I tell people in Australia that I teach Indian cooking, it invariably elicits one of the three following responses:
1. 'Oh, curry! I love curry . . . What curry are you making?'
2. 'Oh, I can't eat Indian food, all that chilli!'
3. 'Oh, Indian food is so heavy and rich, all that cream and ghee!'
    Here are my 'myth busting' responses to these myth-induced statements:

Myth 1: It's all curry to me

While what is called 'curry' has come to symbolize Indian food in the West, no dish of that name exists in traditional Indian cuisine. The word has now become widely used on the subcontinent as a descriptor for dishes when these are written in English, but it is a European construct. An example might serve best to demonstrate this: *poosanikai poriyal* and *sakkaraivallikizhanghu vadhakal* are both traditional Tamil preparations. In the cookery book from which I make these dishes these are translated as 'pumpkin curry' and 'sweet potato curry' respectively. I can see no shared word between them in the Tamil version to equate to 'curry'. It is generally accepted that the word 'curry' and its definition as a highly spiced gravy-based dish are both of British invention. How this came about is not agreed upon, however: the most popular theory is that curry derives from the Tamil word *kari*, meaning a sautéed dish of spiced meat or vegetables (depending on who is translating it). An alternative, or prefacing, theory is that the British picked up the word *caril* or *caree*, which the Portuguese had adapted from *kari*, and used it to describe the food that Indians ate with rice. To my mind though, the origins of the word are nowhere near as important as understanding that curry is *not* an Indian dish. In the often-quoted words of the doyenne of Indian food, Madhur Jaffrey, 'the word curry is as degrading to India's great cuisine as "chop suey" was to China's'.*

Myth 2: It's too 'hot'

A statement from someone that they find Indian food very 'spicy' is often accompanied by a look of fear, as what they mean is that they expect it to be hot with chilli. In historical terms, chilli is a relatively new food in India. Admittedly, it has been avidly absorbed but it is not used to make all food blisteringly hot; in fact, there are many Indians who do not enjoy a lot of chilli in their food. In the north, it is ordinary practice for a plate of fresh green chillies to accompany meals. If an individual wants to 'spice' up his food with chilli, they take a bite of one and chew it with a mouthful of food. This allows each person to adjust the level of chilli to suit themselves and the cook is freed from the impossible task of trying to create a level of heat in a dish to suit everyone who eats it. The use of chilli does become more pronounced as you head south but the cooks there know how to tame it by balancing it out with sour ingredients and spices such as fenugreek. That is not to say that there are no 'chilli' hot dishes to be enjoyed. Red chilli powder is a fundamental ingredient in street food around the country—but even this is not always burning hot—and restaurants can often be generous with it in order to avoid being charged with serving 'bland food'. There are many different varieties of chilli in use from the Naga, one of the hottest chillies in the world, to the Kashmiri, a mild variety that is widely used to add colour and a less intense chilli flavour to food.

Myth 3: It's too rich

Authentic Indian food is not universally heavy and fattening, but the food served up in your local Indian restaurant usually is. This is partly because

---

* For a recent example of this, please see 'The Pros and Cons of Curry Powder' by Bee Wilson, *The Telegraph*, 20 March 2011, www.telegraph.co.uk/foodanddrink/8380898/The-pros-and-cons-of-curry-powder.html, last accessed on 5 August 2013.

its genesis is in the opulent imperial food of the Mughals; partly because its cloying richness is what patrons of such restaurants have come to expect of Indian food; and partly because it's easier to cook with a lot of fat. You can certainly eat such food in India, particularly in restaurants or at weddings: Indians too like to treat themselves to the sort of food that they do not ordinarily eat at home. Many domestic cooks in India actually tend towards frugality with fat and oil, using only a little to initially liberate the flavours from spices, afterwards using water as the cooking medium; what they turn out is light, fresh, bright and full of contrasting and complementary flavours and textures.

CULINARY YOGA

A typical Indian meal* aims to balance flavours and textures so as to provide conclusive satisfaction to the diner's taste buds and leave him or her replete and not craving any particular flavour. Indians believe that for a meal to be balanced, there must be six flavours on the plate: bitter, pungent, astringent, sour, salty and sweet. To create textural satiation, soft items like rice are partnered with crunchy ones like papad. In its basic form, an Indian meal comprises a cereal such as rice or wheat-based bread paired with cooked pulses (dal); at least one seasonal vegetable dish; a dairy item such as curd; pieces of raw radish, carrot or cucumber; and a tangy pickle or chutney. A non-vegetarian meal would add a meat- or fish-based dish to this basic platter. Innumerable variations of this basic culinary theme are to be found across India.

Often while writing this book I felt overwhelmed by the enormity of what I had taken on. Whenever I described a dish or a culinary practice, I was all too aware that myriad versions of it exist. In my head, I heard a distinct female Indian voice saying: '*That* is not the way we do it in our community.' In the end, I had to accept that I was going to have to generalize about the food and food culture of India, and that I was never going to capture all the subtle differences that exist. So, dear reader, you

* Class, caste, community, wealth, religion and gender affect what any individual might eat at a meal. When I write of a 'typical meal', my model is that of a middle-class family of Hindu background. Variations on this are noted throughout this book.

should expect to encounter detours and side trips away from the paths I have mapped out for you: enjoy them.

THE COMMONS

Green leafy vegetables

One of the best aspects of doing first-hand research for this book was that I enjoyed many meals in private homes all over India with people from all sorts of backgrounds. I ate with royalty, a Hindu monk, Jain jewellers, politicians, Sufis, farmers, tribals, Rajputs, traders, Brahmins, Sikhs, Paharis, Moplahs, Christians and traditional and modern families. In doing this, I discovered that there is one thing that all Indians eat no matter where they are or who they are and that is green leafy vegetables. They cook these in different ways and with different flavouring ingredients, but all Indians eat these and most eat them every day. Even in places such as Spiti, in the high Himalayas, people collect wild spinach in the summer and dry it so that they can have greens throughout the winter months when snow covers the land and prevents the growth of any vegetables.

Dairy products

Milk has a very important place in the Indian diet. As the product of the 'holy' cow (for devout Hindus), it is believed to bring spiritual as well as nutritional benefits to its consumers. Adult Indians have customarily not drunk a lot of plain milk, and rather altered it into other products for consumption. Milk used in India comes from cows and buffaloes.

CURD

Curd is made by seeding fresh milk, which has been boiled and cooled to room temperature, with a small quantity of curd left over from a previous batch, and leaving it to sit overnight in a warm place. Plain curd is a universal accompaniment to meals in India. It is also used in various sweet and savoury dishes.

BUTTER

Butter was traditionally made in India by churning curd to separate the milk fat from the whey; when produced in this manner, it is called 'white butter' (and is akin to European-style cultured butter). Butter is not widely used in Indian cooking (*see Ghee*) and tends to be added as a garnish to prepared food.

BUTTERMILK

Churning curd to make butter separates the whey from the solid fats; this residual liquid is called buttermilk. It is widely consumed as a drink with meals and used in cooking.

GHEE

To make ghee,* butter is boiled until all the water evaporates and it gives off a nutty aroma. This liquid is then cooled and decanted to separate off any sediment. What remains is pure fat that can be heated to very high temperatures—ghee is traditionally used to fry food—and stored for long periods without refrigeration. In Hindu dietary philosophy, ghee is considered a ritually pure food and food cooked in ghee is safe for anyone to eat; even a few drops of ghee sprinkled on a dish can 'purify' it. Ghee is used to prepare sattvic food and is an essential ingredient in many Indian sweets, particularly in the northern and western parts of the country. Ghee made from buffalo milk is considered superior as it has a higher fat content than that made from cow milk. Ghee is also believed to have medicinal qualities and is prescribed for a wide range of ailments.

PANEER

Paneer (cottage cheese) is made by adding an acid such as lemon juice or vinegar to milk, causing it to split into solids and whey. The solids are gathered in muslin or a perforated container and placed under a weight to push out any remaining liquid and form a spongy block.

KHOYA (*see Varanasi, pp. 87–88*) and CHHENA (*see West Bengal, pp. 128–29*) are other dairy products used across India.

Roti

This is the everyday bread of India, also called chapatti. It is made from unleavened dough of flour and water that is rolled out into thin, flat rounds

---

* The 'Indian' terms used for the foods in this section are Hindi words (some have been naturalized into English)—as it is the official language of India—but there are many other languages in use in the country and different words may be used for the same item across the regions.

the size of a small dinner plate and cooked on a slightly concave iron pan called a tawa. Once the roti is cooked through it can be held over the flame of the fire to make it puff up. Roti is commonly made from *atta* (wholewheat flour) but there are regional variations in which it is prepared from a wide range of grains and legumes.

Dal

Dal is the generic term used in India for legumes/pulses—plants that have pods with tiny rows of seeds inside, and are harvested and dried. Pulses can grow in adverse conditions and still produce an abundant harvest, and are generally inexpensive. A large variety of dals—more than anywhere else in the world—are grown and used in India, and these are the major source of vegetable protein for much of the population. Dals are used to produce an incredible variety of savoury and sweet dishes but these are most typically cooked with water, spices and other flavourings into a potage, which is also called dal. *Urad* dal, red lentils (masoor dal) and chickpeas (chana dal) are among the most widely used pulses in India and the country is the world's biggest producer of these.

Khichri

Indians of all backgrounds have been eating this mildly spiced potage of dal and rice for thousands of years; it is a seminal dish of Indian cuisine.

Spices

Spices are used extensively in cooking throughout India. The use of a particular set of spices, and blends of these, contributes significantly to creating distinct flavours of regional cuisines. Spices used in different dishes can often be very similar. The difference in flavour is arrived at by varying the proportion of these and/or the way the spices are prepared (cooked in oil or dry-roasted) and at which point of the cooking process they are added to the dish. One of the most universally used spices is turmeric powder, made by grinding the dried rhizome of a plant of the ginger family. Turmeric adds an earthy note to food. It is considered to have antiseptic properties and is usually rubbed on fish prior to cooking. When describing dishes throughout the book, I have tended to mention only the spices that are most distinctive in that preparation. Even if I have not listed turmeric, it is likely that it has been used, except in sweet dishes.*

---

* I have not mentioned salt very often either but you can take it as a given in any savoury dish in the book.

'Masala' is a blend of spices. 'Garam masala' typically describes a highly aromatic blend of ground cinnamon, cardamom, cloves, black pepper and cumin. There are as many variations of this as there are cooks in India. Garam masala is often added to a dish just before it is fully cooked.

Papad

A thin, crunchy wafer made from ground dal and flavourings such as cumin, asafoetida, black pepper and chilli. There are over thirty different names for papad all over India.

Gur

Also called jaggery. This ancient sweetener is made by boiling freshly pressed sugar-cane juice until it forms a fudgy solid mass. In the Bengal region, gur is also made from the sap of the date palm and in the south from juice extracted from the bulb-like stem of the flower of the palmyra palm.

Chutney

Chutney is a freshly ground preparation served as a relish with meals. It is made from a vast range of food items including, but in no way limited to, coconut, curd, fruit, vegetables, fresh green herbs and peanuts. Chutney is an Anglicization of the Hindi word *chatni*, and the chutney of cooked fruit, spices, sugar and vinegar eaten in the West is a condensation of all chatni into one singular representation of the genus.

Mutton

The word 'mutton' is used in India to denote goat meat. It came into use during British rule (the word denotes the meat of a mature sheep in the British Isles). The predominantly hot climate of much of India is not conducive to raising sheep, although these woolly beasts are raised in some cooler mountain regions. Sheep meat, where it is available, is also referred to as mutton, but as a general rule when you see 'mutton' on a menu in India read 'goat'.

Karhai

This is a cast-iron or stainless steel pan shaped like a wok, with the addition of a curved handle on either side of the rim, and it is used throughout India. Many regions have their own distinct traditional cooking pots and utensils but many of these are gradually disappearing from use in modern kitchens in favour of more standardized items. Having spent much time in kitchens throughout India I can confidently say that the pressure cooker is the most universal cookware item on the subcontinent.

Thali

This is a circular metal platter with a raised rim on which a complete meal is served. Food is laid out on a thali in a certain order with many of the items, such as dal, served in small bowls (called *katori*s in Hindi). A full meal is also referred to as a thali.

COOKING TECHNIQUES

Grinding

Spices and flavouring ingredients such as onions, garlic, ginger and fresh herbs are commonly prepared for cooking in the traditional Indian kitchen by grinding to a paste. Dal, grains and meats—for preparations such as kebabs, parathas, etc.—are also ground. There are many different sizes, shapes and styles of grinding devices used across India but these are typically made from stone, with the exception of the 'mixie', an electrical appliance that is popularly used to grind foods these days.

Dry and wet dishes

The application of the descriptor 'dry' to a dish in the West would mark it as unappetizing, but this term is used in India to describe sautéed or stir-fried dishes that do not have a sauce. 'Wet' dishes are those that are cooked in a sauce and are commonly described as 'gravies' in India.

Roasted

A 'roasted' preparation in India rarely indicates an item cooked in an oven, as it would in Britain or Australia. In India, to roast something means to fry it in oil or dry-roast over a pan until it is well browned. In one restaurant kitchen, I watched as a batch of 'roast chicken' was prepared by deep-frying it.

Baghar

A tempering of whole spices and seasonings quickly fried in hot oil or ghee and added to a dish as it finishes cooking.

A NOTE ON SPELLINGS

The transliteration of words for food and cooking from various Indian languages into English has resulted in the existence of various spellings, and there is not necessarily a commonly accepted version. In such cases, I have chosen to stick with one consistent spelling throughout the book. When you are travelling in India, or reading other material on Indian food, you will inevitably come across spellings of words different from those I have used in this book.

NORTH INDIA

PUNJAB AND HARYANA

FIELDS OF GOLD

PUNJAB

Nearly 5000 years ago in what is now western Punjab, there was a thriving metropolis called Harappa. It had well-planned streets and solid brick residences with bathrooms and toilets that emptied into a superb drainage system. Its 20,000-odd citizens—a large population in the Bronze Age—ate a diet based on cultivated cereals and pulses. Wheat, barley and millet were ground and the resultant meal powder mixed with a liquid to form dough; this was shaped into flatbreads that were cooked on metal or clay plates or in mud-plastered ovens—prototypes of the tawa and the tandoor that are still items of daily use in India. Dried peas, moong and *moth* dal were boiled to form a potage or ground and shaped into small cakes and fried. Spices such as mustard, fenugreek, turmeric and ginger were used to give an additional flavour to meals. These were hand-ground between two pieces of stone consisting of a large flat base and a smaller rounded piece held in the hand and moved up and down the base to crush the spices in between. This method of preparing spices is still commonly used in villages and by urban cooks dedicated to the exceptional flavour this particular style of processing yields.* The Harappans domesticated sheep, goats and buffaloes and the milk of these animals was churned into curd and butter. They were very fond of eating meat and fish, which they

* While collecting recipes in Nizamuddin *basti* (village/community) in Delhi some years ago, one of the cooks I worked with made *shammi* kebabs for me. She ground the meat and the flavourings together on the stone and the resulting kebabs were superlative in flavour and texture. This inspired me to carry a grinding stone back to Australia, which I use in my city apartment.

3

probably roasted over coals on a spit, basting the flesh with oil pressed from sesame or linseed or in the animals' own fat.

Harappa was part of a network of 1000 or so settlements spread out across the Indus river basin, forming one of the world's earliest urban civilizations. The complex civic organization of Harappa was replicated across these population centres as were the food habits, and the whole is collectively referred to as the Harappan civilization. The types of cereals, pulses and other foods cultivated in the Harappan settlements differed, depending on the environmental conditions, but the methods used to process these for eating were consistent. Around 1500 BC, Harappan society seems to have collapsed and disappeared. There are many theories as to why this might have happened but no definitive answer. The most popular—and dramatic— story of their demise claims that the people who came to be called Aryans charged into India on their horses and destroyed the Harappans and their urban infrastructure. The truth, if it is ever established, will undoubtedly be far more complex than this simple tale, but it puts a full stop to India's earliest history and facilitates an easy transition into the next historical period when India's dominant Hindu culture was born.

There is little that is undisputed about the so-called Aryans but, for the sake of argument, let us accept that they arrived into India from Central Asia and that they were horse-riding nomads who herded animals and lived on a diet largely composed of meat and milk. What is indisputable is that they did not replicate the metropolitan lifestyle of the Harappans. The Aryans' itinerant lifestyle would have left them ignorant of urban living and the technology required to build and sustain it; if they did destroy the Harappans, it might have been because the latter appeared alien in their permanent brick enclaves. Their arrival in India caused, or allowed, the Aryans to give up their wandering ways, but they preferred an agrarian life living in small village communities: a lifestyle that has endured for the majority of India's population for the past 2500 years or so. (Only recently, in fact, has it been disrupted by the exodus of people from rural hamlets into India's precipitously expanding cities.)

Food would have played a decisive role in the settlement of the Aryans in India. It is believed that it was the lack of food, due to changed environmental conditions, that caused them to migrate out of Central Asia; and the abundance of it in India—for themselves and their herds—that made them give up their itinerant lifestyle for a more stable one. The Aryans became cultivators of cereals, pulses, rice, sugar, fruits and vegetables. They would not have had the knowledge required to create agricultural bounty before they arrived on the subcontinent, therefore they must have learnt of plant cultivation after this migration. Given that the Harappans were good at growing things, it seems that they would have been the obvious teachers. The way the Aryans prepared their food also had strong similarities with the cooking practices of the Harappans. Meals were based around grains that were ground and cooked as unleavened breads or cakes, and legumes and rice boiled and variously flavoured. This culinary evidence suggests that Aryans absorbed significant influences from the Harappans and must not have annihilated them. It seems more likely that they absorbed the Harappans and their skills into their culture.

Meat must have been essential to Aryan survival in the steppes of Central Asia where there were few other food sources. However, their carnivorous habits diminished in India, partly because a much wider array of food became available to them. Milk and milk products such as curd would have also been important in the pre-India Aryan diet, but raising animals on the more verdant land of their new home—and not having to continually move them around—would have resulted in greater yields of milk and therefore more extensive use. Once they got the hang of agriculture, the Aryans probably became very good at producing vegetal food and vastly increased the range and yield of produce. Apart from grains, pulses and rice, there were gourds, onions, cucumbers, leafy greens, radishes, mangoes, citrus fruits, pomegranates, bananas and jackfruit. The number of spices in use expanded to include long pepper, cardamom, cinnamon, nutmeg, cloves, cumin and coriander. The availability of these spices is evidence of the development of trade because all these spices, except pepper, are native to places other than northern India. Oil was pressed from various seeds such as sesame, linseed, safflower and mustard. Wild honey was used to sweeten foods early on and by the fifth century BC, the Aryans had advanced the cultivation of sugar cane such that there was ample supply of it. Juice extracted from the canes was processed into various products such as gur, and these were in common use. The scribes of the party of Alexander the Great (*see below*) considered the abundance of sugar products they saw in Indian marketplaces as a wonder worth noting.

A consequence of having an assured, abundant supply of food was a considerable increase in the population, inevitably leading to tensions over ownership and control of resources. Circa 1000 BC, north Indians were also not ethnically homogeneous; there were aboriginal tribes and likely remnants of Harappans among them—a disparate mix with potential for social disharmony. To maintain communal stability and ensure continued productive working of the land, the Aryans devised a system of social organization, generally referred to as the caste system, which allocated everybody a place in the cultural hierarchy. This system averted the need to enslave people to get them to work, but their place in it was deemed immutable. If you belonged to the Shudra caste, you were a labourer of some kind; if Brahmin, you served as priest, teacher or scholar and did no manual work.

A complex set of rules around food was an integral part of the caste system. These rules were more about contact than about what food a member of a particular caste could or could not eat. Anyone could take food from a Brahmin but a Brahmin could take food only from someone of his own caste, unless it was deemed 'pukka'. Food was rendered 'impure' if handled by a lower-caste person or if adulterated with a foreign substance. As a general rule, a person did not accept edibles from a lower caste but applying ghee, butter or curd, in theory, rendered any food 'pure' and acceptable. Within households there were rules around eating meals. Brahmin men ate by themselves; a host did not eat with his guests; and women and children ate separately. These ancient habits linger on in modern India: if you are invited to a meal in an Indian home, you might find that the convivial part of the visit takes place prior to the meal; once the food is served, all attention is focused on eating and little conversation ensues. In a traditional home, the women of the family will likely serve you but not eat with you.

The development of Aryan/Hindu culture occurred gradually across the Vedic period (1500 to 150 BC), called so because it was the time when the oldest scriptures of Hinduism, the Vedas, were composed. It was also the time when the integral styles and techniques of north Indian cuisine, particularly its vegetarian genre, were laid down. Vedic life began in north India and was concentrated in the Punjab region, eventually spreading into the Gangetic plain. The food ordinarily eaten in the modern Indian state of Punjab still embodies these ancient roots although it has absorbed a few other strands of influence over the past two millennia.

Punjab is a geographical region that historically included the Punjab province of Pakistan and the modern Indian states of Punjab, Haryana and Himachal Pradesh. It is named for the five rivers that dissect it and have been the source of the water and rich alluvial soil that have made Punjab eminently amenable to agricultural interventions since the time of the Harappans. Punjab was heavily forested in its primordial state and the Aryans had to clear the land to create new fields for the agriculture that had become essential to them. In the great Indian epic, the Mahabharata, the fire god, Agni, is said to have devoured the forests of Punjab; the more prosaic truth is that it was man who ignited the jungles to clear them. The central story of this marathon tale concerns a civil war waged between two related families over landownership. On reflection, the region's earliest appearance in literature as the site of a fracas could be seen to be prescient since Punjab's history of great productivity is counterbalanced by one of conflict—the former undoubtedly an issue in the latter.

In 326 BC, Alexander the Great came overland into Punjab, where he defeated the Indian King Porus in his campaign to conquer the known world. (The Greeks believed that the world's end was Punjab.) Coriander seed and cumin—two spices widely used in Indian cooking—are native to the Mediterranean and it is possible that these came into north India with Alexander's armies. Tales of the wonder and bounty of India caused various other peoples to make incursions into Punjab, but none had the impact of the Muslim invasions that began in the tenth century AD and culminated in the capture of Delhi—a city positioned on the eastern edge of the Punjab—in the early thirteenth century by Turks from Afghanistan. In AD 1526, Zahir-ud-din Muhammad Babur, a native of what is now Uzbekistan, captured Delhi via the Punjab from its Turk rulers and founded the Mughal dynasty. The Mughals fashioned Delhi into a fabulous city and built its matching pair in Lahore, with Punjab serving as a busy corridor linking the two.

Now, a Mughal emperor did not travel light. The retinue accompanying him on any substantive journey included 100-odd camels and assorted pack animals just to carry the food supply and equipment needed to set up the imperial kitchen and dining area. In its entirety, the emperor's caravan was a slow-moving body; covering the 260-odd miles between Delhi and Lahore would have required a considerable number of halts during which the imperial kitchen would have been put into operation. The Mughals were very interested in food and not shy of trying new edibles. To satisfy their culinary curiosity, local foods would have been sourced for the royal table and local cooks brought in to create their specialities. In this way, Mughal cuisine absorbed foods and techniques used in Punjabi cooking; this was a two-way process and Mughal influences entered the kitchens of Punjab via the royal journeys and from the Muslims settling in the region.

The assimilation of Muslims into the Hindu Punjab was not a peaceful process. The communal violence it wrought caused Guru Nanak to found the Sikh religion in the fifteenth century with the tenet that 'there is no Hindu, there is no Muslim'. Nanak preached the existence of one immortal being and universal brotherhood in the hope of preventing fights over the supremacy of any particular god. Later, in the nineteenth century, the Sikhs found themselves twice in battle with the British for control over Punjab. While these skirmishes raged, the Punjabis got on with the business of agriculture. There are reports of men fighting battles alongside farmers who continued to work their fields, undisturbed by the havoc around them. In 1947, the British partitioned Punjab between India and the newly formed Pakistan. The resultant interchange of people between the two countries—Hindus and Sikhs fleeing into India and Muslims into Pakistan—and the violence that ensued devastated the region.

Two thousand years of living in a region, which by its God-given strategic location and fecundity has invited upheaval, have made the Punjabis a resilient people, and agriculture remains the region's economic forte. Punjabis embraced modern industrial agricultural production methods during the Green Revolution of the 1960s and '70s, and Punjab has since earned the alternative name of the 'granary of India' as it produces 20 per cent of the country's wheat along with significant annual yields of rice and millet. Its milk production is the third largest in India while sugar, maize and fruit are its other important crops. Maintaining its ancient agrarian-based economy but harnessing it to modern technology has served Punjab well. Its inhabitants enjoy one of the highest per capita incomes in India, but the backbone of the state remains smaller, family-run farms. The influence of agricultural life is evident in Punjab's traditional food. It is hearty and robust to sustain physical work; focused on seasonal foods gathered from the fields; and comprises everyday dishes that can be easily put together at the end of the day or left to slow-cook while all family members, including women, work on the farms. It is also generously enriched with dairy products—reward for a hard day's toil.

A variety of breads made from wholewheat flour are the mainstay of Punjabi cuisine, just as these were for the Harappans. Simple rotis cooked on a tawa are eaten daily; parathas stuffed with mashed, spiced potato or grated radish or cauliflower and shallow-fried in oil or ghee are popular for breakfast, accompanied with curd (dahi) and a vegetable pickle; naans and kulchas cooked in a clay oven called tandoor are also commonly eaten. A traditional tandoor is shaped like a large, tapered jar that opens at the top and has a small vent at the bottom. Wood is burnt in the tandoor until it transmutes into charcoal at which point the oven is ready for use. Flat rounds of prepared bread dough are slapped on to the side of the tandoor with a concave cloth-covered pad called a *gaddi* (though I have seen some cooks do this with bare hands). The temperature inside a tandoor can reach 400 °C and food cooks very quickly. The naan, a leavened bread made with refined-wheat flour, gains its characteristic 'teardrop' shape as it 'drips' down the side of the tandoor in the minutes before the heat causes it to set. It is retrieved from the oven with a long metal hook that leaves a telltale hole in the bread. Meats, fish and vegetables marinated in various mixtures of curd, spices, ginger, garlic, fresh herbs and tenderizing agents such as raw papaya and lemon juice are also cooked in the tandoor on metal skewers or suspended from hooks in the case of a whole fish or chicken. The smouldering coals and dry heat of the tandoor impart a distinct flavour and aroma that are particularly pronounced if these are basted with ghee or oil as this drips on to the coals causing them to 'smoke', thereby adding another layer of flavour to the food. (*See Delhi chapter on p. 77 for more on tandoori chicken.*)

A tandoor can sit above the ground or can be buried such that the opening is at ground level; small tandoors can also be moved easily and it is believed that these were once carried by armies and traders. The tandoor requires much less fuel than an open fire—the only other option for those on the move—and since it encloses its fire, it prevents inadvertently signalling the activity to potential enemies. There is no clear understanding as to when and where the tandoor was first used. Ovens resembling tandoors have been found in the remains of Harappan settlements, but there is evidence to indicate that it was in use in the mountainous areas of Afghanistan in pre-Harappan times; the common use of the tandoor for everyday cooking and the well-developed range of breads baked in it in Afghanistan suggests its longevity there. The tandoor may not be used exclusively in Punjab, but it has become strongly associated with Punjabi cooking. Guru Nanak exhorted people to build communal tandoors, to be used by all residents of a community to bake their daily bread, in the hope that sharing a tandoor would help break down caste barriers. In line with this edict, the practice of using communal tandoors became established in villages and urban laneways in Punjab. It is not known if this impacted the changes Nanak anticipated but it did have socio-economic benefits. Using a communal oven saved fuel costs and gave women an unfettered opportunity to exchange information (some might say 'gossip'). The popularity of tandoor-cooked foods in restaurants in urban centres in Punjab would seem to indicate that a communal tandoor intended for domestic use is no longer a feature of metropolitan laneways.

In the winter months in Punjab, a richly spiced purée of mustard greens is eaten, accompanied with roti made of ground maize and a knob of fresh, soft, crumbly gur. This classic combination is called *sarson ka saag* and *makki ki roti*. Mustard has been grown in Punjab for millennia and its oil-rich seed is an important commercial crop. After harvesting the seed—which will be pressed to yield cooking oil—the green leaves are collected and traditionally cooked in the farm kitchen. These days, time-deprived and farm-less urbanized Punjabis turn to restaurants to partake of this 'comfort food'. *Gajar ka halwa* is another winter dish made from grated carrots cooked with sugar, milk, cardamom and plenty of ghee; at its best, it's a glorious creamy mass that warms you inside like a hug from your grandmother. Gajar ka halwa is often eaten alongside *aloo puri*, deep-fried bread stuffed with spiced potato—a combination guaranteed to supply anyone the energy to undertake hard labour in the fields.

Rice and sugar cane are both harvested in Punjab in the autumn and paired to produce *rao ki kheer*, a seasonal sweet dish of milled rice cooked with sugar-cane juice and jaggery. Plain cooked rice is not served in a Punjabi home as this indicates that someone at home is ill, so it is fashioned into pulao, biryani (indicative of Muslim influence), khichri or, at the very least, flavoured with cumin seeds. An exception is the common pairing of plain rice with the slow-cooked dish of spiced red kidney beans called *rajma*. For just over half of the population of Punjab, beans and pulses are vital to the daily diet. 'Meatier' dried beans such as red kidney beans, whole Kabuli chickpeas (a variety larger and creamier than the smaller desi chickpeas) and black-eyed beans are used in Punjabi cooking more extensively than in any other region of India. Perhaps the best-known vegetarian dish of Punjab is *ma ki dal*, a slow-cooked dish of whole black lentils, which might include a few red kidney beans and chickpeas in the mix depending on who's making it. It takes the heat of a slow-burning charcoal fire to cause the black lentils to yield into the creamy unctuousness of a good ma ki dal. As gas burners have replaced traditional wood/coal stoves in urban kitchens, this is another dish that has become a popular restaurant staple. (A pressure cooker might be used to make this dish in a modern home kitchen but while this shortens the cooking time, it also short-changes on flavour.) *Chhole bhature*, a combination of chickpeas (*chhole*) slow-cooked in a spiced tomato sauce and deep-fried bread (*bhature*), is a classic Punjabi brunch dish, also popular in restaurants nowadays.

The creamy texture of ma ki dal is helped by a generous endowment of ghee. A meal without dairy products would be inconceivable to most Punjabis and they are particularly fond of home-made white butter such that they will take their own butter to restaurants to slather it over hot tandoor-cooked breads. Buttermilk (*chhachh*), the liquid residue collected during butter production, is chilled and flavoured with cumin seeds and salt or sugar, and served with meals. It is also used to make *kadhi*—a word that sounds very much like 'curry' when pronounced—a dish of dumplings made from *besan* (chickpea flour) served in a gravy (also thickened with besan) of buttermilk spiced with red chillies, cumin, fennel seeds and asafoetida.

Rice and milk form the base of Punjabi sweet preparations such as *kheer*—whole rice cooked in sweetened milk—and *phirni*—ground rice or rice flour cooked with milk and sugar and flavoured with rose water, raisins and almonds or pistachios. (There is an Indo-Muslim sweet dish of the same name, also called phirni, but it is made of wheat-flour noodles cooked in sweetened milk.) *Panjiri* is a Punjabi sweet made of wheat flour or semolina cooked in ghee to which sugar, dried fruits and natural gum are added and the mix formed into balls (laddoos). These are eaten during winter to ward off cold weather ills and also given to women who are breastfeeding.

Paneer is another dairy product used extensively in Punjabi cuisine, particularly to provide substance to vegetarian dishes. It is not a new food but rising prosperity has seen it being used far more generously and extensively in recent times. (Even Western-style foods, such as pizzas, have been subject to 'paneerification' in Punjab and parts of north India.) Punjabi vegetarians obviously reject eating animal flesh but they are not as stringent about avoiding onions and garlic like some vegetarians in other parts of India. This may be due to Muslim influence or because most of the state's inhabitants are Sikhs who do not subscribe to the same philosophical beliefs that cause Hindu vegetarians to reject odiferous foods of the *Allium* genus. Muslim influence is also evident in Punjabi cuisine in popular non-vegetarian foods such as *seekh* and *shammi* kebabs and rich meat curries. (*See Delhi chapter on p. 75 for more.*)

A person, such as a tourist, who is reliant on commercial food purveyors for meals will not find it difficult to sample Punjabi food anywhere in India and this fact has partly informed my writing this book. This is not due to any prejudice against Punjabi-style food; when done well, it is delicious and embodies much of the history of north India in its style and flavours, but it is only one of India's many regional cuisines and is not the sole exemplar of subcontinental cuisine. This chapter therefore serves not only as a guide to what to eat in Punjab but perhaps also what to avoid elsewhere in the country. There are many reasons for the dominance of Punjabi food in restaurants and eateries across India. Not least amongst these is that Punjabis pioneered the commercial hotel and catering industry in modern India, particularly in the north. It was their style of cuisine that made up menus when restaurants serving Indian food first appeared in India and Indians came to expect this style of food when eating out. (*See Delhi chapter on pp. 76–77 for more.*)

Recommendations

Amritsar was founded in 1577 by the fourth Sikh Guru, Ram Das, beside a bathing pool famed for its healing powers. There is a historical nexus in India between pilgrimage sites and trade; where pilgrims congregated, traders followed, or it might have been the other way round. Amritsar was located on a major trade arterial that fed into the famed Silk Route; a strategic positioning that brought wealth, growth and a splendid Sikh gurdwara, known as the Golden Temple or the Harmandir Sahib. The temple and the complex surrounding it are literally and spiritually the heart of Amritsar. The streets and lanes of the old city radiate out from it and it is the Sikh community's holiest shrine.

Time momentarily stops when one first catches a glimpse of the Golden Temple. Taking a meal in **Guru ka Langar**, its huge communal canteen, is a timeless practice. Anywhere between 10,000 and 50,000 people eat here every day; on weekends and festivals, this number can rise to 100,000. The dining room seats 3000 people at a time and operates twenty-four hours a day; feeding 50,000 people in a day requires fourteen seatings of 3000 every hour and a half. A meal at the *langar* is a simple and enduring one: roti, dal, pickles, kheer. Volunteers prepare all the food. You can see them at work in the pristine, factory-sized kitchen stirring dal and kheer in giant vats, peeling huge piles of onions and washing mountains of dishes. They no longer make the daily quota of 100,000 rotis by hand as that task has been taken over by a machine which mixes the dough, spits it out in small pieces, flattens these into discs, sends them into the oven, brings them out again when cooked on a conveyor belt, and spits them into a basket from where they are collected by human hands and taken to the dining room for distribution.

Everybody eating at Guru ka Langar is served exactly the same food, and everybody eats together (in community or in *sangat*) seated on the floor in long rows called *pangat*. There are no exceptions to this with respect to the food, while chairs are available for those who cannot sit on the floor. Even the great Mughal Akbar ate the same meal as the commoners among whom he sat when he visited the temple in the late sixteenth century. Eating like this is Sikh philosophy put into practice: by insisting that all people eat the same food and sit together while doing so shows that all human beings are equal before God. Besides being open almost all the time, Guru ka Langar is open to all and the meals are free of charge.

Once all the diners are seated in pangat with a stainless steel plate each—issued at the door—the meal commences. Servers bearing large baskets of freshly baked rotis walk along the rows, dropping these into the upturned palms of each person; more servers come and dispense the other food items on to the plates after which they continue doing rounds of the dining room, dishing out food as requested. You can have as much to eat as you care for but you must eat all that you take. When the meal is over, everyone leaves together, carrying their utensils and dropping these into the washing bins located outside. A meal at the Golden Temple is an experience not to be missed.

The traditional food of Amritsar is very much that of the rest of Punjab but the city owns two native food items: Amritsari kulcha and Amritsari fish. The Amritsari kulcha is a crisp, flaky roti made with refined flour; it is stuffed with potato, onion, black pepper, chilli, cumin and dried pomegranate seeds (*anardana*) and cooked in the tandoor. As soon as it is drawn from the oven, the kulcha is given a generous coating of butter burnishing it a rich golden. Pieces of the bread are used to scoop up an accompanying dish of chickpeas cooked in tangy tamarind gravy. Amritsaris eat their indigenous kulcha for breakfast or lunch, along with lassi, a drink made with sweetened curd, or sweet milky tea (though, sadly, commercial soft drinks seem to be replacing both), and eateries that specialize in serving these usually close up by late afternoon. Top picks in Amritsar for kulchas are **All India Famous** on Maqbool Road, a basic roadside dhaba (*see below*) where hundreds of kulchas are cooked and consumed every day. **Kulchaland** on Ranjit Road (opposite M.K. Hotel) is slightly more upmarket with an indoor fan-cooled section as well as an outdoor eating space. Both places open by 8 a.m. and their service is perfunctory but friendly.

The highways of north India are dotted with basic eateries called dhabas that provide meals to truck drivers and other travellers. Punjabis dominate the ranks of truck drivers in India and the food typically served in dhabas is made to suit their tastes; hence, there is a strong association between Punjab and dhabas. A typical dhaba offers tandoori roti, dal enriched with butter, spiced chickpeas, dishes of spiced seasonal vegetables such as potato and cauliflower, lassi and hot, sweet, milky tea. Non-vegetarian dhaba fare tends to run to tandoori chicken, meat kebabs, butter chicken and spiced mutton stew. The presence of a contingent of trucks outside a dhaba is usually a sign that the food is good—though it can also suggest the availability of liquor and gambling!

A dhaba is a rustic, and often open, structure with well-worn chairs and tables and a few charpoys for tired truckies to snooze on. Food gently simmers in pots atop wood stoves—usually located at the front of the shop where it can be seen by all—ready for immediate consumption. Indian truck drivers spend at least twenty days a month on the road and they rely on dhabas to provide meals to sustain them for the daily battle that driving in India can be. Decent meals are probably the one thing they have to look forward to so they won't settle for anything less than hearty, tasty, nourishing—and inexpensive—fare. I have spent a lot of time on the road in India—

gaining plenty of first-hand experience of how truly abysmal driving conditions are—and I have eaten some terrific food in dhabas. It has recently become quite fashionable among urbanites to drive out to roadside dhabas to enjoy a feast of home-style Punjabi cuisine.*

Dhabas are not confined to transport routes; the word itself has become a catchphrase for any basic eating joint in a rural or an urban location. City dhabas may have a more extensive menu and the surroundings might be more salubrious—at the top end of this, there are a few five-star hotels in India that have restaurants that mimic the traditional dhaba. Amritsar is renowned for its dhabas, such as **Kesar da Dhaba**, an eating joint with a proud record of serving meals since 1916. Located in a narrow lane in the old city, it has spread out over time to occupy several shopfronts on either side of the alley. The most popular meals here are the daily thali combos of Punjabi classics such as ma ki dal and chhole, along with a paneer dish, raita, pickles and roti. Opposite the dining room is a shopfront—part of the same business—in which you can see open cabinets lined with racks filled with small clay pots of phirni; each pot is adorned with a thin film of silver leaf the weight of a butterfly wing. This ethereal substance, called *varq*, is edible, though tasteless, and dissolves in your mouth. (No, it will not 'grate' on your teeth.) Varq is purely decorative and was brought into use by the ornamentation-loving Mughals. Phirni is at its best when set in traditional terracotta dishes as their porous quality permits the moisture of this milky sweet to evaporate so that it sets to a perfect texture. In winter, Kesar da Dhaba makes a 'gold standard' gajar ka halwa.

Chowk Passian, East Mohan Nagar
(0183) 2552103

Bharawan da Dhaba is another old favourite with Amritsaris. It has evolved into a full-fledged restaurant and the menu has extended to include plenty of modern items, but its best offerings are Punjabi

---

* Please note that the following recommended eating establishments are all to be found in the maze of the lanes of 'old' Amritsar. All are well known and any rickshaw-wallah will be able to take you to any of these if you just mention the name of the venue. I was not successful in pinning down the exact opening hours for some places but most are open for lunch and dinner.

classics enjoyed via the Punjabi thali, featuring a 'legendary' ma ki dal, spiced chickpeas, *shahi paneer* (a 'royal' dish of paneer in a sauce of rich spices, cashews, onion and garlic), a simple pulao of rice with cumin seeds and strands of crisped onions, accompanied by naan or paratha and rounded off with a small clay dish of phirni.

Hall Bazaar (near City Hall)
(0183) 2532575
8 a.m. to 11.30 p.m. (7 days)

In Amritsar, my rickshaw-wallah was delighted with my choice, **Punjabi Dhaba**. He told me that it is his favourite place to eat at as the food is the 'best outside of home'. The thali make-up conforms to the formula: dal, chickpeas, spiced potato, a paneer dish, pickles and tandoori roti. It is located down a narrow lane and you need to look for the sign, which is visible from the main street.

Chowk Goal Hatti, Gali Arorian, Hall Bazaar
(0183) 5099162

The nonagenarian **Gurudas Ram Jalebiwala**, located at the intersection of several lanes in Katra Ahluwalia in the centre of the old city, is an essential stop to sample one, or two, of the famous jalebis made here. This sticky, sweet curlicue is universally found across India nowadays but Amritsaris are said to be especially fond of it. It is made from a basic refined-flour batter, piped into hot ghee or oil in spirals and cooked until crisp. Then it is briefly soaked in hot, saffron-infused sugar syrup to take on an orange hue and then cooled down enough for you to bite into it and release a gush of the syrup it has absorbed into your mouth. Heaven for those with a sweet tooth, this can be enjoyed here from early morning to late evening.

Most food offerings in the vicinity of the Golden Temple are vegetarian but when Amritsaris, and pilgrims in the know, need to fulfil carnivorous desires, they visit **Parkash da Dhaba** (also called Parkash Meat Shop) for a bowl of rich mutton stew cooked with curd, tomatoes, onion and a 'secret family recipe' garam masala. This is the only item served at this very basic dhaba and it is only available between 1 p.m. and 6 p.m. Despite the shabby surrounds, people from all walks of life come here to eat and the food sells out every day. There is a branch of Parkash on Maqbool Road, which has a more extended menu of meat dishes. It is in this part of town away from the sanctity of the temple precinct where Amritsar's best-known non-vegetarian offering, Amritsari fish, is to be had. Pieces of a locally caught river fish called *singhara* are coated in a batter of chickpea flour flavoured with *ajwain* (carom seeds) and red chilli powder and fried. Cooked properly, the batter coating sets crisp, sealing the fish inside and causing it to steam and develop a melt-in-the-mouth texture, hence the more popular name for this dish of *makhan* (butter) fish. **Makhan Fish & Chicken Corner** is a fairly modest dhaba in appearance but its proprietors share what appears to be an Amritsari fondness for celebrity and the claim to be the most 'famous' place to eat Amritsari fish: the product could be considered to justify the proclaimed popularity.

21A, Near Madan Hospital, Majitha Road
(M) 9815193241

Surjit Food Plaza on Lawrence Road is another popular place for Amritsari fish.

3-4 Ground Floor, Nehru Shopping Complex, Lawrence Road
(0183) 3294334

Aam papad, fruit leather made from mango pulp, is popularly eaten as a digestive after a meal of rich Punjabi specialities. As the name suggests, **Old & Famous Puni Lal Aam Papad Shop** is 'famed' for this particular item. You will find aam papad elsewhere in India but at Puni Lal it is dressed with lemon juice, red chilli powder and rock salt and eaten as a snack that enlivens the palate with an explosion of sweet, sour, spicy and pungent flavours. The latter is derived from *kala namak*, a purple-coloured rock salt that gains its colour and distinct flavour from the sulphuric impurities it contains.

Lawrence Road, Near BBK D.A.V. College

If you want to try Punjabi food in its natural setting—on a farm, that is—Punjab Tourism runs an interesting farm-stay programme. It has a register of rural homes all over Punjab whose owners host guests and allow them to enjoy an experience of regional life and eat genuine home-style Punjabi cuisine.

www.punjabtourism.gov.in

HARYANA

Until 1966, Haryana was part of Punjab. The border drawn on a map to create this division formally acknowledged long-existing linguistic and religious differences between the region's Punjabi-speaking Sikhs and Hindi-speaking Hindus, by giving the latter their own state. It was the fundamental nature of these differences that resulted in the cleavage of one state from the other as the two share a history as the crucible of Indian civilization, success in modern farming and almost indistinguishable food habits. The preceding discussion about the history and food culture of Punjab applies equally to Haryana but to give the state its due share of attention, I will further expand on some aspects on the shared culture here and note the Haryanvi distinctions.

Before the Ganga gained supremacy as India's premier sacred river, the Saraswati, which flowed through what is now modern Haryana, was worshipped in the *Rig Veda* as the 'best of all rivers' and was said to 'pour milk and ghee'. What the latter statement implies is that the Saraswati watered a region of arable plains on which crops could be abundantly produced and a good number of cattle reared for milk. This consistent availability of food enabled early Vedic culture to flourish there. The Saraswati—now known as the Ghaggar—eventually dissipated into a chain of ponds that only fill intermittently with good monsoon rain, but Haryanvis continue to live in a land of plentiful milk and ghee. Modern Haryana has one of the largest dairy industries in India. Every day, the state produces nearly three times more milk per person than the national average. A fair amount is utilized in the commercial production of dairy products sent out of the state; the rest is consumed locally.

Haryanvis domesticate cows and buffaloes. Given the choice, they prefer the rich sweet milk of the buffalo, which is also more plentiful as the *Bubalus bubalis* is much larger than a cow. When you visit a village home in Haryana, you might well be offered a glass of fresh, creamy buffalo milk instead of tea; and if you prefer the latter, you can be sure it will be very milky. In a Haryanvi village home, milch animals are milked in the evening. The milk is boiled (to sterilize it) and left to cool until it is just warm. A portion of 'sour' curd or buttermilk left over from the previous day is added to some of the milk and the mixture left to sit overnight to curdle and form soft curd. In the morning the fresh curds may be eaten for breakfast; some will be churned into butter that is generously slathered over hot breads, and some further refined into ghee. The chhachh thrown off during butter-making can be chilled and had as a drink or used in cooking. Chhachh is taken as a digestive and you will find it a common addition to any meal served in Haryana.

I have been intrigued by the sky-scraping apartment blocks, office buildings, business centres and shopping malls that have arisen over the past eighteen years from the fields of Haryana to form the city of Gurgaon (which abuts Delhi and is part of the National Capital Region, or NCR). This fast-paced urban centre looms in contrast to much of the rest of the state as most Haryanvis work in agriculture and live in villages. Agriculture is as highly mechanized in Haryana as in neighbouring Punjab, and the state is one of the largest producers of foodgrains such as wheat, barley (*jau*), millet (*bajra*), maize and rice. Haryanvis use all of these grains to make rotis, which are the mainstay of their daily diet. Breads prepared from wheat flour are the most common and eaten throughout the year; others are seasonal such as makki or *bajre ki roti* prepared from the late-autumn harvest of maize and finger millet. Parathas stuffed with lightly spiced potato or a seasonal green like *bathua* (*Chenopodium album*) and drenched with butter are commonly eaten for morning meals. Chickpeas are another major crop in Haryana and the flour ground from these is used to make crisp besan ki roti.

Haryana is also a major producer of basmati rice. While rice is regularly eaten, Haryanvis have a strong preference for breads and other dishes made with grains. They like to make khichri with millet and sorghum (jowar) cooked with moong dal and flavoured with cumin, asafoetida and ghee. In summer, they cook cracked wheat (*daliya*) with milk and sugar to make a type of porridge, which they eat hot as this dish is held to have cooling properties. If rice is to be served as part of a meal, it is often flavoured with cumin seeds and ghee or some other flavouring. Plain rice is traditionally served with kadhi.

Close to 90 per cent of Haryanvis are Hindu, and Haryana has one of the highest vegetarian populations among all Indian states. As it is a wealthy region, this would appear to be a statistic shaped by religious piety rather than economic necessity. Fresh seasonal vegetables are vital to the daily Haryanvi diet. A simple village meal might comprise freshly cooked roti paired with a dish of stir-fried leafy greens such as mustard, fenugreek or spinach, along with pickle, chutney and chhachh. Other common preparations are *aloo palak* (potatoes cooked with spinach), *gajar methi* (winter dish of carrots cooked with fresh fenugreek leaves) and *sookhe chane* (chickpeas cooked with fresh fenugreek leaves and spices). Dal is also cooked with leafy greens.

Haryana shares its more arid southern border with Rajasthan and the two vegetables commonly associated with the cuisine of that princely state— *kachri* (a small, sour 'paddy' melon that grows wild among other crops) and the bean-like *sangri*—are used in Haryanvi cooking too.

Haryanvi dishes are seasoned with combinations of ginger, garlic, red chilli powder, fresh green chillies, black pepper and cumin seeds. A flavourful, freshly made chutney always accompanies a meal. Chutneys are made from a huge variety of fresh seasonal fruits—mango, banana, grape, pomegranate, guava, kachri, tomato—and vegetables—green peas, bathua, green coriander, cucumber, mint, *pabri* (a type of marjoram)—ground or finely chopped and mixed with combinations of the above ingredients. Curd and chhachh are also used to make chutneys.

Recommendations

National Highway 1 (NH1) runs right through Haryana connecting Amritsar (Punjab) to Delhi. It is one of the busiest roads in India and drivers tend to pass along it between these two major cities with nary a glance at what Haryana might have to offer. As a counter to this lack of visitor attention, the state tourism is said to have pioneered 'highway tourism' by supporting the development of wayside amenities such as restaurants, motels and gardens to attract motorists to stop over in the state. Among the most successful of these highway attractions are traditional dhabas where travellers can stop to enjoy a meal of Haryanvi/Punjabi specialities, although these have actually been absorbed into the 'highway tourism' concept rather than being a product of it.

Dhabas have nestled alongside the highway in Haryana for at least half a century, providing decent meals to the drivers of the thousands of trucks plying the route every day. The otherwise nondescript highway town of Murthal (near Sonepat) has become quite renowned for its dhabas and people now drive there just to eat. You can't miss the string of dhabas along NH1 here because of the mass of the parked vehicles of patrons. All these places serve 'pure vegetarian' food and most are open round the clock—and are reportedly busy even at 3 a.m. **Sukhdev Vaishno Dhaba** claims to be the biggest dhaba in the world. Its success has seen it develop a 'multi-cuisine' menu but avoid the 'continental, south Indian and Chinese' offerings and choose from the seasonal menu of good local vegetable dishes and breads such as sarson ka saag, aloo methi (dry dish of potatoes and fenugreek leaves) and *gobhi* parathas (parathas stuffed with cauliflower).

(0130) 65440166
www.sukhdevdhaba.com

Among other dhabas, look for **Gulshan Vaishno Dhaba**, which claims to be the oldest eatery on the Murthal 'block', and **Pahalwan Dhaba**. These two haven't quite reached the heights of Sukhdev's success but you will find truck drivers (as opposed to tourists) eating here. You can't go wrong in either, eating stuffed parathas served with white butter, *dal makhni* and lassi or sweet, milky tea.

Haryana Tourism runs a farm-stay programme, through which visitors can stay at approved farms to experience agricultural life. Depending on your choice of rural idyll, you can learn about local dairying, bee-keeping, horticulture or perhaps join in the harvesting. Home-cooked meals are a feature of all the farm-stays so this is a good way to sample authentic local cuisine. Most farm-stays listed on the site are within an easy day's drive from Delhi.

www.haryanatourism.gov.in/farm/farmtourism

THE VALE OF EARTHLY DELIGHTS

On his deathbed, the Mughal emperor Jahangir is said to have asked to see the earthly paradise of 'Kashmir' once more before he departed for *firdaus*, the heavenly gardens of paradise. The dying royal specifically meant the Vale of Kashmir, the sixty-five-mile-long majestic green valley lying between the Pir Panjal range and the high Himalayas, which his dynasty loved. Up until 1846, the term 'Kashmir' applied only to this vale; in this year, the British defeated the erstwhile Sikh rulers of the region and parcelled it up with Jammu, Ladakh, Baluchistan and Gilgit to form the princely state of Jammu and Kashmir. As a reward for aiding them against the Sikhs, the British handed over the rule of this huge territory to Maharaja Gulab Singh, who founded the Hindu Dogra dynasty that reigned until 1947. After Independence, the princely state was divided—very uneasily—between India and the new nation of Pakistan. Today, the modern Indian state of Jammu and Kashmir encompasses the territories of the Kashmir Valley, Jammu and Ladakh. Its borders remain contentious, however, with claims to its various sections being made by Pakistan as well as China. The three regions have different geographies and cultures so I will present them to you separately.

KASHMIR VALLEY

Hindu legend has it that the Kashmir Valley was once entirely covered by a lake that was home to a devil. To rid the region of this scourge, a powerful being—there are variations as to whether this was a goddess or a holy man—cut out a hole in the lake wall, causing the water to drain out and take the devil with it. According to this story, the renowned Dal,

Nagin, Wular and Manasbal lakes are sizeable remnants of this fabulous waterbody. (We will return to these real waters a little later.) There is archaeological evidence of human habitation in the Kashmir Valley circa 3000 BC. It first comes into literary record in the Mahabharata, the events of which are believed—but by no means universally—to have occurred around this same time, and the Kashmir Valley is considered to have been an important region in early Vedic civilization. Around 3 BC, the region became a vassal of the Mauryan Empire via which Buddhism was introduced. It was a philosophy that the religiously inclined inhabitants seem to have taken to, as Kashmir became an important centre for Buddhist learning. By the ninth century AD, Hinduism had reasserted itself as the dominant creed. In the fourteenth century the Afghan Shams-ud-Din Shah Mir captured Kashmir and introduced Islam. When the Mughal emperor Akbar conquered Kashmir two centuries later, he would have found that a fair proportion of the Valley's population had converted to his faith. The Afghans gained control of Kashmir again after the decline of the Mughals; the Sikhs wrested it from them in 1820 and the British took it in 1846, which brings us back to where we started this chapter. All these rulers left imprints of their culinary cultures on the Kashmir Valley.

In more recent historical times, after the fourteenth century that is, there have been two cuisines in existence in the Kashmir Valley: that of the Muslim community and that of the Hindu Pandit community. The latter are Brahmins who came into the Valley when the Saraswati River, along which they had settled, began to dry up. (It is also said that they were invited to establish themselves there after the aforementioned great lake had been drained, and it makes me wonder if perhaps it took the Saraswati with it as this mystical river is said to have flowed through Kashmir.) A distinguishing characteristic of Kashmiri Pandits is that they are avid meat eaters, a practice considered unusual for high-caste Brahmins (although they are not the only community of this ilk who regularly eat animal protein). One possible theory to explain this uncharacteristic habit is that when the practice of eating meat became infra-dig for Brahmins down on the Gangetic plains—where Vedic culture was evolving—those living in the isolated Kashmir Valley did not hear of this and kept eating meat. Looked at more pragmatically, if the Pandits had given up meat, they would have had very limited food sources to last the long, frozen winters of the Valley. Another explanation is that Pandits sit at the apex of the Brahmin caste and perhaps from their exalted position they felt no need to take on practices established by those below them and give up a significant food source that they enjoyed. Kashmiri Muslims share the Pandit fondness for meat preparations.

One of the best-known dishes of Kashmiri cuisine is the meat curry called *roghan josh*. When prepared in a Pandit kitchen, this dish is flavoured with cloves, cardamom, cinnamon, red chilli powder, ginger powder, fennel and asafoetida. When a Muslim friend made roghan josh for me in her Srinagar kitchen, she prepared the flavour base by pounding suet with garlic, fresh ginger, *pran** and whole red chillies in a large mortar; when she began cooking it, she added cloves, cardamom and cinnamon. It is in the details of the dishes that the differences between Kashmiri Pandit and Muslim cooking are found. Pandits do not use onion and garlic but prefer to distinctly flavour their food with asafoetida, fennel and ginger, and more often use powdered spices. Muslims, on the other hand, use alliums generously and more often employ whole spices.

Traditionally, Pandits did not eat chicken or eggs (believing both to be dirty), but this attitude has now changed and both have been accepted into the Pandit pot. Neither Kashmiri Pandits nor Muslims eat pork or beef but both communities eat fish. The politics of a divided Kashmir and the violence arising from it have driven most Pandits out of Kashmir over the past few decades but many retain the hope of returning to the Valley where they had peacefully coexisted for hundreds of years with their Muslim neighbours. In continuing this exploration of Kashmiri cuisine, I will write of it singularly as the dishes prepared by Pandits and Muslims are very similar once the differences noted above have been taken into account.

Rice, the region's staple food, has been continually grown on terraces in Kashmir for thousands of years. Since the Valley freezes over in the winter, rice is a kharif crop, planted in May–June and harvested in October–November. Many different varieties of rice—some with names evocative of the region's history, such as Begum, Musk-ki-Budji, Qadir Baig and Mughal—have traditionally been cultivated in the Valley. Short-growing cultivars are preferred and basmati has become prevalent. Kashmiris eat rice either plainly boiled as an accompaniment to meals or made into complex

---

* Unfavourable weather conditions in 2011 caused a poor harvest of the Kashmiri shallot called pran (*Allium cornutum*), a sweetish member of the onion family that looks like a giant garlic bulb encased in a papery golden skin, and sent its price soaring, resulting in considerable consternation in the Kashmiri Muslim community as this is an essential component of a traditional Muslim wedding feast in the Valley.

rice dishes such as a pulao, which might constitute a meal in itself when accompanied by a few side dishes.

Wheat is another significant crop grown in Kashmir. It is ground into flour and used to create a diverse and distinct array of Kashmiri breads of variegated taste and texture. The *tsot* is a small, round and chewy bread topped with sesame seeds that looks somewhat like a bagel. The *kulcha* is a bun-shaped bread with a 'short' biscuity texture—created by working pieces of butter into the dough rather than melting it and mixing it in—glazed with egg yolk and baked in rows on the side of a clay oven. *Baqerkhani* is made by layering refined-flour dough with ghee and shaping it into rounds, which are pressed out thinly on a wooden board and baked until crisp; the process is similar to making puff pastry and the finished bread has the texture of a flaky pastry. *Sheermal* is a yeasted, slightly sweet bread scored to look like it is 'striped' and glazed with egg or saffron, which gives it a 'reddish' colour. (Incidentally, I have found that the names and shapes of these breads are sometimes used interchangeably.) Kashmiris eat these breads for breakfast and again in the afternoon, accompanied by tea, and buy them fresh twice daily from local bakeries. (In writing this, something has just occurred to me: I once spent several months working in an urban Muslim village in Delhi and remember noticing that most families bought the bread for each meal from bakeries, whereas Hindus always made their roti at home.) There are about 6000 bakeries in Srinagar alone—one in easy reach of any home—and if you are in Srinagar you will see a flurry of activity around these early in the morning and again around 4 p.m.

Tea in Kashmir is taken in two different styles. *Qahwa* is prepared from green tea, cardamom, cinnamon and almonds. (The proportions will vary according to an individual family's taste and income.) The first activity in the morning in any Kashmiri household is to make qahwa. It is usually brewed in a samovar—a large metal kettle with a spigot—and it is sipped in small cups throughout the day. *Nooncha* (*noon* meaning savoury, and *cha* meaning tea) is brewed from the same green tea leaves as qahwa, but these are boiled for ten minutes or so to create a distillate; more water is then added along with a pinch of bicarbonate soda and the brew boiled again; finally, milk and a pinch of salt are mixed in and the finished nooncha is strained into cups and garnished with a little dollop of cream and a sprinkle of crushed almonds. (These finishing touches vary; I am describing the deluxe edition.) The use of bicarbonate soda gives nooncha its characteristic 'pink' colour. This tea is usually served after meals, sometimes with the addition of sugar.

Kashmir's expansive lakes are the source of two important foods, fish and the root of the lotus plant. Fishing is a huge industry—thousands of fishermen work from Wular Lake alone—and the catch is predominantly made up of carp and native snow trout species. Fish is a daily food for many Kashmiris and it is commonly cooked in a stew-like dish with white radish (*munj gaad*) or apple (*choont gaad*), or fried and served in a spiced gravy with apple. *Nadr gaad* is fish cooked with lotus stems (*nadru*). The lotus stem, or more properly rhizome, is harvested from the lakes and extensively used in cooking. The stems can be coated in rice-flour batter and fried to form crispy batons (*nadr monji*); finely grated and mixed with spices and arrowroot to form patties (*nadr monji ver*); cooked in spiced curd (*nadr yakhni*); stewed with chicken and spices (*nadr kodu*); and used to create a vegetarian version of roghan josh (*nadr roghan josh*). A little more human intervention has created a unique food source on the Dal Lake. The *demb-hanz* are traditional aquatic gardeners who cultivate produce in beds formed from lake weeds and mud that float on the lake. These beds can be towed behind a boat to move them to a more advantageous position, and when this is found they are secured to the lake floor with long bamboo poles. Water-loving fruit and vegetables such as tomatoes, melons, cucumbers and mint are grown on these mobile beds.

Babur, the progenitor of the Mughals, famously complained that there was no 'good' fruit in India. My interpretation is that there were none of the cool-climate fruits available that he recognized from his home turf of Afghanistan. By the time his grandson Akbar arrived in Kashmir, the Mughals had discovered the pleasure of tropical mangoes but still prized temperate fruits above all others. Recognizing that the conditions in Kashmir were perfect for apricots, cherries, grapes, quinces, almonds and pears, they introduced these species to the region and championed the development of indigenous apple species. Fruit from Kashmir, wrapped in soft silk–cotton, was carried on foot by a series of fleet messengers to the imperial table in Delhi in the Mughal era. Kashmiri cooks picked up the practice of adding fruit to savoury dishes from the Mughals and they still cook stews of lamb/ mutton or chicken with apricots, pomegranate or plums; fish with apple and sautéed eggplant with fennel seeds, red chilli, turmeric and quince (*vangun choont*).

The temperate spring and summer climate of the Kashmir Valley allows for abundant production of fruit and vegetables during this part of the year, but when the ground freezes over in the winter there is little that can be grown. Fresh and dried foods are now brought into Kashmir from other parts of India to fill this lack, yet this has not long been possible and Kashmiris have traditionally dried and preserved many fruits, vegetables and fish for use in winter. Dried fruits and nuts are used to embellish rice and meat dishes. *Shufta* is a Kashmiri dessert made of ghee-roasted dates, apricots and nuts simmered in a cardamom- and saffron-infused sugar syrup. Kashmiri cooks do not indulge much in sweet dishes, preferring relatively simple desserts such as shufta, *modur pulao* (sweet rice embellished with dried fruits and nuts) and *phirun*, a firm, custard-like dessert made with ground rice or semolina cooked in milk and set in small clay pots. This is not to say that Kashmiris do not like sweet things—there are numerous bakeries and shops selling biscuits and cakes in Srinagar so somebody has to be eating these—but they just don't have the habit of finishing a meal with dessert.

The addition of a few strands of saffron—the dried stigma of the flower of *Crocus sativus cashmirianus*—is an inevitable addition to a Kashmiri sweet dish and to several savoury ones. Kashmiris can afford to be generous with this ethereal and precious—it is the world's most expensive spice—ingredient, as they grow some of the best saffron in the world in the Pampore region, just outside Srinagar. Saffron imparts a golden hue to food and the Kashmiri variety gives a particularly good colour and flavour. One of the reasons it is so expensive is that it has to be picked by hand and, come harvest time, 100,000-odd people are employed in Pampore to do this work. If you are visiting Kashmir in October, you should make a note to travel to Pampore to see this harvest event. Red and gold are auspicious colours in India and Kashmiris like adding these to food. *Mawal* is the dried, velvety red flower of the edible cockscomb (*celosia*) and Kashmiris use it to add a bright red colour and flavour to food, particularly foods served at weddings. (In fact, red is the traditional colour that Hindu brides wear on this momentous occasion.) Kashmiri red chillies are an elongated variety that have relatively mild capsaicin content but full flavour, and, most importantly yield a bright red colour to food. As further proof that Indian food is not all 'hot', Kashmiri chillies are now grown extensively in other parts of India and the powder made from them dominates the chilli market. While we are on the subject of flavouring foods, let me tell you that Kashmiris make small cakes of ground spices and mustard oil called *ver*, which they dry in the sun until all the moisture has evaporated. A typical ver could include any or all of the following: salt, red chilli, *urad* dal, black cumin (*syah zeera*), black cardamom, cinnamon, clove, cumin, nutmeg, fennel, ginger powder, coriander, green cardamom, bay leaves, fenugreek seeds and coriander seeds; a Pandit ver would have asafoetida while a Muslim one will have onion and garlic. Regardless of its make-up, ver is used in the same way in any Kashmiri kitchen; small bits are broken off and added to cooked dishes. Walnuts grow profusely in Kashmir and chutneys of walnuts ground with green and/or red chillies, curd and salt are regularly eaten with meals. Plums, pomegranates and cherries are other foods used to make chutneys to accompany meals or snacks.

A typical meal eaten in Kashmir will comprise rice or bread, a meat/fish dish and some vegetable dishes such as *haak* (stir-fried seasonal greens). Haak is made with local varieties of spinach, radish or turnip leaves or the leaves of kohlrabi, a perennial member of the cabbage family, though it looks more like turnip, which Kashmiris are very fond of. The crisp, crunchy body of the kohlrabi can be sliced finely and cooked with the leaves in *monji haak* or cut into thicker slices and simmered in a spiced curd-based gravy (*monji kalia*). (I was made to eat kohlrabi as a child and its slightly peppery flavour did not appeal to my juvenile sense of taste; when I encountered it again in Srinagar though, I found it suited my adult palate much better.) Any variety of haak is cooked simply in mustard oil with chilli and salt and either a little asafoetida or garlic depending on religious affiliation. *Nadr haak* (lotus stems cooked with greens) or *vangun haak* (eggplant cooked with radish leaves) are other staple vegetable preparations. Another classic Kashmiri vegetable dish is *gogji rajma* (turnips cooked with red kidney beans and ver). The Kashmiri term for a Pandit is Batta/ Bhatt and, within this community, vegetarians are known as Dal Battas and meat eaters, Nen Battas. The latter are definitely in the majority but vegetarian dishes of Kashmiri cuisine also largely derive from the Pandit kitchen: such as *dum aloo* (potatoes cooked in thick curd gravy spiced with red chilli, aniseed, ginger, asafoetida, black cardamom, bay leaf and clove) and *dum gogji* (turnips cooked in spiced curd). *Guchchi* are a variety of morel mushrooms that grow wild in the hills of the Kashmir Valley (and neighbouring Himachal Pradesh). Kashmiris collect these—along with other edible fungi—and dry them for keeping over a long term. These are quite precious and used judiciously in dishes such as *guchchi pulao*, crafted for special occasions.

Vegetarians will find a sufficient variety of dishes available in Kashmir to make them feel attended to, but the glory of Kashmiri cooking is in the meat dishes. Goat or lamb—the cooler climate allows for the breeding of these woolly animals—is traditionally preferred though chicken has become widely used in recent times. Curd and aromatic spices such as cinnamon, black/green cardamom, clove, bay leaf and red chill are common ingredients in Kashmiri meat preparations (add garlic and onion to this list in a Muslim household), which include *yakhni* (lamb stewed in thick curd sauce); roghan josh (lamb stewed with red chillies); and *kalia* (lamb stewed in thin sauce). Mutton or chicken can be substituted in any of these dishes, with a slight adjustment of the flavouring ingredients in the case of poultry. Meat is also cooked with seasonal greens such as fresh/dried fenugreek leaves (*methi maaz*) or green coriander (*dhaniwal korma*). All these dishes are eaten with rice or roti. For taste and textural contrast, a meal might include a 'dry' meat preparation such as kebabs made from minced meat and served with chutney or *kabargah* (lamb ribs poached in a stock infused with whole aromatic spices, coated in a paste of curd and red chilli powder, and deep pan-fried).

Some of these meat dishes are essential to the customary Kashmiri Muslim wedding feast called *wazwan mishani*, a gargantuan meal that is the apogee of Kashmiri meat cooking and is always prepared by professional cooks called *waza*. The wazwan is the final of the three mishani meals held to mark different points in the engagement and wedding of a Kashmiri couple. Tradition demands that seven set dishes be served at each mishani: *tabak maaz* (lamb ribs poached in milk and spices and braised in butter); *rista* (small meatballs in a saffron and fennel sauce); roghan josh; dhaniwal korma; *aab gosht* (lamb pieces cooked in a milk-based gravy); *murghi korma* (chicken cooked in rich onion gravy); and *gushtaba* (large meatballs in curd sauce). Meat for gushtaba and rista is pounded on a flat wooden stone with a walnut-wood mallet—because it does not splinter—until all the fibres are broken down and the texture is smooth and silky. The menu for the first two mishani meals is typically confined to these seven dishes served with rice, some supporting chutneys and a sweet dish. The mishani wazwan, however, is a no-holds-barred affair, with forty dishes not being unusual. It is considered inhospitable on the occasion of a wazwan to serve more than one or two vegetable dishes, but with changing tastes and modern health concerns, you might find a few more vegetarian dishes in the line-up. Various chutneys and curd accompany a wazwan.

Wedding guests sit in fours around a large copper plate (*tarami*) to share the wazwan. The plate is piled high with rice and the dishes are added to this in sequence. Each diner makes a tunnel into the rice mound from his position around the communal platter and mixes in a portion of the various dishes on offer. Depending on the number of preparations being served, the tarami is replaced with a fresh one at intervals throughout the meal. Guests are offered the use of a *tasht-naar*, a portable washbasin and pitcher, to wash their hands during plate changes. Qahwa is the drink of choice at a wazwan.

In a traditional Kashmiri kitchen, food is cooked on a *dan*, a clay 'oven' that is more like a cooktop, with three or four holes in which pots are contained and heated by a wood fire. Kashmiri Pandits prefer to cook in earthenware pots. Kashmiri Muslims are happy with metal pots but a true wazwan feast must be cooked over a wood fire to ensure that the food tastes authentic.

Recommendations

. . . .

A sojourn on a houseboat on Dal Lake in Srinagar is the wish of most visitors to Kashmir, and there are plenty available on which to gratify that desire. Meals are usually included as part of the accommodation and I suggest that you choose a houseboat that will prepare Kashmiri-style food for you. (It might take a bit of negotiation to ensure that it is not prepared in line with the cook's interpretation of what it is that they think will suit your outsider's palate.)

To experience the 'heaven on earth' that Kashmir has long been reputed to be, I stayed at **Butt's Clermont Houseboats** on the western side of Dal Lake in splendid isolation from the suburbia of bumper-to-bumper houseboats at the Dal Gate end. In doing so, I was following a line-up of luminaries including George Harrison, Ravi Shankar and a Rockefeller, who have all stayed here since the father of the current host, Mr Butt, inherited these charming, ornately carved boats from their British owner in 1946 on his final departure to England. Each boat has a view directly over the lake and to the mountains beyond.

My request for my meals to be furnished with traditional Kashmiri cuisine was met with an enthusiastic response from the cook and I enjoyed any number of dishes prepared, from nadr along with murgh dhaniwal korma, *ninya* (lamb) pulao, yakhni, lake fish cooked with turnips and roghan josh. There was an endless supply of qahwa and home-made walnut cookies for afternoon tea. One evening, I arrived 'home' from my culinary explorations of Srinagar's older precinct to be greeted by Mr Butt who excitedly presented me with a local speciality that he had sent a staff member in the town to buy for me. It turned out to be a delicious fudgy chocolate cake. It did have walnuts in it and as it was the British who set up the houseboat system for which Kashmir has become famed, I figured that this item deserved a pass as 'local'.

Mr Butt can arrange an early-morning 'food tour' of the lake on small, agile commuter boats called *shikaras*. Accompanied by a flask of hot tea, and local breads picked up from a baker's boat along the way, you can watch fishermen at work; observe the floating vegetable gardens up close; inspect the freshest of produce at the floating market and try some wild Kashmiri honey. Just down the road from Butt's, past Hazratbal Mosque, there is a local market where you can sample kebabs with chutney and/or sweet semolina halwa eaten with roti.

On Dal Lake, Hazratbal
(0194) 2420325
www.buttsclermonthouseboat.com

If you prefer a more 'urban' houseboat environment to the country-estate ambience of Butt's, contact the reputable Houseboat Owners Association for assistance in finding a boat with good culinary credentials.

www.houseboatownersassociation.org

You are never far from a bakery in Srinagar so you can easily get fresh bread for breakfast. There are bakeries around Dal Gate—you can't miss these; just watch where the locals are heading in the morning or look out for the baskets or trays of baked goods on display. A cup, or three, of tea is essential with these—milky nooncha is the proper accompaniment but qahwa is fine if you prefer that—and you will find tea stalls ready to supply you near the Dal Gate bakeries. If you are in a residential area, you will see that people take their bread home and have tea there.

Srinigaris call **Qayaam Chowk**, close to Dal Gate, 'the barbeque', as there is a cluster of simple cafes that specialize in serving meat kebabs cooked over charcoal. Try the elongated seekh kebab with walnut chutney.

Mughal Darbar is a reliable place in which to sample Kashmiri dishes. You can order a 'wazwan' of dishes if you are up to it (or don't have an invite to a Kashmiri wedding) or enjoy a singular meat dish such as gushtaba, accompanied by pulao and seasonal greens. There is an interesting situation at Mughal Darbar (and this is not unusual in India): there are two independent restaurants of this name operating in the same building. Note that the recommended venue is on the first floor.

First Floor, Residency Road
Noon–3 p.m., 7–10.30 p.m. (7 days)
(0194) 2482202
www.mughal-darbar.com

You can dine in more 'elevated' style in the elegantly informal **Chinar Restaurant** located in the former hilltop palace of Maharaja Hari Singh. You can enjoy a simple, but meltingly exquisite, grilled local rainbow trout, nadr yakhni, succulent seekh kebabs with tangy pomegranate and onion chutney or turnips cooked with leaves. If you fancy them, more elaborate dishes like rista, gushtaba and *mirch wangan korma* (mutton stew flavoured with red chillies and spices like cardamom and cinnamon) are on offer. Finish the meal with the delicate saffron phirun.

The Lalit Grand Palace Srinagar, Gupkar Road
(0194) 2501001, 2501002
12.30–3 p.m., 7.30–11 p.m. (7 days)

JAMMU

The Jammu region lies south of the Pir Panjal range that demarcates it from the Kashmir Valley. Its land undulates from the high hills of the range— covered with snow in the winter—through a temperate region of low hills to a subtropical belt along its border with Punjab. The varying terrain and climate affect the type of foods that can be grown in these subregions. For instance, mango can be grown in the warmer parts but not in the hills. The major food crops of Jammu are rice, wheat, corn, pulses, potatoes and mustard, all of which are important ingredients in the regional cuisine. Jammu's modern food culture has several distinct elements. Muslims in Jammu eat the same style of food as eaten in the Kashmir Valley and dishes from this cooking tradition are popular in local restaurants as are Punjabi-style dishes. Jammu's native Dogri cuisine is not as easily accessed outside domestic kitchens though several items from this culinary tradition are readily accessible to any visitor lacking an invitation to dine in a Dogra home.

The Dogras are the indigenous people of Jammu and make up more than half of its population. They are predominantly Hindu yet not singularly joined by religion. There are Muslim and Sikh Dogras, united by a shared language (Dogri), cultural practices and location—they live mostly in Jammu but also in neighbouring Himachal Pradesh and Punjab. Until Independence, Jammu and Kashmir was ruled by Dogra Rajputs. Dogri cuisine shares strong similarities with the food of Himachal and, to a lesser extent, that of Punjab. Despite geographic proximity and shared governance, the commonality of features between Dogri cuisine and traditional Kashmiri cooking is not as strong as it is with that of these other two states. A distinct difference between Dogri and Kashmiri cuisine is that the former is largely, but not exclusively, vegetarian.

Pulses form the base of traditional Dogri cooking. Arguably the best-known dish of Jammu is made from red kidney beans (*rajma/rajmash*). These are typically cooked with onions, garlic, turmeric, mustard oil and red chilli. (There will be many variations of this and strict Hindus will replace onion and garlic with asafoetida.) The key to gaining the best flavour in this dish is to cook it slowly in a clay or brass pot over a wood fire. Modern cooks may not have the time or inclination to make rajma in this way but they love eating it and, consequently, it has become a standard dish in Jammu dhabas. A plate of rajma is popularly eaten with rice and a zesty chutney of dried pomegranate seeds (*anardana*) ground with green chillies, curd, ginger, cumin and mint. Pomegranates grow wild in the lower hills of Jammu and the village of Peerah is surrounded by stands of trees bearing this fruit; its 'main street' is also lined with dhabas renowned for their triad of rajma, rice and anardana chutney, accompanied by a generous tumbler of melted ghee to mix into the food as required. There is such a number of dhabas in Peerah trading in this culinary combination that the owners have formed a 'union' and agreed to charge the same price so that no undercutting takes place and all get an equitable share of the passing trade. You will find rajma and rice served in dhabas across Jammu and it is not clear whether it is the proximity of the pomegranate orchards or the fact that the village lies on a particularly curvaceous stretch of the main Jammu–Srinagar highway (causing road users to take a break) that has resulted in Peerah becoming something of a mecca for this dish.

Raungi (black-eyed beans), chana (chickpeas) and *kulthi/kulath* (horse gram) are other pulses commonly used in Dogra cooking. Along with rajma, these are cooked in various styles including *madra/madhra*, a preparation of spiced curd to which cooked beans are added. To make madra, spices such as cinnamon, black/brown cardamom and cloves are tempered in hot ghee to release their flavours; the heat is then reduced and curd added and cooked slowly to absorb the flavours of the spices and thicken slightly; when the 'oil' from the ghee starts to separate, cooked pulses are added to complete the dish. *Maa ka madra* is prepared from whole black urad dal. Madra is an essential component of a Dogra wedding feast (*dham*) and dried fruit might be added to it if it is intended for such a festive occasion.

Maani is another common Dogra preparation using pulses. Cooked beans, such as chickpeas, are mixed into an unctuous gravy flavoured with mustard oil (the common cooking medium in Jammu), whole fennel seeds, ground cumin and coriander, *amchoor* (dried green-mango powder) and asafoetida, and thickened with *besan* (chickpea flour). *Dal puth maani* is another Dogra culinary triad of a dal-based dish—such as *kulthi ki dal*—rice and maani that constitutes a complete meal. The Dogras like to have a tangy or 'sour' dish at a meal as they believe this helps digest pulse-based dishes and balance the flavours. Along with anardana chutney, madra and maani, the repertoire of tangy Dogra dishes includes *kaddu ambal* prepared with pumpkin (*kaddu*) cooked with fenugreek, tamarind, jaggery, red chillies, turmeric and cumin.

A distinct, though not unique, technique of Dogri cuisine is to add a hot coal to some mustard oil and place this in a pot containing a prepared dish and cover the pot. This process infuses the food with a smoky flavour and is called *dhuni*. Dishes subjected to this process are denoted as dhuni-wallah, for instance *khatta meat dhuni-wallah* or *rajmash dhuni-wallah*. Khatta meat is a traditional Dogri non-vegetarian preparation of mutton cooked in mustard oil with garam masala (typically cinnamon, cloves, cardamom, bay leaves), red chillies and a sour ingredient—khatta means sour—such as ground anardana, amchoor or dried mango pieces. The trick lies in cooking it slowly such that it develops a dark, almost black, colour and the flavouring ingredients 'stick' to the meat. Khatta meat is ideally cooked over a wood or charcoal fire as the coals can be manipulated to provide the slow gentle heat required to achieve a superlative taste. However, this traditional method is not always followed because of time constraints and a preference for cooking over a clean and easy gas flame.* Tradition predominates when it comes to cooking food for a Dogra wedding, though, and the prescribed nuptial dishes of madra, ambal, plain rice and *meetha pant* (sweet rice flavoured with aniseed or fennel seeds and dried fruit) will always be cooked over coals in brass vessels. (A dham does not include meat dishes.)

Daily family meals for Dogris typically include seasonal leafy greens; over the course of the year, these would include mustard greens, different varieties of spinach including wild *bathua*, fenugreek leaves and the tops of carrots. People living close to forested areas might collect wild greens such as *kasrod* (fern tendrils) as well. The greens are chopped or torn into smaller pieces and simply stir-fried with a little garlic, ginger, cumin, turmeric, coriander and green chillies. Or, they can be added to other dishes such as *aloo ka oriya* (potatoes in curd–mustard sauce).

A distinct food of Jammu is a cheese called *kalari*. It is traditionally a product of the hills, made and eaten by hill people of both Kashmiri and Dogra ethnicity. Kalari originated as a way to preserve excess fresh milk. To make it, milk is heated to simmering point and a coagulant such as sour whey or citric acid (the use of this commercial product is more recent) is added. The resulting curd is kept simmering until the heat gradually denatures its protein content—forcing out the water in its structure—and firms it up. The cooked curd is then cooled and shaped by hand into palm-sized slabs. The finished cheese is placed on tree leaves, pine needles or clean cloth and pressed under a weight for a day or so to force out any liquid remaining in it. The result is a firm cheese that can be stored and easily transported, and be cooked to a high temperature because it has so little moisture left in it. In Jammu, kalari is fried on a hot tawa until it is crisp and brown on the outside. It can either be eaten on its own or sandwiched in a soft bun in which case it becomes *kalari kulcha*. (This particular kulcha is a white, slightly spongy bread, distinct from the wholewheat tandoori kulcha of

---

* Getting gas for the kitchen is not that easy, though. Piped gas is very slowly coming into use in India, and in very select locations. Liquefied petroleum gas (LPG) comes in heavy red cylinders that have to be delivered to homes, and it is hard work for the workers charged with moving these around. Spend any time in India and you will not fail to see gas cylinders being delivered. The government also places restrictions on the amount of gas a household can access each year and there is a lot of 'under the table' trading that goes on around this commodity.

Punjab.) The inside of a cooked kalari has a gooey, stretchy texture and is similar to the Middle Eastern *haloumi* and Italian mozzarella, both of which are cheeses produced by cooking curd.

Recommendations

Jammu Tawi is the major city of Jammu and the winter capital of the state. The Tawi River flows through it, dividing it into the so-called old and new cities. If you visit the area designated as the 'Old Heritage City' and wander around (or if you want to be more specific, ask for directions to Pucca Dunga, Kachi Chawni or Purani Mandir), you will find numerous street vendors selling kalari kulcha. Also look out for the distinctive Jammu street food called *kachaloo chaat* made from cooked taro (*kachaloo*) dressed with tamarind chutney and chaat masala. If you want to eat in a cafe proper, you can try the popular **Pahalwan di Hatti** for both kalari kulcha and rajma.

Gol Market, Gandhi Nagar, Old Heritage City
(0191) 2431383
7 a.m.–10 p.m. (7 days)

Paras Ram di Hatti was started by Paras Ram in 1940 and is still run by his family. This dhaba is modest in appearance but enjoys legendary status for its non-vegetarian dishes. Come here to try khatta meat.

Old City, Near Panjtirthi
10 a.m.–7 p.m. (7 days)

Nilaya is located in the art-deco palace that was the former home of Maharaja Hari Singh, the last ruling monarch of Jammu and Kashmir. It offers a range of Dogra specialities such as khatta meat dhuni-wallah, aloo ka oriya, madra and meetha pant.

Hari Niwas Palace, Palace Road
(0191) 2543303, 2543180, 2547216

LADAKH

The high-altitude desert landscape of Ladakh sits in stark relief to its administrative sibling, the Kashmir Valley. At 11,000 feet, green comes in small patches—an apricot orchard, a stand of chinar trees, an irrigated field—yet the region has breathtaking majesty. Precipitous mountainsides stretch up into a sharp blue sky (on a good day, that is, else it can be quite grey) and down into valleys cut through by the freezing waters of the Indus and several of her tributaries; this is all the water Ladakh has. It rarely rains here and the evaporation is so high that the air is desiccated of moisture. The land is covered with snow for almost half the year, a natural circumstance that up until recent times left Ladakh completely isolated in winter. Yet, Ladakhis have thrived in this harsh environment for thousands of years, largely because they have developed sustainable agricultural and culinary practices around what their land is capable of giving them.

Ladakh and Kashmir were both on subsidiary routes of the legendary Great Silk Road, which ran all the way from China to the Mediterranean, and share general historical experiences, but Ladakhis are predominantly Buddhist and genetically of Tibetan origin. The region was once a province of Tibet and the connections with that country are so strong that Ladakh is often referred to as 'Little Tibet'. The King of Leh had to call on the Mughals for assistance to beat the Mongols back into Central Asia and thwart their intended takeover of his kingdom in the seventeenth century. In return, he had to send an annual tribute to the emperor in Delhi and build a mosque in Ladakh, but the winter isolation and harsh climate meant that there was little to be commercially gained there, so the Mughals left the region alone. In this way, the environment can be seen to have protected local culture.

In Ladakh, food is traditionally produced on small-scale family farms of just a few acres. The growing season is short and the most productive crop is barley. This grain is the staple food of Ladakhi cuisine (as, indeed, it is throughout the trans-Himalayan region). After harvesting, it is washed, sun-dried, parched on hot sand and winnowed to remove any vestiges of husk. The prepared barley can be eaten whole or ground into a meal called *namphey/tsampa*. In its simplest form, it is mixed with liquids such as butter, diluted rice beer, buttermilk or sugar and butter to make soft, uncooked dough called *kholak*, which is eaten with tea. A range of breads and noodles are also made from namphey, either on its own or mixed with wheat flour. Yes, some wheat is also grown in Ladakh.

Ladakhis share the Kashmiri habit of starting the day with freshly baked breads collectively called *tagi*. *Tagi khambir* is a thick, chewy round of bread leavened with an indigenous yeast product called *pul*, though baking powder has begun to replace this as the raising agent of choice. Khambir is cooked on an iron or stone griddle laid over a fire either supported on stones or laid on top of one of the cook holes of a *thup*, the Ladakhi oven, with smouldering dung or wood beneath it. The bread is placed briefly in the coals to finish it off. There are different types of tagi, all of which are variations on this theme. *Tagi thalkhuruk* is the same dough baked entirely in the ashes of a fire. It reminds me of the Australian bush bread called damper. *Tagi mer-khour* has butter and egg white added to the dough. Bread is often eaten with apricot jam. This golden-orange fruit grows abundantly in Ladakh and is believed to be indigenous to nearby China too. It was first cultivated in India and travelled into the Middle East via ancient trade routes—or it could have been the other way round. Ladakhis enjoy apricots poached in syrup and served with curd as a breakfast or dessert dish. The sea buckthorn shrub grows wild in Ladakh. *Chastu ruru*, its small orange berries, are unusual as they contain saturated and polyunsaturated fats and fifteen times the vitamin C of oranges. (You've got to hand it to mother nature—this is an ideal plant for people who live in cold, harsh climates.) Sea buckthorn is an important commercial crop in the trans-Himalayan region as there is great demand for it from the cosmetic and vitamin industries. Ladakhis turn it into jams and squashes.

Lunch or dinner in a Ladakhi home would typically be *thupka*, a soupy stew of meat, vegetables and barley/wheat noodles and/or namphey. What goes into this one-pot meal will be determined by the season and what is available in the house. Noodles for thupka are pressed into shape by hand: a practice that might derive from the use of barley flour, which is not as glutinous as wheat flour and therefore does not roll out as easily. Pressing dough into small ear and cup shapes is also a commensal activity shared by women sitting in the warmth of the hearth. Thupka is finished with a generous dressing of the dried yak cheese called *chhurpe*. (If you are familiar with Italian food, think of Parmesan cheese sprinkled on a hot bowl of minestrone soup.) *Skyu* is a dish made with ear-shaped noodles served in a thicker sauce than thupka, and a little more like eating a bowl of pasta. While the Italian theme seems to have come in, let's say then that Ladakhis use as many spices in their cooking as Italians—that is, very few—with chillies being the most common. *Mok-mok* (momos) are steamed dumplings stuffed with meat or vegetables that originated in Tibet. Throughout Ladakh, these are served in a bowl of light soup prepared from meat bones or with red chilli chutney. It takes time and patience to prepare mok-mok and so home preparation is usually limited to special occasions.

Given the short growing season, it is not surprising that fresh green vegetables—of the sort children, and some adults, living in more temperate climates detest—are highly prized in Ladakh. In the short summer, leafy greens such as spinach, sugar beet (leaves), white radish (leaves, taproot), peas and Chinese cabbage are grown and cooked fresh; some are also dried so that they can be used when fresh food is not available. Green vegetables are mixed with curd or buttermilk to create *tangthur* (similar to raita) or added to thupka. Peas are boiled, dried and ground to a meal that is added to bread for flavour. The application of modern agricultural methods has allowed for a greater variety of vegetables to be grown—and more fresh food is trucked in from other states—but these additions tend to be cooked in a traditional style such that a contemporary thupka might include a rich melange of vegetables.

Ladakhis rear sheep, cows, yaks and goats and take milk from all these and process it to produce curd, butter, *labo* (soft cheese) and chhurpe; the whey left over from butter production, *chhurkhu*, is used in cooking. Yak's milk—with its high fat content, which is 5–7 per cent compared to 3–4 per cent in cow's milk—is highly prized in such a cold environment. Milk and butter are used to make Ladakhi tea called *gurgur cha*, so called for the sound that is made when the tea, hot water, salt and dairy products used to produce this drink are churned together in a long tube creating a vacuum that disperses the fat globules of the milk and butter into the hot water. The finished gurgur cha is poured into an earthenware kettle that sits in another pot to keep it warm—like a solid tea cosy—and small cups of this are drunk through the day. In earlier days, poor Ladakhis drank *chhang*, a mildly alcoholic beverage brewed from fermented barley, for they could not afford to buy or barter for imported tea, but had plenty of grain at hand.

Recommendations

Leh is the main urban centre of Ladakh. Improved access has turned this once-enigmatic city into a tourist mecca. Restaurants and cafes serving *menu touristica* abound here. The good news is that many of them serve some Ladakhi specialities. You will not find it hard to get a bowl of thupka (if the noodles are long and thin, they are from a packet and not handmade) or a plate of mok-mok. If you are staying in a family-run guest house that provides meals, ask them to make you the local fare; Ladakhis are proud of their culture—even as they eagerly take on modernity—and will probably be delighted that you asked.

The **Women's Alliance of Ladakh** is at the centre of an organization of 15,000 Ladakhi women concerned with maintaining traditional Ladakhi culture and raising the status of women within it. The centre includes a vibrant cafe where local foods are served. Come here for a (late) breakfast of khambir, apricot jam or local honey, gurgur cha, and/or poached apricots with home-made curd. Other dishes are available in the day and local food products are up for sale. Women run workshops on traditional Ladakhi skills like making apricot oil from kernels.

Near Himalayan Hotel
11 a.m.–4.30 p.m. (Monday–Saturday)
(01982) 257293
www.womenallianceladakh.org

Dzomsa on Fort Road is an unpretentiously earthy storefront for the strong anti-plastic movement that has spread in Leh. You can refill water bottles here with filtered water at minimal cost. You can also have a breakfast of khambir with home-made butter and apricot jam; namphey porridge with apricots; a glass of apricot or buckthorn juice; and as much gurgur cha as you like. The store stocks dried apricots, apples, carrots and jars of local vegetable pickles that you can buy.

HILLS OF PLENTY

People were living in the lowland hills of the Himalayas, in the region now known as Himachal Pradesh, as early as the third millennium BC. It is not clear whether they belonged to Harappan culture or were indigenous people whom the Harappans pushed out of the Indus Valley, though the latter is the predominant theory. As the Aryans pushed their way through Punjab into the Gangetic plain, they settled into the region bringing large tracts of arable land under cultivation. This fertile ground ran up several river valleys separated from each other by high hills and mountains; the fact of this geography made it impossible for any single ruler to gain control over the whole region and a number of distinct and separate tribal republics developed in various places. By the fifth century AD, many of these republics had come under the control of Hindu Rajputs. In the sixteenth century, the Mughals gained control of some parts of the region but the difficult terrain prevented them from infiltrating too far inwards and their influence lessened in proportion to the distance from the plains. After the decline of the Mughals, the Sikhs laid claim to the region; it was then wrested from them by the British during the Anglo-Sikh wars of the nineteenth century. After Independence, the twenty-eight independent princely states of the region were brought together to form a Union Territory that, in 1971, became the state of Himachal Pradesh.

On a map, Himachal's borders delineate a region that runs from the Punjab border through to the Tibet Autonomous Region: in between is a greatly varied topography. The land begins to rise from the plains in gently undulating foothills that grow into snow-covered mountains accessible only in the summer months and culminate in the towering, uninhabitable peaks and glaciers of the greater Himalaya. It is from these heights that the rivers that dissect the region and create its fertile valleys begin. Climatic conditions are equally diverse: the high Himalayan region receives almost no rainfall and is desert-dry; lower down the mountains, the rainfall is ample and supports subtropical forests and large areas of lowland orchards. Water is also taken from the state's rivers to irrigate these orchards and Himachal is the largest producer of apples in India earning it the moniker of the 'Apple State'. The British introduced commercial production of orchard fruit, including plums and pears as well as apples, into Himachal in the nineteenth century. While these fruits are abundant in season, they have not been incorporated into local cooking in any significant way. Fruit not sent to inter-state markets is transformed into jams and cordials—another British influence—enthusiastically bought as souvenirs by the many tourists who visit Himachal. Other commercial crops include wheat, barley, rice and vegetables, which are all part of the daily diet in Himachal.

While Himachal's discrete communities are now officially part of one unified state, each has retained its distinctive culture to varying degrees. These differences can be heard in language, seen in architecture and traditional clothing/headwear and experienced in celebrations of festivals and weddings. Each community also has its distinct agricultural and culinary practices though these can be hard to discern for the visitor. Himachal is one of the most scenic regions of India, incredibly popular with tourists (the same ones who buy the jam). Tourism brings important financial benefits, but it has also led to the proliferation of the standard Punjabi-influenced tourist menu in eateries across the state. To be fair, the predominance of Punjabi fare on menus in Himachal is not entirely inauthentic as the region was part of the greater Punjab region until 1947. The culinary explorer need not be entirely disheartened as there are opportunities to sample local cuisine if you are prepared to step off the orthodox tourist trail a little. Or, if you are prepared for a bigger expedition, you can travel to Spiti for a truly unique experience of one of Himachal's distinct regional cultures and its associated cuisine.

During my exploration of Himachal, I spent some time at The Judge's Court, a heritage hotel in Pragpur in Kangra district. The chef there asked me what I would like to eat; 'Himachali food' was my reply. He looked at me perplexedly and said, 'Madam, if you can tell me what dishes you require, I will make them.' It was my turn to be perplexed. I had come all the way to this particular hotel on the understanding that I would find local cuisine and this response left me feeling frustrated, but then

I realized my mistake. 'What I would like,' I said, 'is Kangra cuisine.' With that, the chef happily reeled off a list of dishes he could prepare for me. My point is that there is really no such thing as 'Himachali cuisine', though there is a body of dishes that have become categorized as such. (I have made a similar observation in the introduction about regional food in general.) Having travelled extensively across Himachal, I would say that this repertoire of dishes represents the local cuisine quite well generically, and it is often minor alterations that differentiate a dish from one area to the next. Given the limits of this book, I ask you to accept the headword 'Himachali cuisine' and first explore the commonalities across the state, then look at regional variations.

Despite their internal cultural diversity, 95 per cent of the people of Himachal are Hindu, making it the most homogeneous state in India. The type of food eaten every day is similar across its regions: various dals and beans cooked with spices into stews of varying consistency; seasonal vegetable dishes; wheat- and barley-based flatbreads and plain rice accompany meals. Dairy products are eaten with every meal and curd is used extensively as a cooking medium. Home-made butter is also churned from curd and the leftover whey/buttermilk is used in cooking. Himachal is not a particularly 'vegetarian' state and meat dishes are well liked though not necessarily included in every meal. Mustard oil is the usual cooking medium and chilli, coriander, garlic, onion, asafoetida and pomegranate seeds are typically used to flavour dishes. In the higher mountain regions, there is a tradition of collecting and drying both cultivated and wild leafy greens such as spinach and fenugreek as well as mushrooms in the warmer months, drying these and adding them to dishes throughout the winter months. It may no longer be critical to stock up on winter supplies in some parts of Himachal but the habit of collecting and using dried greens and other foods endures.

Himachali dishes to look out for include *siddu*, a large steamed bun made from wheat-flour dough and stuffed with various fillings such as spiced spinach or potato. A speciality of the Kullu region, it has become popular across Himachal. It is not dissimilar to the steamed buns of Chinese cuisine and given that Himachal was crossed by trade routes that ultimately ran through to China, I wonder if that might have been an influence in the development of this food item. *Sepu wadi* is made from ground *urad* dal which is tied in a cloth and weighted to push the liquid out and create a firm paste; this is then sliced, fried and served in a spiced sauce. The term *madhra* is used in Himachal for dishes made from dried beans such as chickpeas (*chhole*), red kidney beans (*rajma*) or black-eyed beans (*raungi* or *lobhia*), and it is a dish with many regional variations. *Kheru* is a creamy, soup-like dish made of curd beaten to a smooth texture and cooked with *besan* (chickpea flour)—curd can curdle when heated and adding besan prevents this—and tempered with garlic, ginger, cumin, coriander, dried fenugreek leaves (*kasuri methi*) and asafoetida. A variation of this is *jhouli*, a gravy made with curd and besan flavoured with garlic, red chillies, coriander and asafoetida, and served with plain rice. Fresh/dried greens might be included in a jhouli. *Chhachh* mutton is goat or lamb cooked in buttermilk and spices; lamb is raised in Himachal and Himachalis are said to prefer its meat.

Aloo palada is a dish of potatoes in curd gravy, flavoured with cumin, cinnamon, cardamom and asafoetida. *Pahari murghi* is a stir-fried kind of chicken with onions, cinnamon, garlic, bay leaf, red/green chillies and garam masala. Paharis are the traditional inhabitants of the hill regions of Himachal, Uttarakhand, Jammu and Kashmir and Nepal. Paharis are a major community across this region. They speak a multitude of dialects of Pahari language but are basically agriculturists raising wheat, barley, rice and vegetables along terraced hillsides as well as goats, water buffalo and sheep for milk and meat. Their influence is considerable in the cuisine of Himachal and, across the Himalayan hills, there is a shared Pahari style of cuisine. Other Pahari foods normally eaten in Himachal are a chutney ground from sesame seeds (*til*), fresh coriander, garlic, green chillies and curd, and *bhang ki chutney*, which is prepared from ground hemp seeds, cumin and lemon juice.

Recommendations

....

SHIMLA

It was the British who began the tourist industry in the Himalayan hills when they adopted Shimla as their summer retreat in the nineteenth century. There was no connecting road at that time and carting the equipment and supplies to set up house for the summer was a major logistical exercise afforded only by the very wealthy. This kept Shimla a very exclusive playground of about 1000 Englishmen that it took 20,000 Indians to keep in the style to which they were accustomed. There was not a large enough local population to do this work so the British brought in people from other parts of the subcontinent. These foreigners, European and Indian, also brought in their food habits and this began to affect those of the locals. It is a process that has not ceased and the food available in Shimla now represents the massive number of tourists that swell the town almost all year round. There are a couple of opportunities to sample local cuisine though. **Goofa** restaurant at Ashiana Hotel has a menu of Himachali specialities including chickpea/chhole madhra, sepu wadi and siddu. Goofa means 'cave' in Hindi and the cool depths of one are replicated here, making it popular with novelty-seeking tourists.

Hotel Ashiana Regency, The Ridge, Lower Bazaar (0177) 2621572

Shimla itself is far from the exclusive holiday destination it once was but those who can afford exclusivity should stay at **Wildflower Hall**. This luxurious resort, perched atop a hill in lush, peaceful environs thirteen kilometres from Shimla town, offers guests the opportunity to eat Himachali-style dishes at their very best and also to learn how to cook these. The a la carte menu always has a selection of local dishes but the best way to get a taste of the region is to order the grand Himachali thali. On my visit, this included a rich kheru; a simple tasty dish of moong dal flavoured with garlic; raita with pomegranate seeds; a Pahari-style dish of cauliflower and potatoes cooked with mustard seeds, green and red chillies and coriander; sepu wadi in a sauce of puréed spinach; *murgh dhalya dharia*, a local dish of chicken coated in an unctuous sauce of green coriander and curd flavoured with asafoetida; lamb cooked in buttermilk and a dessert of *boondi*, small crisp balls made from chickpea-flour batter soaked in sugar syrup. These were supported by a dizzying array of pickles and other titbits that I lost track of in the end, so I stopped noting and just sat back and let it consume me. These dishes are made in a professional kitchen and likely have much more finesse than those you might encounter in a private home, but the chefs at Wildflower Hall actively seek out local cooks to learn from and use local recipes for inspiration. Guests can elect to take an afternoon cooking class to learn how to prepare a selection of Himachali dishes. Once a week, a tasting of wines made from locally grown fruit such as pear, peach, plum and rhododendron flowers (this tree is native to the Himalayas) is held in the bar. If you are familiar with rich, full-bodied grape-based wine, try to prevent yourself from comparing these less complex fruit wines to those, and you might be surprised at how drinkable some of these are.

Next to Chharabra Village on the Shimla–Kufri Road
www.oberoihotels.com

KULLU VALLEY

The Kullu Valley is the most popular tourist destination in Himachal. In Manali, its regional centre, it is possible to eat Punjabified versions of Chinese, Israeli, Continental, Italian, Thai, Bengali, Gujarati and Mughlai food but almost impossible to find any local cuisine. The best food advice I can offer, if you are visiting Manali, is to avoid joints offering 'fresh seafood' (it's a long, long way to the sea) and 'exotic' international cuisines and head straight to **Johnsons Café** for oven-roasted trout. These are raised locally in ponds that are kept filled with water from the Beas River. If you visit during the apple season, look out for their excellent crumble made with local fruit.

Johnsons Lodge, The Mall
(01902) 252316

Sai Dry Fruits on the Mall in Manali stocks locally grown and produced food products such as sun-dried fruits, almonds, pistachios, honey, cordials, jams and teas: good for snacks, sustenance for long mountain drives or walks and gifts.

4 Ram Bagh Market, The Mall (just above the bus stand)
(01902) 253275

The road from Manali to Naggar takes you through miles of terraced fields of wheat, corn, potatoes, vegetables and rice and fruit orchards. It gets cold in the winter but the region sits just below the snow line and has very productive agricultural land. You can enjoy the bounty of a domestic garden at **Poonam Mountain Lodge** in Naggar. The home-style meals served here are supplied from whatever is growing in the family's garden and orchard plot, supplemented with home-made dairy foods produced from fresh milk from the cows down the road. I

ate a jhouli-style dish of potato, garlic, ginger, cumin and a local spice
called *phirn* spooned over nutty local red rice and a madhra of a small
pink bean called *rong*—a word used in Himachal to describe several
varieties of oval-shaped, shiny-skinned *Fabaceae*. In deference to the
Vishnu temple adjacent to the lodge, all the food served is vegetarian,
but the host Ravi can arrange for a fishing trip to a local river to catch
local trout and cook and eat it in situ.

Below Naggar Castle
(01902) 248248
www.poonamlodge.com

If you find yourself anywhere near Naggar, you must take a detour
to Jana to eat at the dhaba there—as far as I could ascertain, this
place does not have a proper name nor an address but a local taxi
driver will know where to find it. Else, just get yourself to Jana and
start asking people on the roadside. This is a dhaba of the most basic
kind: open-sided, dirt floors, tables and bench-seating fashioned
from a variety of pieces of wood and a rough stone fireplace. Do
not let appearances faze you; you can eat some truly delicious local
food here. On the day I visited, a huge haul of oyster mushrooms
and wild spinach had been collected from the nearby forest. These
jungli fungi were simply stewed with turmeric, cumin and salt to
enhance and preserve their natural flavours. The spinach was treated
with an equally light hand, cooked with nothing more than chopped
tomato and salt. The dish of rong had a smoky flavour due to slow
cooking over a *chulha* (*see below*). The roti was made from ground
local corn and came with a pot of nutty home-made ghee to drizzle
over generously. A light, fluffy siddu stuffed with a paste of ground
coriander and green chillies was an extra I didn't actually need but
managed to squeeze in. A selection like this is the extent of the menu
each day. If the owner/chef of this dhaba were producing such food
in a Western country, he would be hailed as a culinary hero and
probably have his own television show as well.

All the food served at the Jana dhaba is cooked on a chulha, a
traditional low-slung 'cooktop' fashioned from mud, cow dung
and straw. Several holes are shaped into the top and pots of food
are placed on these to cook from the heat of the wood/charcoal fire
beneath. Pots can be moved off these apertures on to the solid part

of the top to cook gently or stay warm. A chulha is a very special thing; each one is unique, made by hand and shaped to suit the space it occupies and the needs of its owner and built low to the ground to accommodate the traditional Indian style of squatting while working. As there is less space between the ground and the cooktop, it requires less fuel to do its work. Chulhas are regularly replastered; when they can no longer be patched up, they are broken down and rebuilt from scratch. Each chulha is said to impart its own flavour to the food cooked on it—from the type of wood burnt in it and the local clay it is made from. You are unlikely to see a chulha in an urban environment but keep an eye when travelling through the mountains as roadside tea shops are still powered by them and the best chai is brewed over them.

KANGRA

The Kangra Valley runs through Himachal's western flank and is distinct from the elevated territory of most of the rest of the state. The land here undulates only gently and the climate is semi-tropical, allowing for the production of a diverse array of food crops. Indeed, it is the most densely populated region of Himachal. Kangra borders Punjab and there is great similarity in the foods but Kangra does have its own cuisine, noted particularly for its sweet and sour flavours. You can best sample Kangra dishes at **The Judge's Court**, a country hotel adjacent to the medieval heritage village of Pragpur. This whimsical, Edwardian-era manor is surrounded by a huge flourishing garden, the produce of which mirrors the bounty of food grown in the region. Depending on the season, carrots, cauliflower, cabbage, turnip, pumpkin, ladies' fingers, radish, banana, mango, lychee, grapes, papaya, peaches, walnuts, guavas, cucumbers and oranges from the garden are used to create meals. The milk used comes from a small herd of cows reared on the property. The Kangra-style feast presented to me included a madhra of green peas cooked in curd; garden-fresh ladies' fingers cooked with small red onions; whole urad dal cooked with *amchoor* (dried green-mango powder), asafoetida and fenugreek leaves; and a Kangra version of Pahari chicken—there is a Kangra dialect of Pahari—redolent with smoky-black cardamom grown in the mountains near Chamba (*see* *below*). The meal ended with a dessert called *meethe chawal* (sweet rice), a dish of plain cooked rice dressed with a syrup of local jaggery, cashew nuts, dates and sultanas.

Jai Bhawan, Pragpur, District Kangra
(01970) 245035
www.judgescourt.com

CHAMBA

Chamba, in the far north-western corner of Himachal, is best known for its ancient Hindu temples and Chamba *dham*, the traditional feast served at weddings. The matrimonial ceremonies of any true Chambian would be considered incomplete without this particular meal. In theory, the whole village—to which the bride and/or groom belongs—is invited to the dham. This does not quite apply in modern, and rapidly expanding, Chamba town but any dham needs to be held in a huge hall, as the invitation will be widely extended (including to stray foreign writers). Even in a capacious venue, the meal has to be served in shifts to accommodate everybody. Guests sit on mats in long queues on the floor with plates before them. Professional servers pass along, dishing out food in a prescribed order: plain rice with a dal; Chamba madhra (*see below*); another type of dal and more rice; a sweet rice dish; *khaddi*, a soupy dish prepared from buttermilk and curd; and a sweet tamarind chutney called *khatta*. I was assured that the last dish was so effective in aiding digestion that within an hour of eating the dham, I would not feel its presence in my stomach. (This did not prove true in my case.) The distinctive Chamba madhra is made from local rong cooked with roasted curd, green and brown cardamom and cinnamon. The curd is roasted by cooking it in oil until it turns golden and develops a curdled look: treating the curd thus drives out all the water and allows it to stay longer; it also gives it a unique flavour somewhat like the smell of freshly baked yeasty bread and this flavour is imparted to the madhra. The brown cardamom grows wild in the nearby mountains and adds another characteristic layer of flavour.

Lacking an invitation to a Chamba wedding, you can visit the restaurant at **The Iravati**, a hotel that serves the dishes that make up a

Chamba dham. You can recreate a wedding feast of Chamba madhra, khaddi, khatta, meethe chawal and dal. A dham is always vegetarian but here you can add meat *darawala*, a Chamba preparation of meat cooked with pomegranate seeds. This fruit has long grown in the region and was traditionally used to prepare khatta, but tamarind from south India is used now. *Chansider*, a rich soupy chutney of jaggery, dried fruit, nuts and cardamom, is another local relish to try. The Iravati also lists several dishes prepared from *guchchi*, a morel native to the Kinnaur region. Guchchi is a rare and valuable food that can fetch up to 100 dollars per kilogram in city markets. It is in season in October; if you happen to be visiting The Iravati then and they have it, you must try it.

The Iravati, Opposite Maidan (HPTDC Complex)
(01899) 222671
www.hptdc.nic.in

Chamba owns several other distinct eatables: *chuk*, a fiery condiment made with ground chillies and spices; *jaris*, a digestive of coconut, fennel seeds, betel nut, green cardamom and sugar chewed after meals; and a dark, wild honey imbued with the floral essence of the region.

SPITI

It takes ten hours by road to cover the 200-odd kilometres between Manali and Kaza, Spiti's district headquarters. There is no other option to get into the area—unless you want to do some very serious trekking—but, fortunately, the scenery is spectacular all along the way and what awaits you at the end of the journey is worth it all. As you ease into Spiti along its river valley, initial impressions are of a harsh, inhospitable landscape intimidated by towering mountains that appear to fold on and over into forever. It's a valid impress as the average height of the region is 4500 metres and the average rainfall is negligible: water comes largely from mighty rivers that churn wildly with snowmelt, so cold that they are barren of aquatic life. Yet people have successfully inhabited Spiti for 1500 years, possibly longer. It is one of the most isolated places on the planet, which has resulted in the perpetuation of its traditional and remarkable lifestyle. Unlike the landscape, Spitians are a warm and hospitable people.

My culinary journey in Spiti was organized by the social enterprise **Ecosphere**. To best experience authentic Spitian life, I trekked through the region escorted by a local guide and stayed in village homes along the way. Life in Spiti is ruled, almost despotically, by the reality of surviving the freezing winter months. In the warmer months, a Spitian village is a hive of activity—food, firewood, fodder, medicine and fibre are grown, gathered, prepared and stored for the winter when the villages will be covered in snow and isolated from each other. It is only in the past two decades that Spiti has moved from a barter economy to a monetary one, which has necessitated producing a cash crop, such as green peas, in the warmer months. Every able-bodied person in a village is involved in this. Upon our arrival at our first homestay, a call announcing us was sent out across the terraced fields surrounding the village where our hostess was working with her suckling baby tied to her back. She came up to the house and cooked us a quick lunch of rice and freshly picked peas—which we ate with curd made from the milk of house cows—and returned to her labour until sundown.

Spitian women stay within the immediate environs of the village to do their share of the summer work. The men move further away; some shepherd animals to fatten them on the highland pastures revealed by the melted snow. Across the region, wild foods such as leafy greens, small onions and mushrooms are foraged for and dried to provide flavour and essential nutrients to meals throughout the long winter. Medicinal plants are also collected during this time: my guide Norbu's father is a traditional doctor and Norbu has accompanied him since boyhood on summer forays to collect medicinal plants, many of which he pointed out to me as we ambled along.

The mainstays of the Spitian diet are barley and dairy products. The former is a cereal crop that grows well in the high altitude and can be brought from germination to readiness in the window of the snowless months. Barley is used from breakfast through to the evening meal, mostly ground into flour from which various food items are prepared. In its simplest form, barley flour is cooked with water and salt into a porridge called *tsampa*; *chirual* is a variation made by adding pieces of dried curd to the mix. *Tirik* is an unleavened flatbread prepared from barley flour, shallow-fried in oil and eaten for breakfast accompanied by fresh curd and perhaps some jam—of commercial provenance, as the climate of Spiti does not support fruit growth. (There are some wild berries that grow locally, though, including those of the sea buckthorn, a thorny shrub that thrives in the harsh conditions. Sea buckthorn berries are dense with vitamin C and are so mouth-puckeringly sour that they are inedible without the addition of a sweetener. The berries are commonly harvested for commercial use in a variety of food, vitamin and skin products.) A dough of barley flour is used to make small dumplings—not unlike Italian gnocchi—cooked in a savoury stew called *skew* prepared from dried spinach, mushrooms and onions. *Churad* is a dish of these same barley dumplings boiled and dressed with sugar, melted ghee and gratings of *chhurpe*, a pungent, Parmesan-like cheese made from the whey left over from butter-making, by tying it in cloth and hang-drying. The churad is unexpectedly delicious. Barley-flour dough is also used to create small stuffed dumplings called momos, made on special occasions. My presence in Norbu's home village of Deemul was occasion enough for a large batch of these to be made, partly by my own hand as Norbu's father gave me a lesson in making these. A smooth, pliant dough was prepared; we pressed small pieces by hand to create thin casings; we filled these with a mixture of goat-leg meat finely ground with onion, turmeric, garam masala, salt and a judicious amount of dried red chillies; and we twisted the corners together over the filling to seal them. The finished dumplings were stacked in a triple-tiered steamer and placed over a wood-fired stove—in the centre of the living room—to cook. This was timed for the end of the working day and as I sat in anticipation of reaping the benefits of our production, the room filled with family members returning from the harvesting. While the momos cooked, a large bottle of home-made arrack distilled from barley was brought out to add cheer to the occasion, along with whole grains of sun-dried, dry-roasted barley eaten as a tasty, nutty snack called *yuag*. The hot momos were served with red chilli chutney and clear broth made from the bone of the leg of mutton we used, and flavoured with dried wild onions.

Spitians rear sheep, goats, cows, yaks, dsos (a cross between a yak and a cow) and donkeys, the latter being the only breed not used for milk.

During summer, sheep and goats are taken to the highlands to graze and cows are kept in the village for milking. Yaks and donkeys are important members of the labour force so they carry loads in both situations. Fresh milk from these animals is turned into curd, butter and cheese. As the name suggests, butter is an essential ingredient in the 'butter tea' drunk in Spiti. This beverage is made with a mixture of brewed black tea, salt, hot water and butter. All the ingredients are put in a long cylinder. A snug-fitting pestle is inserted into the filled cylinder and pulled up and down—it reminded me of a bicycle tyre pump—to create a suction, which forces the dispersal of the butter into the tea creating a smooth, uniform texture. Butter tea is enthusiastically consumed across the high Himalayan region and said to be most efficacious in keeping people warm in the freezing weather: all I can say after tasting it is that it is an acquired taste and not one that I am ever going to acquire. I found *chatang* (black tea with salt) far more to my liking.

Spitians are almost exclusively Buddhists, yet unlike the rest of India their spiritual practices have little impact on their diet. There are few Buddhist edicts against eating any particular food—at least in the Tibetan tradition practised in Spiti. Even the popular notion that Buddhists are vegetarians is not accurate. (Norbu told me that it was forbidden to eat fish but given the absence of these from the icy local waters, this does not represent a particularly onerous abstinence.) Living in the extreme environmental conditions that they do, Spitians have not had the bounty available to them such that they can afford to reject too many foods. In the winter months, meat is an important food. Before winter sets in, some animals are slaughtered: some fresh meat is cooked, some hung up to dry—the winter air is almost devoid of moisture and acts as a natural preservative—and some treated for storage. My breakfast in Deemul included a generous portion of *guyma*, a sausage made with goat's blood, finely ground offal, barley and spices contained in a casing made from the animal's intestine. The finished sausages are hung to dry and eaten through the cold months after cooking in a little oil. Animals' trotters and other bones are used for soup; the skin is used to make leather and the hair woven into blankets and clothing during winter when there is no work to be done outdoors.

Large trees are rare in Spiti; the ground is covered by highland pasture—in summer—and sparse low foliage so it comes like a fairy-tale surprise to suddenly discover yourself at the edge of a Spitian village as there is not much to hide these. The traditional stone-and-mud houses blend into their surrounds and appear to be perched precariously on steep-sided terrain whereas they are actually firmly glued to it. They are able to absorb the tremors caused by the Himalayas stretching themselves upwards by about 5 cm every year. Spitian homes play an important part in feeding the families. Grasses that have been collected and dried in the summer are stacked on the flat roofs, to feed animals during the winter, along with the firewood used for cooking and heating. Spitian homes stretch over several levels and, in the winter, animals live in the bottom storey and continue to provide milk and meat. Other foods are hung or stored in various places throughout the house.

Spiti borders the Tibet Autonomous Region. Spitians are ethnically of the same race as Tibetans; they speak dialects derived from the Tibetan language family and share the same Buddhist traditions. It is more a matter of a line on the map that separates Spitians from Tibetans but a huge chasm that separates them from the rest of India. You would have noticed from my descriptions of Spitian food that spices are used very sparingly; the style of cooking too is almost identical to that of Tibet. When I asked Norbu what constituted special-occasion food in Spiti, his answer was 'Indian food', indicating that India is an exotic place to Spitians. Much effort has been made recently to bring Spiti into closer contact with the India to which it officially belongs. More and more roads are being built into the region, making Spiti less isolated and bringing in, among other things, new foods that do not properly belong to the region and cannot be grown there. Satellite television has infiltrated the remotest villages and this is effecting change in the traditional Spitian society but much remains the same and through the culturally sensitive conduit of Ecosphere, you can experience a timeless way of living.

(M) 9418207750, 9873098017
www.spitiecosphere.com

CELESTIAL DINING

It's the breathtaking views of snow-capped mountains, vertiginous valleys and densely wooded hills of Uttarakhand that capture the attention of most visitors, but mine is more often drawn to admire the terraced mountainsides where the region's food supply is largely grown. One look at a run of these micro-fields stacked up steep inclines and you will understand why the traditional food of Uttarakhand is hearty. Most people who live here are involved in agricultural work, and climbing up and down these terraces requires serious exertion in itself, let alone the actual labour of farming, so significant calorific fortification is required. Over the past millennia or so, as he worked on his hard-wrought mountainside fields, an Uttarakhandi farmer might have found himself being passed each day, particularly in the warmer months, by others exerting their energies ascending the mountainsides on pilgrimage to the holy sites of the region.

Uttarakhand is popularly described as the 'heartland of Hindu identity' because it holds so many places sacred to the Hindus—the Badrinath Temple, one of India's four holiest *dham*s (occupying the northern cardinal point of this ultimate quartet of Hindu spiritual pilgrimage); the Kedarnath Temple, said to have been built by the Pandavas (protagonists of the Mahabharata) to atone for their sins after they won the battle of Kurukshetra at a huge cost of life; the holy city of Haridwar; the ashram town of Rishikesh; and the sources of the holy Ganga and Yamuna rivers. It was the natural fortification of the montane landscape and the impenetrable jungle of the sub-Himalayan plains along the southern edge of Uttarakhand that preserved these sites from Islamic intrusion. The strong vegetarian food ethos of Uttarakhand is both influenced by, and reflects, its importance as a place of Hindu spiritual pilgrimage, and perhaps limited Muslim influence—although the plains now house a sizeable Muslim population. Some things have changed around these ancient monuments though—most pilgrims now travel in cars!

Uttarakhand—meaning 'northern division' in Sanskrit—is the region's old name but the state only came into being in November 2000, when it was separated from Uttar Pradesh, to which it had been unhappily joined since Independence. The modern state is divided into two divisions, Garhwal and Kumaon, the boundaries of these equating with those of older kingdoms of the same names. The people are generally referred to as either Garhwali or Kumaoni, depending on which division they are native to. (For the sake of brevity, I will collectively refer to them as Uttarakhandis.) They share an Indo-Aryan ethnicity and are predominantly Hindu, yet have cultural differences. Each group speaks its own language, although both are dialects of the same parent Pahari language. (Pahari means 'hill people' and collectively refers to the native peoples of the hilly region of the Himalayas from Pakistan to Nepal.) There are some differences in their food habits but these can be subtle and arise from the use of unique local flavourings, seasonal foods and cooking methods. The commonalities between cuisines are more prevalent, so I am going to talk of their food collectively, noting any regional variations along the way.

Uttarakhand's soil is remarkably fertile for such a hilly region—the plain along the southern border with Uttar Pradesh proved particularly fecund once the jungle was removed from it in more recent times—and produces good crops of rice, wheat, barley, chillies, potatoes, millets, vegetables and sugar cane, all of which play significant roles in local food habits. A typical meal in Uttarakhand would be plain boiled rice, roti, one or two seasonal vegetables, dal and a chutney or two. A meat dish might replace one of the vegetable dishes in a meat-eating household. At its basic, it's a meal that is not particularly different from those eaten across most of central India but it is in the constituent ingredients that the distinctions lie.

Legumes (dal) and beans play important roles in the daily diet of Uttarakhandis. Of distinctive note is the use of a local variety of black soybean called *bhatt*. This variety cooks quickly and turns mushy so it is used to make a thick soupy dish called *bhatt ki churkani*; it is also commonly used in a winter dish called *rus*. This is made by cooking a mixture of beans— which might, depending on who is making it, include red kidney beans, chickpeas, *urad* dal and black-eyed beans as well as bhatt—until these are soft and straining off the cooking liquid to create a stock, which is then thickened with powdered rice and flavoured with ginger, garlic, chilli and cumin, and served with a spoonful of melted ghee drizzled on top. The leftover beans are used to create *badil*, a type of cake made by mashing and cooking the beans with carom seeds (*ajwain*), asafoetida, garlic and ginger until the mixture solidifies into a firm mass that is spread out on a tray to cool and firm up, after which it is cut into diamond shapes and served with a chutney.

Gahat or *kulath* (horse gram) is another distinctive dal eaten throughout Uttarakhand. This small round pulse—varying in hue from pale green to rusty pink—is typically included in the leguminous line-up of rus. It is the main ingredient in a dish called *phanu*, in which it is ground to a paste with onion, garlic and ginger and used to make a thick pancake that is cut into pieces and served in a spiced gravy also made from ground gahat. Phanu can be made from other dals such as urad, a pulse not unique to Uttarakhand. It is used here to make distinctive dishes such as *chainsu*, a thick potage of ground and roasted urad dal spiced with asafoetida, coriander seeds, cumin, red chilli and black pepper. Dals such as urad and moong are also soaked and ground to a paste with a few spices, shaped into patties, called *badi* or *mangodi*, and dried in the sun, preserving these for year-round use. Badis are typically added to gravy-based vegetarian dishes in Uttarakhand. Wet dishes of the type we have just discussed are usually served with rice.

Like most Indians, Uttarakhandis like leafy greens. The most common varieties eaten are colocasia, mustard, fenugreek and radish leaves, a local spinach called *pakadi pala*, tender fern fronds (*lingdi*) and stinging nettle (*bicchhu booti*). On a day-to-day basis, these leaves are usually cooked by stir-frying in a little mustard oil with cumin seeds and salt. *Kafuli* is a more complex dish of leafy greens such as spinach and fenugreek, cooked with various spices including turmeric, chilli, cumin, asafoetida and coriander until it softens to a thick purée; a little ground rice or *besan* (chickpea flour) is added to thicken the dish. *Kappa* is a similar dish of cooked green leaves but it is prepared with curd. Stinging nettles and fern fronds are wild foods collected from the forests along with honey and mushrooms; it is likely that Uttarakhandis traditionally collected a wider variety of local species of edible/medicinal plants from the forests.

The large Pahari cucumber is a variety of the *Cucurbitaceae* family considered a native of Kumaon. It is grated and mixed with curd and a paste of ground mustard and fenugreek seeds and finely chopped chillies to make Pahari raita, or cooked with dal or badi in a spiced gravy. (To those accustomed only to green cucumbers, the Pahari variety can look as if it's rotten—even though it is not—as it turns an autumnal orange when ripe.) Uttarakhandis also like to sauté vegetables such as pumpkin or potato with spices to create 'dry dishes' eaten scooped up with rotis: *aloo ka gutka*, a dish of potatoes cooked with ginger, asafoetida, red chillies, cumin seeds, turmeric and coriander leaves, falls into this category. In the winter months, Uttarakhandis eat the large white radish called *mooli*. Its green leaves are stir-fried, and its long taproot is cooked in a spiced stew called *thechwani* or finely sliced (raw) and mixed with curd, lemon, green chillies and ground hemp (*bhang*) seeds.

You will have picked up that the most commonly used spices are cumin, coriander seeds, red/green chillies and asafoetida. The last is often used in Indian cooking as a substitute for onion and garlic. Devout Brahmins and Vaishnavites avoid eating these odiferous alliums, particularly during festivals and pilgrimages. As the temple at Badrinath is dedicated to Vishnu and draws a huge number of pilgrims, and as Uttarakhand has a significant Brahmin population, there is quite a lot of onion and garlic avoidance, hence the extensive use of asafoetida. Having said that, Uttarakhandis do prepare dishes that include onion, garlic and asafoetida, as this resinous spice is believed to aid the digestion of beans and pulses and prevent flatulence.

There are several unique spices used in Uttarakhand: *jamboo*, a spice similar to cumin; *gandherian*, a type of angelica similar in flavour to asafoetida; and *jakhya*, a small green leaf that tastes like mustard. Bhang, or hemp, seeds are another Uttarakhandi spice. These high-protein, oil-rich seeds have a mild nutty flavour and are used roasted and ground either to thicken cooked dishes and add flavour and nutrition or, perhaps most famously, mixed with curd, cumin and lemon juice to make *bhang ka raita*. Farmers grow hemp as a rotational crop as the plants return nutrients to the soil. Although hemp is a plant of the cannabis family, its seeds are not intoxicating. Given the impressive nutrition profile of bhang though, one could suggest that it might intoxicate your body with goodness.

The British annexed Uttarakhand in the nineteenth century—after providing assistance to the local rajas to beat back the Gorkhas of Nepal—and also treated it as a place of pilgrimage of sorts, establishing numerous hill stations to which they retreated from the summer heat of the plains. They established orchards in Uttarakhand and the production of apricots, peaches and apples is still a significant industry. These fruits are exported to other parts of India or used for British-style products such as jams and cordials (eagerly bought by tourists), but not extensively used in cooking.

Where these fruits are most likely to be utilized is in the tangy chutneys that accompany a typical Uttarakhandi meal. In addition to orchard fruit such as apricots, chutney might be prepared from a small local pomegranate called *dadim* or a mix of coriander leaves, green chillies and juice of *galgal*, a variety of citrus native to the Himalayan hills. The juice is concentrated by heating it to create a product called *chukh*, which can then be stored and used all year round.

As there has never been a lot of open pasture for cows to graze on in Uttarakhand, if these animals are kept, they are largely fed on grasses and leaves foraged from the forests. It is quite a lot of work to collect sufficient fodder, every day, for an adult bovine so Uttarakhandis do not keep more than a few cows. This, combined with the fact that the milk yield from hill cows is smaller than that from pasture-fed ones, has meant that milk has never flowed profusely in Uttarakhand. As a consequence, there is a restrained use of dairy products. Ghee is used in cooking but it tends to be drizzled over a dish at the end, while mustard oil is the everyday cooking medium. Unique Uttarakhandi sweets such as *baal mithai* and *singodi* are also made from milk as these are only eaten as special festive treats (not necessarily the case these days). Baal mithai is a dark brown fudge-like sweet made by cooking the reduced milk product called *khoya* with sugar until it caramelizes; the hot mixture is poured into flat, shallow trays to set, after which it is cut into small rectangles and coated with small white *dragees* (sugar balls); if sold without this decorative layer, it is called 'chocolate'. (I have eaten a lot of baal mithai and prefer the 'chocolate' form as the crunchy texture of the dragees interferes with that of the fudge and also makes it too sweet.) Singodi is confected by whipping khoya with sugar and wrapping the resultant dense cream in cones made from the leaves of local oaks.

Sweets such as baal mithai and singodi are usually bought from professional confectioners. *Rot* and *arsa* are sweets customarily served at Garhwali weddings and prepared in domestic kitchens (which is not to say that these might not be outsourced from commercial suppliers these days). Rot is a flatbread made with a dough of wheat, milk, ghee, green cardamom, aniseed and gur, cooked in a small amount of ghee on a tawa. Arsa is a smaller, deep-fried bread made with wheat flour, ghee, gur and a resin collected from local trees. *Jhangora ki kheer* is an Uttarakhandi version of this common Indian dish made from a variety of millets cooked in milk. *Mandua* is a variety of millet commonly used in Uttarakhand to make rotis and a simple porridge called *faanu*.

Recommendations

. . . .

If you recall, I owned up a few paragraphs earlier that I have eaten a lot of baal mithai. That's because I have spent more time in Uttarakhand than in any other state of India. It is not easy to sample Uttarakhandi cuisine in situ as most commercial establishments are focused on providing tourists with food they are already familiar with or what the proprietor divines they will want to eat. There is no shortage of the type of Chinese/Punjabi/Mughlai/Continental/pizza/dosa/momo joints that are found in tourist spots all over India. There has been little improvement in gaining access to local food, outside a private home, in recent times, though most of these opportunities derive from Uttarakhandis opening their homes to paying guests. Before I make some specific recommendations, I am going to provide you a few general pointers to gaining some authentic tastes of Uttarakhand.

The indigenous Paharis of Uttarakhand generally eat two meals a day, a mid-morning 'lunch' and an evening dinner, filling in the gaps with plenty of cups of tea. As you travel around Uttarakhand, you will notice many tea shacks along the wayside. I recommend leisurely stopping at as many of these as you can handle cups of tea. This beverage will be served to you milky and sweet and depending on the proprietor will be additionally flavoured with ginger and/or cardamom, or other spices. Many years ago, in north-eastern Kumaon, I was served a cup of tea with pepper in it. I still remember it as it was so delicious.

People making pilgrimages to the various sacred sites of Uttarakhand now tend to drive, not walk, and tourists who have come for the scenery are inclined to do most of their sightseeing from the windows of a car, getting out of the said vehicle largely for tea breaks—at the aforementioned shacks—or meals at the numerous dhabas found along the more popular road routes. Dhabas are, by definition, basic eateries but they can serve up some pretty good fare though this might not always be strictly 'local' in style. You will often find that dhabas in Uttarakhand serve dishes made from local legumes and beans, flavoured with local spices and served with local rice; sometimes you might even get roti made from millet or barley. My advice then is to inspect the cooking pots of any eatery that looks like a dhaba and, if it smells good, try it. (The food will almost inevitably be vegetarian so you won't have to worry about any unpleasant carnivorous surprises if you want to avoid eating meat.)

Almora in Kumaon is considered to be the epicentre of baal mithai production. Legend has it that this confection was created here. There are numerous sweet shops along the main avenue where you can avail of this moreish sweet. You don't have to travel to Almora though as baal mithai is commonly sold throughout Uttarakhand. My favourite baal mithai–wallah can be found in Bara Bazaar in Nainital opposite the vegetable stalls there. (The sign is in Hindi but the display of baal mithai is easy to spot.)

I have fond memories of visiting **Chotiwala** restaurant in the ashram town of Rishikesh in the first week of my first visit to India eighteen years ago. I can't recall if they had Garhwali/Uttarakhandi specialities on the menu then as they do now, largely because I had no idea in the early stages of that trip that India even had different regional cuisines, and would not have thought to try anything I wasn't familiar with from my experience of eating in Indian restaurants back home. The fact that this enduringly popular restaurant has chosen to feature a good selection of regional dishes on its menu is a clear sign that there is an interest in local cuisine. If there are enough of you, order a feast of all the Garhwali dishes on the menu: rus, mandua roti, aloo ka gutka, Pahari raita, bhang raita, bicchhu booti saag and jhangora ki kheer.

Swargashram
(0135) 2430070
www.chotiwala.com

Sitla Estate is a charming colonial-era bungalow set amid acres of fruit orchards and serves as home to its host and a 'home away from home' for guests. Meals here are largely provisioned from the estate's own vegetable garden, cows and local suppliers. If you make a request to have a meal of Kumaoni dishes (which you are welcome to do), the surrounding forest might provide additional items for your plate. On my visit, I was served chicken dry-cooked with local spices (one of the few meat dishes I have been served in Kumaon outside the homes of my friends). Wild forest honey and home-made jams prepared from orchard fruit are served at breakfast.

Vikram Maira, Mukteshwar, Nainital
(05942) 286330
www.sitlaestate.net

The best way to get to the heart of Uttarakhandi culture and food is by visiting local villages where villagers welcome paying guests into their homes. These homestays are often set up through programmes designed to empower village women, who, because of their typically onerous daily responsibilities such as collecting cattle feed, tending fields, keeping the house in order and cooking meals (in case you are wondering, their husbands spend a lot of time sitting at those tea stalls I mentioned earlier), have few avenues to earn any independent income. Opening and maintaining a guest room in their homes and cooking a little extra is work they can fit into this schedule that rewards them with financial gain and personal success. I have not been able to visit **Sarmoli Village Homestay** in Munsiari in north-east Kumaon but it is highly recommended. I intend to get there, even if it is only to try the local caraway seed* halwa for breakfast. Not only can you stay in a village home and eat local cuisine in Sarmoli, you can also elect to live like a villager for a day and cook meals over a traditional wood-fired mud stove.

Malika Virdi, Village Sarmoli, Munsiari, District Pithoragarh
(M) 9411194041
www.munsiari.com

....

* Caraway is often translated as *shahi jeera* in Hindi but these are actually two different spices. Both belong to the *Apiaceae* family and look similar, but caraway has a slightly sweeter flavour than shahi jeera.

CAPITAL FARE

Delhi can be as old as anybody wants it to be. In the Mahabharata, a splendid city called Indraprastha is said to have existed beside the Yamuna River—where modern Delhi now sprawls—circa 1450 BC. Archaeologists have yet to unearth any material evidence to support the existence of that gleaming metropolis with a golden-pillared, jewel-studded pavilion at its centre, as described in this epic tale, or indeed to show that there was any type of developed civilization in the area before 1000 BC. At this time, the people historically referred to as Aryans pushed into the area from the north. They settled in small villages, living in huts made of mud and wood, and brought the land around them under cultivation with cereals, pulses, vegetables and fruit. In clearing the land and making it productive, these ancients laid the foundation for the glorious city that Delhi would one day become.

Everyday food in early Delhi comprised unleavened wheat breads eaten with stews of dal and vegetables; rice cooked with dal and flavourings; seasonal fruit; honey and jaggery; butter, curd, milk and roasted meats. The range of foods available and the complexity of dishes developed over time although the basic style of a meal changed little. Around 500 BC, meat eating appears to have become taboo for high-caste Hindus, possibly in reaction to the growing popularity of the doctrine of non-violence preached by Jains and the Buddha, who delivered two important sermons near Delhi around this time.

Delhi's first (and evident) significant building was a fort constructed sometime in the eighth century by the Hindu Rajputs who ruled the region. This stone stronghold proved ineffective in holding off the Turks of Central Asia when they swept down across Punjab and captured Delhi in the late twelfth century. It was these Turks who gave Delhi its first truly magnificent edifice, a nearly seventy-three-metre-tall stone-and-marble minaret called the Qutub Minar. On its completion in 1220, the Muslim call to prayer was rung out from this tower: Delhi was now an Islamic city, ruled by men who titled themselves 'Sultan', a term meaning Muslim sovereign. The Delhi Sultanate, as it came to be known, ruled over various configurations of India from Delhi until 1526. In the Middle Ages, the urbane courts of Persia were admired across the Arab and Turk world as the ultimate in Islamic sophistication; Delhi's Sultans enthusiastically replicated the cultural refinements of Persia. They insisted on the use of Persian as the language of their courts and of poetry—even though it may not have been the language they used for personal communication. Persian etiquette, dress, law, art and cuisine were also imitated. This is not to say that local factors did not come into play but these were slotted into a larger, Persian-inspired framework.

In the fourteenth century, Ibn Battuta, an Islamic judge from Morocco and self-proclaimed 'traveller of the age', arrived in Delhi and was promptly installed in the Sultan's court as a lawmaker. (That Battuta did not speak Persian was no bar to his employment.) This gave him passage into the highest echelons of Delhi society and his diaries include descriptions of the food eaten at court and in the homes of the Muslim aristocracy. Amongst the dishes typically served at the royal feasts Battuta attended were whole roasted sheep; rice cooked in ghee served with chicken; pastries stuffed with minced meat, almonds, walnuts and other nuts; and an array of sweetmeats fashioned from sugar, ghee, nuts, dried fruit and floral essences. A rose-flavoured *sharbat* (a cordial) was served at the beginning of the meal. The hallmarks of medieval Persian cuisine were dishes of meat cooked with rice; meat cooked with fruit; and a generous use of nuts, dried fruit and distilled flower essences such as rose water to flavour both sweet and savoury dishes. All these can be seen in the food Battuta describes.

Babur, the founder of the famed Mughal dynasty, liberated Delhi (and India) from Sultanate rule in 1526 and, perhaps to help him settle into the city, he elected to keep on several of the royal cooks who had worked for his vanquished predecessor. The deposed Sultan's mother bribed one of these cooks to poison Babur's dinner. The robust Mughal survived the attempt on his life and had the offending cook skinned alive and the mother thrown into jail to rot. Babur famously complained that there was no good fruit, meat, bread or cooked dishes available in India—having been poisoned early on may not have helped this opinion. Babur was a man of very definite tastes; what he wanted was the food of his native Uzbekistan, typically meat dishes eaten with wheat breads. When his daughter arrived in Delhi to join him, he greeted her with what he considered a desirable feast: roasted sheep with bread and fruit. Perhaps Delhi's food was too sophisticated for him.

Babur's rule was a short one; he died in 1530 and was succeeded by his son Humayun (1530–56), who was succeeded by his son Akbar (1556–1605). When the reign of the so-called Great Mughals ended in 1707, it was Babur's great-great-great-grandson Aurangzeb (1658–1707) who saw it out. Dynastic stability contributed to Mughal success: at the apex of their power, they ruled the subcontinent across the north, east, west and south into Karnataka, and were unimaginably rich. Tamil Nadu and Kerala ultimately eluded them and their dogged determination to bring this region under their auspices contributed to their eventual decline. The Mughals considered themselves gods on earth and spared no expense in ensuring that they were housed, clothed, entertained, transported and fed as though they were immortals. Such display was also expected of them by their subjects who seemed to want to go along with the fantasy that they were being ruled by divine beings.

Babur's heirs retained his taste for the meat-focused cuisine of Central Asia—with the exception of the ascetically inclined Akbar who preferred vegetarian food and only ate meat to conform to the expectations of his monarchical role—but they also shared the Delhi Sultans' admiration of Persian culture. The food that the Mughals served at royal feasts was not dissimilar, albeit more elaborate, to that served by the Delhi Sultans. The Mughals used imperial feasts as a display of their wealth and power yet they themselves rarely ate at these. Their meals were taken in the privacy of their harem, possibly to avoid being seen in public engaged in such a human act as eating, or of only possessing a human appetite. Various writings suggest that, on the whole, the Mughals ate moderately; not one of them is ever described as being gluttonous with food (drugs, alcohol, sex, religious fervour perhaps), but they all shared a strong interest in the culinary arts. Apart from the Islamic prohibition on pork, the Mughals had few inhibitions about food and possessed curious palates, always seeking out new tastes whenever they travelled across their territories. If a newly discovered dish took their fancy, they would co-opt a cook just to prepare that singular dish. The imperial kitchen became a melange of cooks from across the Mughal Empire, Persia and Central Asia: culinary intermingling was inevitable.

Food and cooking were of such importance to the Mughals that the imperial kitchen operated as an independent government department with its head reporting directly to the emperor. The food budget for the court was 1000 rupees a day, a fantastic sum for the time, allowing for the generous procurement of food exotica. Meals were served on white cloths laid on the floor and guests sat on cushions and leant on bolsters to eat. The royal cooks were encouraged to devise ever more elaborate dishes to delight their master and impress his guests. Meat, poultry and game that had been variously roasted, stuffed and stewed formed the nucleus of a meal often adorned with finely beaten sheets of gold and silver; generous quantities of expensive imported almonds, pistachios and walnuts were added—chopped, ground or whole—to meat, rice and sweets and a lavish selection of the finest sweetmeats and fruit ended the meal. On occasion, tea was offered to guests: this beverage was a novelty as it came from China and was not yet grown in India (*see pp. 162–64*).

The use of elaborate spice mixes was another hallmark of Mughal cuisine, a practice noted as distinctive because it was not common in other Indian cooking in the Mughal era. Many spices had to travel long distances to be used in the Mughal kitchen: black pepper and green cardamom from south India; cinnamon from Sri Lanka; nutmeg, cloves and mace from a small group of islands nestled between Sulawesi and New Guinea; saffron from Kashmir and asafoetida from Afghanistan. Spices were expensive commodities and therefore highly desirable additions to imperial meals. In most other Indian kitchens, spicing was usually quite simple, limited to whatever spices grew locally and were therefore inexpensive. The now ubiquitous garam masala of cumin, cardamom, cinnamon, cloves and black pepper is typical of the spice mixes originally developed for the Mughals, imbuing their food with distinctive flavour and the ethereal perfume of wealth. And the Mughals liked their food perfumed: royal vegetable plots were irrigated with rose- and musk-infused water; meat animals were fed on fresh herbs and perfumed grasses; ground pearls, gold dust and saffron were mixed into food and chickens intended for imperial consumption were massaged with musk and sandalwood oil.

In the kitchen, these foods were turned into an endless variety of dishes but there was a consistency in the pattern of a Mughal meal. A dish of rice and meat, such as biryani or pulao, was essential (*see pp. 91–92 for differences between the two*): the Mughals ate wheat-based bread with a meal—breaking off pieces to scoop/sop up the food—and rice was always served as a dish on its own, as in the Persian tradition. Various kebabs—in the Indian context, this means a patty/croquette-style item rather than skewered pieces of meat—fashioned from ground meat and spices were served as starters. An array of meat dishes was the main focus: rich stews such as *dopiaza* in which the onions are included in two ways; one portion is sautéed as a base and cooked with the meat and the other fried until golden, ground to a paste and added at the end of the cooking time; korma of meat cooked in a rich curd-based sauce with plenty of onions; and *haleem*, a slow-cooked porridge of meat and broken wheat; whole chickens, fish and sheep legs stuffed with rice, eggs, spices, nuts and mincemeat; and meatballs, called *kofta*, made of mincemeat served in a rich sauce of cream and nuts. Despite the attention the vegetables received in the garden, they were a mere side attraction at a Mughal meal, often cooked in well-spiced, nut-enriched curd sauces (just like meat). Mughal cooking employed plenty of onion and garlic and they had a preference for dishes that combined sweet and savoury flavours—another Persian culinary trait—and meat was often cooked with fresh and dried fruit.

Among the smorgasbord of sweet items that finished a Mughal feast was *kulfi*, an iced confection made from thickened milk mixed with sugar, nuts and saffron, poured into conical moulds and frozen in a mix of ice and saltpetre—a substance India had plentiful supplies of. Babur had also complained about the lack of availability of ice in India. By the time his grandson was reigning, ice was regularly shipped from the hills of Himachal Pradesh down the Yamuna into Delhi—where the kulfi is said to have been invented in the Mughal kitchen. There is a Persian precedent for this dessert though and the name derives from the Persian word for 'lock'. The Persians were very fond of sweets and the Mughals replicated this taste. Under their rule, there was a significant increase in the amount of sugar cane grown across their landholdings. This was not intended merely for the gratification of their palates; sugar was a valuable commercial crop especially if exported to places such as Persia.

Fabricated sweet treats took second place to fruit for the Mughals: Babur pined for it and all his descendants were connoisseurs. Collectively, the Mughals encouraged significant development in the production of local and imported fruit species. Native varieties and/or fruits grown in India never really lived up to their standards, with the exception of mangoes. They rhapsodized over this fruit and actively promoted its cultivation and the development of new hybrids. For their other fruit needs, they preferred imported produce from the cooler climes of Samarkand, Afghanistan and Kashmir—the emperor's personal supply was often carried from these places into Delhi (or wherever needed), wrapped in cotton wool by a relay of careful foot runners. Anybody who grew fruit to sell in Mughal India could do so free of taxes and good specimens commanded high prices. It was a widespread practice for people to rent out their gardens to cultivators looking for more space to grow fruit. The Mughals were introduced to the pineapple—a native of South America—by the Europeans: it captivated them and they had it cultivated in the gardens of their palace in Agra where it grew in thousands. The Mughals took to gifting this fruit to European visitors to their court: a present that might have proved disappointing to the foreigners who were likely hoping for a diamond or at least a real cashmere shawl in accordance with what they knew about the emperor's staggering wealth.

Ironically, it was the Persians who dealt the fatal blow to the failing Mughal Empire when they raided and sacked Delhi in 1783. The so-called Lesser Mughals hung on to imperial life until 1857 but the scope of their dominion had been reduced to the grounds of their palace in Delhi. Despite looming destitution and failing health, the last Mughal emperor, Bahadur Shah, continued to take great pleasure in hosting feasts of fancy dishes even though his delicate constitution prevented him from taking no more than a little quail broth.

The influence of the food of the Mughals—and their Sultanate predecessors—on the cuisine of India is too extensive, and too deeply dispersed, to enumerate here but you will encounter it in other places throughout this book. Mughal emperors were the movie stars—but with a lot more power over life and death—of their time. People were just as desirous of emulating their habits as we are of the purported habits of famous starlets (eau de Mughal would have been a sure success). But there was also an added fillip: imitation was flattery to the Mughals and a courtier's successful attempts to recreate, possibly even surpass, the emperor's practices could win him favour and influence at court. If nothing else, it would demonstrate to others that you were important enough to have been to court to see what the emperor wore, said, ate; this in itself held enormous social cachet. The Muslim and Hindu aristocracy that attended Mughal feasts would have gone home to their own cooks and asked them to replicate the dishes they had eaten—they may have even managed to bribe a royal cook for a recipe. In turn, their guests would have gone home and described the dishes to their cooks and asked them to recreate those. Descriptions of the type of food the emperor served in the palace would have also filtered out into the bazaar where even the humblest citizen could hear about what the great men were eating. It was only the wealthiest citizens who could have afforded to emulate the food of the emperor but that would not have prevented others making versions of these dishes altered to suit their financial ability. In this way, the culinary influence of the Mughals percolated down into the general population over time. After the British crushed the Revolt of 1857 and took control of Delhi, they exiled Bahadur Shah to Burma (now Myanmar). This left the royal kitchen staff without an employer: they had to find work in other courts and private establishments, taking Mughal influence into these and eventually to the wider population.

Religious and cultural affinity meant that the influence of Mughal cooking is most evident in the cuisine of modern India's 160-million-strong Muslim community. There is a distinct repertoire of dishes eaten by Indian Muslims across India that can be referred to as Indo-Muslim cuisine. The dishes include all those listed in describing a Mughal feast, albeit in less rarefied versions. The hallmarks are the predominance of meat dishes—indeed, much non-vegetarian cooking in India reveals Muslim influence; a generous application of ghee or oil; the use of curd to marinate meats; plenty of onion and garlic; and a preference for complex spice mixes of cardamom, cinnamon, bay leaf, fennel and black pepper. The sweet called halwa is also a staple. The word 'halwa' is of Arabic origin; in the Middle East, it is used to describe a firm, crumbly sweet made with ground sesame seeds or other nuts mixed with sugar or honey. In India, halwa is made from ingredients as varied as semolina, ground dal, banana, bread, dates, nuts and sweet potato cooked with ghee, sugar syrup and a little cardamom until it forms a soft unctuous mass. Local foods have influenced Indo-Muslim cooking creating distinct regional versions but these still conform to the basic culinary framework. For example, rice is the dominant grain in south India and is typically boiled and eaten with meals but Muslims prefer to eat bread so the Muslim community in Kerala makes bread from rice. Rice-based dishes such as biryani, however, retain an important place in Indo-Muslim cuisine and are essential at weddings or celebratory feasts.

The dishes of Mughlai cuisine inevitably feature on Indian restaurant menus around the world. When the British were in India, they often employed Muslim cooks as they knew how to prepare meat dishes—with the exception of pork—and were not limited by caste issues around food.

In creating meals for their own *burra sahib* (big man), these cooks looked to the type of food they thought befitted such a personage: Mughlai food for Muslim aristocracy, in whose kitchens they had learnt their craft. Some cooks would not prepare simple food for their master even if he requested it. The type of food eaten in the household a particular cook served was an issue of honour for him and to maintain high prestige it was essential that the people he cooked for ate grandly. As a result, many of the British who resided in India came to conceive of Indian food as Indo-Muslim cuisine and, even if they knew any different, preferred these dishes. When Indian restaurants began to open in England in the nineteenth century, largely to serve men who had returned from India and had developed a taste for 'curry', the menu had Mughlai-style dishes they were familiar with and these have ultimately become enshrined on the menus. The other influence was that Mughlai food is seen as the 'haute cuisine' of India, the type of food served at weddings and on special occasions and therefore the type of food people would pay for in a restaurant as it was something they could not, or would not, prepare at home.

The Muslim population of Mughal Delhi was not inclined towards agricultural work, preferring to dwell within the city walls with their brethren. It was Hindu farmers and peasants who lived in villages outside the walls of Delhi and produced the town's food supply. The emperor assigned a number of these villages to each member of his aristocracy and they collected taxes as income—a portion of which was paid into the royal treasury. The emperors understood well the essential role played by agriculturists in the well-being of their subjects and the economy, therefore Hindu farmers were not taxed so heavily as to deprive them of an adequate livelihood. Provided the season had been merciful, the Hindu inhabitants of Delhi continued to sustain themselves with meals similar to those of their antediluvian ancestors: unleavened breads; potage made of dal, wheat, corn or barley meal and rice; buttermilk left over from making butter; seasonal leafy greens; fruit; and sweet dishes made from milk, rice, jaggery and honey. This style of food has remained constant across rural north India until this day.

Hindus also lived within the city walls, serving in the roles of their caste. There were not enough aristocratic Muslims in Delhi to populate the court with the requisite number of nobles befitting an emperor. Rajputs, the Hindu nobility, were therefore encouraged to join the court and boost the numbers. Hindu scribes were employed to do much of the bookwork.

Banias, the Hindu mercantile class, were needed to conduct trade. Rajputs were meat-eaters and took significant Mughlai influence into their food but Banias were strict vegetarians and very caste-conscious. They ate only in their own homes, never at court. Their food did not absorb Muslim influences but that did not mean they did not eat well. Delhi's Banias became wealthy and their vegetarian cuisine is finessed and delectable. Unfortunately, it is not available in restaurants.

Recommendations

Shah Jahan (1627–58) had a particular passion for architecture. He indulged it by building a brand new city, naming it Shahjahanabad, now referred to as Purani Dilli (Old Delhi). The city was spread over seven square miles, encircled by a thick stone wall. A wide, tree-lined boulevard called Chandni Chowk bisected the city and down its centre ran a canal that carried water into the imperial palace—now called Lal Qila (Red Fort)—to feed the fountains spouting across the emperor's domicile. In its heyday, Chandni Chowk was a dynamic marketplace where all sorts of exquisite, expensive items were traded vigorously. There were also several coffee houses, a Persian-influenced innovation, where men congregated to drink coffee, smoke hookahs and gossip; the food of emperors must have been discussed. Chandni Chowk remains a very dynamic bazaar but its wares are somewhat more downmarket than they were in the seventeenth century and tea is now the preferred drink, sold by street-side vendors to men who do not have time to dandy. Fortunately, for the food curious, you can still find tastes of Delhi's glorious past along Chandni Chowk.

Exchanging sweetmeats was vital to social and commercial interactions in Mughal Delhi. Sweets were offered to guests when they entered a home. Merchants offered confections to their clients to nibble on while they haggled, to literally 'sweeten the bargain'. Traditional sweets are made from finely ground nuts, pulses, fruit and sugar. Considerable expertise is required to craft these basic elements into delicate confections. Delhiites, then and now, have always found it prudent to leave the preparation of these to professionals. The iconic **Ghantewala** in Chandni Chowk has been selling sweets since

1790; in fact, one of the later Mughal emperors was said to have been fond of its product. You will find a variety of exotic-looking sweets on offer in this modernized store but the most authentic are the deceptively simple yet exquisite *piste ki lauz* (pistachio sweet) and *badam ki lauz* (almond sweet).

Ghantewala, 1862-A Chandni Chowk
(011) 23280490, 23241851
8 a.m.–9 p.m.

Chandni Chowk would have to be a contender for the most hectic place on the planet and it can be tough making your way along it, so fuel yourself with a jalebi or two from **Old and Famous Jalebi Wallah** as you pass by. 'He' has been making jalebis for the passing crowds for a century! **Parathewali Gali** is another of Delhi's old and famous eating places. Look for Kanwarji Raj Kumar's sweet shop opposite Central Bank in Chandni Chowk and turn down the lane adjacent to it. As is obvious from the name, this dog-legged lane is famous for the stuffed fried bread called paratha. There are varying dates as to when parathas began to be sold from this location, ranging from 1839 to 1870, so we can safely place it in the nineteenth century. Paratha-style breads are mentioned in Mughal recipe books; perhaps it was an out-of-work royal cook who started selling them here! Several simple dhabas in the *gali* produce 'bespoke' parathas. You choose your filling(s), which might be cauliflower, potato, chilli, peas, paneer, radish, crushed papad, banana or cooked dal; a piece of dough is broken off from a larger mother ship, rolled out, stuffed and cooked. Your crisp, hot paratha is then presented to you on a plate accompanied by potato curry and various zingy pickles and chutneys.

You can often see kulfi-wallahs selling this frozen confection all over Chandni Chowk. Some still freeze it in earthenware pots filled with ice and salt/saltpetre, as in the Mughal era. Others use a more modern, portable metal ice box perched on the back of their bikes. The moulded kulfi is held in place in this box, dramatically drawn out—like swords—and unsheathed as required. As has long been the tradition of street-side ice-cream vendors the world over, kulfi-wallahs often ring bells to attract customers. Kulfi is frequently paired with *falooda*, slippery vermicelli noodles made from cornflour or arrowroot. (Falooda is also a drink that we will meet further on.) Emperor Jahangir (1605–27) was very fond of falooda eaten with cream and fruit. If eating kulfi in a street challenges your food safety threshold, try **Gianiji ka Falooda**, which has been serving kulfi since 1947.

Fatehpuri Mosque, Chandni Chowk

Gianiji has its dedicated band of supporters who declare that it serves 'the best kulfi falooda in Delhi' but **Roshan di Kulfi** draws the same recommendation from others. Roshan is located in Karol Bagh: a bazaar nowhere near as ancient as Chandni Chowk but almost as hectic.

2816 Ajmal Khan Road, Karol Bagh
(011) 25710045, 28722728
7 a.m.–10 p.m.

At the western end of Chandni Chowk is Gadodia Market, Asia's largest wholesale spice market. Just past the market are shops selling a huge variety of pickles. On the sidewalk adjacent to these, you might see people sitting with small scales and small piles of lumps of a dark resinous substance; this is asafoetida, a latex extruded from the root of a perennial herb of the parsley family. Asafoetida has been used in Indian cooking for millennia but in minute quantities, due to its pungent odour. Further past the pickle shops is Gali Batasha ('sugar meringue lane'), populated by sugar merchants who sell different types and grades of sugar to professional confectioners. (*See the 'Chaat' section for further recommendations in Chandni Chowk.*)

Down a narrow passage off a side street on the south side of the landmark Jama Masjid, you will find **Karim's**. This restaurant has been operating from the same place, run by the same family, since 1913 but its origins can be traced all the way back to Babur. According to the family history, their forefather came to India from Saudi Arabia to make his fortune as a soldier in the Mughal army but ended up as Babur's personal cook: destiny had indeed been kind and a lineage of imperial cooks began. After the Revolt of 1857, the British placed restrictions on the activities and movements of Muslims in Delhi and the descendants of Babur's cook went into exile outside the city. They did not return to Delhi until 1911 when one of the family, Haji Karimuddin, set up a small street stall selling roti, *aloo gosht* (spiced stew of meat and potatoes) and dal to the massive crowds that had come to Delhi to witness the coronation of King George V. Two years later, Karimuddin opened Karim's. Many of the recipes used at Karim's have come down from the Mughal court. These are considered family heirlooms and the composition of the spice mixes used is a closely held family secret. Each morning, the cooks place orders for the masalas they require for that day and these are then ground by family members and sent over to the restaurant. Karim's is renowned for serving some of the best Mughlai food in Delhi. Ideally, you should give yourself over to a carnivorous feast when you eat here. Try any of the kebabs on offer such as the satin-smooth *Shahjahan* version followed by *Akbari murgh masala* (chicken marinated in spiced curd) or *pasande* (pieces of mutton taken from the shoulder, beaten flat and scored with a knife then cooked in a creamy sauce of onion, garlic, ginger, curd and spices). I also have it on good authority that Karim's brain curry is excellent—if you like that sort of thing.

16 Gali Kababian, Jama Masjid
(011) 23264981, 23243342
7 a.m.–3.30 p.m., 6–11 p.m.

Long before Shahjahanabad was even an emperor's dream and before the Mughals swept into India, Ibn Battuta declared Delhi the 'jewel of Islam in the East'. The urban village of Nizamuddin is a living remnant of that time. At the heart of Nizamuddin *basti* is the shrine of the Sufi saint Sheikh Hazrat Nizamuddin Auliya, who lived here in the thirteenth century. He was an important religious figure in his lifetime—said to fly to Mecca and back each night on a winged camel!—and his tomb remains one of the most important pilgrimage sites in India. Nizamuddin chose to settle here, as it was quiet and away from the hustle of the metropolitan development around Qutub Minar. He created a place where people of all backgrounds could come and be fed—literally and spiritually. If the great saint were to return on his magic dromedary, he would find his tradition unbroken since his death in 1325. Only that Nizamuddin is no longer a quiet rural retreat.

Before India's partition in 1947, Delhi was a city with a predominantly Muslim population of one million citizens. In anticipation of this event, and in the period immediately following it, refugees from the Punjab flooded into Delhi. Many of Delhi's Muslims fled to the newly created Pakistan and, in this interchange, Delhi found itself a city of nearly two million inhabitants, largely Hindus. People were traumatized and fearful; tensions between Hindus and Muslims ran high. The mostly Muslim residents of Nizamuddin found themselves living in a hostile place, where they had suddenly become a minority. As the city grew rapidly around them to accommodate its new population, they closed ranks behind the walls of their once-rural village and maintained the distinct culture, habits and language—Urdu—that had defined Delhi for centuries. In my mind, Nizamuddin is like a piece of Islamic Delhi that was broken off and preserved. Life in the basti still adheres to its traditional patterns: pilgrims visit Nizamuddin's shrine in huge numbers; the faithful fill its mosques; burqa-clad women pass along its narrow lanes and the aromas of kebabs and biryani perfume the air.

Wander the labyrinth of lanes and galis of Nizamuddin and you will see food everywhere. Simple dhabas and stalls sell everyday Indo-Muslim fare: various kebabs, meat stews, *keema matar* (mincemeat cooked with green peas), *nihari* (spiced dish of mutton slow-cooked overnight and eaten for breakfast in the cooler months; said to have nourished Babur's army) and halwa. You will also see many bakeries— some of which look medieval and possibly are—where breads such as naan and *sheermal* are cooked in large tandoors. Around lunchtime, you will see men, women and children hurrying home bearing newspaper-wrapped parcels of warm bread bought fresh from these bakeries to accompany their meals. Surrounding the main square are several hotels outside which crowds of people squat, patiently waiting to be fed. After praying to Nizamuddin at his shrine, pilgrims buy meal tickets from these hotels and distribute them to the hungry, who in turn present them to the respective hotels for a simple meal in exchange.

Ghalib's, opposite Ghalib Academy on the main lane into the basti, is famed across Delhi for its delicately textured but robustly flavoured *seekh* kebabs. If you prefer to eat in more refined surroundings— where you can sit, for instance—there is **Dastarkhwan-e-Karim**, an upmarket branch of Karim's where you can have a simple meal of kebabs and fresh bread or a full-blown feast of rich Indo-Muslim style dishes.

Dastarkhwan-e-Karim, 168/2 Hazrat Nizamuddin West
(011) 24350018, 24350024
12.30–3.30 p.m., 6.30–11.30 p.m. (Mondays closed)

....

POST-PARTITION CUISINE

The line partitioning India from newly created Pakistan ran through the centre of Punjab. In the wake of the consequent violence, a huge number of people fled the region and sought refuge in Delhi: most arrived grateful for their lives but with little else and many had to be housed in makeshift camps. They were a mixture of agriculturists who had lost their lands and urban dwellers from places like Lahore who had lost their city. Some were able to resume their previous occupations but others had to invent ways to earn a living in their new circumstances. With so many Punjabis in Delhi, the demand for familiar food was strong and people living in the camps often lacked access to cooking facilities. Sensing the need and the opportunity, various individuals set up makeshift street stalls selling fried snacks and simple Punjabi dishes such as the combination of chickpea stew and fried bread called *chhole bhature*; hard work and ingenuity saw some of these stalls evolve into restaurants and Punjabis also pioneered the catering industry of modern India.

Before 1947, there had been restaurants in India, catering almost exclusively to the British population and the Indian elite. There were restaurants owned by Indians—and these were always staffed by them— but they were there to run a business and please their customers. The menus usually featured a few Anglo-Indian dishes, else the food was European in style. Simple cook shops and food stalls had long existed in India but the restaurant concept was foreign. Indians who could afford to eat in a restaurant would have had a cook, and possibly kitchen staff, at home so why pay for something that you could get for free. Caste and dietary taboos were also barriers to restaurant dining, as was sitting at tables and using cutlery when most Indians were accustomed to sitting on the floor and eating with their hands. What happened in Delhi after 1947 was that restaurants opened to serve Indian-style food intended for Indians. As the people opening these restaurants were Punjabis, their cuisine dominated the menus. As it turned out, it was a successful formula so when eateries opened elsewhere in India, they often copied it. Because of their commercial success, the Indian government consulted and employed Punjabi restaurateurs and caterers in the development of national hospitality training programmes and this was another factor that saw Punjabi cooking proliferate in restaurants across India.

Recommendations

Perhaps the single most important contribution to the development of the Indian restaurant model came from Kundan Lal. He arrived in Delhi as a Partition refugee from Peshawar in Pakistan. To earn a living, he set up a street stall selling tandoori chicken. This style of chicken was a novelty in Delhi at the time and found a very appreciative audience. On the strength of this, Lal opened a more permanent establishment called **Moti Mahal**: a restaurant that at the height of its success was 'the' place' in which to dine in Delhi, and inspired many imitators. Lal is often credited with 'inventing' tandoori chicken but it is arguable that he just popularized it commercially. We can certainly thank him for the ubiquitous presence of chicken tikka on the typical Indian restaurant menu. The kitchens of Moti Mahal are also said to be the birthplace of that other restaurant fixture, the butter chicken—a dish of chicken cooked in a thick, spiced tomato sauce generously enriched with butter. You can still visit Moti Mahal in Old Delhi though its days of glory are well behind it. It looks like the maintenance budget ran out circa 1979 but the food, particularly the chicken tikka, remains excellent.

3703 Netaji Subhash Marg, Daryaganj
(011) 23273011, 23273661
Noon–midnight

Bukhara has been called the 'best Indian restaurant in the world' and it is a popular haunt for celebrities, socialites and politicians. If you are fond of tandoori food, you must try its *tandoori phool gobhi* (pieces of cauliflower dipped in a batter of *besan* and spices, and cooked in the tandoor until the batter sets crisp and the cauliflower steams inside it so that its texture is silky); *ma ki dal* that has been slow-cooked overnight; *sikandari raan* (leg of mutton marinated overnight and cooked in the tandoor); and naan the size of a small flying carpet!

ITC Maurya Sheraton, Diplomatic Enclave
(011) 26112233
12.30–2.45 p.m., 7–11.45 p.m. (7 days)
www.itchotels.in/hotels/itcmaurya/bukhara-restaurant.aspx

Bukhara is wonderful but it is a budget buster and therefore an occasional treat for most people. As an alternative, **Moti Mahal Deluxe** has good tandoori food, a relaxed, homely atmosphere and less hefty prices. This was my neighbourhood tandoori joint when I lived in Delhi some years ago and my favourite dish there was paneer tikka, cubes of marinated, spiced paneer skewered with onion and capsicum and subjected to the magic of the tandoor.

M-30 Greater Kailash 1
(011) 29230480, 29240480

Punjabi cuisine is often defined by the hefty home-style fare served in dhabas—such as the enduring **Kake da Hotel** on the outer circle of Connaught Place—but a spate of restaurants serving a more refined, modern take on Punjabi food have recently opened in Delhi. **Punjab Grill** is one of these. You can start your meal with pistachio lassi, move to tandoori lobster and finish with candied white pumpkin!

Select City Walk, Saket
(011) 41572976
Noon–midnight

Delhi's tradition of culinary innovation continues at **Varq** restaurant that offers diners 'progressive Indian cuisine', a food style that applies European cooking technique to traditional Indian dishes and uses local ingredients in new ways. It is a style that was pioneered in London but has only recently emerged in India, and Varq is its first outing in Delhi. (More restaurants serving this type of food will have opened in Delhi by the time you read this.) A selection from the menu might include chicken kebabs cooked on skewers of sugar cane; salmon fillets roasted in the tandoor; tamarind sorbet; crispy duck breast with roasted coconut sauce; spinach cooked with water chestnuts and raita infused with roasted garlic that is so good you will want to keep it all to yourself. Traditional Indian sweets such as jalebi and kulfi are deconstructed into things of visual and gustatory beauty. I think the Mughal emperors would be delighted with the experimentation and fussing that goes into creating the food at Varq.

Hotel Taj Mahal, 1 Mansingh Road
(011) 23026162
12.30–2.30 p.m., 7–11.30 p.m.

CHAAT

The word chaat comes from the Hindi verb 'to lick' and is applied to a range of snacks or light meals served from street-side carts, sweet shops as well as modern food courts. A typical chaat is a composite dish made of a crisp fried item dressed with a dollop of curd, a lick or two of sweet-and-sour tamarind/mango chutney, crowned with various garnishes and sprinkles of chaat masala (a pungent spice blend of rock salt, black pepper, red chilli, *amchoor*, cumin, asafoetida and a little sugar). Not all chaat conforms to this exact formula; for example, fruit chaat is simply chunks of fresh seasonal fruit sprinkled with chaat masala. I have been unable to determine the definitive origins of chaat but as Delhi is renowned for it, here is as good a place as any to introduce you to it. You will find chaat sold across India, particularly in the north. I will describe the more common types of chaat but there are myriad regional variations with respect to constituent ingredients and names. Ultimately, the magic of chaat lies in the various combinations of tastes and textures: smooth, crisp, silky, spicy, sweet, sour and pungent; just as one of these hits your palate, the next moves across it. One mouthful of chaat tastes different from the next because you will have picked up a slightly different combination of ingredients. The best part of any chaat though is the mix left in the dish at the end; this is so tasty that you cannot help but lick the plate, hence the name!

Golgappa (Pani Puri)

A golgappa is a crispy hollow puff, the size of a golf ball, made of semolina or wholewheat flour, into which a hole is pinched on top and a few pieces of plain boiled potato are dropped in, after which it is filled with mint and/or spicy tamarind chutney and *jal zeera* (tangy chilled broth prepared from amchoor, dried melon called *kachri*, ginger, chillies, cumin seeds, peppercorns and rock salt). To eat a golgappa, you convey the whole thing into your mouth, keeping the hole uppermost so that the liquid does not spill out, and bite in: the result is a taste and textural sensation. Golgappas are taken one at a time and you receive them in a small bowl. It's up to you how many you have. When you have had your fill, you drink the liquid left in your bowl or ask for more if you love to have your mouth on fire.

Aloo chaat

Chunks of potato, fried crisp and golden, sprinkled with salt and chaat masala makes up aloo chaat. Alternatively, the fried potato cubes can be dressed with fresh mint and tamarind chutneys.

Aloo tikki

These are patties of spiced potato fried golden and dressed with curd and chutneys, garnished with crunchy *sev* (thin crisp noodles of chickpea-flour batter pushed through a fine sieve into hot oil), fresh pomegranate seeds and green coriander leaves, and finished off with chaat masala.

Papdi chaat

Constructed from a base of small, flaky pastry biscuits (*papdi*) layered with boiled potato cubes, this features cooked chickpeas, curd, chutney and various garnishes. You use the crisp papdi to scoop up the toppings. Crushed papdi is sometimes also sprinkled over other chaat such as *aloo tikki* to provide that additional crunch.

Raj kachori

The origins of this particular chaat can be traced to Delhi's Bengali Sweet House. It comprises a tennis-ball-sized fried wheat puff called *kachori*, stuffed with everything in the chaat-wallah's armoury.

Dahi bhalla

Urad dal patties are fried then soaked in water and wrung out—which gives them a spongy texture—and dressed with curd, tamarind chutney and garnish of sev and/or fresh pomegranate seeds to create the deliciously soft *dahi bhalla*.

Samosa chaat

The samosa, a crisp pastry envelope stuffed with spiced potato, dressed with curd and tamarind chutney, makes samosa chaat.

There is no end of options for eating chaat in Delhi and every Delhiite has an opinion on where the best chaat is to be had. Here is a list of some of the best I know.

Recommendations

In Chandni Chowk, look out for old-timers **Shree Balaji Chaat Bhandar, Ashok Chaat Bhandar** and **Lala Babu Chaat Bhandar**: the first renowned for a variety of chaat and the other two for their speciality—golgappas. As the name suggests, **Nataraj Dahi Bhalle Wala** specializes in dahi bhalle. **Haldiram's** has good chaat offerings and it's fun to go in and look at the sweets and observe all the people in this busy store. **Bishan Swaroop** has been serving fruit chaat since 1923 and is considered by many to be Delhi's finest purveyor of this sinless treat.

Shree Balaji Chaat Bhandar, 1462 Chandni Chowk
Noon–10 p.m.

Ashok Chaat Bhandar, 3611 Chowk Hauz Qazi
(M) 9891764351
10 a.m.–10 p.m.

Lala Babu Chaat Bhandar, 77 Chandni Chowk, Near Kumar Cinema
(011) 23282806
11 a.m.–8 p.m.

Nataraj Dahi Bhalle Wala, 1396 Chandni Chowk
(011) 65364631, (M) 9811167400
Noon–8.30 p.m.

Haldiram's, 1454/2 Chandni Chowk
(011) 28833007, 28833010
10 a.m.–11 p.m.
www.haldirams.com (lists other branches in Delhi)

Bishan Swaroop, 1421 Chandni Chowk
(M) 9212364070
10 a.m.–10 p.m.

Prince Paan is my absolute favourite for chaat and I have consumed numerous golgappas and raj kachoris here. **Bengali Sweet House** and **Sweets Corner** are good, centrally located options for any or all of the chaat items listed.

Prince Paan, M-Block Market, Greater Kailash 1

Bengali Sweet House, 27-37 Bengali Market
(011) 23319224, 23311855
8 a.m.–11 p.m.

Sweets Corner, 1 Sunder Nagar
(011) 24359261, 41507000
8 a.m.–11 p.m.

CENTRAL INDIA

PLAINS FARE

The Aryan civilization pushed across India from west to east—from Punjab into the vast alluvial plain of Uttar Pradesh (UP) through which the Ganga runs much of its course. Immersion in this sacred river is believed to offer spiritual boon to human beings, although belief is imperative to such gain. Of more evident benefit is the fertility that Mother Ganga bestows on the land. UP is said to be the birthplace of Hinduism, the point where the nascent culture of the Aryans evolved into a fully realized system of living. The fertile soil supported that development by allowing agriculture to thrive; a stable and generous food supply allowed the people who grew it to flourish, literally and culturally. UP houses some of the oldest and holiest places of Hinduism: Varanasi, Rishikesh, Haridwar, Allahabad, Vrindavan and Mathura, where, as legend has it, the god Krishna was born. It is also home to 200 million people, making it the most populous state of India.

UP borders Delhi, from where Islamic influence spread into the region. In 1503, Sikandar Lodi, Delhi's reigning Sultan, moved his capital to Agra. Again, in the mid-sixteenth century, Akbar moved the Mughal capital from Delhi to Agra. Later, his grandson Shah Jahan built India's most iconic monument, the Taj Mahal, in Agra. As the Mughal Empire started to unravel and subsequently decline in the eighteenth century, the region of Awadh, with Lucknow as its capital, became the centre of Muslim power in India and developed its own distinct culture and cuisine.

As you travel away from the urban madness of UP towards its Delhi border, the region gradually evolves into a green-and-gold patchwork of fields—shades altering with each new crop and season—that have been productively worked for thousands of years. Much of the agricultural land in UP is still owned by small independent farmers, some of whom continue to

work their land in a way that has changed little over the millennia: wooden
ploughs drawn by oxen can still be seen furrowing the soil, and colourfully
clad field workers plant and pick crops by hand. Agriculture remains the
backbone of UP's economy; the state is a major commercial producer of
wheat, rice and sugar cane; vegetables such as potatoes, peas, eggplant, ladies'
fingers, cabbage and carrots; various dals; livestock and dairy products; and
fruit such as banana and mango. These foods have been grown and eaten in
the region from the time when the soil was first turned and they remain the
mainstays of daily food. A typical meal in UP comprises wheat rotis and/or
rice, a dal, a dry vegetable dish and a gravy-based one accompanied by curd,
pickles and chutney. Common spices are turmeric, red chilli, asafoetida,
cumin and mustard. Sweets are not necessarily eaten with meals, and more
usually enjoyed as snacks between meals. Half the population of UP is
vegetarian and the other half would include a meat-based dish—typically one
that shows Muslim influence—in a meal, although economics determines
how often a family can afford to eat meat.

As you travel through rural UP, the perennial dark, glossy green of the
mango tree is a distinct hue of the landscape. Orderly stands of these trees
fill domestic gardens and sometimes appear to stretch endlessly across large
commercial orchards. The mango is native to India and both its leaves and
fruit are auspicious. Strings of mango leaves are hung up across doorways to
signify welcome; the fruit is a symbol of everlasting love and a motif based
on the shape of the mango—purportedly the inspiration for the paisley
pattern—is often used in traditional Indian textile designs. Mangoes grow
all over India and each region supports different cultivars of the 1000 or
so reported varieties—many of which exist only as a few trees. UP has the
largest area in India under mango cultivation and is a major producer of
the Dussehri, Chausa, Ratna and Langda varieties. Ripe mangoes are eaten
as fresh fruit; cooked with curd and spices to make savoury dishes; made
into sweet dishes; and puréed and dried in thin layers to create fruit leather
called *aam papad*. Green mangoes are also used in cooking, often turned into
pickles or eaten sliced and sprinkled with salt and spices as a snack. In the
mango belt around Lucknow, green mango is cooked with sugar, semolina
and spices to create a dish called *shakramba*. Certain varieties are designated
as 'sucking' mangoes in which the juice is sucked out via a hole made in the
top of the fruit. India produces more than half the world's mango crop and
some of its finest varieties. There is a catch to enjoying mangoes in India:
they come into season in the wickedly hot summer months, but Indian

mangoes are so magnificent that they almost make it worth enduring the heat for. Wooden carts piled high with mangoes for sale on the streets are found all over UP and, as the summer progresses, different varieties come into readiness.

VARANASI

Varanasi has been continuously inhabited since the twelfth century BC, making it one of the world's oldest living cities. It is also one of India's holiest places; in Hindu tradition, it is a 'crossing place' where gods and goddesses come down to earth and mortals can access the divine. A Hindu who dies in Varanasi is believed to attain enlightenment and release from the eternal cycle of reincarnation. The city rises up on the left bank of the Ganga and along its six kilometres of river frontage are numerous ghats (steps) leading into the river, abuzz daily with sacred and temporal ritual. In the early morning, pilgrims worship the Ganga by immersing themselves in it while next to them others clean their teeth, bodies and clothes. As evening sets in, the river twinkles with light from the hundreds of leaf boats filled with flowers and lit candles floated on it in salutation; at night, Manikarnika Ghat—where the dead are cremated on wood pyres— is a dramatic and moving sight. It is this riverfront spectacle of human activity that draws pilgrims and tourists alike but culinary explorers need to leave the riverside and immerse themselves in the labyrinthine old city, or Vishwanath Khanda, behind it. There is no shortage of human interest here either; as you wander the maze of lanes* you will discover numerous temples busy with people paying homage to their favourite deities including Annapurna, the goddess of sustenance, at Annapurna Bhavani.

Hindus believe that cow's milk is the purest food and therefore eminently suitable for the gods. Idols are often washed with milk while milk-based confections are taken to temples as offerings. India's temple towns are renowned for excellent sweets and Varanasi is no exception. It is famous for confections made from *khoya*, milk transformed by slowly boiling until all the water is evaporated from it, leaving a firm, pliable mass. During this

* I have been unable to find a definitive map of the old city of Varanasi, and the names of various lanes can be hard to ascertain, likewise the names of the many sweet shops and food stalls that line these. I will give addresses where I can else I recommend just wandering around and trying places that appeal—my best finds have been ones that I have just stumbled upon.

process, it is continually stirred with a flat ladle called a *khunti* to prevent the milk sticking to the pot and burning. The putty-like product is blended with sugar, nuts, fruit and other flavourings and fashioned into a vast array of sweets such as barfi, *peda* and gulab jamun. Khoya Gali in the old city is dedicated solely to the wholesale production and sale of khoya—you will know if you happen upon this lane even before you see the stacked rounds of khoya as it emits a distinct dairy smell. As you wander along, keep an eye out for men rhythmically stirring large cauldrons over fires—they are usually engaged in making khoya for an adjacent sweetshop. When pilgrims buy sweets to offer to the gods, they also take a few for themselves, a sweet reward for devotion. **Shree Rajbandhu** on the corner of Kachori Gali near Vishwanath Temple is one of the best stores for khoya-based sweets in Varanasi. The *halwai*s (confectioners) of Varanasi typically inherit this role and come from families that have been in the business for generations.

In addition to its spiritual benefits, milk is believed to give strength and calm to those who consume it, making it an ideal food for pilgrims who have expended their energies travelling to Varanasi and want to meet their gods in a tranquil state. Milk is also a permitted food for those undertaking a *vrat*, or religious fast, a regular practice of pilgrims when they visit holy places. In the lanes of the old city, there are always milk-based delicacies to enjoy, all year round. In the winter, look out for a sweet dish called *rabri*. This is made by boiling milk in a wide iron pan; the milk is not stirred and as the puckered skin forms on top, it is removed with a small bamboo splint and put back into the milk until all the liquid in the milk has evaporated leaving a thick, soft mass of milk solids; this is cut into squares and submerged into a thin saffron-scented custard. Over the course of an afternoon and into the early evening, I watched an elderly man, in a small booth in **Kachori Gali**, painstakingly make a batch of rabri. He served it in small portions sprinkled with crushed pistachio nuts in earthenware dishes; at twenty rupees a serve, it was expensive compared to the cost of other food items in Varanasi but it sold out quickly. All this man makes is rabri: he is an artisan, and if he were working in a small city in France or Italy, he would be considered a national treasure. In Varanasi, rabri is eaten in the evening. *Mallaiyo*, another winter speciality, is eaten in the morning. It is made by leaving a mixture of thickened milk and cream outside overnight for dew to collect on it, which causes the mix to foam. This foam is collected and sweetened with jaggery and sold by street-side vendors in earthenware bowls in the old city.

Varanasi lassi is made from rich, creamy curd instead of the more austere buttermilk that this same-named drink is commonly made of. Varanasi lassi-wallahs put a portion of curd into a jug along with water or milk, sugar and flavourings such as rose water or cardamom, and amalgamate these ingredients by inserting a wooden pestle and rhythmically twirling it between their two hands. Perhaps it is this particular motion and/or the quality of the curd that gives Varanasi lassi its unparalleled taste. Traditionally, lassi was had in Varanasi in summer—in winter, lassi-wallahs made rabri—but the city became so famous for this item that it is now made all year round to supply the demand for it. There are lassi-wallahs throughout the old city. The first time I visited Varanasi, I was wandering the lanes of Vishwanath Khanda when a man sitting cross-legged in a stall with dusky-pink walls and nothing more than a large jug, a wooden pestle, a stainless-steel bowl of curd and a few containers laid out in front of him caught my eye. I wasn't quite sure of what he was selling—it was my first trip to India—so I pointed to the items in front of him and nodded. He then set about making me a lassi in a calm, ritualistic manner. The finished product was ambrosial: cold, frothy, creamy, sweet and tantalizingly perfumed with just a hint of rose water. I tried over the next week or so to find him again but I couldn't; fortunately, I had taken a photograph of him so I knew I wasn't imagining it! On the corner of Kachori Gali is a popular lassi shop where bottled water is used for those concerned about local water quality.

Milk is also transformed into superb masala chai in Varanasi, where it is still served in traditional clay cups, called *kulhad*. Once you have finished your tea, you throw the cup on to a pile on the ground to break it and dispose of it; this practice assures customers that the cup they are given has not been used by anyone else and therefore does not present any risk to caste purity. Drinking hot, milky spiced tea from an earthen cup gives it a distinct flavour that I love. It was not that many years ago when bought tea was almost always served in clay cups especially in trains. Now, railway tea vendors use plastic or Styrofoam cups as do most street-side chai-wallahs. It's a situation I have constantly bemoaned because of the loss of flavour in the tea and because I thought that breaking the cup on the ground and letting it dissolve back into the earth it came from was environmentally friendly. I recently read an article though about how many trees are cut down to fuel the kilns in which the clay cups are fired and I felt chastised in my opinion, although I still grumble about the plastic cups. To sample the best chai in Varanasi, you have to get out into the lanes of the old city—your hotel tea just won't pass muster—and the best time is early morning when you can stand around a stall with the locals, watching the day unfold. As you make your way around the galis, you will see people selling thick, fresh curd to householders who collect their daily portions in stainless-steel pails.

Visitors to Varanasi do not live on milk products alone but, aside from these, the city does not appear to have its own distinctive cuisine. There are traditional eating patterns that you can follow though. In the morning, after a dip in the Ganga and a blessing at the temple, it is customary to eat *kachoris* (fried bread stuffed with a paste of lentils flavoured with asafoetida) with gingery potatoes or spiced chickpeas. Kachori Gali, which runs from the river up through the old city to Vishwanath Temple, is where locals and pilgrims come in the morning for kachoris followed by a jalebi or two and perhaps a glass of hot milk in the winter. I am a jalebi aficionado and the best I have ever eaten were from a sweet shop in the old city on **Nepali Khopra**, diagonally opposite Baba Perfumes. The consumption of meat and alcohol is officially prohibited in Varanasi; many food stalls do not use onion or garlic in their food either, as these items are considered detrimental to spiritual purity. Asafoetida, as used in kachoris, is often substituted for these. Restaurants catering to tourists in Varanasi do serve meat and alcohol and also use onion and garlic: all very well, but if you want something more genuine, you will need to eat from hole-in-the-wall spots such as a cookshop on Nepali Khopra where I ate an evening meal of lightly spiced sautéed spinach, dal and a potato curry with thick, freshly cooked wholewheat roti. The whole lot cost me twenty rupees and it was tasty and wholesome—better than anything I have eaten in a proper restaurant in Varanasi. The following day, I took my lunch from another small cookshop that caught my eye as I passed by with its small but alluring display of dishes. From these, I chose fresh seasonal green peas mixed with beaten rice; chickpea fritters dressed with sweet and salty curd; and *gujias*, sweet pastries stuffed with khoya, all served up on a leaf plate. The proprietor makes all the food himself, something different every day. You will know if you find this particular cook as he has a sign saying 'Photographs 10 Rupees'! If you buy a meal though, he will let you take a snapshot for free.

If you want to get into a special Varanasi frame of mind, there is a government-run shop in Kachori Gali where you can buy sweets that have been laced with bhang, a narcotic preparation from the female flowers of the marijuana plant. Lord Shiva and Krishna are both believed to have been fond of bhang and it is legal in Varanasi. Bhang is also ground into a paste and used in a sweet milk-based drink called *bhang thandai* that you will see being prepared and sold along the ghats. Be warned that ingesting bhang can be very potent!

LUCKNOW

Until the fourteenth century, the region of Awadh, of which Lucknow later became the capital, was as mired in Hinduism as Varanasi. The region is said to take its name from nearby Ayodhya, the birthplace of the great hero of Hindu mythology, Lord Ram. His brother Lakshman is believed to have built a fort near Lucknow and given his name to the city. After 1350, Awadh came under the control of the Delhi Sultanate and, in the sixteenth century, was subsumed into the Mughal kingdom. To manage their vast landholdings, the Mughal emperors installed regional governors to oversee affairs on their behalf. The governors of Awadh, known as nawabs, enjoyed particular imperial favour but, as the great Mughal Empire began to disintegrate, they took the opportunity to assume direct control over the region they had been babysitting. It was the fourth nawab, Asaf-ud-Daulah, who made Lucknow the capital of Awadh.

Awadh was a very productive agricultural region and the nawabs' treasury a very rich one because of this. The nawabs were great admirers of the Mughals and emulated them in spending copiously on cultural pursuits, establishing Lucknow as a centre of Muslim refinement and power that rivalled, and later outdid, Mughal Delhi. The Awadh nawabs enjoyed particular acclaim for the food they served at court. The dishes they served were essentially those of Mughlai cuisine but with their own distinctive take by toning down the robust elements indicative of the Mughals' rustic Central Asian heritage—the Awadh nawabs were of more sophisticated Persian origin—to create more refined versions. The nawabs preferred cream to curd (and are credited with perfecting korma by replacing the curd used in it with cream); lamb (softer meat) instead of mutton; and a subtler use of spices than that favoured by the Mughals. They particularly did not like spices to overpower the fragrance of the local rice they used to make pulao, a dish they preferred over the biryani so beloved of the Mughals. In fact, biryani was not served at royal Awadhi feasts for the nawabs considered it somewhat barbaric in style and lacking sufficient polish to represent them in public; it did make it to the royal dining cloth at more informal, private meals, however.

The pulao* of the Awadh nawabs was created by partially cooking rice in a stock called *yakhni*—variously described as being made from thirty or so kilograms of meat or from chickens fed on musk and saffron—then layering the rice in a pot with cooked meat and saffron-infused milk sprinkled over the top, then sealing the pot with dough and leaving it to cook slowly over hot coals. (This cooking method is called *dum pukht*, and I will come back to it shortly.) This dish was reportedly so tasty and delicate that it felt as if the rice were melting as it went down one's throat. One of the most famous dishes of the Awadh nawabs was a pulao that appeared to be adorned with real pearls; this was, in fact, an entirely edible artifice made from egg mixed with silver and gold tied at intervals in chicken gullet and cooked. Awadh's nawabs had lured the best cooks from the kitchens of the Mughals and other Muslim courts by offering them unbeatable wages. It was very prestigious for them when these cooks invented novel dishes and they loved nothing better than a bit of culinary trickery to show off the elite skills of their well-chosen kitchen staff. Noted instances of such edible illusions include: sweet conserves made from meat; a meal of individual dishes of pulao, korma and kebabs that had been entirely fabricated from sugar; and what appeared to be a perfect pomegranate made from almonds, pear juice and sugar.

The nawabs' cooks had the abundant produce of Awadh to utilize in creating culinary fancies for their masters but, in 1847, crop failure in the region led to a devastating famine. To provide some measure of relief, the reigning Nawab Asaf-ud-Daulah employed huge numbers of people to work on building a monumental congregation hall, the Bara Imambara. The famine lasted a decade and so did the construction. The nawab also employed a contingent of cooks, recruited from the bazaar and not his own kitchens, to provide meals round the clock for the army of labourers. They filled huge pots with meat and vegetables, sealed the pots with dough, set them on coals, and placed more coals on the lid, to slowly cook what was within. One day, the nawab was visiting the building site and smelled the savoury aroma emanating from these pots; he went to investigate, took a taste and was so pleased with it that he sent his own cooks to learn this technique, which is called dum pukht. It is a style of cooking that has become synonymous with Awadhi cuisine—as it was perfected under the

---

* The preparation method described here would be more familiar to Indian cooks as that for biryani, but in traditional Awadhi cooking it is called pulao.

nawabs' remit—but it was a technique that the Mughals had used and has its origins in the Persian practice of burying pots of food in hot sand to cook.

Awadhi cuisine is particularly renowned for its fine kebabs, especially the tender *kakori* made from leg meat—in the nawabs' time, this would have been lamb but mutton is now more likely to be used—pounded to a pulp with onion, garlic, khoya, clove, nutmeg, mace, green and brown cardamom, black and white pepper, dried coconut and white poppy seeds, wrapped around iron skewers and grilled over hot coals. There are two different stories about the origins of this kebab. The first goes that the nawab invited some British officers to dinner and one of these guests was overheard complaining that the *seekh* kebabs were coarse. The nawab was horrified and held crisis talks with senior cooks and advisers to come up with a finer kebab. After ten days of intense trials, a silken-textured kebab was achieved by pounding meat for ten hours. The complaining officer was summoned and presented the new kebab, which he declared a triumph: I imagine the moments between his first bite and his appraisal as a climactic scene in a film. Apparently, it was a cook from the village of Kakori who had devised the successful kebab so they were named for that place. The second story is that the kakori kebab was devised for Nawab Wajid Ali Shah who had lost his teeth and could not chew—despite which he managed to become quite corpulent. You can pick the story you prefer. I think the nawabs would have preferred the former: it was of intrinsic importance to them that they were seen as supreme beings so the story of triumphing over the taste buds of a foreigner who represented the powerful British would sit better with them than that of a fat, toothless man who needed his food puréed. Awadhi cooks also refined the *shammi* kebab, a fried patty of spiced ground meat stuffed with finely chopped mint leaves, green chillies, onions and raw mango and reportedly invented the *galouti* kebab, similar to the shammi though not stuffed.

The *nanbai*s, or bazaar cooks, who operated cookshops in Lucknow's marketplaces, were renowned for their excellent kebabs. The nanbais were also available for hire to work in private homes; people still go to Bawarchi Tola, a street in the old city, to contract cooks to cater traditional Awadhi cuisine for festive occasions. An unidentified Lucknow bazaar cook is credited with creating a bread called *sheermal*, in which water is replaced by egg, and milk, ghee and a little sugar are added. The finished dough is rolled out in thin rounds, pricked with a fork, brushed with saffron-infused milk and cooked in a tandoor.

The final Awadhi culinary legend I am going to tell you is also about bread. Apparently a nawab was in the habit of throwing pieces of stale bread to the poor when he passed by them in the city. One day, a cook picked up some of these pieces, took them back to his own kitchen, deep-fried them—perhaps to sterilize them from their sojourn on the road—dipped them in hot sugar syrup and poured reduced milk over them to create a pudding called *shahi tukra*. 'Shahi' means royal and 'tukra' means piece, but it is not known whether this dish was ever presented to the nawab or whether the name came about because it was first made with royal discards. However, it has become part of Awadhi cuisine.

Like Delhi, Lucknow was a Muslim city surrounded by agricultural land worked by Hindu farmers and labourers. They produced the food crops that fed the nawabs and city residents. There were Hindus living in Lucknow itself, filling roles at court and working as clerks and traders. The nawabs were said to have a preference for lamb meat as it did not cause problems for Hindu guests, and their cooks also incorporated Hindu vegetarian cooking into their repertoire. They enriched dal with cream to make it suitable for royal repasts; one cook is said to have tempered it with a gold coin (removed before serving). Meat dishes such as *murg mussallam* (stuffed whole chicken) were adapted to be made with cauliflower instead; vegetables were cooked dum-pukht style and kebabs created from spinach and corn.

The British had been scheming to gain control of Awadh since the eighteenth century but the Awadhi nawabs maintained their own against the avaricious advances of the foreigners until 1856 when the East India Company annexed their kingdom and exiled the last nawab, Wajid Ali Shah, to Calcutta. Lucknow lost its court, but the refined artistic culture it had spawned continued to be lived out, albeit in ways adjusted to the means of various levels of society. The much-touted courtly manners of the Lucknavis seem to have largely disappeared from public life—at least in my experience of the streets and eateries—but traditional Awadhi cuisine is still enjoyed in Lucknow.

Recommendations

Dining is a royal experience at **Oudhyana**. In this plush restaurant with its elegant eggshell-blue walls, glittering chandeliers and garden seating, you have to sit at chairs and tables instead of lounging around on carpets, cushions and bolsters in true nawabi style, but its Awadhi-style food is imperial. Slightly reminiscent of the culinary trickery of the nawabs is an elaborate vegetarian kebab made from khoya. The biryani is cooked on the dum and the magnificent shahi tukra is definitely not made from roadside pickings.

Taj Residency, Gomti Nagar
12.30–2.45 p.m., 7.45–11.30 p.m. (7 days)
(0522) 2393939

Falaknuma serves Awadhi cuisine and provides guests with a panoramic outlook over the city. Often when the view from a restaurant is good, the food isn't—but that does not hold true here. You can try all the Awadhi specialities such as kakori, galouti and shammi kebabs; chicken or mutton dum biryani; and shahi tukra. The menu is broader than these standards though. A particular Lucknavi speciality is fish cooked in a sauce of finely ground cashew nuts and saffron seasoned with black pepper. Vegetarians are not excluded from enjoying equally decadent dishes such as paneer stuffed with khoya and cooked in a cashew gravy. In the Awadhi tradition, drier dishes such as kebabs are eaten first followed by the 'wet', sauce-based dishes that are mopped up with various breads. To finish, sweet dishes include *kesar phirni*, a delicate ground-rice pudding flavoured with saffron, and a good shahi tukra.

Hotel Clarks Awadh, 8 Mahatma Gandhi Marg
(0522) 2616500, 2616509
www.clarksawadh.com

Chhote Nawab serves traditional Awadhi kebabs but you could diversify and try the *mahi tikka lasuni*, a delightfully garlicky fish kebab, or the vegetarian kebab made with spinach and soft paneer. For something meatier, order a plate of grilled mutton chops marinated in a mix of curd and ground almonds. *Nihari*, a mutton stew, eaten with the soft, spongy bread called kulcha, is a classic Indo-Muslim dish. Lucknow bazaar cooks have a reputation for serving up the best version of it in the country and, if you want try it in situ, the best place is **Haji Sahib's** at Akbari Gate between 7 a.m. and 10 p.m., else Chhote Nawab does a good version. Vegetable dishes change with the season: during the winter, look out for *gobhi methi* (cauliflower cooked with fenugreek leaves, curd and green chillies); in the summer, try jackfruit biryani. Chhote Nawab makes an irresistible version of shahi tukra. It has a different name here: *zauk-e-shahi*, made of honey-soaked toast layered with saffron cream and garnished with pistachio, dried fruit and *varq*, or delicate silver leaf.

Sagar International Hotel, 14-A Jopling Road (0522) 2206601

To experience Lucknow bazaar cooking, visit the popular **Tunday Kebabi**, which, according to its own advertising, has 'ruled the hearts of millions right from the common man up to the most magnetic personalities and celebrities for more than a century'. There is a flourish of the famed flowery language of the erstwhile Lucknavi court in this statement but Tunday's kebabs really are good. The way to eat the patty-like beef or mutton kebabs is to break off a piece of bread, in this case sheermal, and press down into the centre of the kebab, squashing it and scooping it up at the same time. For extra relish, add some slices of onion, grated radish and coriander leaves that come with these. Next door to Tunday is **Bismillah ki Biryani**, a simple eating joint with a considerable reputation for tasty chicken or mutton biryani.

Naaz Cinema Road, Off Aminabad Main Chowk

Next to the UP Press Club on Rani Laxmi Bai Marg is a cluster of slightly more upmarket places specializing in kebabs. These are well patronized by Lucknavis.

A special winter treat in Lucknow is *nimish*, traditionally made from sweetened milk to which a piece of cuttlebone is added and the mix placed in an earthen pot that is left out overnight under moonlight. In the morning, the froth that has formed on top is collected, garnished with pistachio nuts and eaten immediately. Nowadays, the cuttlebone is often replaced with cream of tartar and the reactive process takes place in the refrigerator. If you go to **Akbari Gate** in the old city area of Lucknow in the winter months, you will see a small crowd of men gathered there, each standing behind an identical conical glass case holding what looks like captured white cloud, which is really a large dish of somewhat more corporeal nimish (kept cool perched on a large block of ice). The vendor opens a door in the back of the case and scoops out a serve of his product into small dishes for customers.

Nimish is also eaten in other parts of UP and is alternatively referred to as *malai makkhan*. But things get a bit confusing here as malai makkhan, or cream butter, is also the name given to a another regional dish that is made by beating unsalted butter to a frothy cream and adding sugar and saffron to it. In Lucknow I was told I was being served nimish, but it had a firmer substance than milk froth, and I wonder if it was not actually malai makkhan. Either way, whichever confection it was that I ate, it was a winter speciality and it was delicious.

NECTAR FROM THE FORESTS

Technically, Madhya Pradesh (MP) is not the exact geographic centre of India but, on a map, this huge state—the largest in India—appears to occupy that position. It stretches between Uttar Pradesh, Rajasthan, Gujarat, Maharashtra, Odisha, Jharkhand and Chhattisgarh, holding them together as the mainland. Across the massive girth of MP, the fertile north transitions into the dry, rocky plateau of the Deccan and the southern peninsula; along the way, the state covers a diverse terrain: dry, rocky plains; scrub-covered hills; runs of fertile alluvial soil; and more than 30 per cent of India's remaining forests. The state is a major producer of soybean, pulses and wheat, and the latter two are the staple foods of its population.

The people of MP are predominantly Hindu. Most live in villages and their food is similar to that eaten in rural Uttar Pradesh. A typical meal would be something like this: dal cooked as a simple, spiced stew dressed with crisp, fried onion; *lal bhaji* (leafy greens sautéed with a little oil, cumin, turmeric, red chilli and salt); bitter gourd fried with spices; raw, seasonal vegetables such as radish, cucumber, carrot and onion accompanied by pickles and home-made curd; with fresh fruit or a sweet based on milk and rice to finish. Along the border areas, the food eaten can take on aspects of the respective neighbouring state. Boiled wheat-flour balls called *bafta*, almost identical to the *bati* of nearby Rajasthan, accompany meals in the Malwa region of western Madhya Pradesh, while a dish of fresh corn cooked in ghee, milk and spices called *bhutte ka kees*, popular in Indore, is also eaten in neighbouring Maharashtra (where it bears the same name). On the eastern edge of MP, where the climate and the vegetation begin evolving into the tropics of Odisha, rice is ordinarily eaten with meals.

MP is also home to a significant population of adivasis, an umbrella term for the diverse ethnic and tribal groups believed to be the indigenous people of India. There are over 350 tribal groups in India and every state, except Punjab and Haryana, has tribal populations. The adivasi people traditionally lived in the verdant forests that once covered much of India where they hunted animals and gathered wild food and medicinal plants. Some tribes also practised shifting agriculture whereby they would plant out a piece of land with crops such as millet, harvest it and then set fire to the field to allow it to regenerate—they may have cleared this land by burning it in the first instance—and moving on elsewhere. The gradual transformation of India's surface from natural forest to agricultural, industrial and metropolitan use has been disastrous for the adivasis. They have often been forced to resettle in areas where the land is so poor that no one else wants it because it can't be worked for profit, and their standards of living and education are generally dismal. The adivasis of MP, predominantly the Gond—some of whom have become successful farmers—and the Bhil people, retain the rights to collect minor forest produce such as wild honey, tree resins (some of which are used in food) and *tendu patu*, the green leaves used to make small cigarettes called beedis. They also collect the sweet flower of the mahua tree and distil it to make a clear, floral-tasting white spirit of the same name. The mahua flower can also be eaten and the seeds crushed and boiled to obtain oil that the adivasis cook with. It is a precarious existence, though, eking out a living from the forest in modern India.

BHOPAL

Bhopal, the capital of MP, is a gracious city with a thriving cosmopolitan arts culture; a bustling old quarter of beguiling lanes, bazaars, mosques; and genuinely friendly people. The city has grown up around two adjoining lakes believed to have been created in the eleventh century when the ruler of Malwa, Raja Bhoja, had a local river dammed. It is speculated that the raja established a town on the spot where Bhopal now stands but there is nothing concrete to support this claim. It was not until six centuries later, when Mohammed Khan arrived into the area, that the firm historical foundations for Bhopal were laid. Khan was a trusted general in Emperor Aurangzeb's army. In the unstable political climate that followed the death of his employer Khan began to acquire territory in the Malwa region and eventually fashioned this into his own state and built the city of Bhopal as its capital. In the nineteenth century, the Bhopal court gained particular distinction for being presided over by female rulers, who ran it from behind wicker screens so as to maintain purdah.

The Bhopal royals took their culinary inspiration from Mughal cuisine, encouraging their cooks to create inventive variants on dishes such as kebabs, korma and biryani. Notably, this included *rizala*, a korma-style dish of chicken or mutton cooked with curd, white poppy seeds, green chillies and coriander and a distinctive 'Bhopali biryani' perfumed with star anise and *kewra* water. Traditional Bhopali-style Indo-Muslim cuisine strikes the perfect balance between Awadh's rich, heavy cooking and Hyderabad's hot, spicy food: a culinary achievement that mirrors the city's geographic position as a crossing point between these two cities.

Recommendations

Overlooking the city on Shamla Hills is the former residence of the Bhopali royal family, the **Jehan Numa Palace**, now a heritage hotel. Imperial cooking lives on here in the two restaurants, in dishes such as a rizala of chicken; *nalli gosht* (lamb shanks cooked in a gravy flavoured with nutmeg and kewra water); Bhopali korma and *tawa tabalchi* (an assortment of five seasonal vegetables—in winter, this might include locally grown potato, cauliflower, ladies' fingers, and carrot—each cooked separately and served accompanied by an individual sauce). Please remember that Bhopali-style dishes are served only at dinner.

157 Shamla Hills
(0755) 2661100
www.hoteljehanumapalace.com

The restaurant at the heritage property **Noor-us-Sabah ('light of day') Palace** has excellent views across the Bada Talab ('big lake') and features a selection of Bhopali cuisine including chicken korma, mutton cooked with star anise, biryani and chicken rizala.

VIP Road, Koh-e-Fiza
(0755) 4223333
www.noorussabahpalace.com

Filfora was enthusiastically recommended to me as one of the best places for authentic Bhopali cuisine, so it was a bit off-putting to find the menu heavily populated with Indian, Chinese and tandoori dishes. Closer inspection, followed by some sampling, revealed *keema kaleji* (richly spiced mincemeat); an unctuous chicken rizala; and chicken biryani. They also serve *raan* (marinated, spiced and roasted leg of goat), but you have to order it twenty-four hours in advance. For sweet lovers, there is a local version of *shahi tukra* (*see Lucknow in Uttar Pradesh chapter*) garnished with pistachio-studded cream.

Jyoti Cineplex Compound, Zone 1, M.P. Nagar
(0755) 4289979, (M) 9752781786

Near Filfora, **Laziz Hakeem Hotel** is well regarded by Bhopalis for its biryani—which is pretty much all they serve—available in chicken, mutton, egg or fish versions. The latter is a deceptively simple dish of pieces of lightly fried fish buried under aromatic garam masala–spiced rice, the grains golden with ghee and sparkling with flavour.

187-A, M.P. Nagar
(0755) 4252183
10 a.m.–11 p.m. (7 days)

In the old city, **New Medina Hotel** is recommended for its biryani along with other Indo-Muslim dishes such as *nihari*, mutton *paya* (trotter stew), chicken *dopiaza*, *seekh* kebab and a kewra-scented ground-rice pudding (*phirni*) served in clay dishes. The biryani is made of long-grained rice and flavoured only by the stock in which it is cooked. It comes with a perky chutney of curd, garlic and green chillies. This is a simple cafe but the staff are friendly and helpful.

Ibrahimpura
(M) 9893381794
11 a.m.–11 p.m. (7 days)

For a genuine Bhopali breakfast, wander the lanes of the old city around the **Jama Masjid** and look for Bhopali *poha* (flattened rice) mixed with *sev* (crisp noodles of ground lentil flour). Sev is also eaten with paratha and pickles for breakfast, and generously crowns many snacks. Also look out for *mawa jalebi*, a local take on the jalebi. This distinctive dark-purple sweet is made of a dough of the reduced milk product called *khoya* (aka *mawa*), which is shaped into big knots, fried and soaked in sugar syrup. Look out for big bowls of these prominently displayed on sweet-shop counters and tea stalls.

ALL THINGS RICE

Chhattisgarh officially came into being as an autonomous state of India on 1 November 2000, created from the Chhattisgarhi-speaking districts of eastern Madhya Pradesh. Bordered by Uttar Pradesh, Jharkhand, Odisha, Andhra Pradesh, Maharashtra and Madhya Pradesh, it is a landlocked state and much of it remains undeveloped. Nearly half the state is covered in virgin forest and is home to more than thirty tribal groups, who make up one-third of the population. Most Chhattisgarhis still live in villages but since achieving statehood the Chhattisgarh government has focused on developing mineral-based industries and thermal power generation, leading to increasing levels of prosperity and a growing rate of urbanization. Yet, the ugly steel mills ringing the capital of Raipur and the power plants and factories along the main highway are only fragments against a bucolic landscape of the cultivated fields of the central plains, the gentle green northern hills and lush tropical jungle of the Bastar plateau in the south.

Rice is the major crop and the biannual harvest—kharif (summer) and rabi (winter)—yields such a bountiful supply that the region is popularly referred to as the 'rice bowl of India'.[*] Rice is also the major food of Chhattisgarhis and their traditional cuisine demonstrates ingenuity in creating variety from an inexpensive, readily available food product. As a whole grain, rice is eaten in three forms: *bhaat* (plain boiled rice); *paige* (rice eaten with the water it has been cooked in, flavoured with curd, onion, tomato and chilli); and *baasi* (rice left overnight it its cooking water

---

[*] A moniker that is also used for other rice-growing regions of India such as the Cauvery delta in Andhra Pradesh.

to ferment and become a little sour). It is when rice is ground into flour that it really comes into its own in the Chhattisgarhi kitchen.

Paan roti is a flatbread made from a thick dough of rice flour mixed with chopped onions, tomatoes, green chillies, coriander and caraway. A ball of the dough is pressed between banana, flame of the forest or mahua leaves and snuggled into the coals of a fire to cook. When it is ready, the leaves are peeled off and the hot roti eaten with chutney for breakfast or a snack. Other varieties of Chhattisgarhi rice roti include: *dhuska* (shallow-fried on a tawa); *chusela* (deep-fried like a wholewheat puri); and *cheela* (a larger version of chusela). Cheela is categorized as a roti but technically it is a soft rice pancake. Rice dough is also shaped into various types of noodles. *Fara* are rolled noodles steamed and stir-fried with sesame, garlic, chilli and coriander leaves. To make *muthiya*, rice dough is pushed through a sieve and the resulting noodles steamed and then mixed with similar flavourings to those used with fara. Cooking the same noodles in sweetened cardamom-flavoured milk yields *doodh fara*, which is eaten hot or cold for breakfast or dessert.

Sugar cane is another important crop and the conversion of the harvested cane into gur is a traditional industry in the state. This product is customarily mixed with rice to create a variety of sweet dishes: *arsa* are small round sweets made from rice flour cooked in a thick gur syrup until it forms a stiff dough, balls of which are then deep-fried; *dehori* is a dish of dumplings prepared from rice and curd and soaked in syrup; and *rassota* is a seasonal dish of rice-flour dumplings cooked in freshly pressed cane juice. Those of you who have read the chapters on nearby Bengal and neighbouring Odisha will pick up on a similarity between the syrupy sweetmeats of those states such as *malpua* and *rasagulla* and these, although Chhattisgarhis prefer to create 'dry' confections by making a thick syrup that sticks to the sweet instead of one that drips.

Various titbits for snacking or adding crunch to meals are prepared from rice. *Lai burri* is a snack prepared from a mixture of unhulled puffed rice, curd, red chilli and sesame seeds; it is rolled into balls, dried in the sun and fried when required for consumption. *Thethari* is a savoury biscuit prepared from a dough of rice flour, *besan* (chickpea flour), *ajwain* (carom), red chilli powder and ghee/oil, that is shaped into crescents or curlicues. Various papads are also prepared from rice flour. Reliance on rice as a commercial crop in Chhattisgarh potentially threatens the problems associated with mono-cropping—although it has been going on for a very long time and the harvest keeps giving—but other crops such as wheat are increasingly being cultivated, particularly as the production of this cereal is less labour intensive than growing and harvesting rice. Also, as more Chhattisgarhis take up opportunities to work in the state's natural-resource industry, agricultural labourers are dwindling in numbers.

A typical meal in Chhattisgarh comprises plain cooked rice with a couple of vegetable dishes, one of which will be prepared from leafy greens. Chhattisgarhis eat more than 100 different types of seasonal leafy greens (*bhagi*) round the year. Wild greens are collected from forests and the edges of ponds and waterways and other so-called weeds, and the leaves of vegetables, shrubs and trees are harvested from domestic gardens. Some examples of the types of bhagi eaten are young leaves of neem, a variety of the canna plant, onion leaves, creepers, drumstick leaves, radish, bitter gourd and pumpkin leaves and *bathua*, a spinach that grows wild in cultivated fields. Bhagi of any variety is ordinarily sautéed with a little mustard oil, garlic, cumin, dried red chillies and tomato; onion can be added depending on which variety is in the pan. Flowers are another food item commonly eaten by Chhattisgarhis. These are collected from neem, banana, drumstick, mahua and laburnum trees, among others species, and cooked either as bhagi or dipped in a rice-flour batter to make *pakora*s (fritters).

Chhattisgarhis also sun-dry leafy greens, vegetables, flowers, wild mushrooms, bamboo shoots and green mango pieces to preserve these for use all year round as the intense heat of the Chhattisgarh summer makes it difficult to grow many vegetables. Sun-dried foods are collectively referred to as *suski*. Game meat, fish and shrimps are also preserved by drying in the smoke of a fire, and these impart a 'smoky' flavour to any dish to which they are added.

The words *dubki* and *dubka* mean 'jumping into water' in Chhattisgarh and are used to describe a one-pot dish in which small dumplings, made from ground *urad* dal or besan, are cooked in a vegetable gravy prepared from onions, garlic, ginger, coriander, turmeric and tomato. *Kadhi dubki* is made by using curd or buttermilk thickened with besan flour to create gravy. Yams such as the grey, rough-textured *sooran* (elephant foot yam; *Amorphophallus*), pumpkin and sweet potato are cooked in dubki style. Preparing dubki dishes means that a woman can put together a meal and leave it to cook slowly while she carries out the daily time-consuming task of cleaning her kitchen and stove by plastering it with a mixture of cow dung and mud. Dairy products are not widely consumed in Chhattisgarh and cows are often kept as a source of dung for this daily domestic task, and for fertilizer, more than for milk.

Chhattisgarh is not a state dominated by a vegetarian-food ethos but its low socio-economic profile has meant that many Chhattisgarhis have not been able to afford meat too regularly, so vegetarian food predominates in traditional meal patterns. When it comes to animal protein, Chhattisgarhis like to eat goat, chicken and freshwater fish/shrimps caught in local waterways. These might be cooked by coating them with a paste of onion, ginger, garlic, turmeric and chilli and wrapping them in leaves to cook on coals; very small fish and shrimps are put in a leaf bowl and cooked in the same way. Fish and shrimp are also pickled. Chhattisgarh tribals eat a more extensive range of animal food (*see below*).

Other traditional foods to look out for are *mesu* (fermented-bamboo pickle eaten as a side dish or added to cooked dishes as a spice); *gulgul boghi* (ball-shaped confection prepared from wheat flour, pumpkin pulp and gur); *khurmi* (diamond-shaped sweet glazed with thick gur syrup); and *bafauri* (snack or breakfast dish prepared by crumbling cooked dough balls, made from ground chana dal, and mixing these with coriander leaves, chopped green chillies and salt). (The last dish shows an influence from western Madhya Pradesh.)

Depending on who is telling the story, the indigenous tribes of Chhattisgarh have inhabited the region for anywhere between 10,000 and 50,000 years, but let's not quibble over a few ten thousand years as no one disputes their ancient habitation. Until relatively recently, they have relied on the forest, jungles and waterways for their food supply—which meant they did not eat grains—but as agriculture and industry continues to encroach on the wild lands of the state they are increasingly being forced to adopt a more settled lifestyle and take on the food habits of a settled people. Wild foods are not completely lost to them though and they collect honey, yams, leafy greens, flowers, worms, small birds and red ants. These ants are either eaten live with salt or ground to a paste with garlic and chilli to produce *lal cheente ki chutney*. (The ants have become the best-known food of Chhattisgarh since celebrity chef Gordon Ramsay visited the region and ate some for a television show.) The Chhattisgarhi tribals are particularly fond of pork and would have hunted wild boar in the past. All domestic chickens in existence trace their ancestry back to the indigenous Indian junglefowl, *Gallus gallus*. Chhattisgarh has ten distinct species of chicken that live in the jungle of the Bastar region, including the black-fleshed *kadaknath*: these are no longer common—attempts are being made to revive their numbers—but such birds would have been another food source for these tribal people.

A typical tribal meal is a potage of unpolished rice cooked with yams or other root vegetables, leafy greens or flowers and chillies, or *madiya pej*, a soup prepared from the starchy water drained off cooked rice, that is cooked again with a little salt and eaten mixed with a tangy chutney. In Bastar, a broth called *aamath* is made from bamboo shoots.

The tribals of Chhattisgarh are dab hands at brewing various alcoholic drinks and no gathering, great or small, passes without the sharing of a cup or two of a fortifying beverage. *Salfi* is a milky-white drink derived from the fishtail palm (*Caryota urens*) that grows profusely in the region. The palm sap is tapped by making a slash in the tree and suspending a clay pot under the gash to collect the liquid that oozes out. This sap is non-alcoholic when taken immediately but it has a high sugar content, so the hot climate causes it to ferment quite rapidly if it is kept for a few hours. A distilled liquor is made from the dried flowers of the mahua tree and *thanda* is the name of the local rice beer.

Recommendations

A must for the culinary explorer is a visit to one of the many weekly haats, where tribal people gather to sell or barter produce and other goods, as this is the best way to gain first-hand experience of tribal food and drink. There are said to be 200 or so haats operating on a weekly basis throughout Chhattisgarh, each running on a particular day. A popular haat is held on a Friday at Lohandiguda (sixteen kilometres from Jagdalpur) in Bastar, a region dominated by tribal people. At this haat, you can try red-ant chutney, salfi, mahua, rice beer served in leaf cups and squares of a jelly-like sweet made from coconut and gur.

Prior to Independence, various parts of Chhattisgarh were independent princely states, and several of these erstwhile royal families have converted their family palaces into boutique hotels. Tourism is still a fledgling industry in Chhattisgarh and a palace-based visit is probably the best way to enjoy the state and its regional cuisine, else it is hard to find local cuisine outside of a home. The nearly 300-year-old city of

Kawardha is located in the central plains district of Kabirdham. Here you can stay at the beautifully restored and maintained **Kawardha Palace**, a 1930s' edifice of finest Italian marble set amidst acres of garden. The menu here is dictated by the seasonal produce gathered from the kitchen garden and fruit trees. You can enjoy a grand feast in the dining room or sit outside around the fire and watch while simpler, but no less tasty, dishes such as chicken cooked with fenugreek greens in a clay pot are made for you over a clay stove. Culturally sensitive visits to local tribes can be arranged including sampling tribal cuisine.

Palace Kawardha
(07741) 232085, (M) 9424772108
palacekawardha@gmail.com
www.kawardhapalace.com

Kanker was once at the heart of the princely state of Bastar. The colonial-style **Kanker Palace** was originally built as a viceregal guest house in the Raj era and gifted to the Kanker royals after Independence. Surya Pratap Deo, aka 'Jolly', fronts this family-run hotel. In addition to fulfilling his duties as a hospitable host, he is also a passionate cook. He and his family are dedicated to preserving and sharing the heritage of Kanker and Bastar (where they have farm property that is also open to guests) including the traditional cuisine. Jolly will happily give you cooking lessons in Chhattisgarhi cuisine and take you on a 'food tour' of local villages (both by pre-arrangement).

(07868) 224238, 222005, (M) 9425226506
kankerpalaceheritage@gmail.com
www.kankerpalace.com

Chhuikhadan Palace is the latest royal residence to open its majestic gates to tourism in Chhattisgarh. There are only three rooms in this eighteenth-century palace but these are decorated with frescoes and are full of atmosphere. There is little formal ceremony stood on here and guests enjoy meals of local dishes en famille with the erstwhile rulers.

District Rajnandgaon, 120 km north-west of Raipur

FOOD FROM THE HEART

When I awoke after the overnight leg of my train journey from West Bengal to Patna, to my first glimpse of rural Bihar, I felt I was travelling on hallowed ground. The rice fields I could see outside the window have been continuously cultivated for more than 2500 years, and perhaps the Buddha even walked past these very fields on his wanderings in these parts in the fourth century BC. At that time, Bihar was part of the Magadha kingdom, one of the great 'countries' of ancient India, which encompassed Bengal, eastern Uttar Pradesh, as well as Odisha at the zenith of its power. The Magadha kings ruled from the sixth to the fourth centuries BC and kept their capital in Bihar, first at Rajgir and then at Patna. They were eventually ousted in the third century BC by Chandragupta Maurya, the founder of the empire that eventually expanded, most famously under the watch of his grandson Ashoka—who was born in Bihar—to rule almost all of India. These pan-Indian empires were able to span out from Bihar because there they had iron and plenty of rice.

The Ganga bisects Bihar into uneven northern and southern sections; along with its tributaries, this sacred river is a major source of water for agricultural production in north Bihar. The southern region looks flat to the eye but actually slopes four feet per mile towards the river, draining any accumulated water towards it. Not ideal natural conditions for producing rice, which grows most productively in waterlogged soil, but the rulers of ancient Bihar oversaw the development of an extensive system of channels to ensure that the water stayed where it was needed. Improved growing conditions led to a surplus production that could be traded or used to feed armies. Iron came from Chhotanagpur (now in Jharkhand) and was used to produce advanced agricultural tools (enabling greater crop yields) and weapons (for well-fed armies). Because the Magadha and Mauryan kingdoms were so vast, they were able to bring much of the march land—the area along the border of two states that is often an area of conflict and instability—under productive cultivation because there were few borders, thus increasing the acreage on which food was grown. And then there was north Bihar, a fecund belt of agricultural plain between the Ganga and the base of the Himalayan foothills annually enriched with a thick layer of topsoil washed down from the mountains and from river flooding. All in all, Bihar was an abundant source of food with which to feed the development of classical Indian civilization.

Rice remains an important commercial crop, and long-grained, aromatic Patna rice, widely considered to be the world's best rice, is grown along the Ganga in the north. Each region grows a different variety, or more than one, depending on what grows best there. If you ask a Bihari 'what is the most common meal eaten in Bihar', there's a good chance the answer will be *dal–bhaat–chokha*. The bhaat is rice—we will get to the other two items further on—and Biharis are very fussy about their rice as it is the lifeblood of their cuisine. They will likely have a preference for the flavour of the rice grown in their region, but they understand which variety is best for which dish and will override communal allegiance in favour of the best flavour or texture. At times, the dal part of this trio might be replaced with *maad*, the starchy water strained off the cooked rice. It's almost an inviolable rite for Bihari Hindus to eat khichri, a mildly spiced porridge of rice and lentils, with ghee, papad, pickles, curd and chokha (mashed vegetables), at least once a week, usually on Saturday. Beaten-rice flakes are eaten with sugar and curd (*dahi–shakkar chuda*) as breakfast or mixed with savoury ingredients such as fresh peas in winter and eaten for *nashta* (breakfast or afternoon tea). Rice flour is used to make roti or a light batter to coat deep-fried items; whole or ground rice is cooked with milk and sugar to make the sweet dish known as *kheer*.

One of the most distinctive food items of Bihari cuisine is *sattu*, a flour made from chickpeas soaked in salt water, sun-dried, roasted in a pan filled with hot sand* and ground in a stone mill to a fine flour. Traditionally, this high-protein food is tied up in a cloth and carried by

---

* Parching grains in hot sand ensures an even heat such that all the grains are evenly roasted and none get scorched; you will often see street vendors in India roasting peanuts thus. The sand is sieved off when the process is complete.

field workers; when they need a meal, they knead the sattu with a little water, salt and chilli to form a soft dough off which they break pieces to eat. *Ghenvada* is sattu kneaded with sugar and ghee to make sweet dough eaten in the same way. *Sattu ka sharbat* is a drink made by blending sattu with roasted cumin powder, lemon juice, salt, finely chopped green chillies and water. This concoction is drunk in the summer as it is believed to cool the body. Sattu is also an essential component of what has become the quintessential symbol of Bihari food, the *litti*. This stuffed dough ball was originally a speciality of northern Bihar but is now omnipresent at roadside cafes and homes across Bihar. Litti paired with mutton curry has become a standard dish at Bihari weddings. To make litti, sattu is mixed with salt, black cumin, chopped coriander, garlic and a little oil from an existing mango or lemon pickle and stuffed into a hollow shell of dough that is then folded over and sealed to enclose the sattu. (There are many versions of this filling but the use of pickle oil is non-negotiable.) The finished litti is roasted in the coals of a fire—preferably coals from burning dried cow dung—and when cooked they are tossed around in a piece of cloth to remove the ashes. To eat litti, a hole is pushed in the top and a little ghee poured in. Litti is eaten with chokha, a vegetable mash of coal-roasted vegetables, most commonly potato and eggplant, mixed with onion, coriander leaves, salt, green chilli and mustard oil. It can also be made with *parwal* (small gourd) or *ool* (elephant foot yam).

Bihar is a major producer of vegetables such as eggplant, cauliflower, ladies' fingers and cabbage, and Biharis enjoy eating vegetables. Less than a third among Biharis are vegetarians although they seem to have a preference for vegetarian food. Even meat-eating households tend to limit their consumption of animal protein to weekends or special occasions, and there is a general avoidance of meat on Tuesdays and Thursdays by Hindus. No doubt there are religious factors at work here but economics may have also contributed to this observance. Since Partition, Bihar has been one of the poorest states of India and it is likely that people simply could not afford to eat meat even if they wanted to. It will be interesting to see if meat consumption rises with the state's improving prospects. As a broad rule, Brahmins are usually vegetarians, but there are many Brahmin communities in India that do not subscribe to a meat-free diet and the Maithil Brahmins of north Bihar are one such. They are followers of the goddess Shakti and since she demands sacrifice, usually of a goat, as a demonstration of devotion to her the Maithil are not shy of eating the resulting meat, though what they consume more often than *maas* (mutton) are fish dishes. This community also has strong cultural links with Bengal (where the cult of Kali, another sacrifice-demanding goddess and an avatar of Shakti, is strong) and this is evident in their dishes such as *machchak jhor* (fish cooked in mustard paste). *Kankorak chokha* is a Maithil version of chokha, made from the meat of crab that has been roasted in its shell; the cooked meat is removed and mashed with a little mustard oil, green chillies and lemon.

In addition to dal and bhaat, most Bihari meals will feature at least two vegetable dishes, collectively called *tarkari*, one of which might be a chokha. Biharis like to cook vegetables, particularly leafy greens, in *bhunjia* style (lightly stir-fried in mustard oil—the common cooking medium—with garlic, ginger, salt and perhaps a few spices, depending on the vegetable in use). Another style of tarkari is to cook vegetables, especially potato, eggplant, beans, bitter gourd, ladies' fingers and pumpkin, in a gravy prepared from ground yellow mustard seeds, turmeric and *kalonji* (nigella)—a preparation with flavourings similar to those commonly used in neighbouring West Bengal.

At various times throughout its long history, Bihar has been joined with Bengal within a singular administrative territory; this close relationship is evident in the Bengali influences absorbed into Bihari cuisine. Apart from the mustard-based sauce, Biharis cook vegetables such as potato and *jhingi* (ridge gourd) in a thick gravy prepared from ground *posto* (white poppy seeds), just as Bengalis do. *Panch phoron*—the five-spice mix of fennel, mustard, fenugreek, cumin and nigella of Bengali cuisine—is regularly used by Bihari cooks.

In the early sixteenth century, Bihar came under the control of various Islamic rulers beginning with Sher Shah Suri, then Akbar and finally the nawabs of Bengal, until 1764 when it fell to the British. The Muslim influence is most evident in the use of garam masala—I was given a Bihari recipe for this that used cardamom, black pepper, bay leaf, cumin, mace and nutmeg—in meat and vegetable stews and the so-called 'Bihari kebab'. In this last dish, pieces of mutton are marinated (in a paste of onion, garlic, chilli and various spices), skewered and grilled over charcoal. (From my experience, I was unable to work out what exactly made these kebabs uniquely 'Bihari' but so they are called.)

Bihari cuisine is very often described as 'simple', a misleading term as I found that there is a certain refinement to Bihari food. Spices are used judiciously to impart flavour which is just slightly understated and thus intriguing; ingredients are cut finely; and the quality and seasonality of foods is of paramount consideration. It's a subtle thing and you need to sample good Bihari home cooking to 'get' it! Some examples might serve to give an idea. There is a fair selection of dishes that have come into everyday use in Bihar from the west of the subcontinent—it is more usual for this to be described as an influence from eastern Uttar Pradesh but that depends on how you read your map—and Bihari cooks give their own unique touch to these. The dish of chickpea-flour dumplings served in a gravy of curd and *besan*, flavoured with asafoetida and turmeric, called *kadhi* is much lighter, with smaller, delicate dumplings in Bihar where it is called *kadhi buri*, than any version I have eaten elsewhere (and kadhi is a dish that could almost be called pan-Indian). *Ramsall* or *besan ki sabzi* is a dish of noodles made from besan cooked in a gravy of tomato, red chilli, ginger, cumin, *ajwain* (carom seeds) and mustard paste—almost identical to Rajasthan's *gatte*, except that the noodles are cut much finer in Bihar. Indeed, they were so petite in a version I enjoyed that I thought the dish was made from corn kernels; also, the use of mustard paste is a distinct Bihari addition. A Bihari friend told me that the food of his state is 'light' because the weather is very humid for much of the year and that eating 'heavy' dishes in such a climate makes people sluggish.

As you can see, chickpeas in the form of sattu or besan are an important food in Bihar. Besan differs from sattu in that the shell/skin of the chickpea is neither removed nor roasted before it is ground into flour. *Ghugni*, a dish of whole pre-boiled chickpeas cooked with onion, garlic, tomato, cumin and garam masala, is customarily eaten at breakfast or as an evening snack. There are all sorts of variations; in winter, it is made with fresh green peas (*matar ghugni*) and I was served a version prepared from chickpeas, beaten-rice flakes and moong beans that had been lightly stir-fried with mustard seeds, turmeric and curry leaves. The delicate green leaves of the chickpea are also eaten as a fresh green vegetable in Bihar or cooked with garlic and ginger, packed into jars with mustard oil, and set in the sun to create a pickled vegetable for year-round use. A typical Bihari meal would not be complete without at least one pickle (achar), and there are many different pickles produced throughout Bihar: *nimbu ka achar* (lemon pickle) and *aam ka achar* (mango pickle) are arguably the most common. I was served a red chilli pickle, *lal mirch ka achar*, prepared from a milder red chilli—of the type used to make paprika—coriander seeds, turmeric, mustard oil, aniseed, salt, cumin, black cumin and ajwain. This latter spice is actually a tiny fruit that tastes similar to thyme as both contain thymol. Rajasthan produces almost all of this spice but it is used extensively in Bihari cooking, adding a distinctive flavour note to it.

While rice is an essential food in Bihar, reflecting its eastern influences, various flatbreads (rotis) prepared from wheat flour and other ground grains are also widely consumed. A typical meal pattern in Bihar would be to have rice at lunch and roti with the evening meal; breads are also eaten for breakfast. *Phulka*, a thin roti dry-roasted on a griddle and then puffed over the coals/flame, paratha stuffed with sattu and small, ethereal puris made from rice flour are some of the typical breads I ate in Bihar. Bihar's other dietary mainstay, dal, is most commonly prepared from *arhar/toor* (pigeon pea), a yellow dal indigenous to eastern India.

The fertile alluvial soil of the north supports significant production of fruit including bananas, pineapples, mangoes and lychees. The latter are grown around Muzaffarpur and are famed across India: indeed, these are so delicious that it's almost worth enduring the summer heat of the Indian plains to sample them during their short season. Mangoes are another summer fruit that Biharis make into a cooling summer drink called *aam ka panna*, made by roasting raw green mangoes and mashing the cooked flesh to a pulp with red chillies, salt and cumin. Sugar cane is an ancient crop of Bihar and, over the millennia, various areas have developed their own distinctive regional sweets. Munger in southern Bihar is known for *motichoor ka laddoo*, a round sweet made from besan, ground almonds, sugar and ghee; Silao, near the ruins of the ancient Buddhist university town of Nalanda, is known for *khaja*, a flaky wheat pastry deep-fried and soaked in sugar syrup; and the holy town of Gaya has several sweets to its name. The best known is *tilkut*, a light and flaky toffee-type sweet made from white sesame seeds (*til*) and gur, traditionally in winter. As it is only made from two ingredients, tilkut sounds simple but the process is complex. A syrup made from gur is worked and stretched until it becomes thick and opaque; tennis-ball-sized pieces of this firm fudge are then rolled in sesame seeds and pounded with a flat hammer to disperse the seeds throughout the sweet and break them up somewhat, but not crush them such that they release their oil. Tilkut is also made from refined sugar and is lighter in colour than *gur tilkut* (though, in my opinion, the latter is much tastier). *Lai ka laddoo* is another round sweet made from ground amaranth seeds (*ramdana* or *rajgira*), sugar and khoya. *Kesaria peda* is also made from khoya blended with sugar and saffron while *anarsa*, a deep-fried biscuit-shaped sweet, is made from soft dough of rice flour, sugar, khoya and sesame seeds. The Vishnu Temple at Gaya is one of the five holy places in India where Hindus go to make offerings to their departed ancestors, and as the speciality sweets of this town are the 'dry' ones, this makes them portable such that pilgrims can easily take them home to share their visit to Gaya with their living relatives. All these sweets are bought from *mithai-wallah*s (confectioners). Less complex sweets such as *makhane ki kheer* are made in home kitchens.

Makhanas or fox nuts are the edible starchy seeds of a species of water lily (*Euryale ferox*) harvested from the base of ponds. These hard-cased seeds are roasted and hammered open to reveal the spongy white makhana 'nut'. These nuts are cooked with milk and sugar to make kheer. As makhana is not a cereal, it is often eaten during Hindu religious fasts that require the avoidance of cereals. Makhanas are also fried in ghee and eaten with salt and pepper—quite like popcorn!

Recommendations

Unfortunately, it was very difficult to find any place in Bihar that serves Bihari cuisine outside a home. (The references to my experiences of eating in Bihar are largely to the meals I enjoyed in private homes.) My theory is that, as Bihar has been struggling economically for a long time, Biharis generally have not had the disposable income to spend on eating 'outside' food, and that when they do eat out they want something quite different from what they eat at home. In Patna, the capital of Bihar, you can easily eat Mughlai, Chinese, south Indian food and pizza. In Bodh Gaya, a place that draws 10 per cent of the international tourists that visit India, you can eat Korean, Thai, Japanese, Tibetan and 'Continental', just not Bihari. (I was laughed at by the staff in one particular hotel in Bodh Gaya when I inquired whether they served Bihari food.) The only restaurant I could find that serves Bihari cuisine is called Pot Belly, and it is located in Delhi. (It would be going against the spirit of this book for me to recommend a restaurant out of location, but if you just happened to put the name in your search engine of choice . . .) Nevertheless, here are the limited options I found:

Litti started out as a 'travel' food as it could be made from lightweight, portable ingredients with minimum effort. It is fitting then that it is now sold by roadside vendors all across Bihar. If you go to **Mayur Lok** on Dak Bungalow Road in Patna, there are numerous stalls operating here in the evening selling the type of street food that you will find in any reasonable-sized town in India these days. Look for **DK Litti Stall** and you can sample this distinctive Bihari food item, though it is served with salad and chutney rather than chokha. On **Buddha Marg** opposite Patna Museum, there is a row of shops selling khaja, which I was informed was 'as good as what you will find in Silao'. In Gaya, the best tilkut comes from **Shivam Tilkut Bhandar** on Ramna Road, or orientate yourself to the clock tower in the centre of town and adjacent to it you will find a sweet shop selling good tilkut, kesari peda and anarsa.

Luckily, I can finish this brief section with one superb recommendation. Just outside of Gaya, you can stay at Maksudpur Garh. There are two particular reasons that a stay here is very special. First, you will be served delicious home-style Bihari fare, albeit with a royal touch; and second, the property is legally owned by Goddess Bhagwatiji and is administered on her behalf by the current Raja Saheb of Maksudpur, Ajai Singh. Ajai and his wife, Nalini, are committed to preserving the traditional culture of Maksudpur, including its particular food ways.

Rajmandir Palace, Maksudpur Garh, P.S. Khizarsarai, District Gaya (06322) 243001, 243016, (M) 9820898628
www.maksudpur.com/homestay

JUNGLE BOUNTY

The state of Jharkhand, carved off from the southern part of Bihar, only came into formal existence on 15 November 2000 but the region has had its own distinct cultural identity since the time of the Magadha Empire. The British called it the Jharkhand district when they took over control of Bihar in the late eighteenth century. Jharkhand means the 'land of forests' and considerable areas of the state are still under evergreen woodland. Underneath the forests, though, lie major mineral reserves, and modern Jharkhand is a contrast of pretty green hills and farmland, the dramatic rocky outcrops of the Chhotanagpur plateau and mines and industrial sites such as the purpose-built steel town of Jamshedpur.

Nearly half of India's current mineral yield comes from Jharkhand. Indeed, the region has a long history of being mined. Iron ore and the coal to smelt it—used by the Magadha and Mauryan dynasties to develop the superior technology in weaponry and agricultural tools which allowed them to create their pan-Indian kingdoms—were extracted from Jharkhand. The Mughals, who had a strong interest in adornment, encouraged diamond mining in the region. My theory is that Jharkhand was seen as a place to extract things from but not to develop, hence the forests were largely left alone (compared to Bihar, which was heavily developed such that there is little forest left there), and so were the people who lived in them.

Jharkhand came into its current independent existence because of the ongoing agitation for a separate state by the large adivasi/tribal population that has lived there for millennia. There are over thirty indigenous tribes in Jharkhand. Most of them practise an animistic religion focused on the worship of ancestors and their native forests, which to them are sacred groves to be preserved to provide both spiritual and physical nourishment. The tribes collect the leaves of many plants and trees, and cook and eat these as vegetables, typically boiled in a one-pot meal, with various species of wild yams and tubers, chillies and mutton or other meat. *Kanda*, a local variety of sweet potato, is boiled and eaten for breakfast. Spices are not typically used in Jharkhandi tribal cooking. Flowers of trees such as *amaltas*, flame of the forest and mahua are collected and added to dishes. Jharkhandi tribals also make a distilled liquor called *mahuwa/mahuli* from dried mahua flowers (a common practice throughout central India). *Handia/handiya* is a rice beer produced from rice and local herbs; it is always drunk on festive and ceremonial occasions. Fish, frogs, snails, insects and other small animals are caught and collected for eating from forests and waterways. It was traditional practice amongst the Oraon tribe of Jharkhand for a boy to give a girl a dish of fried field mice to show that he was in earnest.

Wild mushrooms such as *rugra*, a type of button mushroom, and *khukri* (oyster mushrooms) are also collected from the forests during the wet season. It is not just the tribal population that like eating these fungi (which they also dry for use throughout the year). The demand is so great from the general population that the government is seriously experimenting with commercially cultivating these two mushrooms. Bamboo shoots are another forest product and are used as pickles or added to cooked dishes. If you visit local markets, you will see some of these foods being sold. You can usually sample handia at the markets as well.

The food eaten by the tribes of Jharkhand is very similar to that eaten by tribals all across a belt that runs from the north-east through West Bengal, Odisha, Jharkhand and Chhattisgarh into Andhra Pradesh. For all these people, the wilderness—jungle, highland, meadow, forest, river, creek—plays a vital role in cultural identity and food security.

Jharkhand's population is a mix of tribals (30 per cent) and people of Bihari origin; the mining and steel industries also draw workers from other central and eastern Indian states. The typical daily food is rice, dal and vegetables, and many prepared dishes are similar, if not identical, to those eaten in Bihar. There are a few dishes that have originated in Jharkhand or have a distinct regional character. *Dhuska* is a small pancake made with a batter of rice and chana dal flavoured with garlic or asafoetida, green chillies and cumin. It is eaten with potato or mutton curry on festive occasions in both states, but is said to have originated in Jharkhand. *Maad jhor* is a dish of greens cooked in the starchy water drained off cooked rice, and tempered with mustard oil and garlic.

Recommendations

Ranchi, the capital of Jharkhand, was the summer capital of Bihar in the colonial era, as its elevated location makes it considerably cooler and less humid than the plains surrounding it. It was once a very popular destination for Bengalis and Biharis to escape the summer heat. While it retains some of that charm, it has taken on a more 'industrial' ambience since Jharkhand achieved statehood and is not a place that rates highly on the 'must see' list of tourists. Most visitors to Ranchi, and Jharkhand, come on business associated with mining and steel, and most eateries aim to please them with south Indian, north Indian and Chinese food! So it is not easy to find commercial places serving regional food here. One option is **Mithila**. The dining room is decorated with paintings from the Mithila region of northern Bihar and the menu features a small selection of Jharkhandi/Bihari dishes. Try the dhuska with *muduwa maas* (rich stew of mutton cooked with curd, chillies, garlic and garam masala) or relish the steamed rice cakes called *pitha* with *ghugni* (spiced chickpeas).

Hotel Ranchi Ashok, Doranda
(0651) 2480759–65
www.hotelranchiashok.com

The only other commercial option for local food I can recommend is to have *litti chokha*, small stuffed breads served with mashed, roasted eggplant and tomato, and *motichoor laddoo*, a small round sweet (*moti* means pearl) made from besan, ghee, saffron and finely chopped nuts, at the popular **Kaveri Restaurant** on the main street of Ranchi (it is located in a shopping complex, not a religious institution as the name of the complex suggests).

9–11 GEL, Church Complex, First Floor, Main Road
(0651) 2560612

EASTERN INDIA

THE SWEET LIFE

Bengalis have always eaten well: their fecund land stretches from mountain to sea, blessed with an intricate patchwork of water sources. The holy Ganga flows eastward across it, shooting off the tributary Hooghly as a parting gesture before continuing on across Bangladesh, turning south to merge with the Brahmaputra in the Gangetic delta and ultimately spending itself into the Bay of Bengal. Its offspring heads due south to the same destination wending through West Bengal to get there, along the way sending off its own progeny. Creeks, swamps, ponds, estuaries and the coastline are further watery boons; indeed the very atmosphere is dense with moisture. Every year, the rivers of Bengal swell with the monsoon, spill over their banks and recede again, leaving behind a deposit of fertile alluvial soil. It's a cycle that Bengali farmers have been living with for millennia and mastered long ago to gain the best agricultural returns from their 'golden land'. We will come back to this produce, but first a little more scene setting.

The abundance of Bengal—which historically includes Bangladesh[*]— was not confined to eatables. By the fourth century AD, Bengal had built such a strong trade with Rome in silk and woven textiles that when the Roman Empire collapsed, the economy of Bengal crashed with it, and took centuries to fully recover from the loss. In the twelfth century, the Delhi

[*] In 1905 the British divided Bengal into East and West provinces, but the outcry this caused forced them to join the two back into one in 1912. In 1946 'East Bengal' was partitioned from India to become the eastern wing of the newly created Pakistan. In 1971 it became the independent country of Bangladesh. Prior to Indian independence, the term 'Bengal' referred to the undivided region—and it has been used as such in this chapter—and there is significant cultural and culinary similarity between West Bengal and Bangladesh.

Sultanate brought Bengal under Muslim rule. The Afghan Sher Shah Suri usurped Mughal power in India for five years in the mid-sixteenth century claiming Bengal as part of his dominion; after his death, Akbar annexed the region, putting it to use as a food bowl to supply Mughal armies and furnish delicacies for imperial sustenance. It also added considerable revenue to the royal coffers as it was one of the wealthiest regions of India. The Mughal-appointed provincial governor, or nawab, of Bengal had assumed independent control of the region by the early eighteenth century; in 1757, the British defeated the last nawab at the Battle of Plassey, bringing Bengal under their control.

The British were not the only Europeans in Bengal. The Portuguese had arrived there first in 1517. By the beginning of the seventeenth century, there were 5000 Portuguese living in settlements along the Hooghly, either engaged in trade in commodities such as sugar and long pepper or in converting the native 'heathens' to Christianity. By the time the British trounced the Bengal nawab, there were Danish, French, Greek, Dutch and Armenian trading settlements all along the Hooghly. The British had created their riverside settlement in the early eighteenth century by amalgamating several villages and calling this fledgling conurbation Calcutta. After 1757, they made it the administrative and commercial capital of their Indian territory. (We will visit Calcutta further on.)

The Europeans were astounded at the beauty of Bengal and the abundance and variety of food available there. Italian traveller Ludovico di Varthema, who travelled to Bengal via a wondrously convoluted route in the early sixteenth century, said the region abounded in grain of every kind, sugar and ginger and anointed it the 'best place in the world to live'. French physician François Bernier, who served Emperor Aurangzeb for twelve years in the late seventeenth century, described Bengal as 'abounding' with wheat, vegetables, goats, sheep, ducks, rice and a profusion of fresh and saltwater fish. As a land laced with waterways and fringed by the ocean, it is not surprising that rice and fish are key elements of traditional Bengali food.

Two types of rice are generally used in Bengal: *aatap*, sun-dried rice that is milled and polished, and *siddha*, parboiled rice that is soaked, steamed and then dried. Processing rice in this way allows the vitamin-rich outer layers to be retained but not deteriorate in the hot and humid climate of Bengal when stored. Bengalis prefer the flavour of aged rice. Plain cooked rice (*bhaat*) was traditionally served with every meal in Bengal though wheat breads now commonly supplant it, particularly during dinner. This dietary change has its origins in the Second World War, when rice was in short supply and people were encouraged to eat wheat instead, and the Bengalis decided they liked it. Nonetheless, rice is eaten at least once a day by Bengalis. Rice is cooked with dal to create various khichris, or boiled with milk and sweetened to create sweet dishes: both ancient ways of cooking rice in India. Relatively more recent additions to the Bengali repertoire of rice dishes are Muslim-influenced pulaos and biryanis.

If rice plays the supporting role in a Bengali meal, then fish is the star, as Bengalis have an absolute passion for it. Only 6 per cent of the population is vegetarian—largely because of this compelling cultural preference for aquatic protein. Even Bengali Brahmins eat fish. Despite their long coastline, Bengalis prefer the 'sweet' flavour of freshwater fish and crustaceans to the 'fishy' flavour of saltwater varieties. They are particularly fond of *ilish* (*hilsa* or *Tenualosa ilisha*)—they have been charged with being 'obsessed' about it—a tropical fish that lives in the estuaries of the Gangetic delta. In summer, the ilish migrate up the rivers that empty into the delta to spawn. Traditionally, it was a taboo to catch ilish during the hot months when they were breeding; instead they were caught and eaten to celebrate the end of summer and the onset of monsoon. Ilish is prepared in a variety of ways including *ilish jhol* (fish pieces cooked in a thin spiced gravy infused with turmeric, ginger, cumin, coriander and green chillies); *bhapa ilish* (marinated in a paste of mustard seeds and green chillies, wrapped in a banana leaf and steamed); or cooked in a sauce of curd and ginger. The flavourful flesh of the ilish is delectable but there is a drawback: it is full of tiny and wiry bones. This presents little problem to the Bengalis though, for they prefer fish on the bone. Some of them have developed an ability to work the flesh off these and dexterously flick the denuded bones into a corner of their mouth; when this debris reaches a critical mass, they discreetly expel it. Ilish is also smoked to 'melt' the bones, but most restaurants served deboned ilish so don't be scared to try it. In a home, every part of the ilish is eaten, including the head. In fact, a festive meal might include ilish in every course, except dessert!

Ilish is found in all the major rivers of Bengal but stocks are declining. The demand for this fish is huge, particularly from expatriate Bengalis who are willing to pay very high prices for it. To meet this demand, it is being fished out of season. This combined with increasing river pollution—which prevents the fish swimming upstream to spawn—means that fewer eggs are being laid and ilish populations are shrinking. As the species becomes less abundant, the prices go up as does the demand by people who like prestige on their plates. If it is not ilish season when you visit Bengal, try other local species like *rui, parshey, koi* (perch), catfish and *bhetki*—a popular saltwater fish despite the general prejudice against the taste of finny sea dwellers. Jumbo-sized estuary prawns—Bengalis like the roe of this species as much as the flesh—and crabs are also popular and available cooked in a variety of ways.

Fish is a symbol of prosperity and fertility in Bengal. Traditionally, the groom's family sends a fish, usually rui, to the bride's as part of the prescribed matrimonial rituals. All this makes Bengalis very fussy about fish and they have considerable expectations of their fishmongers. These men are artisans and it is fascinating to see them at work. They sit with large, upturned curved blades—called *ansh-bonti* in West Bengal—attached to a piece of wood or metal, between their feet. The blade is razor-sharp and on it they can turn a whole fish into delicate boneless fish pieces within minutes. First, the belly is slit open and the gut removed; the head is then taken off and put aside; the body is slid down the blade within a hair's breadth of the backbone; this process continues until the pieces are as the customer has requested. At the end, there is virtually no flesh left on the frame but the customer is likely to take it anyway as fish bones can be used in a dish called *khosha charchari* in which they are cooked with vegetable peelings and stalks—a very domestic dish, not one that has found its way on to restaurant menus yet.

A Bengali does not live on fish and rice alone, of course. Further savour is added to meals with a range of dishes made from seasonal vegetables. Indigenous varieties include pumpkins, gourds, radish, ladies' fingers, jackfruit, coconut, leafy greens including water spinach, water chestnuts and banana. Technically, banana is a fruit—and when ripe is eaten as such—but raw bananas, their tender white stems (*thor*) and flowers (*mocha*) are all cooked as savoury dishes. The pink flower stamens are chopped finely and cooked with spices in a soft stew called *mochar ghonto* or used as a stuffing for potato croquettes called *mochar chop*. Potato is a popular vegetable and Bengalis are among the largest consumers of this starchy tuber in the world. It is a relatively recent addition to Bengal though as it was brought into India by Europeans and is not used in religious ceremonies as it was not around when those were devised! Before the potato came along, Bengalis ate native yams and these are permissible for use in rituals. Europeans also introduced pineapples, tomatoes, cabbage and cauliflower. While these are used every day in Bengali cooking, the latter two are referred to as 'English vegetables'.

The spices used in Bengali cooking would have once been limited to indigenous ginger, long pepper (*Piper longum**), mustard and turmeric. Over time, trade and the influence of the various ethnic and cultural groups that came into Bengal has greatly expanded the range. Muslims brought in their taste for cinnamon, cardamom, clove and saffron; Europeans brought the chilli. The most commonly used spice mix in Bengal is called *panch phoron*, comprising whole cumin, mustard seeds, nigella (*kala jeera* in Bengali), aniseed (or a tiny black seed called *radhuni*) and fenugreek. Both yellow and black mustard seeds are also widely employed, lending a nutty flavour to dishes. Mustard oil is the preferred cooking medium, particularly for fish; the pungent oil is said to turn 'sweet' when heated, thus complementing the sweet-fleshed fish. White poppy seeds are oilseeds used as spices more extensively in Bengali cuisine than anywhere else in India. This might be due to the fact that Bengal was once at the centre of the thriving opium trade run by the British out of India in the nineteenth century. The main market for this opiate was China and the Chinese were very receptive to the high-quality opium produced in Bengal—which also had a local following. The British would pack ships full of it, sail them down the Hooghly, across the Bay of Bengal, through Malacca Strait, into the South China Sea and the ports of southern China: a relatively short and straightforward ocean trade route for the time, therefore a more profitable one. In China, they unloaded the opium and filled the ships with tea and sailed back to Bengal. All in all, it was very lucrative business for the British—many fortunes were made in the opium trade—and they were happy with the way things stood. The problem was that opium was illegal in China and Chinese authorities were not at all pleased with the British pushing drugs on to their populace. They tried twice to fight the British off; that didn't work so they legalized opium cultivation in China, thus ending the demand for the supply from India and put paid to the British opium trade. Processing the opium poppy for its addictive latex results in a large residue of seeds and these found their way into Bengali cooking. These fine ivory-coloured seeds—called *posto*—are ground into a paste and added to dishes to give a nutty flavour, to thicken sauces and to provide texture. *Aloo posto*, a dish of potatoes cooked in a thick gravy made of poppy seeds, nigella, green chilli and turmeric, is eaten as

---

* Long pepper, or *pipali*, is a variety of black pepper. It was once an important commodity for India and was traded in significant quantities with ancient Greece and Rome and later Europe. It is still selectively used in India in cookery and traditional medicine but *Piper nigrum*, that is, *kali mirch* or black pepper, is the variety now most commonly employed in Indian kitchens.

often as the average Briton eats mashed potatoes. Chicken and prawns are other items cooked in the same sauce to create *murghi posto* and *chingri posto*, respectively. Crispy fritters called *postor bora* are made from a thick paste of white poppy seeds ground with green chillies and onions and deep-fried.

Bengalis also have a predilection for sugary treats, and an associated reputation as master confectioners. Some savoury dishes even have a sweet touch such as *chholar dal*, a dish of split chickpeas cooked with coconut and spices to which a little sugar is added. Sugar cane has been a significant crop in Bengal for at least 2000 years—undoubtedly a factor in the development of the collective saccharine-oriented palate—yet it's a historically recent influence that has shaped the sweets Bengal is best known for. During the time the Portuguese were in Bengal, there were never enough of them to do all the work required to prepare their commodity-laden ships for the long journey to the markets of Europe. Provisioning these ships was essential but it was a task that could be outsourced. The Portuguese trained Bengalis to prepare the ships' victuals. In doing so, they taught their native employees to make *chhena* by splitting milk with acid, collecting the curds and draining these to produce a soft, firm mass that is now used as the base ingredient for Bengali sweets such as *rasagulla* and *sandesh*. It is the process by which chhena is made that gives it away as a foreign intervention. Traditionally, Hindus consider 'cutting' milk with an acid as impure and use reduced milk instead to make sweets (*see Varanasi*). Undoubtedly, there are those who would still consider chhena-based sweets tainted, but they do have a popular following all over modern India.

Rasagulla is made by kneading chhena until it forms a smooth dough; pieces of which are rolled into balls and dropped into boiling sugar syrup in which they puff up slightly. Bengalis call the rasagulla a 'snowball', which gives you an idea of its appearance. Sandesh is made by cooking chhena with sugar syrup until it forms a soft, pliable dough that is rolled into balls or pressed into moulds to shape it. It might be that sandesh was not born from chhena but evolved from a much older sweet made of curd cooked with sugar. Sandesh is now being made in an ever-increasing array of flavours such as chocolate, lemon and mango but, in its simplest form, it is popularly offered to the gods for consecration. Chhena-based sweets such as sandesh do not have a long shelf life so freshness is an important quality of these sweets, and the best confectioners produce new batches on a daily basis (at the least). If you visit the Kali Temple in Kalighat in Kolkata, you will see a number of stalls selling sandesh including *karapaker sandesh*, a variety that is cooked for longer to reduce the water content so that it keeps for longer, allowing pilgrims to carry the goddess's blessings home with them as sanctified sweets. Another chhena-based sweet is *pantua* (deep-fried balls of chhena, semolina and ghee soaked in sugar syrup); an alternative name for this is *ledikeni*, named for Lady Charlotte Canning,* the wife of the first viceroy of India, Lord Canning. *Chamcham* is an oval chhena-based sweet flavoured with rose water or saffron and decorated with piped cream, dried fruit and coconut flakes. The process of making chhena-based sweets seems simple but that is deceptive; it requires considerable skill and attention to produce them and even the best Bengali domestic cooks prefer to buy them from a professional confectioner.

Mishti doi (sweet curd) is a Bengali dessert made of sweet thickened milk set overnight in terracotta pots. The best mishti doi has a thick creamy skin, called *matha*, on top: a sign that rich-quality milk has been used to make it. *Lal doi* is sweetened with date-palm sap (*khejur gur*) that imparts a rusty-red (*lal*) colour to it. Mishti doi does not bear any foreign interference and therefore has a rating in traditional Hindu dietary philosophy as a 'cooling' food; as such, it is eaten in the morning but not at night. *Bhapa doi* (steamed curd) is prepared by steaming a mixture of sweetened curd and evaporated milk flavoured with cardamom or saffron in trays. The finished product is cut into squares and has a texture akin to a European-style cheesecake. Indeed, it is often referred to as the 'Bengali cheesecake'—a similar item is made in Odisha and there is some dispute as to whether so-called Bengali sweets are actually Oriya in origin. Any sweet item—or any prepared food—whose name bears the suffix *bhog* has usually been prepared for the gods.

Bengalis pride themselves on possessing sophisticated palates. They like to eat well and are very particular about the quality of food. Many visit the market every day to handpick their fish and vegetables. Among Indians, they also spend the highest percentage of their income on food. Breakfast in Bengal is simple, perhaps mishti doi or a potato dish eaten with fluffy *luchi*s, oval wheat breads deep-fried to a golden colour. When it comes to the mid-afternoon meal, things get a lot more complex. A traditional Bengali lunch is structured in a sequence to ensure that all five tastes—bitter, salty, sour, sweet, pungent—are satisfied. Bitter food is believed to stimulate the

---

* This sweetmeat is variously said to have derived its name after Lady Canning expressed an appreciation for it, either after receiving a gift of this confection or on tasting it at a function.

appetite so the meal opens with something bitter. In summer, it is *shukto*, a light stew of bitter gourd and other seasonal vegetables cooked in milk and spices; at other times of the year, fried neem leaves are served. Next comes a dish of dal and *bhaja*—pieces of fish or vegetables dipped in a spiced chickpea-flour batter and deep-fried until crisp (sometimes also fried without the coating). *Aloo bhaja* is often served and one of the styles is to finely shred the potato and deep-fry it into thin chips. Dal is sometimes also accompanied by dishes of mashed or stuffed vegetables such as *kumro makha*, pumpkin mashed with green chillies, mustard oil, salt and a little sugar (the pumpkin for this dish is often cooked in the same water as a pot of rice and if cooked this way, it is called *kumro bhaate*), or *potoler dolma*, small gourd stuffed with a tangy spice mixture and pan-fried. (Bengalis are very fond of *potol/parwal*, and when it is in season they cook it in a variety of ways.) After this comes at least one fish dish such as *machher jhol* (fish pieces sautéed in mustard oil and simmered in water with vegetables) or a fiery *jhal* (a dry dish of fish, crabs or prawns cooked with ground mustard seeds, panch phoron and red chilli). If a meat dish is to be served, it comes after the fish and before a rice dish such as pulao; plain boiled rice is served throughout the meal. *Ambole*, a jam-like sweet-and-sour dish prepared from fruit such as mangoes and tomatoes, paired with crunchy papad comes next. A sweet dish such as *payesh* (rice or other grains cooked in sweetened milk) and a sweetmeat finish the meal. What type and how many dishes are served depends on whether it is a regular family meal or a festive one. In the evening, drier and richer food is preferred and Muslim-influenced meat dishes often appear paired with luchis. A general principle in Bengal is that 'wet' dishes are eaten with rice and 'dry' dishes scooped up with bread. *Kochi pathar jhol* is a dish prepared from goat meat, ginger, onion, tomatoes and spices such as cumin, coriander seeds, black pepper, red chillies and garam masala, and perhaps a little sugar. It is popularly made for Sunday lunch—and could be said to be Bengali 'comfort food'—and each family will have their own favoured recipe for it.

KOLKATA

The British created Calcutta, once the 'greatest city of the Orient'. They built it up on the land bought from the Bengal nawab; they named it and, for a time, they ruled India from it. Before it became a bastion of British power, Calcutta's raison d'être was as a trading port, a clearinghouse from which the bounty of Bengal (and eastern India) was exported around the world. From the late seventeenth century until the early twentieth century, Calcutta was a vibrant metropolis, abuzz with a multitude of languages spoken by traders who had come there from across India and around the world. The British 'owned' Calcutta but as long as non-British traders working there obeyed their rules and paid the various taxes and duties required of them, they were largely left to conduct their business untrammelled.

In its early days, Calcutta was a rugged place to be in: the climate was hot and the air dense with moisture for most of the year; disease and infection bred virulently and killed off large numbers of foreigners who had no inborn tolerance, either to the climate or local pathogens. The population was predominantly male and many spent their spare time in taverns—drinking, gambling, fighting. In the absence of their own female kind, British men frequently took Indian common-law wives. As the British began to take control of more and more of India, they lavished funds on creating a showpiece capital that materially demonstrated their might. They built monumental public buildings, mansions for homes, private clubs and fancy hotels and their womenfolk began to come out, bringing the final 'civilizing touch' and ousting the native wives. Calcutta was the most Anglicized place in India and it is in modern Kolkata (renamed in 2001) that British influence remains most culturally prominent. Bengalis are particularly passionate about cricket and the middle and upper classes continue to enthusiastically patronize British-style private clubs. The food served at these clubs retains a distinct Anglo-Indian character, such as in various 'chops'—not the meat cutlet that bears this name in Western cooking—of minced meat, fish, egg or vegetables shaped into oval patties, coated with mashed potato and deep-fried. A cutlet in a Kolkata club is a meat or vegetable patty, crumbed and fried. Chops and cutlets have made it out of clubs and into the canon of Bengali cuisine. You will find them in infinite variety on all sorts of menus in Kolkata and as an adjunct to the ritual of the evening *adda*, a time when Bengalis gather with friends and family to chat about the latest in current affairs and/or personal events.

The British achieved what the Mughal emperors never could—consummate rule over the entire subcontinent—but they never conquered the Indian palate. Their influence on Indian cooking was limited and largely confined to the royal and elite classes. Prior to Independence, it was a popular—but certainly not universal—practice in wealthy households to have a meal of 'British' dishes in the evening. Indians of all classes have since developed an avid proclivity for biscuits, an item that was introduced by the British. (India's omnipresent 'Britannia' biscuits are made by a company that was started in Calcutta in the nineteenth century.) In the matter of drink though, the British did affect a most significant change on the habits of Indians. They introduced tea production and the practice of tea drinking to India. (*See Assam for more.*) The British style of pot-brewed tea lives on in homes in Kolkata where freshly brewed Darjeeling tea is drunk in the afternoon. The British also introduced beer brewing and commercial distillation of spirits such as whisky and rum; these alcoholic beverages are as popular as tea.

The British are believed to have received funding from Armenian traders to buy the land on which they built Calcutta. Armenians had traded from India for centuries before the British arrived; Emperor Akbar had many Armenian wives! They were never a large population in Calcutta but they were a consistent presence—there is still a small community of Armenians living there—and an influential one; you can taste the material evidence of this in restaurants that serve Bengali food with a dish called *dolma*—vegetables such as small gourd or eggplant and onion stuffed with rice and minced meat flavoured with mint, coriander, cinnamon and pepper. There were once 6000 Jews living in Calcutta and they made a significant contribution to the economic development of the city but today the most evident reminder of their presence is a culinary one: the famous Jewish bakery and confectioner Nahoum & Sons in New Market. Opened in 1902, it is still run by members of the same family though their clientele has changed over time. It is no longer predominantly Jews—there are now less than thirty in Kolkata—and other Europeans but Bengalis who buy the fruitcake, cheesecakes and cheese-filled pastries called *sambusak* (akin to the samosa) that have been baked and sold at Nahoum for over a century.

Recommendations

....

Oh! Calcutta is a popular upmarket restaurant that serves traditional dishes from across the culinary history of Calcutta. When ilish is in season, they have a special menu of dishes made from this fish, including *ilish dame* (pieces of ilish marinated in a paste of white poppy seeds, curd and chilli; slow-cooked with green chillies, turmeric and mustard oil); ilish fillets simmered in a broth of green mangoes, mustard seeds and coconut milk; and the Raj-inspired ilish baked with Cheddar cheese. Crustacean dishes include *kakra chingri bhapa* (purée of crab and prawn with coconut and mustard, steamed in banana leaves) and prawn cutlets. Vegetarians can try the classic mochar ghonto, aloo posto and cucumbers cooked with fenugreek and curd in a sealed earthen pot in *dum pukht* style (*see Uttar Pradesh chapter*). A perennial favourite is railway mutton curry, a coconut milk-based curry said to have been devised for British army officers who could not cope with chilli-infused dishes. Desserts include a stuffed, syrup-soaked pancake called *malpua* and mishti doi.

Forum 4th Floor, 10/3 Elgin Road
(033) 22837161, 22837164
12.30–3.30 p.m., 7.30–11 p.m.

Bhojohori Manna is a friendly, unassuming restaurant popular with locals for home-style Bengali food. The extensive menu includes shukto; *lal ghonto* (white pumpkin cooked with *ajwain*, or carom); jumbo prawns steamed with coconut and chilli; various chops and cutlets; jhol and jhal made with seasonal fish and crustaceans; and mutton korma with luchi. In summer, they make ambrosial *aam doi* with mangoes; at other times, you will just have to make do with bhapa doi or mishti doi with a thick layer of matha on top.

9/18 Ekdalia Road
(033) 24401933
Noon–9.30 p.m.
www.bhojohorimanna.com

Kewpies is arguably the best-known Bengali-style restaurant in Calcutta. The set thali of the day takes you through a traditional Bengali meal with the food served in clay bowls. The menu changes with the season; in late September, it includes shukto; a small stuffed and fried potol; a slightly sweet moong dal with green peas; fat prawns cooked in coconut milk; a piece of bhetki coated in mustard and coconut paste, wrapped in banana leaf and steamed; eggplant cooked in curd; sweet tomato ambole with papad; mishti doi and rose-flavoured sandesh.

2 Elgin Lane
(033) 24759880
12.30–3 p.m., 7.30–11 p.m.

Aaheli was one of the first in Calcutta to serve traditional Bengali food and it remains a steady favourite with locals. The daily thali includes two seasonal fish dishes; a meat or chicken korma served with luchis; a seasonal vegetable; dal; various crunchy fried titbits; mishti doi and sandesh. The chilled *aam-pora sharbat* (mango cordial) served here has a cult following as it is made in the traditional style from real fruit, rather than the commercial syrup that is now commonly used.

The Peerless Inn, 12 Jawaharlal Nehru Road, Chowringhee
(033) 22280301, (M) 9831780403
12.30–3 p.m., 7.30–11 p.m.

Join the queue at **Tero Parbon** for quintessential Bengali fare: dal with prawns, fresh crab and lobsters, chops and cutlets, jhol, shukto, ghonto, dolma and posto boro.

49C Purna Das Road
(033) 24632016
Noon–4 p.m., 7–10.30 p.m.

K.C. Das is Kolkata's most famous confectioner. Nabin Chandra Das (great-grandfather of the present presiding Das) is credited with inventing the rasagulla in 1868, although it is argued that he did not invent it but just popularized an already existing sweet. The truth is unlikely to ever be established and it hardly matters, for K.C. Das indeed makes exceptional rasagulla and other chhena-based sweets.

11A & B Sidhu Kanor Dahar, Opposite Esplanade Metro Stop Exit
(033) 22485920, (M) 9831056505
7.30 a.m.–9.30 p.m.
Other branches: 41A Bagh Bazaar Street; 57A Ripom Street

Ganguram & Sons are purveyors of some of the very best mishti doi and sandesh in Kolkata.

46C Jawaharlal Nehru Street
(033) 22881184
6 a.m.–10 p.m.

At **Balaram Mullich & Radharam Mullich**, try lal doi, mishti doi and banana-leaf-wrapped sandesh.

22 Park Street
(033) 65218303
6.30 a.m.–11 p.m.

Sen Mahasaya has been making sandesh for more than a century and is very good at it.

40A Ashutosh Mukherjee Road
(033) 24551135
10 a.m.–6 p.m.

Girish Chandra De & Sons operate from a charming old store where they only sell sandesh—moulded into a variety of shapes.

2 Debendra Drive
Corner of Ashutosh Mukherjee Road
(033) 24667708
7 a.m.–10 p.m.

The eternally stylish **Flury's**, once a popular playground for Calcutta's European citizenry, is now a tourist cliché but you will get a good cup of Darjeeling tea here and you can enjoy it in air-conditioned comfort while you watch the crazy world of Kolkata rush by through huge street-facing windows. If you fancy a Raj-style breakfast, the baked beans are good.

18 Park Street
(033) 22297664
7.30 a.m.–10 p.m.

Until 1905, the province of Bengal was made up of the states of Odisha, Bihar and the country of Bangladesh. In that year, the British partitioned it into West and East Bengal; in 1947, East Bengal became East Pakistan and, in 1971, Bangladesh. There is much similarity in the food of West Bengal and Bangladesh, but the cuisine of the latter has a much more pronounced Mughal/Muslim influence. Unfavourable economic, political and environmental circumstances in Bangladesh drive a huge number of dispossessed people across the border into Bengal and many of them end up living in Kolkata. Mirza Ghalib Street is also known as 'Little Bangladesh' and there are several cafes here that serve Bangladeshi-style food. At either **Prince** or **Kasturi**, you can try *bhuni khichri*, a dish of fried meat cooked with rice; *kacchi biryani*, in which raw rice and meat are cooked together (else, rice and meat are usually cooked separately for a biryani) and a *bharta* of mashed spiced fish. **Sholoyana Bangali** is an upmarket restaurant serving Bangladeshi-style food.

37 Purna Das Road, Triangular Park
(033) 24197532
Noon–10.30 p.m.

One of the most important non-European communities in Calcutta was the Chinese. The first Chinese immigrant to Bengal is said to have arrived in Calcutta in 1778. Ten years later, there were a sizeable number of Chinese working in the port, loading and unloading ships. The sons of these men branched out to take up other opportunities in Calcutta such as leather work and dentistry; both these tasks were considered lowly by both Hindus and the British in Calcutta so there was a gap in the market for the Chinese to fill without treading on anyone's toes. The community flourished and Calcutta was one of the first places in the world to have a 'Chinatown', and the only place in India to have one. Restaurants were opened in Chinatown specifically to feed the local Chinese population but over time the wider population of Calcutta discovered these and a Chinese restaurant industry developed. There are still about 3000 people of Chinese descent living in Kolkata, concentrated in the suburb of Tangra. The city has its own version of Chinese cuisine referred to as 'Tangra' type: Chinese-style cuisine blended with local ingredients designed to lure and satisfy the Bengali palate. Spices and curd are employed more generously than they ever would be in traditional Chinese cuisine and the dishes have much more gravy. **Tiretta Bazaar** in the city centre—where the original Chinatown was located before roadwork forced a mass relocation to Tangra—still has a Chinese market. It has become a popular place for breakfast as Chinese women come here and set up food stalls in the morning selling dishes such as Chinese-style sausages cooked with local mustard greens. Out in

Tangra, **Beijing** is well known for its crabmeat balls made from fresh sweet-fleshed local crab and its so-called 'fried' rice, which is actually quite a wet dish and more like a delicious rice porridge.

77/1 Christopher Road, Tangra
(033) 23283998, (M) 9831013380
Noon–11 p.m.

ODISHA

FEEDING THE DIVINE

In 261 BC, Odisha—then the feudal kingdom of Kalinga—was the scene of one of the most momentous, and mythologized, events of Indian history. After leading his soldiers to the brutal defeat of the Kalinga army, the Mauryan emperor Ashoka is said to have looked around the battlefield and, in a pang of conscience for the carnage he had caused, instantly converted to Buddhism. (He didn't give Kalinga back though.) It was an act that had a significant impact on the development of India's religious and cultural life, including food habits. From this point on, Ashoka adhered to the Buddhist tenet of ahimsa, or the avoidance of violence by keeping a 'harmless mind, hand and mouth' and abstaining from harming or injuring another living creature. An obvious corollary of this is a vegetarian diet, though Buddha did not actually demand that his followers not eat meat, just that they should not kill an animal or directly cause it to be killed. If, for instance, a deer fell off a cliff and died, eating its flesh would not constitute an act of violence. Nonetheless, Buddhism was strongly associated with vegetarianism. After his conversion, Ashoka actively promulgated his newfound religion, most famously in edicts carved on rocks and pillars throughout the Mauryan kingdom, which encompassed much of India then. His influence saw Buddhism become the dominant religion in India for several centuries. As a counterweight to this influence Hindus absorbed Buddha into their pantheon of deities as the ninth incarnation of the god Vishnu, and enshrined the practice of vegetarianism as a marker of religious and spiritual purity. This meant that Brahmins, the Hindu priestly caste, had to adopt vegetarianism—when earlier they had regularly sacrificed animals to the gods and later eaten the flesh—to maintain the spiritual high ground expected of them. Hinduism eventually regained religious and cultural dominance in India but its spiritual leaders, largely, continued to abstain from eating meat and thus influenced the development of India's unsurpassed vegetarian cuisine.

Odisha, at one time, stretched from the Gangetic delta to the Godavari River in Andhra Pradesh and was a prosperous region involved in vigorous maritime trade as far afield as Indonesia. Oriya rulers spent lavishly on temple building; by the twelfth century, there were said to be 7000 temples around Bhubaneswar—the modern state capital—alone. In the late sixteenth century, the Mughals arrived in Odisha and annexed it to their realm; while they were there, they desecrated so many temples that non-Hindus have been since banned from entering the most holy of these, such as the Jagannath Temple in Puri. After the dissipation of the Mughal Empire, the Marathas subsumed Odisha into their kingdom and, in 1756, it came under British rule. Odisha's changing leaders had all been keen to claim the region but they collectively ran it down; as it lacked good natural ports, the British ignored it in favour of Bengal.

Today, Odisha is one of India's poorest states. Oriyas still largely live in villages and, despite their land being rich in mineral resources, they benefit little from the profits generated by the huge mining industry there. And yet, Oriyas have one of the highest life expectancies in India and it's likely that their diet plays a significant role in this. Odisha has a 500-kilometre coastline along which several major rivers empty into the Bay of Bengal after snaking their way across the state, watering the fertile delta between the coast and the inland plateau. It is in this region that most of the people of Odisha live. These waterways are rich sources of fish and water for irrigating rice paddies; rice is the largest cereal crop of Odisha and the main food of its population. Oriyas are very fond of fish, and eat it at lunch and dinner, typically fried or cooked in coconut-milk gravy. (It is somewhat ironic that in the place where Ashoka turned vegetarian, only 5 per cent of the population is vegetarian.) Fish is always eaten with plain boiled rice. While Oriyas like fish, it does not mean that they can afford to eat it at every meal, particularly as fish and seafood are becoming increasingly valuable, as the demand for these grows in wealthy urban centres such as Mumbai and Delhi. Oriyas are particular adherents of Hindu fasting practices; on Monday, Tuesday and Thursday, many of them eat only vegetarian food, and it is a vegetarian preparation called *dalma* that is most commonly eaten. Dalma is made from *toor* dal cooked with finely diced green papaya, green banana and seasonal vegetables such as eggplant, pumpkin and gourd. It is spiced with turmeric—Odisha produces some of India's best turmeric—cumin and black mustard seeds or with *pancha phutana*, a mix of mustard seeds, fennel, cumin, nigella and fenugreek. There are as many different versions of dalma as there are cooks in Odisha: coconut and chilli are common additions but vegetables like tomato, cauliflower and beans—commonly eaten in modern Odisha—are rarely added, as these are said to turn mushy during cooking. (I wonder if this is to do with the fact that these are 'foreign' vegetables.) Putting aside the possible addition of chilli, dalma is prepared from indigenous foods; cumin, fennel and fenugreek are also non-indigenous but these came into the region when Kalinga was a great trading kingdom and have been around long enough to have 'blended' in.

Dalma is always served with rice. A traditional meal in Odisha would feature these two along with *khatta* (a sweet-and-sour sticky chutney prepared from raw mango or *ou*/elephant apple), *santula* (a dish of finely chopped vegetables sautéed with garlic, mustard, green chillies, cumin seeds and salt—each cook will have their own variation on this hallmark Oriya dish; one might add a spoon of pancha phutana and another a little fresh coconut) and *saag bhajia* (leafy greens cooked with coconut). Coconut palms grow prolifically in Odisha and coconut oil is traditionally used for cooking; in the north-east of the state, where it borders Bengal, mustard oil is also used. *Badi*, various pulses ground to a paste and sun-dried in small nuggets, are added to vegetable dishes to enhance protein and texture. If fish is part of a meal, a vegetable dish is usually dropped off the menu. Oriyas enjoy eating mutton and chicken but economic circumstances limit its consumption for most, and it is more of a festive dish. Oriya-style meat dishes show a distinct Muslim influence, being typically flavoured with spices such as cinnamon, cloves, cardamom and black pepper.

Rice features in Oriya cuisine in diverse ways. Puffed rice called *muri* or flattened rice called *chuda* with curd and sugar is eaten for breakfast or as a snack. *Pakhala* is a widely eaten porridge-style dish made with boiled rice that is left soaked in water overnight to ferment, then mixed with curd, cucumber, cumin seeds, fried onions and mint leaves. It gets really hot in Odisha in the summer and pakhala is avidly consumed during this time as it is considered to prevent heatstroke. *Badi chura* is a condiment of fried dal ground with green chillies, onion and garlic, papad or fried fish: it is added to dishes for texture and flavour and is believed to aid digestion. *Monda mitha* is a steamed bun made of rice stuffed with cottage cheese, coconut and curd. Oriya cuisine includes a variety of 'cakes', collectively called *pitha*, made from various mixtures of ground rice and dal. Pitha can be sweet or savoury and cooked in various methods: wrapped in turmeric or banana leaves and steamed, baked or cooked like pancakes. *Poda pitha* is made from ground rice, *urad* dal, coconut, ginger and black pepper and can be either baked or steamed. *Amalu* or *malpua* is a pancake of wheat flour and milk or curd, which is soaked in sugar syrup; an array of malpua are prepared across eastern India but this sweet is said to have originated in Odisha. Perhaps the most distinctive Oriya sweet is *chhena poda*, made by kneading chhena with semolina, sugar, cashew nuts and cardamom to form soft dough; this is wrapped in sal leaves and set to bake in a slow charcoal fire for several hours. The resulting cake has a caramelized crust and a moist, dense interior; the taste and texture are like that of a hybrid of a cheesecake and crème caramel. A meal is not considered complete in Odisha without at least one sweet dish and a wedge of chhena poda is often served as part of a meal. Chhena poda is only a recent addition to Oriya cuisine, said to have been invented in the early twentieth century by a confectioner in the town of Nayagarh, who mixed some leftover chhena with sugar and set it in a warm oven overnight. The surplus chhena was left over from making *rasagulla*, a sweet that Oriyas claim to have invented but is now 'lost' to Bengali cuisine. To avoid this happening again, chhena poda is vigorously produced and commercially promoted in Odisha—I was delighted to find it sold by food vendors while I travelled by train throughout the state. It is traditionally made in domestic kitchens, particularly during festivals.

Given the geographic proximity of Odisha to Bengal, it is unsurprising that there is much similarity between the cuisines of these two states. Many dishes share names, albeit with different spellings, but there are subtle differences in the way these are put together. Fish, rice and tropical fruit and vegetables form the basis of daily meals in both states; very similar spices and blends are used and Oriyas share the Bengalis' love of sweets. Oil, ghee and spices are used more sparingly in Odisha and overall the food is less rich than that of Bengal, something that is in part a reflection of the differing economic conditions of the two states.

There are two interesting food-related claims made by Oriyas: first, that many dishes identified as Bengali are actually Oriya in origin; second, that Odisha is home to the largest kitchen in the world. If the first claim is true, then it might be related to the existence of the second. To explore this further, we must visit the coastal town of Puri.

In Hindu mythology, when the god Vishnu was working to preserve the earth, he is said to have stopped at Puri to eat, though it was quite some time after this purported event that Puri made it on to the religious map of India. In the eighth century, the influential Hindu reformer Shankara designated Puri one of his four *maths* or places of learning. Today it is one of the four most auspicious pilgrimage centres, or *dhams*, in India—the others being Dwarka in Gujarat, Badrinath in Uttarakhand and Rameswaram in Tamil Nadu, one at each cardinal point, deliberately chosen by Shankara to ensure that Hindu pilgrims would come to know all of their country. It is a lifetime ambition for devout Hindus to visit all four dhams. When they come to Puri, the focus of their worship is the massive twelfth-century Jagannath Temple, abode of Lord Jagannath—one of the 1000 names of Vishnu—and his two siblings. A small army of 6000 workers minister to the daily needs of the three deities. These workers are divided into ninety-six hereditary and hierarchical orders, each assigned a specific task: they wake the gods; dress them; brush their teeth; take them for public worship; put them down for a siesta; re-dress them in different outfits; dance for them every evening; and feed them. Vishnu's meal stop at Puri has ensured that food has a central role at the Jagannath Temple. Each day in the temple kitchens, fifty-six different food items, collectively called *chhappan bhog*, are prepared by 700 cooks; six times a day, various selections of these food items are offered to the deities. Once the food has received the blessing of the gods, it becomes *mahaprashad*, food so pure that it is said that a dog could lick it and a Brahmin could still eat it without getting polluted. After being consecrated, the food is used to feed the temple workers and is sold to pilgrims: it feeds about 10,000 people a day, which is why there are so many cooks. Mahaprashad is reported to be 'shared by people of all castes and creeds without any discrimination' but non-Hindus are not permitted to enter the temple complex. In 2007, a 'foreigner' managed to gain entry; an act the temple authorities declared defiled all the food in the temple and the whole lot, worth nearly 25,000 dollars, was buried in a pit dug specifically for the purpose.

The chhappan bhog of the Jagannath Temple is cooked by rules prescribed in ancient Hindu religious texts. These require that it be cooked in earthenware pots on wood-fired clay stoves—of which there are 700 hence the claim to being the world's largest kitchen. There is no gas or electricity in the kitchen; only the dim light from small clay oil lamps called diyas lights it. The food itself is *sattvic*—which leads to clarity and equanimity of mind and therefore supports spiritual development—so it is vegetarian; cooked in or laced with ghee; and without onion or garlic. Vegetables such as tomato, potato, ladies' fingers, cabbage, chilli and cauliflower are not permitted, as they were not known in India at the time the scriptures that guide the temple food practices were written down. Few spices feature but coconut is prodigiously used in many dishes. Pilgrims donate coconuts to the temple in significant quantities, but this is not enough to feed the daily multitude of pilgrims. The temple buys most of the coconut crop produced in the surrounding region, along with most of the bananas, fruit and vegetables. I have an image in my mind of the Jagannath Temple as a spiritual factory that provides the principal means of employment and income for the surrounding town and agricultural region, similar to the mill towns of nineteenth-century Britain, only much more sustainable.

The temple's chhappan bhog includes dishes such as dalma, khatta, pakhala and saag bhajia; six distinct rice dishes and about twenty-five sweet dishes, ranging from simple ripe banana and sweet puffed rice through a whole selection of pitha including podi pitha and malpua to *kora* (small, round confection of sweetened coconut) and *suji kheer*. The latter is a dish of semolina fried in ghee and boiled with milk and sugar until it thickens to the consistency of custard. It is made with rice throughout India and is more usually known as kheer; when made for domestic use the grains are not usually fried in ghee. It is claimed that kheer originated in the kitchens of the Jagannath Temple.

The temple food is considered the 'paragon of ritual Hindu food' and sets the standard against which all other temple food is measured. (Partaking of the mahaprashad of Puri is so important to pilgrims that there are special places in the alleys surrounding the temple where they go to smoke hashish to build up an appetite—at least that is what I was told it was for!) Because of this, Puri temple cooks are highly sought after by other temples and private connoisseurs. In the nineteenth century, as Bengal prospered economically under British rule, it also enjoyed a cultural 'renaissance'. Its drivers pushed for social reform and, like the Europeans of the later Middle Ages/early modern period, they looked for guidance to the past, in this case the early Hindu philosophical works known as the Upanishads. Many Bengali reformers were wealthy Hindus and what better than to have a cook in the kitchen who knew how to prepare the type of food prescribed in seminal Hindu texts; and, of course, the ultimate place to get such a cook was just down the road in Puri. Odisha's fortunes, on the other hand, were declining and it is likely that the coffers of the Jagannath Temple—reliant as they were on donations—were not as buoyant as they might have been, leaving temple cooks open to more lucrative offers to go and cook in other places such as Calcutta. Temple cooks are not supposed to receive wages as they work in the service of their lord so they may have seen this as an opportunity to spread religious practices. It is said that Oriya cooks thus brought Oriya dishes into Bengali upper-class kitchens and these dishes eventually dispersed into the wider community, leading to many Oriya dishes being claimed as Bengali: undoubtedly having been 'Bengalified' in some way beyond just changing the spelling of the name.

One food item that is the subject of particular dispute between the two states is the chhena-based sweet rasagulla. Oriyas claim it was invented in the kitchens of the Puri temple more than 300 years ago to appease Lord Jagannath's consort Mahalakshmi for being ignored on the last day of the Rath Yatra. (On this occasion, Jagannath is taken out of the temple and paraded through Puri on a massive chariot; the word 'juggernaut' derives from this event.) Bengalis place the rasagulla more recently decreeing that it was invented in the nineteenth century by a Calcutta sweet-maker for sale to mere mortals. The most likely story is that the rasagulla came into Bengal from Odisha but was commercially produced and popularized in Calcutta. As an interesting side note, the round shape of the rasgulla represents Lord Vishnu's rule of the globe.

Recommendations

....

PURI

Unless you are Hindu, you will not be able to enter the Jagannath Temple to buy the mahaprashad, but you could ask your hotel to arrange some for you. If you want to get a view of the 'world's largest kitchen', you can do so from the rooftop of Raghunandan Library opposite the temple's main gate. The food ambience of the precinct surrounding the temple is distinctly vegetarian. If you want to eat some genuine Oriya food, you will have to really get in with the locals and nosh at the more basic eateries along the roadside. One particular establishment I chose—by the fact that it was full of Oriyas—was a very rudimentary place, nothing more than a few wooden tables and benches set up under a canopy but it had a serious wood-fired clay stove in the corner on which all the food was cooked. The meal I ate, served on a banana leaf, consisted of a generous ladle of dalma paired with a small pile of *bundia* (crunchy pearl-sized 'puffs' made from *besan* batter dropped into hot oil and soaked in sugar syrup; also a chhappan bhog item) and a piping hot stack of puris. To finish, I pretended I was an Oriya and indulged in a large wedge of chhena poda. It cost me about a dollar and it was truly delicious; the locals sitting with me were delighted that I enjoyed their food so much. Contrast this with my visit the previous day to an upmarket establishment advertising itself as specializing in Oriya food. Putting aside the fact that I had to argue with the manager to even get them to prepare any Oriya food, when it did come, it was awful: a greasy travesty of the tasty, clean, light meal I later enjoyed in the roadside cafe.

Another way to enjoy genuine local cuisine is to take a cooking class organized by **Grassroutes Journeys**. The class starts at the local market where you join your hostess to shop for ingredients, after which you return to her home to learn how to prepare dishes such as dalma and the local version of saag bhajia. A lunch or dinner of the dishes ends the class. Grass Routes can also take you on a bicycle journey into the villages surrounding Puri where you can see local agricultural practices and stop for lunch at a roadside cafe where, once you have finished eating, you take your leaf plate and push it through a small window into the waiting garbage disposal unit: a very well-fed cow.

C.T. Road
(06752) 223656, (M) 9437029698
www.grassroutesjourneys.com

On Temple Road, you will find the nonagenarian **Senapati Sweets**, one of the best sweet shops in Puri. It is renowned for chhena poda and 'steam cake', a lighter version that is steamed rather than baked. **Dolmardap** on Sahi Puri is another purveyor of fine chhena poda.

As you travel away from the temple precinct towards the beach, the food ethos becomes less vegetarian; Puri is also one of the largest fishing villages in Odisha. Early risers can go to the eastern end of the town beach to watch the catch come in and be taken to the local fish market. In the evening, at the western end of the beach adjacent to Marine Drive, you can find numerous vendors cooking and selling fresh local fish and seafood—bought at the market earlier in the day. You choose the fish or crustacean that takes your fancy and the vendor cleans it, rubs it with ginger paste; coats it with semolina, flour, turmeric and salt and cooks it in hot oil. The method is not unique to Odisha but it does give you a taste of some local fish. As you eat, you can take in the excited crowds of Bengali holidaymakers promenading along the beachfront.

At times, Odisha is described as a place where a culinary transition from north to south takes place as it shares a part of its border with the south Indian state of Andhra Pradesh. While the similarities between Oriya and Bengal are often noted, the generous use of red chillies, coconut oil and curry leaves in Odisha shows a distinct Andhra influence. One morning in Puri, I was wandering along C.T. Road scouting for something interesting to eat when I saw exactly what I wanted—a man cooking something in a large cauldron at the front of a tiny shop. I don't speak a word of Oriya so I obtained my breakfast by pointing and doing my best version of the Indian head-wobbling gesture—an action that achieves much in the absence of a shared language—and the vendor handed me a leaf bowl of *upma ghugni* (a savoury potage of semolina and dal layered with chickpeas cooked in a gravy of coconut, tamarind and spices, and chopped green chillies) and piping hot vegetable pakoras. This dish was later described to me as 'Tex-Mex' in style as it is made up of an Oriya dish—a chickpea curry called *ghugni**—crossed with one of the south—the savoury semolina or upma. Later that day, I spotted a street-side vendor with a little stall nattily set up on his bicycle surrounded by a small crowd. I pushed through, did my point-and-smile routine and was given a plate of Oriya-style *dahi bara*, soft spongy lentil patties topped with *aloo dum* (potato curry) and ghugni: another local Tex-Mex dish, for dahi bara is usually served dressed with curd in north India.

* Variations of this dish are eaten throughout eastern India and Bihar.

BHUBANESWAR

Bhubaneswar emerged into history in the fourth century BC as the capital of the ancient Kalinga nation. Two centuries or so later, after his life-changing victory over that kingdom, Ashoka used the ports and trade networks established by Kalinga to send missionaries into Asia to spread Buddhism. Over the following 2000 years, the fortunes of Bhubaneswar waxed and waned. Between the seventh and twelfth centuries, 7000-odd temples are said to have been constructed in what is now the south of the city. In the Middle Ages many of these temples were destroyed during Muslim incursions. There are 600 or so remaining temples in Bhubaneswar, earning it the moniker 'Temple City of India', and the city is an important Hindu religious centre. In 1948, Bhubaneswar was made the capital of the modern state of Odisha.

At **Chandan** restaurant in Bhubaneswar, you can enjoy a refined thali that demonstrates the complex and distinct flavours of Oriya cuisine. A delicate dalma is inevitable in the selection of dishes; others might be mutton slow-cooked in a potato-and-onion gravy in a clay pot; *maachcha besara*, fish pan-fried in mustard gravy; a gentle vegetable stew called *ghonto*; crisp, spiced lentil condiment badi chura; and *dahi biagana*, a simple but sublime dish of fried eggplant slices submerged in a sauce of curd infused with curry leaves and red chillies; finished with a sweet, syrupy doughnut made from chhena that is a variation on the rasagulla. You must order several hours in advance to enjoy this meal.

Swosti Premium Hotel, Jaidev Vihar
(0674) 3017000
www.swosti.com

Dalma is the most popular restaurant in Bhubaneswar for Oriya food. Of course, you must try the dalma here. It comes as part of a thali meal, which also includes two different fish dishes (unless you order the vegetarian version); *mansa kassa* (richly spiced mutton curry); banana stem with curd; and a santula prepared with finely chopped green papaya, ridge gourd, eggplant and potato. Dalma is a smart yet unpretentious and affordable family restaurant and it can get quite hectic on weekends.

157 Madhusudan Nagar, Sachivalaya Marg
www.dalmahotels.com (lists all branches)

If you are travelling between Cuttack and Bhubaneswar, make a pit stop at the village of Pahala Kalinga that is famous for Oriya sweets. Only three types of chhena-based sweets are made and sold here: rasagulla, chhena poda and *chhena gaga*—made from a dough of chhena, semolina and sugar that is left to dry out before being moulded into rectangular shapes which are boiled, fried in oil and finally dunked in sugar syrup. The confectioners of Pahala are collectively India's largest producers and sellers of chhena-based sweets.

NORTH-EASTERN INDIA

THE NORTH-EAST

AN INTRODUCTION

A slender corridor of land sprouting from the eastern shoulder of the Indian subcontinent—colloquially called the 'chicken's neck'—joins the region known as the 'north-east' to the rest of India. Comprising the states of Assam, Meghalaya, Arunachal Pradesh, Mizoram, Manipur, Nagaland and Tripura, it connects India to her Asian neighbours, geographically and culturally. The aggregated population of these seven states largely belongs to 120 or so distinct tribal groups, bestowing the region with one of the world's most diverse populaces. Most of these tribes share little, if any at all, genetic material or linguistic and cultural affinity with the Indo-Aryan majority of the mainland. (If the drivers of the north-east did not practise the same road behaviour as the mainland citizens, it would be easy to believe that you were in another country.) The immediately striking difference in the north-east is the East Asian appearance of the people, whose ancestors came to India from Tibet, South China and Burma (now Myanmar) at some antediluvian time. It is likely that they mixed in with an aboriginal population, creating a complex human confluence that is still being deciphered.

Indian history records that the north-east was controlled—in varying configurations—by tribal Hindu rulers up until the Middle Ages when the Koch and Ahom dynasties—both of south-east origin—gained ascendancy. In the mid-sixteenth century, through a local vassal, the Mughals captured the lower part of what is now Assam but struggled to maintain control over the locals whose intimate knowledge of the hilly terrain—and most decisively in this particular power struggle, their superior knowledge of water and boats—allowed them to keep up guerrilla warfare that eventually drove out the Islamic regime. The British were the next to attempt to wrest the north-east. It took several attempts and their success in the Anglo-Burmese war in 1824 before they successfully annexed the region and created Assam Province that encompassed what is now Assam, Nagaland, Mizoram and Meghalaya. Following Independence, the modern states of the north-east were carved out of the province in the 1960s and 1970s, with the exception of Tripura and Manipur, which had been autonomous princely states. During the colonial period, Arunachal was known as the North-East Frontier Agency, or NEFA.

Vast swathes of forest that proved such a useful ally in quelling Mughal ambition in the north-east are still extant and house more than half the known repository of plant and animal species in India. These lush habitats thrive in, and contribute to, a climate that is predominantly subtropical, though this changes with the terrain ranging from the flat river valley of the Brahmaputra river—that cleaves the north-east through its middle—to the glacial atmosphere of the permanently snowbound mountains of the Eastern Himalayas. Between these two extremities, the land is predominantly hilly, and the mountain ridges and gorges of this region provided an isolation that allowed the tribal people of the north-east to develop their unique cultural identities. The wild and cultivated foods of these varied environments have also played an intrinsic part in the development of tribal distinctiveness.

Just as these seven states are collectively called the 'north-east', a commensurate 'north-east cuisine' has been identified, often presented as a homogeneous culinary inventory eaten across the region. Such a category should properly be seen as comprising the distinct cuisine of each state that has developed in response to the unique geography, culture and religious influences; in this book, each will be looked at in its distinctness. Food habits and cooking practices are shared across the region though and, as a starting point, we shall explore these.

Forest, jungle, alpine meadows and rivers have been eternal, abundant sources of food for the people of the north-east, and a vital influence on their cuisine. A widespread—yet not universal—abundance of water from regional rivers and good, reliable rainfall has allowed for profuse cultivation of rice, and the base of a meal in any north-eastern state is a generous mound of this starchy cereal. Many eat it three times a day and are very happy to do so: to them a meal without rice is no meal at all. Some tribes in Arunachal, who inhabit drier hilly areas, practise a method of dry rice cultivation to ensure supply. Rice is usually boiled and served plain. It is also ground, steamed, fermented and roasted to make breads, alcoholic drinks, snacks and desserts. Many cultivars of rice are grown throughout the north-east, with a preference for Japonica or 'sticky' varieties—north Indians tend to prefer Indica or 'dry' types such as basmati—a predilection that north-easterners share with their Asian ancestors and neighbours. Abundance of water means that fish, shrimp, crabs and eels are a plentiful—and traditionally free—source of food, and people across the region share a fondness for aquatic protein. For some tribes, particularly those living by or near a water source, eating fish is a daily affair. If seasonal or climatic conditions prevent the procurement of fresh fish, dried fish is eaten as a substitute. Dried fish is also added to dishes to impart a distinct pungent flavour—depending on how it has been preserved—that people in the north-east have a general preference for (*more later*).

After rice, the most essential part of the daily diet is a dish of 'herbs': leafy greens of cultivated species such spinach, mustard and radish leaves along with hundreds of different wild greens including leaves and flowers of shrubs and trees, ferns, grasses and what might be identified by the less knowledgeable as 'weeds', collected from forests or wherever greenery freely grows. This category also includes the smaller aromatic leaves referred to as 'herbs' in Western cooking, such as coriander, mint and basil. The broad range of herbs used in north-eastern cooking varies across the region according to the type of plants that grow there and developed preferences. Of all the kitchens I visited in the north-east, there was only one where a basket of fresh, vibrant greens did not figure in the ingredients used in the meal prepared for me. People typically eat their herbs boiled, steamed or lightly stir-fried, flavoured simply with garlic, ginger and chilli. (I found that stir-fried vegetables were often described in the north-east as 'fried', making it sound as if these have been cooked in a lot of fat, which is not the case.) More aromatic herbs such as basil are usually chopped and added to dishes at the end of the cooking. The best way to get a sense of the diversity of greens eaten across the north-east is to visit local fresh-food markets and keep an eye out for roadside vegetable stalls. When you see one, get out and have a look as it is likely that some of the greenery on offer has been picked from the nearby forest and you won't see it again thirty kilometres further on.

North-eastern cuisine is commonly described as 'light' and 'healthy' due to the perceived absence, or limited use, of fats. Having seen for myself that pork lard, mustard oil and oil-rich sesame paste are used generously, I can say that the food is not quite as innocent of edible lipids as some have reported. (Admittedly, I did eat meals that were entirely free of any fat, and it is possible that this could be the sum of someone else's experience of food in the north-east.) I think what is distinct in the matter of the 'lightness' of north-eastern cuisine is that there is a limited use of dairy products (though this is not true in higher altitudes). Whether due to geography, climate or culture, the indigenous peoples of the north-east do not keep cows and therefore do not use milk (tea is taken black), butter or ghee in cooking, and the 'heavier' cadence given to dishes prepared using these products is absent from their food. In some states, such as Assam, milk is used to make sweet dishes such as *kheer* (rice cooked in milk).

Another notable culinary commonality across the north-east is that people do not seem to care much for sweets. You will see vendors selling the type of sugar-saturated confections popular throughout mainland India—so somebody must be buying these for such businesses to exist—but I was only once served a sweet dish in a home, and that too because my visit was deemed a special occasion. Many different types of fruit grow in the north-east—these are eaten separately from meals and put to limited use in cooking—and the hills of the Eastern Himalayas are believed to be the indigenous home of citrus fruit. The popular and widely available green-skinned-when-ripe sweet lime (*Citrus limetta*, commonly known in north India as *mosambi*) and the juicy 'orange' (*Citrus reticulata blanco*, which is actually a variety of mandarin; commonly called *santara* in mainland India) varieties are both native. You will see trees bearing generous fruitings of various oranges and limes as you traverse the region, but what is most likely to catch your eye are trees laden with football-sized pomelos. This grapefruit-coloured citrus has a thick skin and a sweet, meaty, pink flesh that is eaten sprinkled with salt, dried red chilli and black pepper as a juicy snack.

Another distinction that marks all the varied cuisines of the north-east—and one that I think contributes to it being described as 'light'—is the limited use of spices. The flavourings most commonly used are garlic, ginger, turmeric, black pepper and chillies, and very often no more. All these ingredients are easily grown in the region. Nagaland has publicly laid claim to ownership of the world's hottest variety of chilli popularly known as *bhoot jholokia* or *raja mirch*; at more than one million Scoville heat units, it definitely ranks as one of the most terrifying chillies known. (Jholokias grow wild throughout the north-east, not just in Nagaland.) In states such as Assam, Manipur and Tripura that have a strong cultural connection with Bengal, the spices associated with the cuisine of this neighbouring state—such as mustard, fennel and cumin—are often used. The absence of a more diverse range of spices might be attributed to the cuisine being more closely aligned with Asian cuisine, or due to the absence of a sustained Mughal presence in the region. Before the culinary excesses of the Mughals influenced mainland Indians towards elaborate spice mixes, most ate food as simply spiced as that eaten in the north-east. Or it could be that fresh foods available in the region taste good enough to not require too much additional embellishment!

Travelling through the north-east I noticed that the produce available was of consistently high quality and sparkling freshness. The varying climatic zones, fertile soils and access to water means that many different types of foods can be grown, that produce does not travel very far and that it reaches the marketplace in prime condition—that is, if a household is even reliant on the market. Most people of the north-east live in rural areas and are engaged in agricultural work. At a minimum, a village home will have a garden patch in which leafy greens and other herbs are cultivated; at least one gourd or pumpkin vine will be trailing over a rooftop or fence; and a couple of fruit trees like banana, papaya, jackfruit or pomelo would be part of the garden. A pig and some chickens might be kept and fed on scraps. Fish can be caught in nearby waterways and some homes have their own ponds to grow fish and collect small shrimps. Also, there are wild foods that can be gathered, such as leafy-green herbs and bamboo. Fresh or preserved bamboo shoots are a popular ingredient in cooking and the hollow stalks of this plant are used as cooking vessels that impart a nutty flavour to the food cooked in them.

Over 250 types of fermented foods and drinks are produced and eaten across the north-east. The regional preference for the taste of these pungent foods might also explain the absence of spices as the strong flavour of these would overpower the relatively subtler taste of spices. Fermented soybeans, bamboo shoots and fish are universal items in cooking across the north-east, though the preferred level of the pungency of these varies: I found that the Assamese prefer a milder flavour while the people of Meghalaya and Nagaland like their fermented soybeans to have a more obvious punch. To make fermented soybeans, the beans are washed, boiled, lightly crushed and placed in a basket lined with banana/fern leaf, or just wrapped in leaves, and left in a warm place for five days or so depending on the season. The fermented beans are mashed to a rough paste and added to dishes or cooked with tomatoes as a side dish. There are regional variations on how this condiment is made and it is known by different names across the north-east; in Nagaland it is called *akhuni* and in Meghalaya, *tungrumbai*.

Fermented bamboo shoots can be prepared simply by slicing and soaking in a bucket of water for several days. The Nishi people of Arunachal chop bamboo shoots into small pieces, pack these into leaf-lined, woven bamboo baskets and place them in a pit in the forest. More leaves are laid on top and weighted with stones to keep air out, and the shoots are left to ferment for one to three months. Whichever method is used, the fermented bamboo shoots add a tangy, lemony taste to dishes.

The most basic method to produce fermented fish in the north-east is to simply wrap up some small fresh fish in banana leaves, tie this parcel up tightly and leave it for several days to achieve the desired level of fermentation. In Tripura, a somewhat more complex method is used to produce a fermented fish sauce called *shidal*. Small, sardine-like fish called *sarpunti* are cleaned, salted and laid in clay pots under a layer of mustard oil; the stuffed pot is buried for three to four weeks. At the end of this fermentation period, the liquid—that is, the shidal—is run off and added to food as a flavour enhancer. This aeons-old product—ancient Romans enjoyed a similarly produced fish sauce called *liquamen*—and others like it demonstrate the strong connection between the north-east and Asia. Shidal is cousin to the fermented fish sauces used in Thailand (*nam pla*) and Vietnam (*nuoc nam*); also, Koreans traditionally bury their beloved *kim chi* (fermented cabbage) in clay pots to develop.

The fermentation process is also applied to rice and other grains to produce alcoholic drinks. Rice beer (also called rice wine) is the most popular of these and there are as many as twenty-four different names for this beverage in the region. Each tribe will have its own slightly varied method of producing rice beer but the basic formula is to take cooked or well-soaked rice, mix it with an indigenous amylolytic starter or 'yeast', pack this mixture into a clay pot and leave it for three to four days in a warm place, usually over or near the kitchen fireplace. After a few days, the fermented rice mix is blended with water and the resultant liquid strained off to produce a slightly foamy, cloudy wine. This is moderately alcoholic and does not keep very well; some tribes distil it over a wood fire to produce a stronger, clear alcohol that can be kept for longer. The natural starters used to ferment rice beer are made by blending pulverized wild herbs, such as leaves of edible nightshades, red chillies or ginger with rice flour, and shaping the mixture into small tablets or fish-shaped lumps and sun-drying them. Making these yeasts is a hereditary profession passed on from mother to daughter.

It is common practice across the north-east to feed the leftover grain mash from making rice beer to pigs. It is believed to make the animal slightly tipsy, causing it to sleep, thereby gain weight more rapidly than if it were moving around. The nutrient- and calorie-rich nature of this fermented mash is probably just as important in the fattening process. Agricultural workers in the north-east often drink rice beer throughout the day to provide an energy boost and improve stamina—a benefit attributable to the natural sugars made available in this product by the fermentation process.

The collective cuisines of the north-east could be fairly described as non-vegetarian. There is a general preference for pork and fish, the former easily raised on leftovers, foraged foliage and grain mash; the latter freely caught. Chicken and beef are also eaten, while goat mutton—the favourite meat of the mainland—is in limited use. Some tribes eat a diverse range of wild-animal protein such as frogs, insects and their larvae, and birds. Pork and fish are preserved by smoking, so that in the absence of the fresh item, these can be substituted. Smoking is done in various ways including stringing whole fish, or skewering pieces of pork, and securing these above the smoke from the cooking fire or stuffing them into bamboo hollows and setting the tubes over coals. Even if fresh pork or fish is available, a small piece of the dried version might still be added to a dish to imbue it with additional flavour.

North-easterners prefer to cook food over a fire; they believe it does not taste as well when cooked over gas. Taste is unquestionably a factor in this preference but there is likely an economic imperative too; in the forests of the north-east, free firewood can still be easily collected. In saying that, even the wealthiest rural households, which might otherwise be able to afford to cook every meal over gas, usually retain a wood-fired stove to cook on. Those in more urban environments are usually in possession of a small, portable, timber-fuelled iron cooker that is set up outdoors to create some semblance of cooking over a real fire. A dish that I encountered all across the north-east was one made of eggplant, tomatoes or potatoes—or combinations of these—cooked in the coals of the fire then mashed with salt, a little mustard oil and green chillies to create a flavourful side dish. Another essential presence I pleasurably encountered in the traditional north-east kitchen was that of a lovely cat.

A basic meal in the north-east will be made up of rice, a meat or fish dish, a chutney and a dish of green vegetables: upon this standard there are many regional variations.

EATING GREEN

It is the westernmost point of Assam that connects the rest of India to the north-east, and it is the Assamese people who have the strongest genetic, linguistic and cultural affiliation to mainland Indians. The ancient Narakasura dynasty of Assam features in the Hindu epic the Mahabharata. Irrefutable evidence has yet to be found to prove that the Narakasura kings were more than mythic, but subsequent rulers of Assam liked to claim descent from this exalted clan although they were more likely to have been aboriginal. From AD 350 until AD 1140, Assam—along with parts of Arunachal Pradesh and Bhutan—was known as the kingdom of Kamarupa. It was ruled by a succession of Hindu-aligned dynasties until the mid-twelfth century when the territory—in a reduced configuration—was taken over by the Tibeto-Burman Koch tribe, who were ousted within a century by the Ahoms, a tribe indigenous to the region around the China–Burma border. The Ahoms converted to Hinduism and retained control of Assam until the early nineteenth century when the British annexed the region. It was the Ahoms who ultimately terminated Mughal ambition in the north-east in 1671 by soundly trumping them in a naval battle on the Brahmaputra River.

The Brahmaputra, India's second-largest river, bisects Assam, running the 800-kilometre length of the state from top to bottom, having carved in its wake one of the world's largest river valleys. The fertile land running on either side of this mighty waterway constitutes much of the land mass of Assam, and it is the flattest land in all of the north-east, thus the easiest to bring under cultivation. There is also plenty of water available for growing things and the Assamese are largely engaged in agriculture. In his book on ancient India, *The Culture and Civilisation of Ancient India in Historical Outline*, historian D.D. Kosambi describes Assam as a place 'where every little valley has its own tribal group'. The population of modern Assam remains a diverse mix of tribal people, Indo-Aryan Hindus and Muslims who came into the region from the west and south-east. All these people have wrought various influences on Assamese cuisine yet it shares the core features of north-eastern food, as described earlier.

Xaak is the generic term for leafy greens in Assam and there are hundreds of different xaak collected from waterways, wetlands and jungles: this also includes cultivated species. Xaak can be stir-fried with garlic, salt and a little turmeric or fenugreek or used as a stand-alone vegetable dish or added to meat or fish preparations. The flavours of different xaak range from bitter, astringent, and sour to sweetish, earthy and spicy. The Assamese have long understood that eating a wide variety of greens provides essential vitamins and nutrients. *Saatxaaki* is a dish made of seven types of seasonal xaak, stir-fried in mustard oil.

As in all the north-eastern states, plain cooked rice is the core component of a meal in Assam. Rice that has been ground and sieved to create a fine powder is put to more distinctive use to make sweets called *pitha*. To make pitha, a small amount of rice powder is spread on a hot tawa; the heat causes it to stick together to form a thin roti. A mixture of gur, ground sesame seeds and black pepper is spread over the surface and it is rolled up and removed from the pan. When this was demonstrated to me, I was quite amazed at how the pitha mixture held together with no binding ingredient. My host told me that pitha had to be made with a local variety of rice called *baul chora* as any other rice would 'break': I think that it works because this particular rice is of a 'sticky' variety. There are many variations of the traditional pitha. The prepared rice flour can be made into a batter, flavoured with local fruits such as banana, jackfruit, orange or ripe papaya, and cooked on a greased tawa like a pancake. These might be filled with fresh coconut mixed with gur, ground cloves and fennel. (I noticed that people in the north-east often referred to gur as 'molasses' but it is not the same as the thick, black, pungent syrup of that same name that is a by-product of commercial sugar refining.) *Bor pitha* are small caramel-coloured 'doughnuts' made from a soft dough of rice flour and gur. *Kholasapori pitha* is a savoury item flavoured only with salt and mustard oil, and eaten with pickle or a meat dish. Pitha is customarily prepared at home on special occasions, but can also be bought from commercial confectioners now.

A popular Assamese breakfast dish is made of flattened rice flakes (*chira*), ground rice or sticky rice mixed with sweetened curd or milk. According to local food writer Janice Pariat, this particular combination is a 'plebeian' version of a royal Ahom dessert called *hurung* that is prepared from thick reduced cream and crisp puffed rice drizzled with warm jaggery syrup. A common morning repast for agricultural workers is *poita bhaat*, cooked rice left over from the evening meal, soaked overnight—to cause it to 'ferment' and give it a pleasant sour/tangy flavour—tempered with mustard oil, salt and green chillies: an unrefined but nonetheless tasty and sustaining dish for people who spend their day labouring to produce food. Rice is also wrapped in banana leaves or stuffed into bamboo hollows, cooked over coals and served as an accompaniment to a meat dish, or mixed with gur and curd as a snack or light meal. Of all the north-eastern states, Assam was the only one where I was served dessert, this being *payas* (rice cooked with milk and sugar), essentially the same as *kheer* eaten across mainland India.

Assamese love fish. In most households, it is eaten daily and usually eaten fresh. If fresh fish is not available, then dried fish is incorporated into the meal. Some 'vegetarian' Assamese also eat small fish, getting around this by saying that these fish feed on green plants and thus are 'vegetarian'! Rural households often have their own fish ponds and/or are close enough to a water source where they can freely fish. In a small traditional village in upper Assam, I was served a meal largely prepared from a small haul of fish brought up in a basket from the nearby river. There were tiny, small and middling species in the catch, and various dishes were prepared from these. Some of the smaller fish were wrapped in banana leaf, roasted in the fire and ground with tomato, onion, green chillies, salt and mustard oil to make *maach pitika*; others were coated with salt and turmeric and deep-fried to add crunch to the meal; a few of the slightly larger specimens were skewered and roasted over a coal fire, then ground with oil, onion, ginger and salt to make a chutney; and the larger fish were cooked with fern leaves (*dhekia*) to make a dish called *dhekia tenga*.

A typical Assamese meal always includes a *tenga* (sour) dish. The sourness might be achieved by using lemon, lime, tomatoes, herbs such as dhekia, fermented bamboo shoot or local sour fruits such as *omora* or hog plum (*Spondias mombin*, a relative of the cashew) and *ou tenga* or wild elephant apple (*Dillenia indica*). The latter has a hard casing that is pared away to reveal a crisp 'apple' within, which is sliced and added to dishes. Fish is often cooked in tenga style, but vegetables and *dal bor* (fritters made of ground *urad* dal) are also prepared in this way. A tenga dish has a 'soupy' consistency and is traditionally eaten at the end of a meal to aid digestion.

Another distinct Assamese dish is *khar*, a stew prepared from vegetables such as green papaya or dal flavoured with a product popularly referred to as 'indigenous soda'. This soda is produced by charring a piece of the stem of the banana plant over the fire until it can be crushed into ashes, which are then soaked in water and allowed to percolate for some time. The water strained off this mixture constitutes the soda. (Indigenous soda is also used in cooking by other tribes in the north-east.) The Mishing people of Assam make khar from the leaves of a local variety of black dal. The taste of khar is described as 'astringent'; by including this taste in daily meals, Assamese cooking covers all the tastes—sweet, sour, salty, bitter, pungent, astringent—that the ancient Indian health system of Ayurveda describes as essential if meals are to be truly satisfying and nutritious. Astringent in Ayurveda means 'dry' and 'light'; indeed, when you try khar, you will understand how these words translate, pleasantly, into texture and taste. Commercial bicarbonate soda is now widely used as a substitute for indigenous soda. Khar is taken at the start of a meal to 'clear' the system and set it up for the meal to come.

Pitika is another essential component of an Assamese meal. This term denotes a preparation of vegetables (eggplant, tomato, potato) or fish roasted in the coals of a fire until cooked and mashed with a little salt, green chilli and fresh coriander. Most Assamese share the 'non-vegetarian' preference prevalent throughout the north-east. Aside from fish, duck and pigeon are favourite meats. (I was nearly knocked over when entering the municipal market in Guwahati by a man rushing out carrying a pair of fat pigeons; I concluded that he must have been in a hurry to get these birds into a cooking pot somewhere!) While pork is widely eaten, it does not hold the premier position in the food hierarchy that it does in other parts of the north-east. Assam is home to more than two dozen types of bamboos, and this evergreen grass is of particular economic, cultural and culinary importance. Fresh as well as fermented shoots are commonly cooked with duck and pork, the tanginess of the bamboo 'cutting', and complementing, the richness of these meats. Eating bamboo shoots is held to aid digestion, which makes sense when you consider it is a high-fibre food.

The lines demarcating the borders of Assam have changed dramatically over its long history. At various times, it has included, or been included in, regional configurations with parts of West Bengal and Bangladesh (when that was part of pre-Partition Bengal) and there is a Bengali influence on Assamese food. This is perhaps most notable in a more extended use of spices than is generally found in north-eastern cuisine. Assamese cooking still predominantly relies on combinations of ginger, garlic, turmeric and chilli to enhance the flavour of dishes, but mustard seeds are often used along with judicious amounts of cumin and fennel. The use of these spices is more common in lower Assam as it is contiguous with Bengal, and coconut is regularly used in this part because coconut palms grow there. In upper Assam, the food of various tribes has a much stronger 'Asian' influence. The Singpho food I ate in Margherita district (*see Recommendations*) spoke to me more of Thai and Vietnamese food—and probably Burmese, if I had more experience of that cuisine—than it did of 'Indian' food.

One of the ways Assamese add a bit of crunch to a meal is to include a few bor—fritters made from various flowers, like those of the drumstick tree, water lily, pea plants and coral jasmine or leaves or fine slices of vegetables; these ingredients are dipped in a rice- or chickpea-flour batter and deep-fried. Commonly known as pakoras in northern India, these have a tendency to be quite 'heavy'. What struck me about bor is that when done well these are light and delicate, just like the pakoras I ate in Bihar; I wonder if this might not have been an influence from this central Indian state as the British brought in many Biharis to work on the tea estates in Assam in the colonial era.

TEA

Traversing Assam from Guwahati to its northernmost border at Tinsukia, nearly 500 kilometres away, seems like travelling through a huge tea plantation; the highway is almost unceasingly bordered by luxuriant stands of tea bushes. Assam is one of the largest tea-producing areas in the world, sending out 1.5 million pounds of it annually to satisfy domestic and global demand for this dried leaf. The prevailing climatic conditions in Assam—a cool winter and a hot, humid rainy season—are ideal for cultivating tea and it grows so prolifically that the bushes can be harvested twice in a year. Tea is native to the upper north-east though its scientific name, *Camellia sinensis var. assamica*, seems to indicate that it belongs exclusively to this state. It was 'discovered' in the region in the early nineteenth century when much of the north-east was designated as 'Assam' by the British. Although the words 'tea' and 'India' have become inseparable, it was the British who started the tea industry in India, in Assam, and taught the Indian population how to drink this beverage.

By the early nineteenth century, Britons of all classes were well and truly addicted to tea; they got through some thirty million pounds annually, all of which came from China. When the British fell out with China, circa 1840, as a result of the Opium Wars, it was tough to keep up the supply of tea to Britain: a matter of potentially serious consequence for the British economy and the country's tea-loving populace. It was critical to find an alternative supply. Nearly two decades earlier, Robert Bruce, a British agent stationed in Assam, had noticed the Singpho people in upper Assam drinking a decoction brewed from what he recognized as tea plants. He sent a sample of these to London for official identification and received confirmation that what he had found was indeed a variety of *Camellia sinensis*. Bruce and his discovery were ignored, though, until the crisis with China forced the British to seriously consider looking elsewhere to grow tea. Recalling Bruce's discovery—though he was long dead by then—the first tea garden was established in Assam. The British were initially wedded to the idea of 'China tea' and brought in Chinese plants and two supposed Chinese tea growers—who, it turned out, knew nothing about growing it! This was a dismal failure and they returned to the 'wild' indigenous variety of Bruce's acquaintance, which had by this time naturally interbred with its Sino relative, resulting in the much more civilized, that is, commercially viable, *assamica*. By the late nineteenth century, the Indian tea industry, centred in Assam, was flourishing.

To create the tea gardens of Assam, the British forcibly pushed indigenous tribes off their lands; they were understandably enraged at this eviction and refused to work on the plantations. There could be no industry without labourers to pick and process the tea so the British brought tribal people from central India to do the work. (These people mixed on the plantations and created a new tribe called Bhagania.) This probably did not endear the product of their usurped land to the people of Assam, though apart from the Singpho there were few Indians at all who drank tea and, up until the early twentieth century, almost all of that produced in India was exported to the United Kingdom and its colonies. It was then that the Indian Tea Association realized that its biggest potential market was right in front of it. It took several decades of dedicated work by the association to instil the tea-drinking habit in Indians. They employed travelling salesmen to demonstrate how to make tea in people's homes; had it supplied to factory workers; placed vendors on trains; and opened tea shops. They wanted consumers to drink tea made by infusion in a pot but sellers decided to boil it in milk and add spices and plenty of sugar to make it more appealing to a population with a preference for sweet, milky drinks. The Indian Tea Association did not approve, largely because making tea in this way used fewer leaves. Indians responded very positively to this masala chai, though, and an immeasurable amount of it is now brewed every day by millions of chai-wallahs across India. Indeed, Indians have become the world's largest consumers of tea.

Recommendations

....

GUWAHATI

Guwahati was once Assam's capital, an honour now due to Dispur. Guwahati is modern Assam's biggest city and the place where most visitors to Assam, and the north-east, alight from an aeroplane, train or bus to begin their travels. It has some good places to sample Assamese cuisine.

Khorika means 'stick' in Ahomiya and the speciality of this popular restaurant, run by a local celebrity chef, is pork, chicken, fish and duck skewered and slowly roasted by an open fire. Fish khorika is a trio of small blackened fish paired with a generous spoonful of fresh green chilli chutney, the flesh smoky, slightly chewy and delicious in its simplicity. The menu extends well beyond barbecue into an impressive selection of local specialities such as duck cooked with bamboo shoot, pigeon meat with banana flower and fish cooked in six different Assamese preparations. Meals come with slices of the elongated local lime and a thick mustard pickle. When I sat down to my meal, I reflected on how I had seen most parts of my meal in their raw state during my exploration of the city's streets and markets: plump ducks and pigeons in pretty cages expertly woven from bamboo; baskets piled high with fat green chillies and fresh garlic; and near the restaurant a young boy had co-opted a section of the footpath to display the small fish—the same variety I had eaten as khorika—he kept alive in shallow containers until dispatched to customers.

First Floor, Kamal Plaza, G.S. Road
11.30 a.m.–3 p.m., 7–10.30 p.m. (7 days)
(M) 9435010935

Paradise holds claim to being the first restaurant in Guwahati to serve Assamese food, and has done so for thirty years. Try the peppery pigeon curry or the royal Ahom thali to sample local dishes without having to think about putting a complete meal together: expect a tenga, pitika, khar, fish stew, steamed fish, stir-fried greens and local condiments such as *kharisa* (grated bamboo shoot with green chilli) and *kharoli* (chutney of fermented mustard paste, salt, chilli and soda). Leave room for a serve of delicious 'noble' hurung at the end.

Near Goswami Service, G.N.B. Road, Silpukhuri
10.30 a.m.–midnight
(0361) 2666904

The location of **Delicacy**, under a busy flyover somewhere out of the city centre, might be a little off-putting, but the sign featuring a smiling lady in traditional Assamese dress is a much better indicator of what awaits culinary explorers who make the journey to this well-patronized restaurant. You can order classic Assamese dishes such as duck cooked with bamboo shoot or gourd, fish or potato pitika, papaya khar, tangy tomato-based fish tenga and sweet rice payas.

Junction of G.S. and R.G.B. Roads, Ganeshpuri
11.30 a.m.–11 p.m. (7 days)
(M) 9864747474

Customers of **Laxmi Cabin** are seemingly always in a hurry: they stand at high tables to quickly eat their snack or sweet treat and push off as soon as this is done, only to be replaced by others. Come here to try pitha. You can choose a stuffed pancake-like pitha from the glass showcase and/or a packet of rolled pitha from the counter top. (Its blue-and-white sign is written in Assamese but it's easy enough to spot this place.)

H.B. Road, Kamarpatty, Fancy Bazaar

Baruah Bhavan is an atmospheric, colonial-era Assamese mansion in the older quarter of Guwahati, a block or so up from the riverside. It now operates as a small hotel. Guests can enjoy home-cooked Assamese thalis for lunch or dinner, in a pleasant, domestic setting.

40 M.C. Road, Uzanbazar
(0361) 2541182, (M) 9954024165
www.heritagehomeassam.com

KAZIRANGA

Spotting a one-horned rhino in Kaziranga National Park, a UNESCO World Heritage site, is a rite of passage for visitors to Assam. The area where the park is located is home to the Karbi tribe. If you enter through the central gate of Kaziranga, pass the tourist complex and follow the road around to your left, you will reach **Horlank Namsing**, an outdoor eatery that serves Karbi-style food. The eating area and open kitchen are perched atop a knoll lined with tea bushes, overlooking a Karbi village. Sample *lang dang kitum* (banana flower smoked over a wood fire then mashed with garlic, salt and green chilli); *lank-okrimung* (local river fish smoked in a bamboo hollow; there are chicken and pork versions); and *hanserong* (smoked wild greens)—this selection of dishes deliciously demonstrates how tribal people harness their source of heat and cooking to build additional flavour in their food—and *kangmoi ahan* (wild herbs cooked with indigenous soda). Meals are accompanied by a bright-purple chutney made from the fleshy flower of the roselle plant (*Hibiscus sabdariffa*) ground with dried fish, turmeric and salt. (Roselle is another plant used to add a 'sour' flavour to food in Assam.) In such a setting, a bamboo cup (or two) of the sweetish local rice beer called *horlank* is a necessary meal pairing. This eatery only operates from mid-October to mid-April, as the park closes during the monsoon.

(M) 9854872861
11.30 a.m.–3 p.m., 7–10.30 p.m. (7 days)

The restaurant at **Jupuri Ghar Resort** in Kaziranga serves a good selection of Assamese dishes. These are a little more commercial in their execution than the food at Horlank Namsing but fresh and tasty nonetheless. Try the excellent *patot dia maach* (fresh fish marinated in a paste of onion, yellow mustard seeds and mustard oil, and roasted in banana leaves) and papaya khar.

Kohora, Kaziranga Tiger Reserve
(03776) 294214, (M) 9435196377
11.30 a.m.–3 p.m., 7–10.30 p.m. (7 days; seasonal)

MAJULI

The Brahmaputra River is so wide in upper Assam that it accommodates the island of Majuli, one of the world's largest inhabited river islands, and still maintains wide stretches of water between it and the distant 'mainland' banks. Majuli is home to several tribes like the Mishing, who live almost exclusively along the Brahmaputra or its tributaries, in beautifully crafted bamboo-and-thatch homes raised on stilts. Through the agency of **Help Tourism**, I was able to visit Mishing elder Komala Karta Koman and his family at their home for a demonstration of traditional Mishing cooking. Living alongside a river that rises dramatically every year is challenging, and often dangerous. The size and shape of Majuli is altered every year by monsoonal flooding but once the water recedes, the land is left with a new coat of fertile alluvial soil. The Mishing are skilled cultivators and know how to make the most of these circumstances to grow crops and produce; they also gather wild foods and a Mishing meal always features cultivated and foraged ingredients. A heap of rice is at the centre of any Mishing meal (my hosts were quite dismayed when I ate only a little) accompanied by a dish of chicken, pork or fish boiled with wild herbs and greens and flavoured with turmeric, chilli, salt and perhaps some freshly crushed local black pepper. Chicken and pork are raised on household scraps, pigs on the residue from the production of home-made rice beer. The floor of a Mishing home is woven from bamboo and the weave of the kitchen area is made wider than the rest of the home so that if any food spills it falls down to the pigs below. (I found this quite a convenience for discreetly disposing of the cane stalks that had been used in the fish dish served to me as these were too bitter for my taste and I am sure the pigs got more pleasure out of them than I ever could!)

The Mishing catch fish using a bamboo trap shaped like a large cone with a hollow top. This is pushed down into the water until it touches the bottom and traps any passing fish; the trapper puts his hand in through the hole in the top and pulls out the catch. The fish I ate with Komala were really fresh; in fact, they were still moving and he killed and gutted them while we chatted casually. A chicken had also been freshly dispatched for my dinner, and its innards were skewered and cooked in front of the central cooking fire and eaten with rice beer. The barbecued innards were something of a treat but the rice beer is a daily staple. Komala told me that he drinks it when he comes from the fields for lunch and again when he comes home in the evening; it gives him 'energy'. The Mishing have no concept of 'sweet dishes' and do not like to eat sugary things. I have no idea how old Komala is. He is not a young man yet he is lithe and agile and spends all day working his fields. Perhaps we could learn something from the Mishing diet.

Help Tourism can arrange a 'culinary' visit to Majuli and/or into other village kitchens in Assam.

Milan Nagar, V.I.P. Road, Guwahati
(0361) 2842048
www.helptourism.com

I enjoyed another unique eating experience in Majuli. The island is home to over twenty-two Vaishnava *satra*s (monasteries). Auniati, the largest, houses over 400 monks and it is here that I visited the monk, and registered tour guide, **Nitul Dutta** in his spartan 'cell' where he cooked a meal for me. All the cooking was done over, and in, a fire pit carved out of the smooth clay floor of his kitchen. He prepared a dish of dal and a starchy tuber called *arum* in Assam (this vegetable belongs to the genus *Colocasia*); and stir-fried greens and a pitika of eggplant and potato flavoured with a little mustard oil. The food was simple yet full of taste. While Nitul had happily served me my meal, I had to take my banana leaf plate and banana stem bowl and dispose of it in the waste area; a monk is not permitted to handle used food receptacles. Please contact Nitul if you are interested in visiting the monastery for a meal and a tour. (The latter is not obligatory, and I just went for the food!)

nitul.dutta75@gmail.com
(M) 9508050296

EASTERN ASSAM

The Singpho people have long inhabited the easternmost territory of the north-east. They live in equal numbers across Assam and

Arunachal Pradesh. Their direct relatives live nearby in Myanmar and China, and their language and culture are born of this part of the world, bearing no resemblance to those of greater 'India'. Likewise, their cuisine is akin to that of Myanmar/Thailand with some Indian influence; it is something of an irony that a Singpho habit has been taken up by millions of Indians. You see, it was the Singpho whom Robert Bruce came upon drinking tea in the early nineteenth century. Traditionally, the Singpho did not prune the tea bushes to 'picking' height but allowed them to flourish more naturally as small trees. They prepare tea by sun-drying the leaves for three days and leaving them exposed to dew at night during the same period, after which they are packed into a bamboo hollow and smoked over fire to preserve them and add flavour. The finished tea, called *pha lap*, is then stored in bamboo. The colonial masters of the Indian Tea Association would be pleased to know that the Singpho take their tea black.

In the far north-east of Assam, near the border with Arunachal Pradesh, on the road to Namdapha National Park, is **Singpho Village** restaurant. The food served here is exactly as you would find in a Singpho home. No spice beyond black pepper is used in this kitchen; the zingy, aromatic flavours come from garlic, ginger, green chilli, bamboo shoot, coriander (the South East Asian *Persicaria odorata* variety), mint, basil (a wild local variety called *nitang ban*) and lime. *Wu san tikye* is a dish of chicken mixed with garlic, ginger, mint and finely shredded bamboo shoot, wrapped in leaves—collected from the nearby jungle—and roasted over coals; this dish itself is worth travelling for. Wu san salad is shredded chicken mixed with lots of finely sliced onion, fresh herbs, green chilli and black pepper. The Singpho like to eat pork (*wu*) and both these dishes can be made with pork; there was none to be had the day I visited as the chef had not made it to the market early enough to get hold of some before it sold out. A fish chutney (ground from barbecued fish, small onion, ginger, dried bamboo shoot and basil) and banana flower soup completed our meal. The accompanying rice is shaped as a ball and wrapped in green leaves; you take one of these, centre it on your plate and unwrap it leaving the leaf underneath to eat off.

New Colony Bargolai, Margherita District
(M) 9854440162
10 a.m.–9 p.m. (7 days)

THE GINGER HILLS

In square kilometres, Meghalaya is one of the smallest states in India. However, if its vertical terrain is added to its statistics, it would claim a higher ranking as the land within its borders is predominantly hilly. In 1876, the highest ever recorded rainfall fell in the town of Cherrapunji in the Khasi Hills region and it has been known as 'the wettest place on earth' ever since. This circumstance tends to give the impression that all of Meghalaya is constantly under a rain cloud, but Cherrapunji could not produce its famous oranges if the sun did not shine there for some part of the year. The state does receive good annual rainfall, though, and its subtropical hills and interspersing valleys are lush and green. Forest areas are rich sources of wild food—'nature's gift', as described to me. Much of the rest of the land is cultivated to grow rice and fresh produce and significant crops of high-quality ginger and turmeric.

When the British took over the administration of Meghalaya in the nineteenth century and integrated it into Assam Province, the region was largely the territory of three tribes: Khasi, Jaintia and Garo. This relatively short colonial intervention disrupted ancient tribal rule and ultimately left the state with a unified governance structure, but these three groups remained dominant in number and cultural influence. There are strong differences and similarities between the Khasi, Jaintia and Garo people: their faces reveal a shared genetic link with the people of South East Asia and the Khasi and Jaintia speak a related language but that spoken by the Garo is unique. Differences reportedly exist relating to the foodstuffs they favour and how these are cooked, but several local cooks assured me that in the case of the Khasi and Jaintia these differences are so subtle that the cuisines of these two tribes are almost indistinguishable. Based on this information, I am going to write of the food of Meghalaya collectively and note any distinct cultural variations.

Before exploring the food of the people of Meghalaya, let's have a look at what they 'chew' on more than anything else: betel nut. This so-called nut, *Areca catechu*, is the seed of a tropical palm—introduced into India from South East Asia—that grows profusely in Meghalaya, and is a major crop of the state. Betel nut is grown in other parts of the north-east and mainland India and is taken as a stimulant, digestive and mouth freshener by Indians of all backgrounds, but nowhere is it more enthusiastically, and continually, chewed upon than in Meghalaya. Thin slices of the nut are paired with 'betel leaves'—harvested from the climbing vine *Piper betle*—slaked with lime paste. The betel nut, leaf and lime combination is most commonly taken folded into a wrap, often including spices, tobacco and aromatics such as camphor, and in this format is called paan; in this preparation, dried betel nut is also used. In Meghalaya, betel (*kwai*) is taken in a different format. The whole nut is soaked in water and stored under heavy mats to make it ferment and imbue it with a distinct local flavour. Many people carry a supply of these prepared nuts around, along with a small knife. When they want to chew some betel, they pare the casing away and slice up the kernel, or 'nut', found inside. They pop a few pieces of the tender nut into their mouth and then separately take a section of betel rubbed with lime paste; they might also add in pieces of dried tobacco. (Lamp posts, poles, building frontages and gateways across Meghalaya are covered with white smears caused by people wiping their fingers across these to remove the lime paste used in this process.) Offering betel nut is a sign of hospitality across the subcontinent, but in Meghalaya it is an inviolable social custom to offer it to guests: a meal begins and ends with it, though it is not mandatory to take it.

Other important crops grown in Meghalaya are rice, citrus fruit, guava, pineapple, potato, the aforementioned turmeric and ginger, black pepper and *tej patta*. This last item is the leaf of the native *Cinnamomum tamala* tree; it is dried and used in cooking throughout India. (It is also used fresh, particularly by cooks who have the tree in their garden.) It is often erroneously described as 'Indian bay leaf' in cookbooks. While it is of the same *Lauraceae* family as the bay laurel used in Western cooking, tej patta is a different genus and imparts a cinnamon-like flavour to food, distinct from the citrus/pine flavour of its Mediterranean relative. In Meghalaya, it is typically used to flavour dal.

Local turmeric and ginger, onion, garlic and the green tops of its plant, and a little black pepper are the chief flavouring ingredients used. The ginger and turmeric grown in Jaintia Hills are noted for their quality and local cooks are fussy about how they use these two rhizomes, employing fresh, dried or powdered turmeric and 'light' (newly harvested) or 'strong' (older, slightly dried) ginger quite specifically in various dishes. The Garo like to add indigenous soda to dishes to impart a subtle alkaline flavour to their food. All the tribes of Meghalaya are decidedly non-vegetarian in their tastes and add dried or fermented fish to vegetable dishes, and cook leafy greens in meat stock.

Rice and pork are dietary mainstays in Meghalaya. A typical meal would include a large serving of rice, a pork dish, a green vegetable dish, some small fried fish to add crunch and pungency or a chutney made with dried/ fermented/smoked fish. *Dohnai iong* (pork cooked in the paste of ground black sesame seeds and flavoured with garlic, turmeric and onion) is a popular daily dish. *Tungrumbai* (pork cooked with soybeans, green chilli and black sesame) is typically prepared in the winter. Black sesame is used extensively and these oil-rich seeds are also added to vegetable dishes and dal. Pork cooked with mustard leaves, *wak pura*, is an everyday dish, but the pairing of this rich meat with tangy greens is an exceptional match. Wild mushrooms, foraged from the forests in the early monsoon, are cooked with black sesame and pork. Unsurprisingly, the dish that Meghalaya is best known for is one prepared from pork and rice—*jadoh* (rice meat). To make *jadoh*, pork pieces (with fat and bone) are boiled in a large pot of water along with sliced onion and turmeric; when cooked, the meat is taken out of the water and is separated into fat and meat. The fat is chopped into small bits and added back to the stock in the pot along with local red or white rice, which absorbs all the liquid as it cooks to create the jadoh. The cooked meat is finely chopped and mixed with onion, 'strong' ginger, salt and some stock to make *doh sniang khelh* that is eaten with the jadoh. (This dish is sometimes described as a 'salad'.) There are different versions such as that made with pork liver (*jadoh nierbah*) or chicken (*jadoh syiar*). Jadoh is essential at any festive meal in Meghalaya.

Rice is also used to make various breads and cakes. *Putharo* is a flatbread prepared from rice that has been soaked in water overnight, dried and ground into a fine powder. It is mixed with water to create a batter that is cooked in a slightly concave clay dish over a fire. The way the rice is prepared for putharo causes it to 'ferment' and the finished bread has a soft, spongy texture like a crumpet—it is only cooked on one side as the heat causes it to set all the way through—and a slightly sour taste. It is popularly used to mop up pork dishes such as *doh jem* (stew of offal). The same ground rice used for putharo is made into dough with jaggery and steamed in banana leaves or shaped into discs and deep-fried to produce *pukhlein*. Savoury rice cakes are flavoured with salt and turmeric or stuffed with small pieces of pork (*pudoh*) and steamed in small clay moulds. Rice cakes, either sweet or savoury, are eaten for breakfast or as a teatime snack. If you are visiting Shillong or Jowai, you can find *kong*s (women) who sell home-made rice cakes from large leaf-lined baskets in the markets of those towns.

I visited a village 'slow food' market in Khasi Hills where I encountered an incredible array of wild sweet potatoes and yams, some of which were novel even to my local companion. The people of Meghalaya like to peel these starchy root vegetables and eat them raw as snacks; boil them for breakfast dressed with local honey or palm sap; or fry them like chips.

Recommendations

. . . .

SHILLONG

The Raj-era 'hill-station charm' for which Shillong, the capital of Meghalaya, was once noted is evident only in small pockets now in this sprawling post-Independence city. Before the British came along and created this 'Scotland of the East', Shillong belonged to the Khasi tribe and remains their 'territory'. The best place to encounter Khasi culture and cuisine is Bara Bazaar. This huge marketplace is somewhat of a labyrinth of lanes but it's a pleasure to aimlessly wander and see fresh local produce on display. Meghalaya is a matriarchal society and you will notice that women run most of the stalls. There are small and basic, but very clean, food stalls throughout the market that serve local food, particularly jadoh, to market workers and shoppers. **Kong Nat**'s jadoh stall has a local reputation for its food. (The market is a maze of similar-looking lanes so just ask around inside it to get directions.) The menu changes regularly but a jadoh is always on offer and perhaps pig trotters or mustard leaves cooked with pork.

7 a.m.–7 p.m. (Sundays closed)

You will find the bustling Police Bazaar at the confluence of several roads including the appropriately named Jail Road. Seek out the cheekily named **Restoranto Khasiano**. It's a basic place serving Khasi food that is popular with the locals. Try the pork jadoh with doh sniang khelh.

Jadoh restaurant offers the opportunity to enjoy local cuisine in a somewhat more salubrious, though less atmospheric, environment than the market. You can try jadoh or doh jem (a reminder for the squeamish that this is a stew of pig's intestines and offal), smoked beef curry or *jhur sed* (greens stir-fried in mustard oil).

Don Bosco Square, Laitumkhrah
10a.m.–6 p.m. (Sundays closed)
(M) 9774365583

Upmarket dining in Shillong can be enjoyed at **Tripura Castle**, a heritage hotel. Despite being named for a neighbouring state—this hilltop hotel is part of the summer abode of the former maharaja of Tripura—you can enjoy good Khasi cooking here along with some lovely views across the hills. Of course, there are jadoh and dohnai iong but, for a change, try Cherrapunji chicken, a dish of locally raised bird cooked with garlic and black pepper. There's a catch though—if you want to have a Khasi meal, you need to pre-order and a day's notice is preferred. The upside is that you can be assured that the food is freshly prepared.

Tripura Castle Road, Cleve Colony
(0364) 2501111

MAWLYNNONG

A village in East Khasi Hills, and around 100 kilometres from Shillong, Mawlynnong lays persistent claim to being the 'cleanest village in Asia' after being awarded that title by a travel magazine nearly a decade ago. I did not do a 'white glove' test while I was there, but visual inspection indicated that high cleanliness standards have been unfailingly maintained. Mawlynnong nestles almost unobtrusively in the forest that surrounds it and is incredibly beautiful. Village houses are traditionally made of bamboo and you can stay in one at **I-LA-Jong Guest House**. The family that runs it serves local food for guests, if requested; a Khasi cooking class can also be arranged. Various seasonal ingredients are collected from the forest and garden. A basket of small shrimp might be scooped up from the large backyard pond and cooked with turmeric and finely chopped wild greens. Village-raised pork is also cooked with wild greens and local black pepper and served with a side dish prepared from banana flower—cut fresh from a tree in the garden—smoked over the fire, chopped finely and sautéed in a little mustard oil, onion and green chilli. To arrange a food-focused visit, contact **Help Tourism** (*see the Assam chapter*).

WILD FOOD

Driving through the lush Naga Hills in the gentle winter sun, taking in the majestic views across the interweaving valleys and enjoying the friendly hospitality of the locals when stationary, feels somewhat incongruent with the prevailing idea of this landlocked state as one occupied by 'fierce warriors'. The people of Nagaland belong to fourteen major tribes, each with its own language and customs, but are collectively referred to as the Nagas. (The Nagas also live in the neighbouring states of Assam, Arunachal Pradesh and Myanmar.) They are considered to have made their way into India from Tibet at some distant time; not much else is known of their early history. They lived in isolation in their mountainous north-eastern corner of India well into the nineteenth century. Naga reputation for ferocity is not without foundation: they once collected the heads of slain enemies and comrades alike and displayed these as status symbols, believing that doing so would bring good luck; and twice beat off the British before capitulating to them. They later joined forces with their overlords in one of the most famous battles of the Second World War, in which the advancing Japanese army was stopped at Kohima, the capital, and driven back thus thwarting its plans to take control of India. The Nagas also have a reputation for 'eating anything', and they do indeed have a very broad palate.

A visit to the main market in Kohima offers visitors the opportunity to see just how widely the Nagas eat. Fluffy white rats, pale-green silkworms, coral-pink dragonfly larvae, bags of small frogs, buckets of writhing eels, snails and—most intriguing—whole nests of hornets from which fat caramel-coloured larvae are extracted and eaten: all these are sold here. At the butchers' stalls lining a small lane a little down the road from the market, dog meat is available. The fact that much of the land mass of Nagaland is mountainous has served to insulate it from development and it still contains large tracts of forest. Much of the food described above would have been collected from these or wild waterways (with the exception of the dog meat: I didn't quite get to the bottom of where that comes from) along with lots of different leafy greens and local herbs. Silkworms bought from the market might be boiled then stir-fried with red chilli, garlic, ginger and some *bastenga* (liquid from fermented bamboo shoots) to create *loutsa ga*. Snails are boiled with a piece of smoked pork, a little pork lard, fermented bamboo shoot, roasted sesame seeds and fermented soybean paste called *akhuni* to produce *noyla ga* while hornet larvae are deep-fried, and reportedly taste like peanuts. (I didn't get to try these for economic reasons, which I will explain further on.) Dog meat is likewise boiled with ginger, garlic, turmeric and chilli. Before you start to get nervous about eating in Nagaland (or not, if you relish truly exotic food items), let me explain that the dishes I describe are delicacies and the components expensive. On the day I visited Kohima market, hornet nests were selling for 7500 rupees each (about 150 dollars), an unbelievably enormous sum of money to pay for food in India. Silkworm, dragonfly larvae and dog meat are likewise costly, so if someone suggests that you might be unwittingly served the meat of dog, or perhaps monkey, it is unlikely since a domestic host would be sure to inform you beforehand of the treat in store for you, and a commercial operation is not going to secretly slip expensive dog meat or hornet larvae into your meal. While some of these foods may not appeal to you (and I admit that I too was challenged by some), if we stand back and look at them without prejudice, what we see is a selection of wild, unprocessed foods free of chemicals and full of nutrition. Outside of buying them in the market, Nagas collect such wild foods themselves for domestic use so they need not always be costly.

The cooking methods and flavouring ingredients used in Naga delicacies are the same as those used for everyday dishes—it's just the protein that changes. Pork and beef are everyday meats. More than 90 per cent of Nagas are Baptist Christians—converted wholesale from their ancient animist ways by missionaries in the late nineteenth and twentieth centuries—so there is no religious prohibition on either of these meats, which are typically cooked with bamboo shoot or akhuni. *Thevo chu* is a dry dish of pork with fresh bamboo shoots; *akshi* is pork boiled with dried bamboo shoot; *aoshi* is pork boiled with fermented soybeans; and *nashishi* is beef boiled with fermented bamboo shoots. *Amerso* is chicken boiled with rice and fresh bamboo shoots. Fish rubbed with a mixture of ginger, chilli and salt and smoked in a bamboo hollow is a speciality of the Lotha tribe, but bamboo is widely used as cookware across Nagaland.

Nagas do like to eat vegetables although dishes made from these are not necessarily 'pure vegetarian'. An everyday preparation of leafy greens might be boiled with chilli, akhuni and pork lard; a piece of smoked pork is a common addition to a dish of boiled yams or sweet potato. It is common practice to smoke meat over the fire to preserve it and ensure that there is always some meat available to add to a meal. A family I visited in Kohima had sparrow-like birds and strips of pork and beef strung up above the fireplace in their kitchen. Akhuni is added to dishes as a condiment or cooked as a dish with tomatoes and chillies and eaten with rice. This is one vegetable dish to which meat is not added as it has ample flavour of its own.

Nagas are particularly fond of chillies and these go into almost every dish as unremarked as the addition of salt usually is. The local variety of chilli is called *raja mirch* and presumably it takes its royal title from its legendary potency rather than its size, for it is small and squat. Nagaland is a rural state and most Nagas live in villages and are engaged in agriculture. Twenty different varieties of rice are cultivated and a generous portion of this—plain boiled or steamed—is the basis of every meal. Nagas grow pineapples, small white onions, tamarillo (tree tomatoes), bananas, jackfruit, oranges, passion fruit and mangoes. Even in the 'suburbs' of Kohima, homes have productive gardens with fruit trees, a vegetable patch, pots bursting with greens and herbs, and pumpkin and gourd vines growing over outbuildings, fences and trellises; if the space is available, they will also keep a pig and chickens; the porker—whether residing in a rural or urban pig pen—receives the residue from the production of *zu* (rice beer). A traditional Naga breakfast dish is *nyabe*, sticky rice cooked with sugar and eaten with fried rice bread (a type of puri). Food stalls around Kohima market (behind the main bus stand) sell nyabe but you have to get in early to get a plate.

Recommendations

Nagaland only opened up to tourists in 2000. Given this, the remote location and the sometimes violent political environment (Nagas want to secede from India and become an independent country called Nagalim), tourism is a slowly developing industry. One very successful tourist drawcard is the annual **Hornbill Festival** held in

Kisama village on the outskirts of Kohima. This week-long event was conceived as a vehicle for various Naga tribes to get to know each other a little better and now it draws people from around the world. The main attraction is the programme of events focused on traditional tribal dance, song, dress and ritual but the venue also has numerous food stalls selling tribal cuisine—and pizza! The dishes on offer vary every year but you are likely to be able to sample *axone*, a popular dish of smoked pork cooked with akhuni eaten with rice or mashed yams and boiled wild greens such as fern shoots that is a speciality of the Sumi tribe; fish cooked in bamboo; and a dry dish of beef, Naga onions, chilli and tomatoes. Several stalls serve rice beer in large bamboo cups accompanied by local snacks such as *themo tathty*, a dried beef pickle that reminded me in texture of the dried-fish floss sold in Asian snack shops, and *kerhu tathu*, a dried soya pickle made of cooked, dried soya and black beans mixed with small pieces of dried garlic, ginger and chilli. You can also have a plate of nutty, crunchy dried grasshoppers. (In his book *Nagaland: A Journey to India's Forgotten Frontier*, author Jonathan Glancey is scathing about the food on offer at Hornbill, saying that it has been toned down for tourists. Unless you have the unstintingly adventurous inclination of Glancey to get out into villages in the remotest parts of Nagaland, which also requires ignoring travel restrictions, then the culinary offerings at the festival are not a bad experience of Naga food.)

There are not many hotels offering accommodation in Nagaland so most tourists stay in homestays with local families and these offer the best option for trying local cuisine as your host will usually be delighted to prepare regional dishes for you. **The Heritage** is a charming historic bungalow in Kohima that offers accommodation and serves Naga food.

Old DC Bungalow, Officers Hill
(0370) 2241864

If you are interested in learning about tribal cuisine in Nagaland, go through an ethical and culturally sensitive travel company such as **Help Tourism** (*see the Assam chapter*). Roadside dhabas are another option for sampling simple Naga meals as most customers are locals who just want a low-cost meal of familiar food.

ARUNACHAL PRADESH

THE FAR EAST

Even the dry facts about Arunachal Pradesh mark it as an interesting place: it is the largest state in the north-east; the least populated state in India and one of the most remote; it shares international borders with Bhutan, Myanmar and China; it is the least visited by tourists; and it is home to twenty-six major tribes and myriad sub-tribes. If we flesh out these bare statistical bones, the flavour of Arunachal grows even more enticing. The land flows from the glacial terrain of snow-capped Himalayan peaks along the northern border into high alpine meadows and jungle-covered foothills that unfold into steamy subtropical rainforests and flat plains along the Brahmaputra valley. Most tribes of Arunachal are Tibeto-Burman but the diversity of geography allowed them to develop distinct identities, languages and cultures. In 1837, the British stopped free movement in and out of Arunachal; indeed, until recently, human traffic has remained tightly controlled (non-Indians still require a permit to visit) because of security concerns due to the proximity with China. (The Chinese invaded India through Arunachal in 1962.) This political isolation has meant that many Arunachali tribes have been able to maintain their traditional lifestyles free from foreign influences.

The food habits and preferences of different Arunachali tribes have been as strongly influenced by geography as by culture and religion. The food grown and eaten in the cold, mountainous region of Arunachal bordering Bhutan in the western part of the state is a world away from that eaten in the subtropical hills in the east. Yet some food practices are shared across all the tribes. More than two-thirds of Arunachal is under forest cover, and the region has retained a spectacular biodiversity of plant species. Many tribes still depend on forest produce for much of their everyday food and each has a deep knowledge of edible and medicinal plants. The leaves and flowers of plants I knew only as ornamentals, or weeds, such as *Crepis japonica*—considered to have antiviral and anti-cancer properties—and mountain ebony are eaten in Arunachal. Even Arunachalis, who are not reliant on forest produce for their daily food supply, continue to collect wild foods because they prefer these for taste and health. Almost all Arunachalis live in remote villages, primarily involved in agricultural work; in large part, the land is fertile and receives good rainfall. Agricultural products such as rice, millet, potatoes, soybean and ginger bring in most of the state's income and are important foods in the diet of Arunachalis.

Rice, wild/cultivated leafy greens and meat are the bases of daily meals, though the plate looks somewhat different in the mountainous regions. Religious practice varies amongst Arunachalis; they are Hindu, animist, Buddhist and Christian. Whichever creed they subscribe to, it influences what animal products are, or are not, consumed but they all enjoy meat, and between them they regularly eat pork, yak, duck, chicken, buffalo and fish. Beef, insects and game are other rarer additions to the cooking pot. (An acquaintance told me that he had been served leech curry by the Apatani people in central Arunachal.) The most popular method of cooking meat is to boil it with a simple flavouring of chilli, ginger and salt and perhaps garlic, or to stir-fry it with the same. Pork cooked with fermented bamboo shoot (*ekung*) is another common dish. To ensure that there is always some meat available, it is preserved by smoking over a fire. Vegetables are cooked in the same way with the same flavourings. All of this might sound a little 'plain' but remember this is food that is foraged or caught, or pulled straight from the garden, and the pigs have been fed on the residue from the production of local *opo/apung* (rice beer), so the flavour of meals is derived from freshness and quality not technique and additives. As mentioned, there are tribal and regional variations on this basic food pattern.

Bordered by Bhutan and the Tibet Autonomous Region, Arunachal's western region is one of isolated valleys and hills that rise north to the Himalayan peaks and glaciers of such a forbidding nature that they are largely unknown. Bhutan and Tibet have exerted significant influence over this area and the prevailing local culture is described as 'Tibetic'. The predominant religion is Tibetan Buddhism and the Buddhist monastery at Tawang is Asia's second largest and a major attraction in the region. The locals belong to the Monpa tribes; in physiognomy and dress, they look very like Tibetans and their food is similar to that eaten across the Trans-Himalayan region, much of which is of Tibetan origin.

Monpas grow and eat rice but it is not a grain that grows easily in the cold, dry climate that prevails in most of their territory. Barley (*bong*) is a traditional grain for the Monpa; it is ground into flour and used to make meat- or vegetable-stuffed steamed dumplings called *momo* or noodles cooked in soups and stews. Buckwheat (*Fagopyrum esculentum*) produces a grain-like seed but it is not a cereal. A relative of rhubarb (a native of China), it grows readily at high altitudes and is commonly eaten in the Trans-Himalayan region. The Monpa use ground buckwheat (*teeta phaphad*) to make a naturally leavened pancake called *khura* that is taken with tea, and noodles called *putang* that are cooked with chilli, soybean 'cheese' (*chhura*), meat or dry fish to create a thick soup stew called *putang thukpa*. This last dish is for special occasions but less elaborate versions of *thukpa* (noodle soups) are commonly eaten by the Monpa. Another common dish is made from buckwheat/millet flour mixed with water and cooked to form a thick, bland paste, perked up by adding strong-flavoured local cheese or fermented soybean and vegetables or pairing it with a chutney. The green leaves of the buckwheat plant are dried for use in the colder months when fresh green vegetables are not available and these are often cooked with small dried fish. *Khapse* is a fried bread made from the finely ground seed of the amaranth plant; the green leaves of this ancient food are also eaten.

The Monpa raise yaks for milk and use this to make butter, ghee and a cheese product called *chhurpi*. Hard chhurpi is made by curdling skimmed milk with whey and straining the curd off in bamboo containers. The curd is then cooked over a low fire until it forms a stringy mass, which is wrapped in cloth and pressed under a stone to force out any additional water and set to dry out above the kitchen stove for a month or so until it hardens in the smoke and develops a golden patina. In this form, chhurpi can be kept for some time and is therefore a way of preserving milk. Hard chhurpi is used to add flavour to cooked dishes (not unlike Parmesan cheese in the way it tastes and is used) and pieces are traditionally carried to nibble on over long journeys. Soft chhurpi is a type of cottage cheese made from the whey left over from making butter and its production ensures that no part of the milk supply is wasted. To make soft chhurpi, buttermilk is cooked until it forms into a soft whitish mass; this is put in muslin and hung up to drain. This form of chhurpi is made into soup, cooked with greens or eaten like a condiment with meals as it has a mild tangy flavour.

Rich Amritsari kulchas that are had for breakfast or lunch.

Forest mushrooms native to Himachal Pradesh.

A traditional wedding feast, or *dham*, taking place in Chamba.

A chai stall in one of the lanes of the old city in Varanasi.

A special sweet treat, *nimish*, in the freezing winter at a stall in Lucknow.

A lunch in a village in Madhya Pradesh, comprising dal, fruit chaat, potato–peas sabzi, carrot pickle and wheat roti with fresh butter.

Kebabs in Bihar: these delicious mutton kebabs are slow-cooked and finished with a coating of cream.

Banana flowers, or *mocha*, which are used in a variety of savoury dishes in Bengali cuisine.

A steamed cake in Puri, similar to the *chhena poda*, made with *chhena*, semolina, sugar and cardamom.

The distinctive pomelo salad in Majuli.

A monk's meal in Assam: *arum* cooked with dal, *pitika* of eggplant and potato flavoured with mustard oil, and stir-fried leafy greens.

Rice cakes in Meghalaya: the purple one is made with red rice, the brown one is made with gur, the yellow one has turmeric and the others are all made with ground white rice.

Pale-green silkworms and hornets' nests for sale in the main market in Kohima.

Freshly prepared cottage cheese, Sikkim.

The process of preparing the special Khamti *pasa*, Arunachal Pradesh.

Local snacks at a night market in Ahmedabad.

Seasonal gur for sale in Udaipur.

Evening bread being baked in a wood-fired oven in Panaji.

Freshly made rice bread at
The School Estate, Kodagu.

A shop selling sweets in Mysore,
including the famed *Mysore pak*.

Evening snacks on display at a
street-side stall in Madurai.

A halwa seller in Calicut.

Toddy being tapped from a
coconut tree in Kerala.

Sardines, prepared toddy-shop
cuisine style.

The Monpa eat yak meat but it is an uncommon treat as the animal is more valuable as a source of milk and labour. Yak butter is traditionally used to make the butter tea that the Monpa drink every day. (Cow milk butter is also used now.) This is prepared by churning butter and salt with prepared black tea; it is a brew that warms and sustains people all across the cold zone of the greater Himalayas. Alcoholic drinks brewed from millet, barley, rice or maize, fermented by the addition of locally made yeast called *pham*, are another source of internal warmth.

The cooler climate of the elevated region of western Arunachal supports the production of cool-climate fruits and vegetables such as apples, stone fruit, cauliflower, beans, carrots and cabbage. Much of the fruit is grown for sale, with a fair portion converted to easily transportable dried fruit; the vegetables are used in local cooking with cabbage, carrots and beans featuring as common additions to thukpa and vegetable stews.

There are broad genetic and religious affinities between the Monpa people and the tribes of eastern Arunachal such as Khamti and the Singpho (who also live in Assam), yet the food they eat is worlds apart. Geography and climate are obvious contributors to these culinary differences: the west, with its mountainous terrain and cool to cold climate, has restrained vegetation, while parts of the east are covered with lush subtropical jungle and tracts of fecund soil adjacent to the rivers that flow through the region before merging with the Brahmaputra. Neighbouring Myanmar has had more influence in eastern Arunachal than Tibet; Buddhists in this region tend to follow the Theravada sect of Buddhism that is the dominant practice in Myanmar.

The Khamti tribe of eastern Arunachal is believed to have migrated into the region from Myanmar, where there remains a strong Khamti community. Rice is the main food of Khamti cuisine but rather than boil this, as is the usual practice, they steam it over the fire in two brass vessels: one sits on top of the other, like a double boiler; the bottom pot is filled with water and steam from this rises into the upper pot that is filled with rice and lined with leaves to stop the rice falling through the perforated bottom. If more water is required, it is poured over the rice from top. The slightly cooled cooked rice is shaped by hand into large balls and wrapped in large leaves collected from the jungle to keep it warm until it is time to eat. Each person takes a wrapped rice ball and unfurls it, the leaf traditionally serving as a plate. If you need more rice, you take another ball.

The Khamti prefer to eat sticky rice and a popular method of preparing it is to fill bamboo hollows with local red rice that has been soaked in water

184 The Penguin Food Guide to India

and place these alongside the fire to gently steam away. When the rice is cooked, the hard outer sheath of the bamboo is carefully pared away to ensure that the paper-thin inner sheath remains adhered to it, holding it in a tubular shape and contributing to its nutty flavour. Rice cooked thus is called *kholam* and pieces of it are taken as a snack or eaten at breakfast with fried potatoes and grilled tomato chutney—a combination definitely worth getting out of bed for!

On special occasions, the Khamtis make a cold soup called *pasa*. Having witnessed the complicated preparation process, I understand why it's an occasional treat. To begin, fresh fish are cleaned and filleted and the frames skewered and roasted by the fire. The raw flesh is placed on a wooden board and pummelled with a heavy, sharp knife—or two swords working in unison, as was demonstrated to me—along with garlic, green chillies, ginger, coriander and local green herbs similar to basil and mint, until it melds into a green paste. In the meantime, a huge basket of wild greens (*khumpatt*) are pounded to a pulp in a huge wooden mortar and pestle; this is then mixed with water and the strained liquid is mixed with the herbed fish pulp. And while all that is happening, any meat on the barbequed fish frames is picked off and the frames soaked in warm water for a little time, after which the liquid from this is strained and added to the soup along with the small flecks of cooked fish scavenged from the frames. Pasa is bright green, unbelievably delicious and must be incredibly nutritious.

Everyday Khamti food is a little less demanding. They do not eat beef, but chicken, fish and pork are usually on the menu. Typical dishes are chicken stewed with bamboo shoots or stir-fried with garlic, ginger, red chilli and bamboo shoots; pork is cooked in similar fashion. Chicken is also marinated in garlic, ginger and fresh local herbs and stuffed into a bamboo hollow (or wrapped in banana leaf) and cooked over a fire. Fish is steamed or boiled with wild greens and bamboo to make soup. Mustard greens are boiled with green chillies and, when cooked, the water is drained off and fresh ginger or garlic stirred through, after which the pan is covered briefly to allow the flavour of these aromatics to impregnate the dish. Sweet potatoes and yams are steamed and eaten as snacks or breakfast; a special sweet dish (not unlike *kheer*) is made from milk, new rice, sweet potato, honey and coconut. Pumpkin, beans and banana flower are commonly used in Khamti cooking, and seasonal fruit such as bananas, oranges, pineapple, jackfruit, pomelo and star fruit are enjoyed on their own. There is a strong similarity between the foods eaten by the Khamti and other tribes in the region such as the Singpho.

Recommendations

Arunachal only recently opened its borders to tourists and the infrastructure is still developing. There are not many restaurants to be found outside the capital, Itanagar, and, even then, few serve local food beyond momos and thukpa (though you can get Punjabi and Chinese)—two food items you will easily find in dhabas across western Arunachal. **Hotel Donyi Polo** in Itanagar will prepare local dishes on request.

If you want to experience tribal cuisine in Arunachal seek out a culturally sensitive travel organizer such as **Help Tourism** (*see the Assam chapter*) and ask for a food-focused trip.

Khamti woman Antena Monglon runs **Maunglang Tour & Trade Camp** in the Mishmi Hills of eastern Arunachal. She can arrange for guests to learn about the culture and traditional food of the Mishmi people.

Antena
(M) 9954531131

FAIR-TRADE FISH

Having been exiled from Delhi, Arjuna, a hero of the Mahabharata, winds his way across the mainland to Manipur where he meets and falls in love with a local warrior princess. They marry and their son eventually becomes the king of Manipur. At the time the events described in the Mahabharata are said to have taken place (circa 3000 BC), the dominant tribe of Manipur, the Meitei, were followers of the Sanamahi faith and worshipped the sun and their ancestors rather than the Vedic gods. It was not until the fifteenth century when the king of Manipur became a Vaishnavite (follower of the Hindu god Vishnu) that the Meitei converted en masse to Hinduism. The Meitei make up 60 per cent of the population of Manipur but take up only 10 per cent of its land.

Manipur is shaped like a huge amphitheatre: an outer circle of rugged hills rings a fairly flat valley. Many rivers run off the hills into the valley and empty into the huge Loktak Lake, from which the Manipuris draw a huge supply of fish. The valley's temperate climate and rich soil produces an abundant harvest of rice, ginger, turmeric, oranges, pineapples, bananas, pulses, peas, cauliflower, tomatoes, carrots and pumpkins. This valley is the land that the Meitei live on and perhaps because it is so fertile, they have not needed to spread out (or could not, as they were hemmed in by the hills). The other two major tribes of Manipur, the Nagas and the Kukis, live predominantly in the forested hills.

Manipur shares its eastern border with Myanmar (earlier known as Burma); the Meitei and their next-door neighbours share an obvious genetic relationship. It is said that the Brahmins of Manipur look 'more Indian' than the rest of the population. This suggests that they came in from elsewhere, perhaps at the same time of the shift to Hinduism. The local language also changed at this time to Bangla. So adding those pieces of information suggests that Manipuri Brahmins likely came from Bengal. It has long been a tradition in Manipur to have Brahmin cooks, called Bamons, prepare food for festivals (a practice that has now been adopted by non-Hindu Manipuris), and if they were of Bengali origin then this would show up in their food; and as they were at the top of the social hierarchy, what they ate would have influenced common eating habits over time. The Meitei use more spices in their cooking than is usual throughout the north-east. Dishes are flavoured with mustard seeds, cumin, coriander, fenugreek, bay leaf and asafoetida. It is not a huge list of spices compared to that used in mainland cuisine and is on par with the spices used in Assam, and like that state it shows a Bengali influence. The Meitei are very fond of eating fish, but this is a preference they would have developed long before the Bengalis arrived.

The fishing community that lives on floating islands of the capacious freshwater Loktak—the largest lake in the north-east—supplies more than half of the fish eaten by the Manipuris. The other portion of aquatic protein comes from domestic and cooperative fish ponds. In the capital, Imphal, you can visit Ima Keithel to ogle the bounteous local catch. A collective of women has run this market since 1939. In that year, the women of Manipur revolted and forced the government to take action against monopolistic traders who overcharged for basic foods. To this day, Ima's women traders pride themselves on always charging fair prices.

Nga thongba is a Manipuri fish stew flavoured with mustard seeds, cumin, *tej patta*, red and green chillies, onion, garlic and tomato. It is eaten with rice. A daily Meitei meal would feature *nga ataoba*, fresh fish marinated with salt, red chilli powder and lime juice and fried in mustard oil until crisp; steamed rice; a vegetable stew called *kangsoi* and *iromba*, a chutney that in its classic form is prepared from mashed potato, green chillies and fermented fish called *ngari*. Variations on classic iromba are prepared by throwing into the mix other vegetables like green beans, banana stem or mustard leaves. Ngari is made from small fish fermented in earthen pots. It is used to add a piquant note to other dishes including *sinju*, a crunchy salad of finely chopped, raw green paw-paw, banana stem/flower or cabbage mixed with local herbs, sesame seeds and roasted chickpea powder; it is eaten as a snack or a meal side. Manipuris are particularly fond of a sinju made with finely chopped *yongchaak*, a flat, wing-shaped green bean, also known as 'stink bean' as it has a 'gassy' smell. To prepare it for eating, the outer skin of the bean pod is scraped off with a *yong-khat*, a U-shaped metal implement designed for this purpose. Manipuris are believed to have picked up their liking for pungent fermented fish, bamboo shoots and soybeans from their Burmese relatives. They also like their food hot, employing *u-morok* (*raja mirch*, 'the hottest chilli in the world') to add bite to dishes.

The Meitei relish fish and prawns, as well as meats such as pork and chicken, but they also prepare a wide range of vegetarian dishes, more commonly than all over the north-east. Vegetables grow well in the rich valley soil, and many homes have kitchen gardens, so the ingredients used in vegetable preparations tend to vary with the season. Common vegetarian dishes are *ooti* (dried peas cooked with indigenous soda, green onions and green chillies), *oosoi-ooti* (*ooti* with fermented bamboo shoot); *sana thongba* (paneer cooked in milk flavoured with tej patta and turmeric); and *pakode thongba* (small chickpea-flour fritters served in a sauce prepared from the liquid in which chickpeas have been cooked with asafoetida; this is the Manipuri version of the *kadhi* eaten throughout mainland India). Any dish described on a menu as thongba will be a thick stew. Kangsoi is an everyday dish prepared by boiling vegetables in various combinations with salt and chilli: leafy greens such as mustard leaves boiled with fermented soybeans is a popular format. A kangsoi is not always strictly vegetarian as ngari (fermented fish) or meat such as pork or chicken might be added. *Lomba*, an indigenous aromatic plant that tastes similar to lemongrass, is used to flavour chicken kangsoi. All tribes of Manipur collect local species of wild leafy greens and herbs, as well as cultivated ones such as mustard greens, to eat daily. These might be stir-fried with green chillies and turmeric, perhaps with some dried fish added. Like the French, Manipuris believe that cutting leafy greens with a knife will spoil the taste so these are always shredded by hand in preparation for cooking.

Up in the hills, the cooking pots of the Nagas and the Kukis feature beef, chicken, duck, fish or pork on a daily basis. A typical dish is *voska pok* (pork cooked with mustard leaves, indigenous soda, chilli and ground rice). Dried or smoked meat is often added to a dish of greens. In a traditional Naga kitchen, food is cooked in clay pots. Tea, coffee and cardamom are cultivated in the Manipur hills, though these are largely grown for commerce and sent out of the region. On the other hand, wild mushrooms that are collected from the hills in the wet season are relished and do not often get any further than local kitchens.

Meitei do like to finish a meal with something sweet, be it fresh seasonal fruit or a prepared dessert. *Chak-hao* is made from a local variety of unhulled sticky black rice cooked with gur. *Sanggom kheer* is rice cooked in milk with coconut, cardamom, tej patta and sugar.

Recommendations

....

Circumstances prevented my travelling in Manipur so I am unable to make first-hand recommendations. The Host restaurant in Imphal was recommended to me as a good place to eat Manipuri specialities such as iromba and nga thongba; after that, you are on your own!

Hotel Anand Continental, Khoyathong Road, Majorkhul, Thangal Bazaar
(0385) 2449422

....

BAMBOO AND BAI

On a map, the state of Mizoram looks like it has dripped off the larger north-eastern land mass and come to a stop, sandwiched between Myanmar (earlier known as Burma) and Bangladesh. The people of Mizoram are of several ethnic tribes, collectively referred to as the Mizo, and share linguistic and cultural similarities and an ancestry. Mizos migrated into Mizoram only 300-odd years ago from the adjacent Chin Hills of Burma (where they had landed much earlier after a longer migratory journey from north-west China). Having come from a hill area, the geography of Mizoram must have felt familiar: six or so hill ranges run parallel to each other across the length and breadth of the state separated by deep gorges run through by rivers. Much of the hill region of Mizoram is covered with forests of wild bamboo, and bamboo shoots are vital in Mizo cuisine.

While the abundance of bamboo in this part of India is a boon, in Mizoram it has deadly consequences. Every forty-eight to fifty years, the two main species of bamboo that grow in Mizoram flower—all at the same time—and begin to drop their seeds; these attract black rats, which then multiply to plague-level numbers from gorging on these high-protein seeds. Once they have finished off the seeds, the multitudinous rats head into the fields and lay to waste any crops they can find. In 1959, the rodents were so virulent in their destruction that it led to a serious famine in Mizoram (and a violent twenty-year-long rural rebellion). When the bamboo next flowered in 2003, the government was better prepared with emergency rice supplies and the payment of a bounty of two rupees for every rat caught. If any bamboo seeds can be gleaned before the voracious rodents set in, these are cooked and eaten as 'bamboo rice'.

Mizos predominantly live in villages and towns perched along the ridges of their hilly land. Just over half the population is involved in agricultural work (as per the 2011 Census, Mizoram has the second-highest urban growth rate in India, so there is likely to be a significant shift away from rural occupations over the next decade) and the state produces rice, maize, ginger and grapes for export and domestic supply. In the late nineteenth century and into the twentieth, the Mizos regularly 'raided' the tea gardens of Assam—a habit they likely inherited from their Chin ancestors who were also fond of a good raid on a neighbouring village. To counter this, the British effectively shut Mizoram off to outsiders, except for Christian missionaries, who managed to convert the Mizos, almost wholesale, to their faith. In modern Mizoram, life revolves around the church. Many Mizos attend a service every evening after dinner; most wear Western clothing; and English is widely spoken. Despite this, there is little Western influence on their traditional cuisine. The Mizos have a noted preference for spending money on clothing rather than food, but this does not mean that they do not eat well; their cooking practices show distinct Chinese and Asian influences. Indeed, the people of this part of the world have long known how to eat well without spending a lot of money.

The dish at the heart of every Mizo meal is *bai*. At its simplest, bai is made from shredded greens cooked in boiling water to which some salt is added: that's it, but there are numerous variations. Chunks of fresh or smoked pork or chicken and/or bamboo shoots can be added. It may be prepared from the stalk and leaves of cauliflower and potato, or from a melange of seasonals such as pumpkin, green beans, eggplant and ladies' fingers flavoured with chillies, a local herb called *lengmaster* (similar to basil in taste) and indigenous soda. In traditional Mizo cooking, little fat was used—there is none in bai—as the only fat available was lard, and since a typical family would only be able to raise and kill one or two pigs a year, access to fat was limited. Apart from boiling it, food is prepared by steaming, roasting over coals, smoking and fermenting. The Mizos ferment lard and use it to flavour dishes, a practice that likely arose in the days when they had to preserve fresh produce for long-term use. Mustard oil is now easily available and commonly used; fried foods are consumed more regularly than they would have been a generation or two ago.

Spices are used sparingly in Mizo cuisine. Flavour is first and foremost derived from the use of fresh seasonal produce enhanced with ginger, garlic, onion and chillies. Smoked or fermented meat, bamboo shoots, fish and soybeans (*bekang*) are regularly used for pungency. Leafy greens feature in every meal including various mustard leaves (*antam*), pumpkin leaves and bean leaves; these are also preserved by wrapping them in banana leaves and setting them in the smoke above the fire to ensure constant supply.

A typical Mizo meal is rice, bai, fried potatoes, colocasia or pumpkin, and a chilli-based chutney such as *rotuai* made from green chillies and fresh bamboo shoots. The Mizo are meat-eaters but do not necessarily eat it at every meal. If animal protein is to be added, it might take the form of boiled or fried fish, pork or chicken cooked in bai or in more complex preparations served as sides. These include *vawksa rep* (smoked pork cooked with bamboo shoots and a local herb called *anthur*) and *arsa pok* (chicken stewed with ginger, green chillies and rice). *Arsa buchiar* is a porridge-like dish made from whole chicken that has been roasted over coals then cooked with sticky rice and local herbs such as the celery-like *pardi* that is eaten as a complete meal. *Ar sawchiar* resembles chicken pulao and, like its mainland cousin, is flavoured with green and brown cardamom, black pepper and *tej patta*; the addition of a little rice beer to this dish is entirely a Mizo innovation. Snails, silkworms and dog meat are had as delicacies in Mizoram.

Mizoram is officially a dry state though rice beer is brewed and sold. Ironically, production of a wine sold under the brand name Zawlaidi, made from locally grown grapes—of the *Vitis labrusca* species—has recently begun in Mizoram (presumably for export). The Mizos drink a tea called *zu*; a cup of this beverage sweetened with jaggery is the traditional finish to a meal.

Recommendations

I was unable to travel to Mizoram so I cannot make any first-hand recommendations but Burra Bazaar, the main market in the capital Aizawl, was described to me by a Mizo 'expat' as a good place to see and taste local foods. There are piles of local vegetables, some familiar and some completely exotic, buckets of snails and stacks of whole dressed chickens ready to be taken home to make arsa buchiar. (If you see a stall with a picture of a cute puppy above it, don't mistakenly wander over thinking it's a pet shop: the price quoted on the sign is the cost per kilogram of *ui sa* or dog meat.) On the upper level of the market are simple food stalls serving local dishes such as bai made from green vegetables and fish served with rice and bamboo shoot.

FISH-FUELLED FLAVOUR

The small state of Tripura is bordered on three sides by Bangladesh. Since this country came into being, as Muslim East Pakistan after the partition of India in 1947, non-Muslim Bengali refugees have come into Tripura in such large numbers that they now outnumber the indigenous Tripuris four to one. This has shifted the culture and cuisine of Tripura towards a strong alignment with that of Bengal, but the beginnings of this transformation can be traced further back into the court of the Tripura kings. From the thirteenth century until 1949—when the state acceded to the Union of India—Tripura was ruled by the Manikya dynasty. This enduring lineage claims mixed descent from the Aryan Rajputs of north, west and central India, and indigenous Tripuris. (The last maharaja was highly decorated by the British for his bravery in combat and social reform, a trait that his genetic profile may have contributed to.) The Manikyas were great admirers of Bengal and made Bangla the language of their court. Such an act could only serve to usher in other associated aspects of the culture; once a significant influence comes into a royal court, it inevitably makes its way, over time, albeit in a modified version, into the wider society. This is not to say that the entire population of Tripura has embraced Bengali culture—far from it. The indigenous people, of which the main groups are the Tripuri and the Reang, retain their identities and practices, including food habits; even the food prepared in the royal kitchen has maintained a strong local identity. (Since the Tripuri are the largest indigenous group, and have given their name to the state, I am going to use this term to collectively refer to all the Tripura tribes.)

The landscape of Tripura runs from lush rolling hills and valleys in the north-east to flat plains along the western border. Ample forest cover remains in the hill area; there is good rainfall and distinct wet and dry seasons. The main commercial crop and the mainstay of the domestic diet is rice. Wild and cultivated leafy greens, bamboo shoots, chillies, ginger, potatoes, fish and pork are commonly eaten foods. An unsalted fermented-fish product variously called *shidol* or *berema*, is an essential item in the Tripuri kitchen. It is added to many dishes for flavour including *godhak*, a potage of vegetables (leafy greens, peas, beans, cabbage, bamboo shoot) that is boiled with green chillies, ginger and salt until soft, then mashed and flavoured with shidol. Godhak is eaten every day by the Tripuris and there are endless variations, depending on seasonal availability of vegetables and individual household preference. When the larder is bare, Tripuris cook shidol with chillies, onions and salt or indigenous soda and ginger, to create a simple dish eaten with rice. The small dried fish that shidol comprises are washed and gutted before use. Shidol has a strong aroma and distinct flavour and is usually an 'acquired taste', but anyone who enjoys the fish sauce used in dishes from Thailand to Vietnam should not find it unpleasant. (I substituted it when trying out Tripuri recipes as I didn't have access to shidol.)

Boiling combinations of meat and vegetables flavoured with chillies, ginger and salt to create a potage is the basic cooking method in the Tripuri kitchen. *Muya bai wahan chakhwi* is a more complex stew of bamboo shoots, pork, jackfruit, green papaya (both tropical fruits grow abundantly in Tripura), indigenous soda, turmeric and fresh lemon leaves thickened with a little ground rice. Chakhwi is a potage of bamboo shoots, green chillies, indigenous soda, onions, garlic, pork, fresh lemon leaves and shidol. A royal version of this dish is enriched with ghee and sesame seeds. Tripuris like to eat meat and fish and commonly add fresh or fermented bamboo shoots to dishes containing animal protein, or serve chutney prepared from bamboo shoots, chillies and shidol with meat dishes. A dish simply called *aa* is prepared from fresh fish cooked with green chillies, onions, garlic and shidol.

Despite the evidence I have just given, shidol is not omnipresent in Tripuri cuisine, and cooking methods extend beyond boiling. *Musadang* is a salad of cooked pork cubes tossed with dry-roasted green chillies, finely chopped ginger, onions, garlic and fresh green coriander leaves. *Mosodeng* is a side dish of coal-roasted potato and eggplant mashed with green chillies and onions. Pork or mixed vegetables marinated in ginger, onion, green chillies and coriander leaves stuffed in a bamboo hollow and roasted over coals is another traditional method to turn raw produce into a tasty meal. Rice is also prepared in a similar manner, wrapped in banana leaves. Tripuris do not have much of a sweet tooth, but the proliferation of shops selling Bengali sweets might serve to change that.

I was unable to visit Tripura and cannot make first-hand, or even second-hand, recommendations for places at which to eat Tripuri food. The only information I could glean about eating out in the capital Agartala is that restaurants serving Bengali-style food are numerous and popular. Hopefully, by the time the next edition of this book comes out, I will have made it to Tripura to find out for myself. If you travel there and find good places to eat Tripuri cuisine, let me know.

SIKKIM

SIMPLE PLEASURES

The small state of Sikkim lies nestled between Nepal to the west and Bhutan to the east, and sits south of the Tibet Autonomous Region. In the thirteenth century, Tibetans began to migrate into Sikkim; in 1642, Tibetan Phuntsong Namgyal was crowned the first king of Denzeng (the Tibetan place name for Sikkim) and he initiated a social system based on Tibetan Buddhism. Sikkim essentially remained a Buddhist kingdom until it was annexed to the Union of India in 1975. Not that the Buddhist rule of Sikkim hadn't been challenged, and dissipated, over that time. The Hindu Gorkhas of Nepal invaded in the eighteenth century, took over some territory and remained a constant threat. In the nineteenth century, the British assisted Sikkim to beat back the Nepalese but demanded, and received, control of the Darjeeling region as their price. They later took over the flat fertile land called terai along the southern border, cleared it of jungle and turned much of into tea gardens to work which they brought labourers from Nepal. Given the animosity between Nepal and Sikkim, the politics of this action has been questioned, the suggestion being that this was done to undermine Tibetan influence in Sikkim. If that were the British strategy, it might be seen to have worked since ethnic Nepalis have become the dominant population, although the culture and local religion are a blend of Nepali–Hindu and Tibetan–Buddhist influences.

Before the Tibetans came into Sikkim, it was inhabited by the Lepchas/Rongpas who, like many of the tribes of north-east India, originated from the area around the China/Burma border. The Rongpas called their land 'paradise', an epithet echoed in the alternative names given to Sikkim by the tribes arriving later. The Tibetans called it the 'land of hidden rice', the Limbu 'happy homeland' and the modern name of Sikkim is commonly translated as 'happy house'. In Hindu texts, the region is referred to as the garden of the god Indra. A visit will confirm the accuracy of these descriptors (though the rice is clearly visible nowadays). India's highest mountain, and the third highest in the world, Khangchendzonga (or Kanchenjunga), sits on the border between Nepal and Sikkim. It dominates the skyline (when it's clear enough to see) and sets the geographical tone of the Indian state: from its permanently snow-capped, uninhabitable, farthest perimeter of Khangchendzonga, the land of Sikkim unfolds towards the Indian mainland through less forbidding mountain ranges, deep river valleys and gentle hills. Little of the modern state is flat, and cultivating the land here is not easy (we will come back to this), but because of the tough terrain, swathes of Sikkim's forests are untouched and home to a wondrous diversity of plants, animals, butterflies and birds. While the state is famed for orchids, of more particular interest to the culinary-minded are the twenty-three species of bamboo, producing edible shoots, and over 300 types of wild ferns of which several are edible. The climate, away from the highest peaks, is temperate in the upper reaches and subtropical in the valleys with good annual rainfall; the overall picture is lush and picturesque.

The British were very particular about which parts of the Sikkimese kingdom they wanted because these were the easiest to access and turn to profit by cultivation. The indigenous tribes were made of sterner stuff though and created food-growing areas by terracing the hillsides and drawing water up from rivers or tapping into the rivulets running into these to supplement natural rainfall. Even today, most Sikkimese are involved in agrarian work—organic farming is enshrined in government policy—growing rice, maize, millet, barley, wheat, oranges, tea and black/brown cardamom. This spice grows luxuriantly in Sikkim hills and the state is India's largest producer of *Amomum subulatum*, the smaller of the two species of black cardamom. The pods grow in clusters around the base of the leafy plant; when fresh, these are dark purple and full of sweet, sticky seeds of a flavour that reminds me of the eucalyptus sweets I ate as a child, though the taste is popularly described as camphor-like. The pods darken when dried over a fire, a process that gives black cardamom its characteristic smokiness. Despite the prolific production of this spice, it is used sparingly in Sikkimese cuisine, flavouring only the occasional sweet rice dish and a local bread called *selroti*.

The ancient links between Tibet and Sikkim are evident in the cuisine of this state. Stuffed dumplings called momos and *thukpa*, both dishes of Tibetan origin, are commonly eaten in Sikkim. Thukpa is a broth in which different noodles and combinations of meat and vegetables are boiled to create a 'one-pot' meal. Different types of thukpa eaten in Sikkim are *gyathuk* made with thin noodles; *thenthuk* made with flat noodles 'pulled' off a rope of soft wheat-flour dough and dropped into boiling stock; and *bakthuk* made with small dumplings that look like Italian gnocchi. (Wheat-flour noodles used to produce thukpa are sometimes referred to as 'Tibetan pasta'.) Most Sikkimese live in a far less harsh environment than Tibet's though and are able to collect, grow and eat a wide variety of fresh seasonal vegetables.

As is common across the wider north-east of India, the Sikkimese eat a varied range of ethnic fermented foods. *Kinema* is a fermented soybean product made by adding a little wood ash to cooked and slightly crushed soybean, traditionally left to mature in fern-leaf-lined baskets. Kinema is typically cooked with tomatoes, onion, turmeric and chilli to make a thick 'dry' chutney; more water can be added to this mix to produce a wet 'curry'. I found the flavour of kinema less pungent than some of the other fermented soybean products I sampled throughout the north-east; it reminded me in texture of Japanese *natto*. Kinema is sold wrapped in leaf parcels in markets across Sikkim. *Masu* is the Sikkimese version of fermented bamboo shoot, made by stuffing bamboo hollows with fresh pared bamboo shoots, sealing the ends tightly with leaves and leaving it for a week or two. The Sikkimese pickle a range of vegetables to preserve these for use during the cold winter: *gundruk* is produced by wilting greens like mustard or cauliflower leaves in the sun, shredding and packing these tightly into earthenware jars and leaving these in a warm place for a week to ten days. At the end of this time, the naturally pickled leaves are sun-dried to remove any moisture and then stored. Gundruk is added to soupy dishes and eaten as a pickle. *Sinki*, the tap root of white radish, is fermented in a mud-lined pit for several weeks and the resulting product is added to soups or used as a pickle. A deep-fried, ring-shaped leavened bread called selroti is prepared from a fermented batter of rice and wheat flour mixed with fresh cream or butter, sugar and ground spices such as black cardamom, cinnamon, green cardamom or cloves. Selroti is a special-occasion food, usually eaten with a potato curry or meat dish. Fermented foods along with ginger, onion, garlic and chillies are the main flavouring agents of Sikkimese cooking.

Cows and yaks (these in higher altitudes) are kept as milch animals. Curd, butter, ghee and a cheese called *chhurpi* are made in homes from the milk of these animals. Two types of chhurpi are eaten in Sikkim: a hard type usually made with yak milk and a soft type made from buttermilk and similar to ricotta (*see the Arunachal Pradesh chapter for method*). Sikkimese cooks add soft chhurpi to soup or cook it with fiddlehead ferns—these are crisp and taste like asparagus—onion, green chillies and turmeric to produce a dish called *ningro*. *Chhurpi ka achar* is soft chhurpi mixed with pickled vegetables to make a snack.

If a Sikkimese a family is not of a vegetarian inclination, they will most likely have a pig penned in the yard, its girth gradually increasing owing to a daily feed of the fermented grain left over from making *chhang* (rice beer). Chhang is made from millet, rice, maize, barley, cassava, buckwheat or combinations of these. The most popular fermented beverage, *kodo ko chhang*, is made with millet that has been fermented with a local yeast starter (*khasung*) for several weeks in a fern-lined bucket. When the millet is ready, a portion is mixed with hot water in an elongated container called *tongba* and left to sit for at least five minutes. The alcoholic liquid is then sipped through a straw (to prevent the millet grains being 'drunk' as well); the same batch of millet can be topped up a couple of times with hot water before it loses its pleasant sweet–sour taste and potency. At this point, it becomes pig food. The Sikkimese are renowned for their fondness for chhang as drinking it helps them keep warm through the chilly, often freezing, nights experienced in their mountainous state. Of course, it is addictive too!

When a pig reaches an appropriate size, it is slaughtered and the meat offered to the rest of the village. The following week, another family butchers its pig and the supply of fresh meat is thus regularly available. Sikkimese like to cook pork with mustard greens or bamboo shoots. Some eat beef while goat meat and chicken are commonly eaten. *Pakku* is a local version of mutton curry mildly flavoured with cumin, cloves, coriander seeds, cinnamon, nutmeg and asafoetida; it is paired with selroti on special occasions. While this dish might be mild, Sikkimese do like the bite of chilli in their food and use a fiery local variety called *dalle khursani*, searingly hot at 100,000–350,000 Scoville units. A jar of this small, round fruit, preserved in salt, can be found in most Sikkimese kitchens.

In the wet months, the Sikkimese collect mushrooms from forests and eat them stir-fried with plenty of garlic, a little onion, turmeric and green chilli. When wild varieties are not available, cultivated ones are eaten. I was fascinated by the great number of cars that stopped to buy bags of mushrooms from roadside stalls along the route from Gangtok to Siliguri. It was early evening when I observed this and thought that perhaps they were taking the fungi home to make *phing*, a soup of noodles, meat, mushrooms and other seasonal vegetables, which is a regular dish in Sikkim. *Sinu* or stinging nettles (*Urtica dioica*) are also collected from the forests in Sikkim; the flowers of these are made into a soup and the leaves stir-fried and eaten as a vegetable.

Recommendations

. . . .

Gangtok, the hectic and sprawling capital of Sikkim, is a considerable contrast to the peaceful, slow-paced vibe of the rest of the state. Fortunately, the heritage **Netuk House Hotel** is a charming oasis that was once the home of a wealthy Sikkimese family. Its popular restaurant is renowned for its Sikkimese specialities such as bamboo-shoot curry, nettle soup and pakku. The handwritten menu changes regularly to reflect seasonal availability.

Tibet Road
(03592) 222374
www.heritagehotelsofindia.com
netukhouse@gmail.com

Snow Lion is considered to serve the best momos in Gangtok along with a pretty tasty thukpa. Try the pork momos.

Hotel Tibet, Paljor Stadium Road
9 a.m.–10 p.m.
(03592) 203468, 204962
www.hoteltibetgangtok.com

Taking a meal at **Café Culture** feels as if you are eating comfortably at home. The Sikkimese couple that runs this restaurant is focused on trying to preserve and promote local food traditions. Try the nettle soup, gundruk or ningro, and if it's on the menu, you must try the *chayote*-root curry. This starchy vegetable is the root of a green squash variously called alligator pear, vegetable squash or *choko*. (Under this last nomenclature, it plagued my childhood meals, though my adult self has grown to appreciate it and I was fascinated to eat its delicious roots.) This vegetable is only available in the winter and is a much-anticipated seasonal delicacy (*more below*).

Secretariat Road, Below Royal Palace
Noon–10 p.m. (Sundays closed)
(M) 9434805145
firefoxstay@gmail.com

The Sikkim government has enshrined ecotourism as policy. In practice, this means encouraging and promoting homestays as a preferred accommodation option for visitors to rural areas instead of building hotels there. For the culinary explorer, the great thing about this is that when you are in a homestay in Sikkim, meals are usually included and will likely feature local dishes, especially if you inform your host in advance that you are interested in sampling local cuisine.

I travelled to remote **Hee Bermiok** in west Sikkim to stay with a Limbu family on their small, self-sufficient farm, bordered by Varsey Rhododendron Sanctuary. Limbus are tribals indigenous to the Sikkim hills with genetic and cultural links to Nepal and Tibet. My host family earns an income by cultivating and selling brown cardamom, and the walk up to their home is through several acres of these lush leafy plants—yet this spice was not used in any of the wonderful dishes I ate with them. The open area surrounding their home was a model of typical village self-sufficiency. There was a pen with a large pig and another with several goats, both reared for meat; the chickens pecking around the yard were for eggs and meat; a hive of wild bees for honey; and a few cows for milk, which is used to produce curd, butter, ghee and fresh chhurpi. I had this soft cheese for breakfast, cooked with onion, local red chilli, turmeric and salt, along with a boiled egg straight from the coop and tea from the bushes out in the garden.

In the evening, we sat in the kitchen (kept cosily warm by the clay stove), drinking home-brewed chhang made from a mixture of millet and wheat. As I contentedly sipped away, my hostess produced a meal of traditional dishes. Local pork was cooked with ginger, cumin, garlic, turmeric, a little mustard oil and fresh mustard greens. Chicken—that until an hour or so earlier had been an inhabitant of the yard—was cooked with fenugreek, cumin, red chilli, garlic and ginger and pieces of chayote; this member of the gourd family has a firm texture and is quite bland, but it soaks up the flavours of the food it is cooked with and becomes quite moreish in this dish. The chayote vine is prolific in Sikkim; when it has done fruiting for the year, the root is dug up and eaten. A stew of chayote root cooked with nigella seeds, onion, turmeric and red chilli was also prepared for me. Outside in the garden were tamarillo trees heavily laden with ripe fruit, several of which were roasted in the coals, skinned and ground with black sesame, red chilli, ginger, garlic and a local herb called *ching* (*Heracleum nepalense*; a member of the carrot family with a lemony–peppery flavour), to produce a tangy chutney. To visit the Hee Bermiok homestay, contact **Help Tourism** (www. helptourism.com).

The homestay programme run by the community-based Kewzing Tourism Development Corporation in the Buddhist village of **Kewzing** in south Sikkim was highly recommended to me. Time constraints prevented me from making a visit but you might like to make a trip there to sample the Tibetan-influenced food of the Bhutia tribe. Find out more at **www.sikkimfoundation.org/ village_home_stay**.

WESTERN INDIA

DESERT COOKS

If you have not visited India before and your imagined vision of it includes elaborately moustached men in towering turbans; isolated atmospheric hilltop forts; pink-and-green fairy-tale palaces; and camel caravans passing through a desert landscape, then it is actually Rajasthan you have in mind. The state of Rajasthan, 'the land of kings', was created in 1949 by the union of twenty-two feudal kingdoms once founded by Rajputs, a Hindu warrior caste. There is no mention of the Rajputs in historical records before the fifth century AD: they themselves claim to descend from the sun and moon or, alternatively, from the heroes of Hindu epics, such as Lord Ram. A somewhat less exalted explanation for their later appearance in Indian history is that they were invaders from Central Asia or an indigenous martial tribe given a place in the Vedic social order to control them. By the turn of the first millennium, they were the prominent rulers in north India and thus largely in the frontline when the Muslim invasions of India began. The Muslims might have eventually triumphed over them—with some exceptions—but the Rajputs put up a good fight and their valour won them the admiration of the Mughal emperors. They allowed the Rajputs to continue to rule their kingdoms, provided they paid taxes and tributes into imperial coffers. When Emperor Akbar married a Rajput princess—and several others later—it paved the way for Rajputs to come into Mughal courts; in doing so, they took influences from it back into their own royal domains. These influences are also evident in the princely cuisine of Rajasthan.

Like the Mughals, the Rajputs were enthusiastic meat eaters; when they were out on campaign, a wild animal such as a deer would be an instant source of food, cooked quickly over a fire. Not only did this provide the necessary sustenance but the Rajputs believed that eating wild meat increased a man's virility, courage and strength—all important qualities on the battlefield. A dish developed by Rajputs out in the field is *lal maans* or *jungli maans*, essentially meat cooked with ghee, salt, whole red chillies and a little water, all ingredients easily procured from any village. As the Rajputs did not usually carry frying pans with them when they headed out to fight, meat was cooked on stones heated in a fire. *Maans ke suley* is a slightly more complex Rajput dish of barbequed meat—said to have been invented by the Mewar Rajputs of Udaipur—made by flattening meat pieces with the back of a knife, marinating these in a paste of onion, garlic, red chillies and *kachri*—a powder made from dried cucumber used as a tenderizer—threading the pieces on to skewers, and cooking them over hot coals.

It was not until they were safely ensconced in their forts and palaces though that the Rajputs had the leisure, and the kitchen staff, to experiment with blending new inspiration into their court cuisine. Eventually, their cooking took on the hallmarks of Mughal cuisine: the liberal use of onion and garlic and spices like cardamom, cinnamon and cloves; meat cooked in korma style with rich ingredients such as curd, cream, *khoya* and nuts; and elaborate biryanis and pulaos. The Rajputs added *kewra* (screw-pine essence) and rose water to dishes but in a restrained manner; they did not take on the Mughal predilection for intensely perfumed dishes nor their penchant for sweetness in food. The Rajputs also used more chillies than the Mughals, and they were very fond of eating wild boar. Rajasthani dishes such as *safed maans* (meat cooked in a sauce of white poppy seeds, coconut milk, cashews and curd); *malai maans* (meat cooked in cream) and *mussallam badam–pista ka salan* (meat cooked with almonds, pistachios, cream, curd and a long list of spices) all show Mughal influence; in fact, the name of the last proclaims that it is a Muslim dish.

They might have stopped fighting battles some time ago but Rajput men have retained a fondness for shikar. The drier months were considered the best for hunting; the drier food of the animals is believed to make their meat more flavourful. Meat from animals caught in greener areas was considered of inferior taste and quality; even now, meat from animals farmed in the desert areas of Rajasthan is considered to be the tastiest, and that coming from the uber-dry area around Bikaner to be the best of all. Hunting is effectively banned in modern Rajasthan, with most animals protected by law, but permits can be obtained to shoot vermin such as rabbits. A wild rabbit might be cooked in a pit dug in the ground, heated by a cow-dung fire, wrapped in a layer of roti and another of banana leaves. Apart from the occasional rabbit, modern Rajputs and other Rajasthani carnivores have to make do with mutton and chicken.

The Rajputs have never been a majority population in Rajasthan but as the traditional rulers and landowners, they have had significant influence on Rajasthani culture. In modern Rajasthan, they play significant roles in the tourism industry. This is in part because they own the forts, palaces and hunting lodges that have been so successfully turned into hotels and guest houses throughout the state. And partly because they are hospitable by inclination and elegant hosts. As a visitor to modern Rajasthan, you are likely then to encounter Rajput-style cuisine in hotels and restaurants.

There are two distinct cuisines in Rajasthan, that of the Rajputs and that of the rest. Rajasthan is India's largest state by area but its population density is among the lowest because the Thar Desert, one of the driest places on earth and one of the harshest inhabited environments in India, covers a large part of the state. In its most arid parts, Rajasthan is sand-covered dunes (the ones you might have pictured being traversed by camels); its more hospitable regions are semi-arid and covered with thorny scrub. The average annual rainfall in its western part is 313 mm, the lowest in India. The southern and eastern areas receive more rain—675 mm on average, a total that is the second lowest in India—and are more fertile, but the lack of water in Rajasthan is a huge problem. The state regularly suffers terrible droughts and this has had a major influence on shaping its cuisine.

Brochure-perfect forts and palaces of Rajasthan serve merely as the backdrop to daily life. The state is one of India's poorest and a vast majority of its population lives in villages, growing crops (if the climatic conditions support this) and/or raising livestock. Milk from these animals plays an important role in traditional Rajasthani cooking. Fresh milk, butter, ghee—and the *chhachh* (buttermilk) left over from making this—are used extensively to replace precious water. A glass of buttermilk is had with meals and dal is often cooked in buttermilk to make the ubiquitous *kadhi*. I was given conflicting opinions about the use of ghee in everyday Rajasthani cooking: some people said it was used liberally to add moistness to food in the absence of water, others that it was used sparingly because most villagers could not afford to use it otherwise. My experience is that when traditional Rajasthani food is served in commercial settings, it is most often enriched with ample ghee and what is eaten at home is generally lighter—though people might prefer to add more ghee or butter to their food if they had the means or were not subject to modern health concerns—and that liberal use of ingredients such as ghee is saved for special occasions. As restaurants tend to replicate festive foods, the dishes on offer are usually rich and/or more elaborate. Dishes enriched with ghee and other dairy products are typically spiced with flavourings such cumin, asafoetida, *ajwain* (carom seeds) and ginger as these are believed to aid digestion. Onions, garlic and red chillies are the most commonly used ingredients in Rajasthani cooking, and for poor villagers these might be the only flavourings that they can afford to use on a regular basis. An everyday food item is *lehsun ki chutney*, a relish prepared from garlic cooked in a little ghee and ground with red chillies that paired with roti can constitute a meal for some rural families. Despite the extensive use of red chillies, Rajasthani food is not notably 'hot'; I was told that this was because the use of ghee counteracts the bite of chilli; or it may be that the variety of chilli used is a mild one.

Creativity often arises from adversity and Rajasthani cooks have been ingenious in creating a diverse cuisine from limited ingredients. This is nowhere more evident than in their use of dal. Pulses, or dal, have been grown in Rajasthan since Harappan times and have long been the predominant source of protein for many Rajasthanis. The state is a major producer of chana (chickpeas)—a plant that can withstand drought conditions. *Besan* (flour ground from dried chickpeas) is used extensively to produce a wide range of foods, including *gatte* (soft dough of besan, ghee or curd, baking powder—a modern addition—red chilli, cumin and salt, rolled into sausage-like forms, cut into pieces and boiled). Cooked gatte can be tempered with garlic and chillies, coated with a sauce, used as an addition to kadhi or deep-fried and eaten crisp. *Pittor* is a thick, cooked paste of besan, green chilli and onion that is eaten scooped up with roti. Besan is used for flavour, texture and thickening in kadhi; to make bread (*missi* roti) and create sweets such as besan barfi. Besan *chukki* is made from a crumbled besan *baati* (*see below*), that is cooked with ghee, khoya and sugar syrup to form a fudgy confection. In Marwar (Jodhpur region), a similar sweet called *dal laddu chakki* is made by cooking besan with almonds, khoya, ghee and sugar.

Other dals are just as creatively employed. *Mangoris* are small sun-dried dumplings made from either moong or *urad* dal, and these are often cooked in a sauce made of besan and curd. *Papad*—usually eaten as a crunchy accompaniment to meals—made of besan and/or urad dal are also cooked in a simple sauce of onion, garlic, chilli, coriander tempered with asafoetida and cumin. This dish is called *papad sabzi*; sabzi is the Hindi word for 'vegetable', and it is common in Rajasthan for dal-based dishes to be referred to as vegetable dishes possibly because of the lack of fresh vegetables (*more below*). Ground moong dal is cooked with ghee and sugar syrup into a halwa and a batter of ground urad dal is used to make *imarti* (a syrupy sweet similar to a jalebi but shaped like a crown).

As in the rest of India, dal is also made into various spiced potages, customarily eaten with *baati* (bread shaped like a ball and cooked on coals). Baati is usually made from wheat flour, ghee, salt and a little water although other flours such as besan can also be used. Cooked baati is crushed slightly and drizzled with ghee—if not to be eaten immediately, soaked in ghee—and paired with a bowl of dal: pieces of the baati are broken off and used to scoop up the dal. As baati is very dry, it can be kept for some time and was often taken along on long journeys or hunting expeditions as sustenance. The same dough that is used for baati is also fried, ground into a powder and mixed with jaggery or sugar, dried fruit, nuts and cardamom to create the sweet dish called *churma*. *Dal–baati–churma* is traditionally served at Rajasthani weddings, and it is pretty likely that you will encounter it in restaurants that serve Rajasthani cuisine.

Rajasthan is a major producer of millet, barley, sorghum and corn—the latter grown in the south of the state, which has more water—and all these grains have been used in Rajasthan historically, ground into flour and made into a variety of rotis. Flour from these grains is much harder to work with as they contain little or no gluten; indeed, as gluten-rich and supple wheat flour has become more readily available, the tradition of making breads from these (healthier) grains has ebbed. *Soyta* is a popular winter dish of meat cooked with grains, so you have *bajre ka soyta* (meat cooked with millet) or *makki ka soyta* (with corn).

Rice, because it requires so much water to grow, was till recently a truly luxurious food eaten only by royalty. Extensive irrigation work and the creation of large dams in southern Rajasthan have now altered the use of land from traditional crops to rice, and rice has become a more usual food for Rajasthanis. Irrigation works have not just allowed rice to be grown in Rajasthan; access to more water has also allowed the state to become a leading producer of canola, mustard, cumin, coriander, fenugreek and soybeans. This has made some farmers prosperous yet many smaller farmers, who well understood how to manage limited water, are losing out as the water table drops—as irrigators draw on it more extensively—and cannot afford to dig deeper wells to access it.

Natural lack of water and the extreme heat of Rajasthan made it difficult to cultivate vegetables, so fresh produce did not play significant roles in the traditional Rajasthani diet. In villages, gourds, cucumbers and eggplant might be grown around the village well in the cooler winter but the brevity of this season did not allow for much more than a minimal intake of fresh produce. To get to eat some sort of green food more regularly, the green leaves of other hardier plants such as chickpeas, poppies and fenugreek were collected, sun-dried and stored for use throughout the year. The fruit and beans of two wild plants, indigenous to the Rajasthan desert region, are also collected, sun-dried and cooked as *ker sangri*: *ker* are small berries that grow on low thorny scrub and *sangri* are the dried, bean-like pods of the tree *Prosopis cineraria* (member of the pea family) that grows wild in the desert. To prepare ker sangri, the dried fruit and beans are soaked in water to reconstitute them, then cooked in a gravy of ghee, onion, garlic, curd, *amchoor* (green-mango powder), dry red chillies, ajwain, asafoetida and fenugreek. This dish is tangy and rich and is customarily served at weddings. Dehydrating foods in the sun puts the arid climate to good use, allowing these to be stored and intensifying their flavours. There is now so much more fresh produce grown—due to modern hydro interventions—or trucked into Rajasthan that the need to rely on dried foods has diminished, yet Rajasthanis retain a taste for these foods. In fact, as dishes such as ker sangri become less of a necessity and disappear from home kitchens, they are getting increasingly fashionable in restaurants. An unusual Rajasthani dish is *dana methi ki sabzi* (fenugreek seeds cooked with jaggery, amchoor, dates, asafoetida, red chilli, fennel and cumin). Fenugreek is ordinarily used as a spice, and judiciously at that as it is quite bitter, yet the sweet-and-sour flavours in this dish balance out the bitterness. Amchoor has long been used in Rajasthan to add tartness and acidity to dishes, but with cheap tomatoes coming into the state from Punjab, these are frequently used to replace it. Pickling food has been another important way of preserving fresh produce and meat, and a simple meal or snack might consist of fresh roti eaten with pickles.

Sweet items are often eaten at the start of a meal in Rajasthan and it is common to nibble on something sweet throughout the meal; this might be as simple as a piece of gur. Since sugar cane is not a traditional crop in Rajasthan, sugar-based foods are therefore expensive to produce and have not been everyday items. That is not the case now and Rajasthanis enjoy sweet foods and sweet tea as much as any other Indian. Laddoo, a round sweetmeat, is the most common traditional sweet; at its simplest, laddoo is made from besan, or crushed roasted roti, mixed with sugar and ghee and pressed by hand into a ball. Jaggery is often used to make laddoos as the sticky molasses in it hold the laddoo together. *Gond ke laddoo* are made by mixing tree resin/gum (gond) with ghee, semolina, sugar and *charmagaz*, a mixture of the seeds of pumpkin, musk melon, watermelon and cucumber. It is made in winter in Rajasthan as it is believed to be warming, and is also given to pregnant women and taken to relieve backache. Laddoos are dry and keep for some time, so they can be used when travelling. *Lapsi* is made from broken wheat roasted in ghee and cooked in sugar syrup with cardamom/saffron, coconut and nuts; a little fenugreek may be added to temper its sweetness. Making lapsi is like making halwa, and the ingredients are (or certainly would have been) expensive, suggesting that this dish originated in a royal kitchen, most likely in the Marwar family palace of Jodhpur. Another sweet said to have originated in Jodhpur is *mawa kachori* (a pastry envelope stuffed with a mixture of khoya—aka mawa—crushed nuts and cinnamon); a small hole is made in the top and sugar syrup poured in. This decadent treat smacks of wealthy origins. *Ghevar*, a confection that belongs to Jaipur, is made from wheat-flour batter poured into boiling ghee at intervals to form a light, honeycomb-textured mass that is later either soaked in sugar syrup or—in view of modern dietary restrictions—dusted on top with castor sugar, albeit liberally.

A Rajasthani man I interviewed about the food of his home state told me that the *rasagulla* was a traditional Rajasthani sweet. This confection actually belongs to east India but I think I can explain why he might believe otherwise. There is a very successful company called Haldiram's that runs a chain of sweet shops. A Marwari family from Bikaner started and owns this company, which has played a significant role in popularizing the rasagulla across India by selling it in stores. Bikaner itself is renowned for dried savoury titbits, collectively called *namkeen*, eaten as a snack throughout India. The complete lack of moisture in the air in Bikaner makes its climate ideal for drying food and is said to give the namkeen made there a distinct taste and character that is superior to that made anywhere else in India. Haldiram's started out by making namkeen and still specializes in it.

Marwaris are a very successful trading community in India and hail from the Marwar region of south-western Rajasthan, of which Jodhpur is the main city. A large part of Marwar is desert and has not been home to a lot of agriculture or industry, but it lay on an overland trade route between the coastal ports of Gujarat and Delhi, and Marwaris developed into shrewd but principled traders—and tax collectors. When traffic on these routes began to dwindle in the nineteenth century, Marwari merchants moved out to places such as Bombay, Madras and Calcutta (which is where they discovered the rasagulla) and turned their well-honed business sensibilities to banking and large-scale commerce. It was in these cities that the Marwaris really succeeded—a number of them now rank among the wealthiest people in the world—but they missed the taste of familiar foods. At this time, Indian food would have been almost exclusively regional, and Haldiram's began to provide them with some of the foods they missed.

As a traditional Bania (trading) community, the Marwaris are strict vegetarians, as are more than 60 per cent of Rajasthanis—the second-highest population of vegetarians in India after Gujarat. This high vegetarianism is in part economic: while many villagers raise animals they cannot afford to eat them since they are more economically valuable as ongoing sources of milk than finite meals of meat. There are more intrinsic influences at work in this communal vegetarianism though. It was not only goods that passed along the ancient trade routes that ran through Rajasthan from Gujarat but ideas, particularly religious ones, as well. The Bania communities of Gujarat were strongly influenced by Jain and Vaishnavite philosophy (*see pp. 222–24*), both of which espouse strict vegetarianism. The economic success of the Banias made them very influential and their assertion of vegetarianism an important spiritual practice inspired others in the wider community. There are similarities between the cuisines of Rajasthan and Gujarat though the sharp economic contrast between the two states—the latter is one of the most prosperous in India—shows in the food. As a rule, Rajasthanis do not enjoy the diverse and abundant range of foods eaten in Gujarat, their food generally being more robust and straightforward. This may also reflect the staunch conservatism of Rajasthan, as the state has not been so open to external influences as Gujarat. The fact that it is landlocked without any ports may have historically determined this as there just were not many different people coming into the region.

A typical breakfast for a Rajasthani villager would be roti with pickles or lehsun ki chutney, butter and buttermilk and/or milky tea. *Poha* (flattened rice) cooked with spices is popular, particularly in bigger towns where people might take their breakfast (or morning meal) from a street vendor on the way to work. Lunch and dinner will be similar with a vegetable dish—which in a village might include 'vegetables' such as papad or gatte—dal or kadhi and roti. The more affluent would have two or three vegetable dishes, a selection of pickles and chutney, plain curd, a sweet item and a glass of buttermilk. If meat is eaten, a meat dish would be included. A Rajasthani meal ends with a digestive called *churan*, a selection of sweet, sour and salty items made from dried *amla* (Indian gooseberry), ginger, pomegranate, mango, tamarind, plum and other fruits processed with cumin, asafoetida, sugar and salt.

Recommendations

Tourism is a successful and significant industry in Rajasthan and there is an overwhelming choice of places to visit, stay in and eat at. Rajasthani tourism operators and restaurants that cater to visitors have been remarkably successful in giving visitors 'what they want to eat', which often means the standard Indian restaurant menu or Continental-style food. Fortunately, the more astute have begun to see that local food is attractive to visitors and more places are offering Rajasthani cuisine. You still need to exercise discrimination with these, though, as some operators 'adjust' even this to suit the tourist palate. The dishes available will tend to run to those vegetarian ones described in this chapter—meat dishes are not common unless you eat in Rajput-run places—but hopefully you will also find, because you will be looking, seasonal and regional specialities as you travel around.

Over time, more regional/local dishes will find their way on to menus as visitors like you show an interest in eating them. My tip in choosing authentic places to eat in Rajasthan, apart from the recommendations here, is to look for smaller, family-run, converted heritage homes, palaces (yes, these come in small sizes too), hunting lodges, camps and guest houses that offer meals. Many grand palaces offer spectacular royal Rajasthani feasts, at equally spectacular prices, but my personal experience of these is that unless you are of Liz Hurley's milieu, there is a tendency to treat potential customers with disdain. For instance, I was very keen to eat at the restaurant in Umaid Bhawan Palace hotel in Jodhpur as I had been told they serve excellent local cuisine, but I was treated in such a condescending manner—wrapped in icy 'charm'—that I decided I would rather take the 3000-plus rupees that it would have cost me and spend it elsewhere in Jodhpur.

JODHPUR

Jodhpur is located on the eastern fringe of the Great Indian Desert and is a very dry area. Nowadays, though, the market brims with fresh vegetables, thanks to the development of artificial water catchment in the region. My Jodhpuri guide told me that even though tomatoes had become easily available, and were inexpensive, Jodhpuris did not consider that they endowed the food with a 'good taste' and preferred to stick with traditional souring agents such as amchoor. Millet is the usual grain of the region. Millet roti eaten with chutney and millet porridge, had with curd in the morning and with milk in the evening, are common fare in the villages around Jodhpur. The local version of soyta is meat cooked with millet but it is considered a dish for the wealthy, a 'palace dish'. Jodhpur is the home of mawa kachori and the best place to try it is **Mishri Lal Hotel** in the central bazaar. While you are there, you can try another Jodhpuri speciality called *mogri kachori*, a savoury pastry envelope stuffed with cooked moong dal and onion.

Clock Tower, Nai Sarak
8 a.m.–10 p.m.

Shahi Samosa sells Jodphuri-style *mirchi bada*, a large chilli—which is more like a pepper and not particularly hot—stuffed with a spiced potato mixture, dipped in besan batter and deep-fried.

Clock Tower, 95/B, Nai Sarak

You will receive a friendly welcome at **Haveli Inn Pal** in central Jodhpur. The family-run hotel is housed in an eighteenth-century haveli and the rooftop dining area is evocatively shadowed by Jodhpur's star attraction, the Mehrangarh Fort—the largest in Rajasthan. Look in the other direction and you will find yourself in direct line of sight between the fort and Umaid Bhawan Palace (which looks quite amicable from this distance) with the famed blue-washed houses of Jodhpur spread out below you. The menu is not immediately full of Rajasthani culinary promise, but ask for local cuisine and you shall receive. The dishes I ate included a kadhi flavoured with fenugreek, green onions, chana and neem leaves; *badi* (sun-dried lentil dumplings made from ground moong and *moth* dal) cooked in a gravy of onion, garlic, cumin and curd; a vegetable dish of fresh turmeric cooked with spices; raita tempered with onion, tomato and cumin cooked in ghee; and lapsi, made of wholewheat, jaggery syrup, shredded coconut and fennel seeds, served hot. Lapsi is always served at weddings and auspicious occasions in the Jodhpur region. As all religious rituals in the area start with the breaking of a coconut, this is an essential ingredient in a celebratory lapsi: wealthier families serve it sprinkled with dried fruit and an additional drizzle of ghee on top.

Opposite Lake Gulab Sagar, Near Clock Tower
(0291) 2612519
www.haveliinnpal.com

Roughly halfway between Jodhpur and Jaipur is the secluded and blissfully peaceful **Chhatra Sagar**. This luxurious tented camp overlooks a man-made lake that was created in the nineteenth century when a local nobleman, Thakur Chhatra Singh, dammed a seasonal stream to create a reservoir to capture and store the monsoon rains. It was expected of the Rajasthani ruling class, the Rajputs, to undertake work to create more permanent water supplies for their subjects. Building the lake at Chhatra Sagar nearly bankrupted Thakur Chhatra Singh, but his efforts turned a once-desolate area into a fertile oasis; provided local people with a stable water supply; and bequeathed his grandchildren a unique place in which to open an exclusive resort. 'Sustainable' and 'local' are not just empty words at Chhatra Sagar: much of the food served here is sourced from the camp's own garden—which is fed by water channelled from the lake—or from local producers and only goat meat is used as this is the traditional meat of the region. The staff are all either family members or come from the surrounding villages. The meals served at Chhatra Sagar are not solely focused on traditional Rajasthani fare but are more representative of the Rajput heritage of the Singh family. Rajputs prefer to marry within their own tribes, but they are careful to keep a healthy genetic distance between clans. It is common for Rajputs to marry across India, for example a Rajput girl from Odisha might marry into a Rajput family in Rajasthan or a Rajput girl from Rajasthan will marry into a Gujarati Rajput family, to maintain this distance. In traditional Rajput culture the girl goes to live with her in-laws and she will often influence the food that is prepared in her new home. Thus a typical meal in a Rajput home might include elements from all around India. This is the case at Chhatra Sagar where the extended family ties run across several Indian states and the food served here is of pan-Indian home-style cooking with the focus on quality seasonal produce, and there is always at least one Rajasthani dish at a meal. During my visit I ate badi with spinach; *bajra roti* and *makki ki roti*; a 'white' dal made with skinned urad dal and white spices such as fennel, curd, garlic, coriander and onions; local potatoes cooked with ginger; and *makhane ki kheer*, the starchy white seeds of the water lily—also known as fox nuts or gorgon nuts—cooked in milk and sugar.

You can take a cooking class at Chhatra Sagar with an advance request for such. They will also take you on a tour of the garden and a neighbouring village to see local food production.

Pali, Marwar
(M) 9414123118
harsh@chhatrasagar.com
www.chhatrasagar.com

JAIPUR

Jaipur was anointed the capital of Rajasthan in 1956, and it hasn't stopped growing ever since. At the centre of its sprawling expanse is the 'Pink City', the old walled quarter surrounding the royal palace complex. The streets and lanes of the bazaar area here are truly chaotic but worth braving to visit one of Rajasthan's most stalwart restaurants, **Laxmi Mishthan Bhandar** or LMB. Sadly, recent renovations have removed the fabulous original 1950s' decor and turned the dining room into something resembling a nondescript shopping-mall joint; luckily, they haven't done the same to the menu. The food served in the restaurant is clearly aimed at the tourist market but the Rajasthani thali they serve is as good as it was when I first tried it some fifteen years ago, and it is quite enormous with a good mix of standard and seasonal dishes. On any day you can expect the thali to comprise two different types of baati, ker sangri, kadhi, *boondi raita*, a couple of sweets including besan churma, and papad. Alongside all this will be several seasonal dishes, which in winter might include *dana methi kishmish*—fenugreek seeds cooked with raisins—and cauliflower cooked with asafoetida, turmeric and red chilli. All the food served at LMB is cooked in ghee and is pure vegetarian. If you don't fancy a thali you can order all the dishes separately. Ghevar is sold in the adjoining LMB sweet shop; you will also find it available at numerous sweet stalls out in the bazaar.

Johari Bazaar Road, Biseswarji
(0141) 2565844, 2578845, 2565846
8 a.m.–11 p.m. (7 days)
info@hotellmb.com
www.hotellmb.com

Diggi Palace has a small offering of local dishes including a tasty if standard Rajasthani thali and lal maans. They also offer Rajasthani cooking classes and the beautiful garden is an absolute haven in Jaipur, and a great place to enjoy a local beer or a glass of Indian wine.

Shivaji Marg, C Scheme
(0141) 2373091, 2366120
reservations@hoteldiggipalace.com
www.hoteldiggipalace.com

If you wish to stay in a real home with a charming family, you might like **Sneh-Deep** guest house. You can also eat meals there and enjoy genuine home-style Rajasthani cooking while sitting out on the rooftop.

B-33 Sethi Colony, Govind Marg
(0141) 2604570, (M) 9314880887
snehdeepguesthouse1@gmail.com
www.snehdeep.com

An hour's drive south of Jaipur is a theme-park-cum-restaurant **Chowki Dhani**, reputed to serve excellent and authentic Rajasthani village-style food. I was not able to pay a visit but it might be worth investigating as several of my culinary literate contacts recommend it to me.

www.chokhidhani.com

BUNDI

The walled town of Bundi is located in the greener south of Rajasthan. While the town is relatively untouched by tourism, there is very little distinct local food to be found in the town's commercial eating establishments. One of the nicest places in which to stay and eat is the small family-run heritage haveli **Bundi Vilas**. You take your meals on the terrace here with the fort walls and ramparts looming immediately in front of you (which are lit up at night). All the food is home-made light, vegetarian cuisine and a meal might include stuffed eggplant, dal, potato cooked with garlic, onion and turmeric, crisp vegetable pakoras and mango pickle made from local mangoes.

Opposite Motimahal Ravla Chowk, Balchandpura
(0747) 5120694
www.bundivilas.com

UDAIPUR

Udaipur became the capital of the princely state of Mewar in the mid-sixteenth century. The ruling Sisodia family has records of descent going back 1400 years making them the oldest family in the world. The Sisodias are regarded as the ultimate Rajput dynasty as they did not capitulate to the continued attack of the Mughals who wanted the kingdom to create a clear route through to Gujarat and the fertile Malwa district. The great Marwar hero Rana Pratap spent most of his reign fighting off the armies of Akbar; it is said that Rana Pratap ate rotis of grass when he ran out of food on the campaign trail. Mewar encompassed most of southern Rajasthan where the rainfall is the highest in Rajasthan. Maize/corn is the major cereal grain grown in the region. It is made into makki ki roti; cooked with meat in the local version of soyta; made into pakoras and cooked with buttermilk for breakfast or as a snack. Corn is a monsoon crop so it is eaten fresh during that period and then dried maize is used throughout the rest of the year.

Unfortunately, it's quite difficult to sample local specialities in Udaipur: it is one of India's most beautiful cities and one of the most changed by tourism. The central area around the lake and palace is full of cafes and restaurants catering to tourists who seem to want to eat Western-style baked goods while in India. If you want to sample genuine local food, then get off the main 'drag' and walk through Burra and Bapu Bazaar, from the old clock tower to the new. There are not many eateries in this area but as you progress along **Burra Bazaar**, it evolves from shoe shops into one long food market. There are stalls selling great lumps of what looks like marble and coal but are actually different types of salt, as well as lumps of alum, which is used in pickles to help retain the crispness of vegetables. Then there are people selling gum collected from the forest by the local tribals, the Bhils; this is used to make sweets like gond ke laddoo. Next come spice merchants selling bulk quantities of fresh spices that you must take the opportunity to smell, to experience what the aroma of spices can be. After the spice dealers are the sugar merchants, selling various grades/types of sugar including white discs of purest grade sugar offered as prasad in temples. Alongside are confectioners who make various sweets such as the toffee-like *chikki* or *gajjak*, the production of which emits the most beguiling caramel aroma. As you come into **Bapu Bazaar**, the area opens out into a fresh-food market; in winter, you will see carts piled high with various types of gur ranging from almost black in colour (least refined) to a light caramel colour (highly refined, usually treated with chemicals) and the texture varies from soft and crumbly through firm fudge to hard. It is a tradition during local marriages for male guests to be offered a piece of gur to put in their mouths when they leave the ceremonies and female guests to be given extra gur to take home. As winter is also marriage season, gur sellers are usually very busy at that time and it is interesting to watch people taste, touch and deliberate over which gur they want.

I found that the roadside stalls (outside the tourist drag) were the best places for something resembling a local-style breakfast. Look out for *aloo kofta* (balls of mashed potato flavoured with fennel, mustard seeds, green chilli, coriander and lemon, dipped in a besan batter and deep-fried). Not at all greasy, these are eaten with fried green chillies and a cup of piping hot sweet tea: much better than a bowl of packaged breakfast cereal or canned baked beans in some tourist cafe.

Outside the main tourist area, several restaurants serve authentic Rajasthani thalis. On the day I visited **Natraj**, the thali included black-eyed beans cooked with green capsicum and potatoes; kadhi; kachori stuffed with potato and cumin; and cardamom-scented kheer.

23–24 City Station Road
(0294) 2487488
10.30 a.m.–3.45 p.m., 6.30–10.45 p.m. (7 days)

Bawarchi opposite Delhi Gate (where there are a number of thali joints patronized by locals) serves a tasty thali featuring a seasonal dish of fenugreek leaves cooked with dal and chilli; excellent boondi raita; lentil dumplings; and lapsi.

6 Delhi Gate
(0294) 2414955
www.bawarchirestaurant.in

For a far more glamorous and refined experience, and for local-style meat dishes, try **Udai Kothi** that serves a Rajasthani thali featuring dishes made from family recipes such as a simple but wonderfully flavourful mutton cooked with curd, whole coriander and red chillies. The wonderful views across the lake of the palace are an added bonus, especially in the evening when the rooftop dining room sparkles in candlelight. The hotel also has its own farm called Udai Bagh where all the fresh produce used in the restaurant is grown. A visit to the farm can be arranged for hotel guests or you can stay at the farm surrounded by all that fresh food. At the time of writing, the owners of Udai Kothi were planning to open a Rajasthani speciality restaurant. It might be operational by the time you get there.

Outside Chand Pole, Hanuman Ghat Marg, Pichola Lake
(0294) 6530116, 2432810
info@udaikothi.com
www.udaikothi.com

TRADE FARE

The sea-facing temple at Somnath on the coast of Gujarat is said to have witnessed the dawn of time. As a definitive date for that particular event has yet to be determined, the earliest period for which there is evidence of human settlement in Gujarat is circa 2500 BC. By then, the Harappans had built a port at Lothal on the Gulf of Cambay and were trading with Persia, Mesopotamia and Egypt. This civilization went into decline around 1500 BC, for reasons that remain only marginally understood. From this period until Gujarat was incorporated into the Mauryan Empire, in the fourth century BC, legend has it that Krishna and his clan, the Yadavas, ruled the region from their capital at Dwarka on the far western tip of the Gujarat peninsula. After the death of Ashoka in 232 BC, Gujarat had a succession of rulers in possession of various configurations of the state. Muslim rule was established in 1299 when the Delhi Sultanate defeated the ruling Hindu Chavdas and incorporated Gujarat into their kingdom. In 1407, the Delhi Sultanate appointed a governor, Muzaffar Shah, who declared Gujarat an independent sultanate and anointed himself its ruler. This arrangement lasted for nearly two centuries before Akbar annexed Gujarat to the Mughal Empire, and then, in 1818, the state came under British sovereignty. Meanwhile, the Portuguese had taken control of the island of Diu adjacent to the Gujarat coast, and the southern port town of Daman; Parsis from Iran had been settling in the same coastal area since the seventh century. Throughout this time, Gujarat was (and remains) home to a significant population of tribal and nomadic peoples whose origins are as undefined as the date of the beginning of time.

Gujarat has three distinct geographical regions. Saurashtra or the Kathiawar peninsula—hemmed in by the Gulf of Kutch, the Bay of Cambay and the Arabian Sea—forms the greater proportion of the land mass and sustains the bulk of the population; the topography runs from low hills and marshes in the north-west across a central plain that is arid in some parts and fecund in others. Kutch in the north-east—a smaller peninsula bordered by the deserts of Pakistan and Rajasthan, the salt marshes of the Rann of Kutch and the Gulf of Kutch—is largely barren and rocky with intermittent patches of greenery and fertility. Gujarat's mainland runs from the gentle Aravali Hills in the north to the Damanganga River on the border with Maharashtra in the south encompassing a flat plain of fertile alluvial soil. The diversity of geography has gifted Gujarat with a rich bank of natural resources, including abundant foods, though these are not equally distributed across the state. This in turn has drawn the diverse populace we met in the preceding paragraph. All these factors play out in three distinct regional cuisines, but before we explore these, let's look at some of the commonalities of Gujarati cuisine.

Gujarat has a 1600-kilometre-long coastline yet you are very unlikely to be served fish at a meal. This runs counter to every other Indian state with a coastline where seafood is an important part of the daily diet. In all the coastal states, the percentage of vegetarians in the population is less than 10 per cent, except in Gujarat, which boasts of the highest percentage of vegetarians, at 64 per cent, in all of India. Gujarat is a prosperous state and Gujaratis earn some of the highest average incomes in India. Their collective vegetarianism thus is not driven by economic necessity—there are some for whom this is the case—but more markedly by religious philosophy, particularly Jainism. There are 5.5 million Jains in India: less than 1 per cent of India's total population but 35 per cent of Gujaratis are Jains. The holy hill of Shatrunjaya in Saurashtra is said to be where Adinath, the first Jain *tirthankara*, gained enlightenment at some point in his 592,704-quintillion lifetime. This is arguably an impossible number of years to have lived although it might have been that Adinath was also around to witness the dawn of time. A more concrete date for Jain activity in Gujarat is fourth century BC when the last Jain tirthankara, Mahavira, was active as a contemporary of the Buddha. Jains believe in the sanctity of all life and are vegetarians with a dietary ethos that extends well beyond abstinence from eating animal flesh. Devout Jains do not consume onion, potato, radish, turmeric, ginger, garlic, carrot, sweet potato, yam or any other tuber; harvesting these requires that the whole plant be destroyed, and digging for these subterranean vegetables exposes worms and other small soil-dwelling forms of life to potential harm. Jains also believe that tubers absorb microscopic forms of life (microorganisms) from the soil they grow in and that cooking and eating these foods necessitates killing that life. In Jain cooking, plantain (green banana) is used as an alternative to potato and yam. Multi-seeded fruits and vegetables such as figs and eggplants are not eaten because of the promise of life inherent in them; also, honey is not permitted. Jains eat before nightfall to avoid unintentionally swallowing insects attracted by the light needed to illuminate a meal taken after dark. There is no deviation from the practice of vegetarianism amongst Jains but how rigidly a family or individual adheres to the other 'food rules' will be influenced by the sect they belong to and personal preferences as well as circumstances.

Gujarat's Jain community is a particularly prosperous one. There are many occupations that Jains cannot undertake because of their beliefs: for example, they would not do work that required them to dig into the earth such as mining for gold and precious gems such as diamonds. Yet Jains control the huge Indian diamond industry, which they operate largely out of Gujarat: a corollary is that many of India's finest jewellers are Jains. Gujarati Jains are also successful traders of many other goods. The cultural importance—there are many major Jain pilgrimage sites in Gujarat—and collective wealth of the Jains makes them very influential. A contact of mine from regional Gujarat told me that it was difficult for him to successfully run a non-vegetarian restaurant amidst the strict vegetarian environment there, and he finally had to close down. If you travel there—particularly in Saurashtra and Kutch—you will notice that most commercial food businesses serve vegetarian food. (There are restaurants serving non-vegetarian food but not Gujarati cuisine.)

Vegetarian influence in Gujarat has not only come from the Jains. Gujarat was part of the Buddhist Mauryan Empire and, in the third century BC, Ashoka had a rock edict (exhorting people to practise non-violence) erected near Junagadh, then the capital of Gujarat. After Ashoka's death, the Mauryan Empire survived only fifty years but his promulgation of Buddhism had a long-lasting influence in Gujarat; up until the seventh century AD, there were still several thousand Buddhists in Junagadh and subsequent Gujarati rulers added sentiment similar to Ashoka's original stone edict. Further import was given to vegetarian philosophy and practice in Gujarat by Vaishnavites—those who worship the god Vishnu as the supreme lord. Vishnu's chief function is to keep the world in order by preserving, restoring and protecting it. At the point in time when he was most actively engaged in preserving the world, he is said to have stopped at Dwarka on the Kathiawar coast to rest. Sometime later, Krishna, the eighth avatar of Vishnu, is said to have fled north India—due to the intra-familial violence depicted in the Mahabharata in which he had become unwittingly involved—and set up his capital at Dwarka. Such an epic history made the place a magnet for Vaishnavites. In the Middle Ages Vaishnavite preachers were very active in Gujarat. They successfully converted several local princes and many wealthy Gujarati Banias to their philosophy, which includes adherence to a strict vegetarian diet. Winning over the most influential members of society, the aristocracy and the rich, ensured that the wider community would be influenced to take up Vishnu as their principal god and follow prescribed practices such as vegetarianism. Gujarat's most famous son, Mahatma Gandhi, exhorted others to follow his example and not only renounce eating animal flesh but forgo any epicurean indulgences. Gandhi steadfastly adhered to his dietary principles but Gujaratis on the whole practised the former and ignored the latter, developing a distinct style of food that is variously described as 'vegetarian haute cuisine' and 'India's most diverse vegetarian cuisine'. A key aspect of Gujarati food is balancing taste and texture; to achieve this, a Gujarati meal comprises a considerable number of items. A typical meal would include bread and rice; dal; several vegetable dishes collectively called *shaak*; at least one sweet dish; salted buttermilk; and a selection of side dishes including *farsaan*, pickles and chutney.

Gujarati daily bread is often made from *bajri* (millet). It has long been the staple grain and is one of the state's main crops. A hardy plant, it can be grown in drier, less fertile areas such as Kutch; it is also a nutritious and easily digested grain. Millets—there are many types as the word is applied globally to describe small-seeded grasses—are an ancient food and have been eaten in India for millennia but have largely fallen out of favour, except in Gujarat. (There is now a strong grass-roots movement working to bring millets back into wider use across India.) Pearl millet (*Pennisetum glaucum*) is the most widely used; it produces a dark grey/purple flour. Millet does not have any gluten to hold it together, and dough made from it cannot be easily rolled out as it tends to break up. To make millet dough, a piece is pressed into a circle then patted backwards and forwards between the palms to push it out as far as it can go without breaking—this creates a thick rustic bread called *rotla* (also made from other gluten-less grains such as corn and rice). Hot bajri rotla are customarily 'split' and anointed with ghee to moisten them.

Wheat-flour breads that can be finely rolled out with a rolling pin are called *rotli*. The Gujarati genre of breads also includes *bhakri* (fried bread similar to a paratha) and *poodla* (batter-based, pancake-like bread popularly made from *besan* or ground moong-dal flour).

Dal in Gujarat is ordinarily made from *toor/arhar* (pigeon pea) though other varieties are also used. Gujarati food is noted for its sweet-and-sour flavourings and its dal often has a distinctive sweetness. Gujaratis might also eat sweet dishes through a meal as well as at the end (*more on this later*). All manner of seasonal vegetables are prepared in various styles: this might include sautéed leafy greens; quickly cooked spiced cauliflower; and crunchy salads of raw vegetables. Eggplant-based dishes are popular, the fleshiness of this vegetable providing substance and texture in the absence of meat. Shaak are scooped up with pieces of rotla or rotli. Rice (*bhaat*) comes at the end of the meal and may be plain or cooked with split moong as a khichri. Any form of rice is drizzled with ghee and eaten with crisp papad to counterbalance its soft texture. Kadhi is a soupy dish made of buttermilk (or curd) and besan, with vegetables and various spices added in. There is a multitude of types of kadhi including distinct regional variations: in Kutch, toor dal (and the water it is cooked in) is added to the buttermilk instead of besan. A little sugar or jaggery is added to a kadhi to balance out the slightly sour taste of the buttermilk or curd. Kadhi is believed to aid digestion so it will typically be served with 'heavier' dishes such as those made from eggplant. It is eaten frequently during summer, as the hot weather is believed to make it more difficult to digest food and because it is a cooling dish.

Gujarati cuisine is famed for its variety of pickles and chutneys, which play a supporting role to the major constituents of a meal by adding tang, piquancy, crunch and stickiness. Gujarat, particularly in the north, is one of the hottest places in India, with average summer temperatures touching 50 °C. This historically made it very difficult to store fresh fruit and vegetables and pickling has long been a reliable way of keeping these foods (just as it is in countries with very cold climates). Modern refrigeration has altered the above situation but food habits were set in place long before that was ever imagined. Mangoes, lemons, chillies, cauliflower and carrots are preserved in mustard, peanut or sesame oil with salt and spices. The sesame oil here is made from raw sesame seeds and is quite mild unlike the pungent Asian variety that is pressed from roasted sesame seeds. A wide range of chutneys is prepared from fresh fruit (guava, tomato, mango, star fruit, pineapple, tamarind) and fresh green herbs (mint, coriander) along with coconut, sesame seeds, peanuts, ginger, garlic and fresh/dried chillies. Various combinations of these ingredients are ground, or very finely chopped, and mixed with spices, lime or lemon juice, salt and sugar to achieve a sweet-and-sour flavour. The same ingredients can be mixed into curd to create a type of chutney called raita. A spoonful of chutney is taken at the start of a meal to stimulate the appetite and 'release' digestive juices; it continues to be eaten throughout the meal as an individual dish and/or mixed in with other items.

Farsaan is the collective word used in Gujarat to describe a range of side dishes. Farsaan are also eaten as snacks. A farsaan can be fried, baked or steamed; two of the best known are *dhokla* and *khandvi*. Dhokla is a light, spongy savoury cake made from a fermented batter of besan and curd that is steamed, dressed with a tempering of fried mustard seeds, green chillies and a little sugar and garnished with fresh coconut shreds and coriander leaves. It is served cut into squares. Gujaratis have been eating dhokla since at least the eleventh century. Khandvi are thin, silky crêpes prepared from besan–buttermilk batter dressed with a tempering of coconut, mustard seeds, green chillies and asafoetida. *Arvi na patra* is a crunchy multilayered farsaan of colocasia (*arvi/arbi*) leaves smeared with thick, spiced besan batter, rolled up, steamed, cut into pieces and fried. Within the farsaan category are *nasto*, a vast range of crunchy dry, fried or baked snacks, many made from chickpea flour but not limited to it. Perhaps the most popular is *chidwa*, a crunchy, sweet-and-sour mixture of beaten rice/corn flakes, crisp *sev* or *boondi*, peanuts, fried curry leaves, spices, raisins and grated coconut: once you start on a packet of chidwa, it is hard to stop. Nasto is believed to have been derived from the Gujarati habit of moving around, as traders or pilgrims—modern Gujaratis are keen recreational travellers and make up a large percentage of the domestic tourism numbers in India, hence you will often find Gujarati food available at tourist destinations—as they needed food that could travel and was culturally 'safe'. Gujaratis are often described as the 'most snacking' of Indians, a reputation partly derived from their penchant for farsaan. I wonder though if this reputation doesn't have something to do with the way Gujaratis eat their actual meals as each of the different items are only taken in small quantities: just like eating a series of snacks.

When I first visited Kutch, I was fascinated to see people at their meals take a mouthful of a vegetable dish and break off a piece of jaggery—from a lump sitting on their plates—and put this into their mouths as well. My

European culinary background demands a strict division between savoury and sweet foods at a meal so this was quite a revelation. Once I got over my astonishment, I gave it a try and I liked it. I saw this practice over and over throughout Kutch and when I moved on to other parts of Gujarat, I detected a distinct sweetness in many 'savoury' dishes; I have heard Indians, other than Gujaratis, describe Gujarati food as distinctly 'sweet'—and not always in an appreciative tone. This sweet–savoury combination is also present in other Indian cuisines, but I also find it most discernible in Gujarati food. I tried to ascertain how this had come about. When I asked Gujaratis, I received a variety of answers: one person swore that it was not sweet and that if there was sweetness present it was a foreign incursion planted in the food by Rajasthani cooks; another said it was just something that 'we [Gujaratis] are used to and we like it'; another said that adding jaggery to food assisted in alleviating breathing problems, and that this was a common habit with miners; yet another said that adding sugar to food helped people in humid areas cope with the climate; and finally someone explained that sugar was added to dal to balance out the salty water it was cooked in. All these indicate that there is no definitive answer to my original question. In respect of actual sweet dishes, at least one will be served at the end of a meal. This might be *shrikhand*, an ancient dish made from dewatered curd—hung up in a cotton cloth or weighted to push the water out of it causing it to thicken—mixed with sugar and saffron or fresh fruit such as mango. Shrikhand is also eaten with fried bread called puri in Gujarat as a light meal.

KUTCH

Until 1948, Kutch was an independent state; in that year, the Bombay Presidency was separated along linguistic lines into Marathi-speaking Maharashtra and Gujarati-speaking Gujarat. Geographic proximity saw Kutch attached to the latter, even though the language of its inhabitants was Kutchi. Kutch had more cultural alignment with neighbouring Sind but the events of 1947 saw that region being partitioned off into Pakistan. One of the things that Kutchis shared with other Gujaratis was a tradition of working as traders, although trading in Kutch was more localized and had not made Kutchis as collectively wealthy as other Gujarati trading communities—who had access to good ports and a wider array of commodities. Kutch is renowned for its cultural riches though. Separated from the Kathiawar peninsula by the Gulf of Kutch and the marshes of the Little Rann, Kutch can become an island during the monsoon when these marshes flood; even in dry weather, the main access to Kutch is via a bridge. This isolation has allowed Kutch to retain its unique culture based around traditional village life. The tribals who have long inhabited the region have also been able to maintain their traditional ways, though development is encroaching upon them, particularly on the nomadic pastoral tribes who are losing access to land as it increasingly gets taken over as 'private property'. Kutchi cuisine is simpler than what you will find in 'Gujarat'—Kutchis do not consider themselves Gujarati—but shares basic ingredients and food style.

Kutchis are predominantly rural people so their food tends to be substantial and straightforward. The arid environment makes it difficult to grow many vegetables or fruits; peanuts, wheat and oilseeds are grown in the more fertile southern corner. Traditional Kutchi cuisine is based on millet and dairy products. Garlic and red chillies are heavily relied upon to add flavour, as these are inexpensive and can be dried and stored. Rearing and raising sheep, goats, cows and buffaloes is a customary occupation in Kutch and the main means of income generation. These animals are predominantly raised for milk production; much of this milk is transformed into ghee, as it used to be impossible to transport fresh milk very far at all in Kutch due to the heat, bad roads and isolation. Turning it into ghee allowed it to be kept and therefore transported to and sold in distant markets where it could a fetch a good price. While it might now be possible for fresh milk to be more easily collected and transported, the tradition of making ghee has stayed alive in Kutch. Ghee production means there is plenty of residual buttermilk, and as this is not a product that can be kept, it is used extensively in cooking, often standing in for precious water. A typical meal will inevitably include buttermilk as a drink to start the meal, perhaps flavoured with salt and cumin seeds, and as a kadhi; bajri rotla with ghee and a piece of jaggery would make up the rest. Kutchi cuisine has traditionally not included much of a repertoire of vegetable-based dishes, since it is difficult to grow these in the region. But improvements in roads and infrastructure has meant that easily transportable vegetables (potato, cauliflower, eggplant) are now regularly available in markets, and these have been incorporated into the cuisine.

Recommendations

In the north of Kutch, in the semi-desert Banni region, you can stay at **Shaam-e-Sarhad**, a tourist project owned and run by the Banni people from Hodka Jheel village. Accommodation is in traditional, circular mud houses with conical thatched roofs called *bhunga*s, made of local grasses. This style of construction is very effective in combating the intense summer heat and bhungas are also hardy: most withstood the 2001 earthquake that devastated Kutch while many concrete buildings collapsed. Meals at Shaam-e-Sarhad have the same focus on giving guests an authentic experience of local culture. The Banni people traditionally raise livestock, for milk production, on the grasslands that edge the Rann of Kutch. Changing environmental conditions over the past century have caused these grasslands to diminish. The Banni community are committed to careful, and long-practised, management of grasslands to ensure these endure, so that they can maintain their customary occupation. The ghee, butter, buttermilk and curd—the latter made from sweet, rich buffalo milk—used at Shaam-e-Sarhad is bought locally, and an excursion can be arranged to see a village milking session and the production of these foods. The people are predominantly Muslim—their ancestors came from Sind in neighbouring Pakistan—and socially very conservative. Men do all the cooking at Shaam-e-Sarhad because Hodka women, while responsible for cooking at home, rarely step outside their home compounds. The staple food is bajri, wheat, pulses, meat, rice, buttermilk, milk products and milk-based sweets. A meal at Shaam-e-Sarhad might include bajri rotla, a buttermilk kadhi flavoured with whole red chillies, curry leaves, cumin seeds, green chillies, pepper and star anise; local beans cooked with star anise and green peas cooked with nigella seeds and star anise. The somewhat ubiquitous use of star anise is a distinct Muslim influence.

Shaam-e-Sarhad Village Resort, Hodka Village, Banni, Bhuj (District Kachchh)
(02803) 296222
www.hodka.in

Bhuj was established as the capital of Kutch in the mid-sixteenth century and remains the main city. The 2001 earthquake destroyed much of it but since that time there has been considerable redevelopment, and Bhuj now has a new airport, railway line, a university and a distinct air of prosperity: as well as a much increased pace of life since I first visited it in 1996. Despite the damage wrought by the quake and the subsequent erection of many ugly concrete buildings, Bhuj has retained its medieval centre of narrow streets and bazaars along with a friendly charm and some good places to eat local food.

Annapurna Hotel is an unpretentious cafe serving Kutchi food. On the day I ate there, I had hot bajri rotla—served with a pot of home-made butter to slather on—*tamatar sev* (sweet-and-sour chickpea-flour noodles cooked in tomato sauce); cabbage and potato cooked with cumin seeds; and a splendid shrikhand made from buffalo curd. Annapurna is a workingman's cafe so the food is substantial, inexpensive and tasty. The owner is very friendly and happy for you to make your own 'pick and mix thali' whereby he brings out all the dishes he has available for that meal for you to choose from.

Near Bhid Gate
(02832) 220831, (M) 9825662166
11.30 a.m.–11 p.m. (Sundays closed)

Rasoli is a new restaurant that has yet to develop the character of Annapurna, but it has a more elaborate selection of local dishes on offer served in a spotless, air-conditioned, family-friendly environment. The daily thali includes petite bajri rotla; kadhi; vegetable dishes like fresh fenugreek (methi) leaves sautéed with spices and a sweet–sour eggplant and potato dish; *polda* (chickpea-flour pancakes); sweet semolina halwa and a khichri of rice cooked with moong beans and lightly flavoured with cardamom. Sides include freshly made butter, ghee, pickles and buttermilk. The meal is finished with a digestive called *mukhwas*, made of fennel seeds, split coriander seeds, dry grated coconut, menthol powder and betel leaf.

Abha International Hotel, Siddharth Complex, Jantaghar
(02382) 25451

Farsaani Duniya is a very popular sweet shop: it caught my eye as I walked past because it was so crowded. All the sweets are made on the premises in kitchens and production spaces that sprawl behind the small shopfront. Local Kutchi confections include *adadiya* (a fudge-style sweet made from dried fruit cooked with ghee, black pepper and ginger) and *gundar pak* (a flaky confection that includes *gond*, a local tree gum, in its ingredients). These two sweets are only made in winter but another local sweet called *mohantar*, made from dry fruit, sugar and ghee, is available all year round. If you happen to be in Bhuj in the warmer months, try *gulab pak*, made from rose petals, nuts and milk solids: rose petals are believed to be great for cooling the body.

Chatti Bari Ring Road, Near intersection with Anam Ring Road

SAURASHTRA

Saurashtra, or the Kathiawar peninsula, occupies the middle of Gujarat. Prior to Independence, the region was made up of many small princely states. Despite not being in possession of vast tracts of physical territory, these individual states were often very wealthy largely due to trade in the natural resources they did have, such as diamonds. Kathiawar food shares all the general characteristics of Gujarati cuisine and is particularly noted for its pickles and dairy products. Garlic and red chillies are used extensively to flavour food and it has a reputation of being 'rich and spicy', possibly because of the influence of so many royal households that could afford to use spices generously. Distinct local specialities include *lasana batata* (spicy, garlic-flavoured potatoes); *gatte ka pulao* (fresh green chickpeas cooked with rice and spices); *chawla methi dhokla* (a winter version of dhokla made of ground rice and fenugreek); *dahi dhokla* (dhokla soaked in curd); and *dahi bindoo* (ladies' fingers soaked in curd and fried). Saurashtra has a large dairy industry and citizens of Rajkot have the distinction of being the largest consumers of ice cream in India. This dairy-based confection is a modern entrant into Gujarati cuisine but its appreciation is not limited to the people of Rajkot. It is popularly served as the final fillip at a meal after a more indigenous sweet has been eaten.

In the Saurashtrian town of Wankaner, I was welcomed into the home of a local Jain family for a cooking demo. No one in this family has ever eaten meat or eggs but they are not as restrictive in their eating as rigid adherents to Jain dietary principles would be. Almost everything eaten by the family is prepared at home and the menfolk come away from their jewellery stores to eat lunch with their family. After spending some time watching a selection of typical everyday dishes being prepared at their home, I got to enjoy them for lunch. First up was a dish of eggplant and potato stuffed with a mixture of ground peanuts (a major crop), chickpea flour, red chilli, coriander and 'green garlic'—a fresh herb somewhat like chives. The stuffed vegetables were steamed in a pressure cooker then sautéed in a tomato-based gravy. I ate this with thin, delicate wheat rotli, perfect for scooping up such a substantial dish. Dal and rice were next and a winter sweet prepared from dried ground fenugreek leaves mixed with ghee, sugar, coconut and gond to form a firm fudge. Gond is used in sweets throughout India; among its many properties, it is believed to warm the body and is eaten more in winter. A jug of buttermilk spiced with salt, fresh coriander and cumin was at hand and the large table was strewn with a selection of pickles and farsaan to aid and abet the mains. I did not stay on for the evening meal but I was told it would be roasted eggplant cooked with tomato and fresh coriander; kadhi; bajri rotla and khichri. The family said that this meal pattern rarely changes but the ingredients alter, depending on the seasons.

Saurashtra has the lion's share of Gujarat's coastline and I convinced myself that it must be possible to sample Gujarati-style fish or seafood dishes somewhere—after all Gujarat does have a commercial fishing industry. After consulting a map and doing some research, I zeroed in on a destination on the Saurashtra coast, convinced that fish dishes awaited me. When I explained my mission to my driver he tried to persuade me to visit the island of Diu where fish meals are easily available—as is booze. Gujarat is a 'dry' state where the sale of alcohol is prohibited unless you hold a permit to obtain it. A visitor to Gujarat can get a one-week permit to buy alcohol, but has to declare himself an alcoholic. While Diu is joined to the Saurashtra mainland by a bridge, it is a Union Territory governed by Delhi not Gujarat. Alcohol is not only freely available on the island, it is also very cheap and the place is a magnet for people wanting to get drunk; and the thought of a town full of drunks was not appealing to me. (I have since been told that if you avoid the immediate town centre, with the bars and the drinkers, the rest of Diu is charming.) So we stuck with my original destination and, after many hours of driving, finally reached it. As my driver had predicted, there was not a skerrick of aquatic food to be had anywhere despite the huge expanse of water in front of us. The local cafe owner told us that we 'might' be able to source some fish in a town twenty kilometres away; my driver sweetly went off there and returned several hours later with prawns and several local fish, for which he been charged an exorbitant price. The cafe owner had said he would cook any fish we could get but by the time we procured it, the cafe had other customers and he had become jittery as he felt they would not like fish being cooked in the same kitchen as their vegetarian meals. In the end, the fish and prawns were cooked—very simply—on the sly and we ate our meal in the family's private courtyard. Served alongside were wonderful bajri rotla, which the women had patterned with thumbprints before cooking these over a fire made from coconut shells.

Recommendations

Das Aditya is in the centre of Bhavnagar, a prosperous port and diamond-cutting town; it began operations more than 100 years ago as a small sweet shop. It has now grown into a full-fledged restaurant, thronged at lunch and dinner by locals and visiting businessmen. At lunch, only thalis are served; the contents change every day, but you can expect a spread of seasonal Gujarati vegetarian dishes such as lima beans cooked in curd; peas cooked with ladies' fingers; paneer cooked in a gravy flavoured with mustard seeds, turmeric and green chilli; dal gently enhanced with smoked cloves; kadhi; and *basundi*, sweetened reduced milk flavoured with saffron. You can take spoonfuls of basundi in between the savoury dishes in true Gujarati style or save it to enjoy it at the end of the meal. (Unfortunately, I lost the card with the exact address and contact details for Das Aditya but when we pulled into town and asked a passer-by for directions, we found it pretty easily.)

Limbdi is not a town you would visit for any particular reason but it does have a central location along the major highway linking Saurashtra with Kutch and the capital Ahmedabad, so if you are doing any road travel, there is a fair chance you will pass through it. If you do, stop at **Avantika** for a Kathiawar-style thali of dal flavoured with spices and peanuts; sev tamatar; *sukhi bhaji* (local spinach sautéed with garlic); whole moong dal cooked with red chilli; potato and cabbage cooked with mustard seeds; and whole green chillies sautéed with salt and fresh lemon juice. Bajri rotla, curd, rice, papad and a bowl of miniature gulab jamun round out the meal.

NH8A, Near the New Collector Office
(02753) 260794

If you visit the Jain temple complex of Shatrunjaya, food choices in the nearest town of Palitana are fairly limited. Most visitors are pilgrims and want to remain 'pure' so they stay in one of the many religious guest houses, called dharamshalas, where they are fed austere vegetarian meals. In nearby Adpur, you can stay in the charming heritage hotel **Vijay Vilas**. A converted royal guest house, it is run by the great-grandson of the former prince of Palitana. Much of the food served here is grown in the hotel's extensive garden and each meal is freshly prepared. You should allow plenty of time in your schedule to enjoy sitting in the light- and antique-filled dining room savouring a meal that might include freshly picked ladies' fingers cooked with cumin, turmeric, green chilli and chickpea flour; fresh fenugreek leaves cooked with toor dal; stuffed eggplant; and bajri rotla.

Village Adpur
(02848) 282371
vishwa_adpur@yahoo.co.in

In the former princely state of Wankaner, you can stay in the magnificent art-deco **Royal Oasis**, the summer guest house of the royal family, members of which still reside in the nearby palace. Simple Gujarati vegetarian meals are available and a tour of the palace, including the formal dining room with its expansive spread of grand service used for royal dinners, is included in your stay.

Royal Oasis, Wankaner
(02828) 220000

The Gujarati mainland begins at the north-eastern corner of the Rann of Kutch and is bordered by Rajasthan, Madhya Pradesh and Maharashtra. The geography of this region varies, but it has large areas of agricultural land supported by natural water supplies and man-made irrigation. India's first cooperative dairy was started in Anand—aka 'the milk capital of India'—south of Ahmedabad in

1946. It is now jointly owned by 2.6 million Gujarati farmers and trades under the brand name of Amul, selling an extensive range of dairy foods such as milk, ghee, butter, cheese and ice cream. Amul is also the biggest food brand in India and one of the most successful cooperatives in the world. By operating as a cooperative, it has allowed Gujarati dairy farmers to fare better than their fellow producers in most other states. It is possible to organize a visit to the Amul production facility by contacting the company via their website www.amul.com.

Ahmedabad is the largest city in Gujarat and it was the capital until 1970 when the mantle was given to nearby Gandhinagar. This change of ranking has done little to stunt development in the city. In 2010, Ahmedabad earned the distinction as the fastest-growing city in India (and the pace of life there literally confirms this). The city was founded in 1411 by the then Sultan of Gujarat, Ahmed Shah; in 1572, it became part of the Mughal Empire and still retains a distinct Muslim identity and influence, particularly in the city's older parts. There are more than fifty mosques, including the Jama Masjid with 260 carved stone pillars holding up the domed roof of the prayer hall. If you would like a taste of Ahmedabad's Muslim culture—or if you just need to eat some meat—near Jama Masjid is **Bhatiyar Gali**, a narrow lane lined with small shops and stalls serving typical Indo-Muslim food such as meat and chicken kebabs, mutton samosas and biryani. It can get pretty crowded here in the evening and it's a very rudimentary 'street eats' area. If you want to sit down and enjoy a meal, try **Moti Mahal Hotel** near the railway station. This is still a simple eatery and also very busy but well regarded for its Muslim-style cooking. Their chicken biryani is made of the longest grain rice I have ever encountered, warmly flavoured with brown cardamom, onion, garlic and ginger.

Station Road, Kapasia Bazaar
(079) 22121881
11 a.m. until late

In 1900, **Chandvilas Hotel** in Ahmedabad is reputed to have served the first commercial Gujarati thali. The same restaurant was also famed for its dal made from thirty-eight ingredients and Mohandas

Karamchand Gandhi was a notable customer before he became Mahatma. The Chandvilas closed its doors many years ago but there are now numerous places to enjoy a Gujarati-style thali in Ahmedabad.

Chetna Dining Hall is centrally located and popular with workers at lunchtime and families in the evenings. A typical thali has a selection of pickles, dal, kadhi, several seasonal vegetable dishes, two or three farsaan, rice and papad. I watched the local family sitting next to me with interest: they ordered puris, which they dipped into a dish of spiced potato, then took a bite of a papad, alternating this with a bite of raw onion—Gujarati food mixing and matching at work. Chetna is a basic kind of place but the service is friendly and the food of good value.

Relief Road
(079) 22114278
10 a.m.–3 p.m., 7–9.30 p.m. (7 days)

Pakwan Dining Hall is a very popular restaurant that serves up a generous thali, replete with a most extensive variety of mains and sides. On any day, you can expect a meal comprising buttermilk, dal, several vegetable dishes—including the elaborate stew of seasonal vegetables and coconut called *undhiyu* in winter (*see below*)—a paneer dish, sweet curd, gulab jamun, salad, dhokla, papad, various chutneys and pickles, custard and ice cream; plenty of items to mix up into all sorts of combinations. All the thali places I ate at in Ahmedabad serve the food very quickly, and I felt that I was being rushed to finish my meals: local people seemed to have no problem with this though. They come, they eat, they leave.

Opposite Vadilal Sarabhai Hospital, Ellisbridge, Paldi
(079) 26873290
11 a.m.–3 p.m., 7–10 p.m. (7 days)

Vishalla is located on the outskirts of central Ahmedabad. It has been set up to resemble a typical Gujarati village. While it is evidently aimed at the tourist market, locals also come here as they rate the food and ambience very highly. Avoid coming for lunch if you can as it is a buffet whereas in the evening, you can choose what you like (and have it freshly prepared) from a good menu of traditional

Gujarati dishes. Vishalla also has a small museum of traditional cooking utensils.

Opposite APMC Market, Vasna
(079) 26602422
11 a.m.–3 p.m., 7.30–11 p.m.
www.vishalla.com

If you would like to try a more refined thali in a more rarefied and relaxed atmosphere, visit the rooftop **Agashiye**, where you won't be rushed. It is renowned as one of the best—if not the best—restaurants in Gujarat. You can also purchase an excellent series of cookbooks on Gujarati food that are published by the gift shop in the hotel.

House of Mangaldas Girdhardas Hotel, Dr Tankaria Road
(079) 25506946
www.houseofmg.com

Every evening, the open square of **Maneka Chowk** buzzes with a food market. Locals rave about the food but most offerings consist of Chinese noodle dishes and north Indian street food. I was almost turned off but I ferreted around and found a man selling *methi bhajiya* (crisp fried dumplings made from a batter of fresh fenugreek leaves and besan) served with a tamarind-and-gur chutney and a salad of grated radish, gourd and carrot that is a popular winter snack throughout Gujarat. The vendor refused to take payment from me, saying that I was a 'guest of his country': after a trying day in hectic Ahmedabad this kind gesture revived my flagging spirits. Then I found a vendor selling handmade ice cream that was still in the wooden pails it had been churned in, surrounded by ice and salt to keep it frozen. There was a variety of flavours drawn from local foods such as custard apple, cashew nut, pineapple, almond, and saffron: I was able to sample each of these as the vendor was more than happy to allow me a small spoon of each flavour. If this vendor were making and selling this product in a market in any Western city, he would by now have been eulogized by the media and there would be long queues of people waiting to pay five dollars a scoop for his ice cream. Another busy vendor was selling a local snack called *fafda* (long 'sticks' of fried besan dough sprinkled with a spice mix and garnished with a grated vegetable salad and a thick slick of coriander-and-mint chutney).

Fafda is ordinarily eaten for breakfast and comes in a variety of shapes including a zigzag version called *fanfri*. The following morning, I found myself breakfasting in Maneka Chowk on more methi bhajiya, this time dipped into a bowl of dal. I followed this up with hot jalebis from **Astoria Bhajiya House** at Astoria Gate. (Don't come here for an early breakfast though as they don't really get going until around 9 a.m.) This sweet item is not native to Ahmedabad but reflects the city's Muslim heritage; and I will take any excuse to eat fresh, hot jalebi for breakfast. If you would like someone to guide you around the best places to eat in Ahmedabad, and do a bit of sightseeing in between food stops, then I highly recommend cultural guide Shaikh Mukarram (Jonny). He can be contacted at (M) 9824361058 or mukarram.shaikh@gmail.com.

The south-eastern corner of Gujarat is the state's green belt. It receives ample rainfall, courtesy the south-west monsoon, and produces a wide variety of fresh food including rice and pulses; seasonal vegetables; tropical fruit such as bananas, mangoes and *chikoo* (sapodilla), a caramel-flavoured fruit with a distinctive 'sandy' texture that is a native of Latin America, and was introduced into India by the Portuguese. One of the best-loved dishes of Gujarati cuisine is a melange of winter vegetables called undhiyu, which originated in Surat. It is prepared from sweet potato, eggplant, green beans, yam, green banana, freshly grated coconut and chickpea-flour dumplings flavoured with fresh fenugreek leaves, all packed into a leaf-lined clay pot, which is put into a coal-filled pit to slowly cook and meld into the world's most magnificent vegetable stew: the best undhiyu is said to have ninety-three different ingredients in all.

When the Parsis (*see the Mumbai chapter*) first arrived in India in the seventh century, they landed off the southern coast of Gujarat where they settled and worked as traders and storekeepers. The Parsis have since become concentrated in Mumbai, but until that city was built they predominately lived, worked and traded from Gujarat; Parsis still speak Gujarati among themselves. While the Parsis are renowned for their ability to fit in and adapt, they did not take on the vegetarian food ethos of Gujarat; they make a version of the undhiyu called *umberu*, featuring meat such as lamb, quail, partridge or chicken along with the vegetables. Gujarat's Parsi heritage most visibly lives on in the hamlet of Udvada in southern Gujarat. This small town is an important pilgrimage centre for Parsis and if you happen to visit, try **Globe Hotel**'s Parsi cuisine. Parsis also share the Gujarati love of sweet-and-sour flavour although they likely brought this taste with them from their native Persia.

Near Iranshah Atash Behram (Zoroastrian Holy Shrine), Udvada (0260) 2345243, 2345474

SOUTH-WESTERN INDIA

COCONUT, CASHEWS AND BAKERIES

Ancient Goans preferred to give credence to the gods for the bounty of their land rather than Mother Nature or the ingenuity of mere mortals. The creation story of Goa tells us that Lord Parashurama—an avatar of the god Vishnu—threw his axe into the sea and demanded of the local Neptune that he roll back the borders of this watery domain to the point where his weapon had landed. Geological evidence agrees that in an earlier age the sea did recede along the western coastline of India, widening in its wake the strip of land between the Arabian Sea and the Western Ghats, but the precursor of this retreat was an earthquake, not divine territorial acquisition. This new ground was a generous gift—however it had come—for the human inhabitants of the region but its sandy footing meant it was not well suited to food production. To remedy this, Goans built bunds (dykes) with tree trunks, stones and mud—gradually building these up on the receding tide—to reclaim the land behind the coastal mangroves, building it up with alluvial soil washed down from the Ghats by the annual monsoon. Rice, of several unique varieties, sugar cane and vegetables such as gourds, radishes and leafy greens were grown on this terrain. There was not enough land on which to produce any surplus food, to barter or trade, but combined with the natural culinary bounty of a region blessed with a benign climate (relative to the rest of India) and plenty of water, Goans ate well.

Two major rivers run through Goa, the Mandovi and the Zuari, from which a network of tributaries (extended in time by man-made canals) dissect the lower-lying land, providing water for agriculture and harbouring freshwater species of aquatic protein. Fishing in the Arabian Sea yielded abundant hauls—over 100 types of fish and seafood have been identified along the Konkan coast—most of the year round and while coastal terra firma was not suitable for cultivation, it naturally supported abundant stands of coconut palm with its versatile seed. (*See pp. 357–58 for more on the bounteous coconut.*) Banana, mango, jackfruit, tamarind and spices such as black pepper, ginger and turmeric were other indigenous foods. Cooking was done in clay pots over fires of coconut husks, imbuing dishes with a particular flavour. Fish, coconut and rice still remain the backbone of Goan food.

Until the sixteenth century, Goans were largely left to their own ways, unaffected by the greater movements of Indian history. The region had officially come under the dominion of various Hindu and Muslim rulers but they rarely visited. The vertiginous Ghats made Goa difficult to access from the east; marshy waterways deterred travel in a southward direction along the coast. In their isolation, Goans turned their outlook towards the sea and built a successful commerce, selling spices and other goods to Arab traders who harnessed the monsoonal winds to pull their boats to the west coast of India, and push them back to their homelands when the same winds later retreated. In 1510, these 'trade' winds pulled to Goa a flotilla of Portuguese ships, under the charge of Alfonso de Albuquerque. Albuquerque and his men easily separated the region from the erstwhile rule of the Bijapur Sultans and claimed it for Portugal. This was not the seminal capture of Indian territory by the Portuguese but an expansion of their holdings.

The first Portuguese to set foot on Indian soil was explorer Vasco da Gama who landed at Kozhikode in Kerala in 1498, pioneering a direct sea route to India from Europe. The Portuguese had doggedly persisted in forging this course to gain direct access to the source of the spices that were such a valuable commodity in medieval Europe. (Vasco da Gama is reputed to have made forty times the cost of his initial voyage on the cargo of black pepper he took back to Portugal!) Ultimately, Goa proved to be more amenable than Kerala to this end and the Portuguese made it their capital in India in 1530: from there, they wrested control of the spice trade from the Arabs, consequently ending Venetian dominance at the European end of the Arab spice route.

The arrival and settlement of the Portuguese in Goa not only had a profound influence on local food ways but indeed on the cuisine of all of India. For anyone with even a passing knowledge of Indian food, it is impossible to conceive of it without chilli, yet this 'hot' condiment is not native to the subcontinent: it belongs to the 'Indies' of Christopher Columbus's discovery—Latin America—and it was the Portuguese who introduced it to India in the Middle Ages. Goa is believed to be the gateway from which the chilli began its progression through central and north India, but it seems it may have come into Goa from south India. The Portuguese were very successful in shipping commodities from India and selling these in Europe but they needed help on the ground to negotiate local customs and financial transactions, and procure goods and actually get these on to their boats. In Kerala, they employed local Syrian Christians and Hindu traders, moneylenders and brokers from Tamil Nadu to assist them. Through their contact with the Portuguese, these south Indian businessmen were introduced to the chilli—its piquant bite would have immediately pleased them, accustomed as they were to the taste of hot black pepper and ginger—and they took it back into their own communities. Not only did south Indians have a palate attuned to fiery food, the chilli also proved to be a very functional plant: it was hardy, easy to grow, prolific in poor soil and, unlike black pepper, resistant to mould—an important consideration in the humid south. These properties made it an inexpensive and, hence, popular relish. By the time Goa was taken over by the Portuguese, there were already three varieties of chilli under cultivation in south India. These same communities of financiers and traders followed the Portuguese to Goa and it is likely that they influenced Goans to add chillies to their cooking in the first instance. (*See pp. 279–81 for the onward journey of the chilli from Goa.*)

Had the Portuguese done nothing but introduce the chilli, they would still have made a major contribution to Indian culinary evolution. But they also brought many other foods into India from their other colonies, thus enriching the subcontinent's culinary repertoire immeasurably. Of the foods they introduced, the ones that thrived and became part of the cuisine included cashew nut, guava, *chikoo* (sapodilla), custard apple, pineapple, papaya, peanut, tapioca, corn, sweet potato, passion fruit, tomato and potato, though the latter two did not grow well in the tropical climate of southern India and were not taken into Goan cuisine until much later.

The Portuguese were also interested in local foods. Albuquerque championed the use of European horticultural techniques to improve and develop native fruit, particularly mango; in fact, one of India's most commercially successful mangoes, the Alphonso, is named for him. Xavier and Montserrat mangoes were also named for the Portuguese men who created these hybrids.

Goa's Portuguese community was small, yet divided into a class hierarchy. The upper echelon were the *fidalgos*, high-level government officials often with connections to the Portuguese nobility and churchmen who came out to Goa on a 'tour of duty', their purpose being to make as much money as they possibly could during that tenure. Their position allowed them to maintain a lifestyle as similar as possible to that they enjoyed in Portugal. These men often brought their wives with them and did not form conjugal alliances with Goan women—at least not officially. They were often interested in local foods but, as custodians of the traditions of their own country, their tables were more often spread with dishes with what was familiar, and they could afford to import the foodstuffs, wine and cooks that made this possible. Eventually, the dishes enjoyed by the Portuguese elite dispersed into wider society and became part of the cuisine prepared by families of Portuguese descent who particularly wanted to emphasize this lineage. The distinct Portuguese-style dishes still regularly prepared in Goa are devoid of complex spicing, or often any spicing at all, flavoured instead with wine, garlic, tomatoes and olive oil. These include *caldo verde* (soup made from spinach or cabbage); *sopa de camarão* (prawn soup); *galinha à Portuguesa* (chicken cooked with tomatoes and capsicum); *peixe caldeirada* (fish stewed with olive oil, wine, garlic, onion, potatoes and tomatoes); and various pastry-based items such as *almôndegas* (prawn patties) and *pasteis de ostras* (oyster tarts).

It was all very well to have an upper class to provide cultural guidance but the Portuguese knew they needed numbers to maintain control over their Indian territory. Their Kerala experience—they were driven off by the local populace who did not appreciate their aggressive relationship-building style—had taught them it was best to develop an amicable relationship with the natives. There was a body of middle-class Portuguese men—merchants, priests, artisans, low-ranking soldiers and sailors—in Goa but very few Portuguese women had come along. Albuquerque initiated a policy that encouraged them to marry local women. The intent of this policy was to grow the Portuguese community in Goa and cause the men to stay on there with their new families and contribute to building a stable society, albeit one that the Portuguese governed: an unintended outcome was the development of a new style of food that is referred to in Goa as 'Catholic' or 'Christian' cuisine.

Whoever was in charge of the kitchens of these mixed marriages, either a Goan wife or a local cook, had to satisfy both European and Goan tastes. This class could afford to eat well but did not have the unlimited resources of the fidalgos and had to substitute local foods for imported ones; they used local techniques to create unique versions of Portuguese dishes. Out of this process of exchange and grafting emerged Goa's most famous dish, *vindalho* or *vindaloo*, a slow-cooked stew of pork, garlic, chillies, black pepper and vinegar—an adaptation of the Portuguese dish of meat cooked with wine and garlic called *vinho e alhos*. Vinegar is used extensively in Goan Catholic cooking; initially it was a substitute for the wine used in Portuguese cooking. Goa's climate was not conducive to growing grapes and wine or European-style grape vinegar could not be made, so alcoholic coconut toddy was used instead as a base for vinegar. Genuine Goan coconut vinegar is made from toddy to which a piece of burnt terracotta tile is added and left to mature in wooden barrels for two months. The Portuguese also used toddy, instead of yeast, to make a European-style, oven-baked, leavened bread called *pao*. *Poder*s (local bakers) would deliver freshly baked pao every morning to the homes of the fidalgos for their breakfast. Goans of all backgrounds have now adopted this habit and they eat pao, spread with butter or jam or dipped into spiced chickpeas. Pao is traditionally a soft loaf pulled apart into four pieces but the word is also used to describe leavened bread of various shapes and textures, produced these days with commercial yeast not toddy: partly because the hereditary community of toddy tappers now prefer to do other, better-paid work.

India, on the whole, does not have a tradition of producing raised breads, biscuits and cakes except in Goa where the skill of making baked confections was learnt from the Portuguese. Milk, sugar and almonds used in Portuguese confectionery were replaced in Goa by coconut, jaggery and ground cashew nuts to create unique Goan sweets such as *bebinca*—made from a batter of eggs, coconut, jaggery and ghee poured into a pan in a thin layer, each set slowly over a coal fire before another layer is added. It takes hours of painstaking attention to achieve the desired translucent, jelly-like finish of good bebinca, and it was customarily only made on special occasions such as Christmas. Now it can be bought from bakeries and eaten in restaurants all year round. Another special confection, the *bolo* (a small cake made of a fermented batter of wheat flour, jaggery, coconut and toddy) was made to celebrate the pre-Lent festival of carnival but is now available at most bakeries.

The Portuguese happily availed themselves of the fish and seafood that was so abundant in Goa but this did not quell their preference for meat, especially pork. When a pig was slaughtered in Goa, usually for a festival, all its parts were used. The blood, liver and heart were cooked with plenty of vinegar, chilli and spices and left to 'mellow' for three to four days to make the sticky dense stew called *sorpotel*, typically eaten with a steamed rice cake called *sanna*. Most meat would be taken off the bones and finely ground with chillies, turmeric, cloves, cinnamon, black pepper, garlic, ginger and coconut vinegar, stuffed into sausage skins and left to dry in the sun or smoked over a fire to make Goan sausage, a variation of the Portuguese *chouriço*. It belongs to Goan Catholic cuisine but, when sandwiched between pao, has become a popular snack with Goans of all backgrounds. (There was somewhat of a furore recently when an Indian airline tried to prohibit passengers from carrying Goan sausages on flights out of Goa.) The spare ribs and bones from which the meat is removed to make Goan sausages are cooked with onions, green chillies, the Goan spice mix called *recheio* and tamarind to make *aad maas*. *Assado de porco* is a pork leg marinated in ginger and garlic, then pot-roasted with spices, chillies and *feni* (*more below*); it is popularly eaten for Sunday lunch in Goan Catholic households.

It was not only their native culinary style that the Portuguese brought into Goan kitchens but also influences from their colonies in Africa, Asia and Latin America. *Balchao*, a heady sweet–sour dish of ground shrimps, spices, chillies and vinegar, is derived from the cooking of Malacca, where the Portuguese held the port and shipped out nutmeg, mace and cloves indigenous to that region. *Galinha cafreal* (chicken marinated in a paste of chillies, black pepper, lime and garlic and grilled over hot coals) is believed to have come into Goa from Africa. *Feijoada*, a slow-cooked stew of Goan sausage, beans and tomatoes, can be more definitively traced to Brazil, where a dish of the same name is made with pork and beans.

If coming to Goa to make money was the motivation for many of the Portuguese, converting the natives to Christianity, specifically Catholicism, was the raison d'être for others; some probably held both ambitions equally. The Portuguese encountered more resistance to their offer of spiritual salvation than they had anticipated and resorted to less than subtle tactics, such as throwing pieces of meat on to the roofs of Hindu homes to pollute these and force the inhabitants to convert. Undoubtedly, the Portuguese believed that they were doing the Goans a favour by coercing them to accept Christ as their saviour, but things got really brutal when the Inquisition came to Goa in 1590. Hindus were forced to flee into the hinterland to escape persecution and the regime was so repressive and vicious that native Catholic converts escaped Goa in large numbers. They settled further down the coast in places such as Mangalore after being threatened with having to eat beef—among other things—to prove their religious fidelity: an act that remained a gross violation for people who maintained their Hindu belief that the cow was a holy beast. In the end, the Portuguese had to compromise with native Christians—they needed them to work for them if nothing else—and stopped the forced beef-eating and allowed the upper-caste Hindus who had converted to retain their caste marks and caste in marriage.

Amongst the Hindus who escaped into the inland forests of Goa were the Saraswat Brahmins, a community whose ancestors are believed to have migrated to Goa and India's west coast, from the Saraswati basin in Punjab, when this river dried up circa 3000 BC. Goa's Saraswat Brahmins have their own cuisine; it is similar to that eaten along the Konkan coast and has absorbed some Portuguese influences. It probably best represents pre-Portuguese Goan cuisine, particularly since the Saraswats may have mixed with the indigenous people when they arrived all those millennia ago, while the Catholic cuisine of Goa is a thoroughly assimilated blend of Saraswat and Portuguese food and cooking. There are many dishes that share the same name across these two cuisines, but what goes into these gives them a taste that makes them recognizable as belonging to one or the other.

With around 400 kilometres of sea frontage, and plenty of other waterbodies to haul a catch from, fish and seafood (such as prawns) made into a curry and eaten with rice is the daily food of all Goans, Brahmins and Catholic alike—except the small percentage of the population that is vegetarian. Freshly ground coconut, chillies, turmeric, cumin and coriander form the base of this daily curry, and after this is when you get the differentiation—Hindus use kokum or tamarind to add tang to their fish curry and asafoetida in a prawn curry; Catholics use vinegar and dried mango rind, respectively. Goan Hindus also like to add black mustard seeds and curry leaves to their fish dishes. Seafood dishes common to both cuisines are *ambot-tik* (fish pieces, always firm varieties such as shark, cooked in thin, sour/tangy gravy that, unusually, does not contain coconut) and *caldinho* (a mild coconut-based curry flavoured with cinnamon, cloves, coriander and ginger). If you are eating in restaurants in Goa, you will most likely be served the Catholic versions. Crisp fried prawns or small fish are typically served, in Hindu and Catholic households, as a textural adjunct to curry and rice.

If a touch of sweetness is required to balance the flavours of a curry, the Hindu cook will use jaggery from sugar cane and the Catholic cook, jaggery made from the sap of the palmyra palm. The Portuguese anointed this particular tree *palmeria* or 'palm of excellence', possibly because they were fond of the alcoholic toddy tapped from its young flowers. (Look out for street vendors selling the fruit of the palmyra: these look like small black coconuts but inside are three sweet, jelly-like seeds that taste similar to lychee.) Goan Hindus prefer to use ground dal as the base for sweet dishes while Catholics use nuts and eggs.

Some Saraswat Brahmins will eat chicken and mutton but will not touch pork. They have no religious objection to this meat—and probably would eat wild boar if it were still legal to hunt these—but the Portuguese used pigs to clean out the sewers in their Goan settlements and this practice made the animal completely disgusting to Hindus. *Xacuti* is a meat dish said to have been created in Goan Hindu kitchens before the Portuguese arrived. Typically made of mutton or chicken, the meat is cooked in a paste of coconut, chillies (obviously a later addition), black pepper, coriander, aniseed, caraway, mace, onions, garlic, tamarind and white poppy seeds to form a thick stew. Xacuti is said to hold 'pride of place' in Goan Hindu cooking yet the spicing is very similar to that used in Muslim cooking along the Konkan coast and likely reflects the earlier trade this region engaged in with Arabia.

Vegetarians are better catered for in Goan Hindu cooking as even the fish and meat eaters of this community observe regular fast days where they restrict their dietary intake to vegetarian food. Typical dishes include *tonak* (thick stew of *vatane* or white peas, spices and vegetables); *ros* (coconut-based gravy eaten with rice); *mungcho dal* (curry of green moong dal, coconut, green chillies and a little jaggery) that is made for fasting days. A typical Goan Hindu meal would include at least one pungent accompaniment such as mango pickle or red chilli chutney, crunchy papad and a glass of *sol kadhi*, a thin sauce or drink made from coconut, kokum and green chillies. Tropical vegetables such as banana flower, bamboo shoot, jackfruit, colocasia and drumstick appear in many dishes when in season and a regular daily meal would be finished with one of the many varieties of local bananas. It is not easy to sample Goan Hindu food, particularly the vegetarian dishes, outside of private homes. The best way to do so is to visit one of the spice farms in the Goa hinterland around Ponda that are open to the public and serve traditional food. (*See also Mum's Kitchen in Panaji.*)

The Portuguese introduced and cultivated cashew in India primarily for its crop of nuts, but the tree also produces a red/yellow pear-shaped fruit that gives a sweet, fragrant juice. The skin of the fruit is very fragile, thus limiting its commercial potential as it cannot be easily transported without damage. Portuguese monks in Goa discovered that the juice of the cashew fruit could be turned to valuable use by distilling it to produce a pleasant alcoholic beverage called feni. To create this drink, the juice is gently pressed out of the cashew apples by slightly crushing these in a block, tied together with string, and then applying weight. The extruded juice is poured into earthen pots and these are buried in the ground and left to ferment for several days, after which the liquid is distilled. The first distillation produces a lower alcohol drink called *arrack*; the second and third distillations produce feni, which can have an alcohol content of up to 42 per cent. The best feni is made in situ: when the cashew fruit comes into season, feni makers, called *kazkar*s, head into the hinterland and set up small distilleries in, or near, cashew orchards and get to work. It is a mark of discernment for Goans to obtain their feni direct from a kazkar; they buy their yearly supply in bulk and store it, for feni improves with age. Cashew feni is made only in Goa and cannot be sold in any other state of India. The Goan government has registered a Geographical Indicator (GI) that marks cashew feni as a unique product of a specific location—like Champagne or Parmigiano-Reggiano cheese—that cannot be called by that name, unless it is made in that place. Coconut feni, made by distilling toddy, is another popular drink in Goa, but it is not unique to the state and therefore not covered by the GI.

The British captured Goa from the Portuguese at the turn of the nineteenth century and handed it back to the Portuguese thirteen years later, likely because they did not find it valuable enough. The one thing they did take with them were Goan cooks, who they prized highly because they knew how to cook meat and bake goods European style. Goan cooks were regularly recruited into British households all over India and, partly as a result of this, they have a continuing reputation throughout India as good cooks. When the British handed their Indian holdings back to the Indians in 1947, the Portuguese did not follow suit with Goa; they hung on to it, even though they had neglected it and run it down such that it was no longer the 'pearl of the Orient'. In 1961, Prime Minister Jawaharlal Nehru, fed up with Portuguese procrastination, sent the Indian army into Goa and forced them to leave, though in the end they went easily and no actual armed force was needed.

Many Goans retain strong cultural ties to Portugal—Goans born before 1961 are still entitled to citizenship of that country—and Goa has become a popular tourist destination for the Portuguese. Indeed, with British, German and Indian domestic tourists pouring in, tourism is Goa's main industry. This has had a major impact on the food available in restaurants in the state. In popular beachside areas, which now pretty much encompass the entire Goan coastline, you can eat from 'German bakeries', pizza parlours and cafes serving Japanese, Israeli, Russian and Chinese food. If you want to eat authentic Goan cuisine though, you are going to have to head inland.

Recommendations

Until the early nineteenth century, Panjim or Panaji was a quiet fishing village on the Mandovi River when work began to reclaim the swampy land around it. In 1843, it became the new capital of Goa after malaria and cholera epidemics decimated the population of the erstwhile capital of Old Goa; the port there had also silted up, limiting its commercial viability. Panaji had a working port and, for the modern visitor, the main attractions are the historic residential quarters of Fontainhas and St Thomas (São Tomé) that lie adjacent to the river and port. A calm old-world atmosphere lives on in this 'Latin Quarter', where among the charming colonial homes—painted yellow, green, ochre or indigo, in keeping with the Portuguese building code—are cafes, restaurants, bars and bakeries where you can enjoy authentic Goan food and hospitality.

One of the oldest bakeries in Goa, and probably the most charming one in India, is **Confeitaria**, hidden from the street by the crook of a dog-legged lane. The window of this tiny store does not display its products but is a European-style Wunderkammer of curios and trinkets. Every item produced at Confeitaria is baked in a wood-fired oven: this is fired up in the morning and gradually loses its heat over the day. Different items are baked at different times of the day, depending on the oven temperature: savoury pastry patties that need intense heat go in first, followed by bread, then biscuits and, last of all, cakes. Local confections to try are *dodol* (dark, dense moist cake made from rice flour, coconut and jaggery); croquette-shaped *pina* (small cake of rice flour, coconut and jaggery); *bolinhas* (macaroon-like item of sugar, semolina and coconut); *doce* (halwa-like sweet made from ground dal, cardamom, coconut and sugar, cooked over the coals of the fire in a pan, poured into a tray and cut into triangles once it sets). There is also bebinca and a range of European-style breads including small *paezinhos*, eaten as snacks. If you are visiting at Christmas and Easter, you will find an additional range of items baked especially for those festivals.

31 De Janeire Corte de Oiterio, Behind Presidency Grocery
(0832) 2225791
8.30 am.–8.30 pm. (9 a.m.–noon, Sundays)

Rio Rico personifies the old-world charm of Portuguese Goa. The decor will make you feel like you are dining in a nineteenth-century European opera house. Rio Rico bills itself as serving authentic Goan/ Portuguese dishes such as caldo verde; *peixe albarda de* (fish cooked with onion, tomato and capsicum); peixe caldeirada; galinha cafreal; mutton xacuti and fish caldinho. There are some interesting vegetable dishes on the menu including a tonak of local green beans and a salad of pineapple dressed with salt, cumin, coconut and chopped green chilli. The prawn vindalho is very well accompanied in the local fashion by a glass of cashew feni.

Hotel Mandovi, D.B. Marg
(0832) 2224405
12.30–3 p.m., 7–11 p.m.
www.hotelmandovigoa.com

George Bar is a friendly, inexpensive bar and restaurant serving the gamut of Goan Catholic specialities popular with locals. It is well regarded for its fish and seafood dishes including fish/prawn balchao; fish caldinho; *mackerel recheado*, whole stuffed and baked fish; shark ambot-tik; and prawn curry. The fish and seafood used changes daily, depending on what is available in the market. If you fancy a meat-based meal, there is chicken or beef xacuti, sausage pulao, vindalho, sorpotel, and pork aad maas (only available on Saturday).

Church Square, Opposite Church of My Lady of Immaculate Conception
(0832) 2426820, (M) 9822487722
11 a.m–11 p.m. (7 days)

Panajikars like to come to **Café Tato** for breakfast, so this little eatery is buzzing in the mornings. Try the soft pao with a plate of sweet–sour chickpeas. Coffee is the preferred morning beverage in Goa and it is heavily consumed at Tato. Opposite Café Tato is the gourmet food store Loja Costas where you can purchase canned local dishes such as sorpotel and xacuti if you fancy taking some Goan food home with you.

**G-3 Souza Towers, Rue Travessa De Revolucau,
Near Municipal Gardens
(0832) 2426690
7 a.m.–7 p.m. (Sundays closed)**

Horseshoe, in the heart of Fontainhas, specializes in Portuguese–Goan food. Chef/proprietor Senhor Vasco Silveria attends to the cooking himself to ensure that the food is sent out exactly as it should be, and locals nominate it as the best restaurant in Panaji. You can start your meal with some small dishes such as *choriços fritos* (pan-fried Goan sausage); hand-made prawn wafers; a classic 1970s-style shrimp cocktail made with local shrimps and caldo verde. More substantial dishes include *sukhem tissero*, a heaped plate of clams cooked in coconut with Goan spices; *balchao de peixe*, fish in a coconut-and-feni sauce served with pao; feijoada and *carne de porco assado* (spiced roast pork). For sweet lovers, there is a good selection of desserts including bebinca, cashew-nut cake or the ethereal *serradura* made of vanilla-flavoured whipped cream garnished with crushed biscuits. You can pair your meal with cashew or coconut feni.

**E 245, Rua De Ourem
(0832) 2431788
Monday: 7–10.30 p.m., Tuesday–Saturday: Noon–2.30 p.m.,
7–10.30 p.m. (Sundays closed)
vascosilveria@yahoo.com**

Take a seat on one of the intimate *balcãos*, aka balconies, at **Venite**. Order a feni or a beer and contemplate the two centuries of history that have unfolded near this building. The restaurant is not the same age as its domicile: it has only been operating since 1961 when the current owner's father returned to Goa from Bombay, where he worked in the restaurant industry, to snap up some cheap real estate created by the eviction of the Portuguese in that year and open up his own place. Venite specializes in fresh seasonal seafood so the selection changes daily and you can have it cooked in various Goan styles. Visit Venite for breakfast and try *tisas*, a Goan breakfast dish made of sprouted millet ground into porridge. It's a friendly place so make sure you pack a book in case you end up hanging out on the balcony, feasting all day!

Rua 31 de Janeiro
(0832) 2425537
8.30 a.m.–11 p.m. (7 days)

You can imagine yourself living in colonial Goa when you stay at the 1880-built mansion home that is now **Panjim Inn**. The family that has owned it continuously for over 100 years has moved out to allow guests to move in (though a family member is rarely away from the premises for long) but they have left plenty of four-poster beds, period furniture, art and photographs to give the place a distinct period feel. The spacious veranda houses a restaurant that overlooks the street below; the menu always includes fish curry and rice, the piscatorial content changing daily depending on the local catch. There are also pork vindalho; sorpotel richly spiced with chilli, cumin, coriander, black pepper, cinnamon, nutmeg, tamarind and Goan coconut vinegar; and Goan sausages squeezed out of their skin and cooked in onion–tomato sauce served with pao. According to the chef, the village of Goa Velha (not to be confused with Old Goa), north of Panaji, is the best place to buy genuine Goan sausages. If you think you might like to do your own Goan-inspired cooking (*see below for market and cooking classes*), Panjim Inn has smart, self-contained apartments with kitchens, located on the Altinho overlooking the city.

E 12, Rua 31 de Janeiro Fontainhas
(0832) 2226523, (M) 9823025748
www.panjiminn.com

A short walk up a cobbled by-lane brings you to a Portuguese-style peach-coloured home with a line of tiled tables nestled in the veranda. Step off the street in through the doorway and you find yourself in what, at first glance, seems like a formal family living room but is actually the cosy dining room of **Viva Panjim**. Have a Goan *rumba* (cocktail of cashew feni, rum and pineapple juice) to stimulate your appetite for some of the local pork specialities for which Viva Panjim is famed, such as *assado cadibel* (roast piglet); pork feijoada; Goan sausage pulao; sorpotel and piglet *torradinho* (suckling pig stewed with onions and black pepper). If your fancy runs to seafood, the thick coconut-based prawn curry here is one of the best in Goa and the thick, tangy sauce of prawn balchao is perfect to mop up with pao!

178 Rua 31 de Janeiro, Behind Mary Immaculate High School, Fontainhas
(0832) 2422405, (M) 9850471363
11.30 a.m.–3.30 p.m., 7–10 p.m. (7 days)

Ernesto's is a smart, modern restaurant located in the courtyard of a smart, modern furniture store in the quieter—less touristy—outskirts of Fontainhas. The brief menu includes Goan-style *costeletos de porco* (pork chops marinated in cafreal spices); feijoada of pork and kidney beans served with pao; and sweet serradura. The bar serves feni and has a decent wine list. Worth strolling along lanes less travelled.

49 Mala Fontainhas
(0832) 3256213, (M) 9921207175
11 a.m.–3 p.m., 6.30–10.30 p.m. (Mondays closed)
www.ernestosgoa.com

Mum's Kitchen is outside the well-trodden tourist zone of Panaji, both in location and cuisine. It is well worth a considered walk or a quicker taxi ride to dine there. The owners have an avowed mission to 'save Goan cuisine' from the fate befalling it in 'multi-cuisine' restaurants across the state. There are no concessions to the tourist palate here, just really tasty food made from recipes collected from Goan mothers of all culinary persuasions. Mum's Kitchen serves classic Goan Catholic dishes and a good selection from the Goan Hindu kitchen. A meal is a must for vegetarians to try dishes such as *caldeen* (cabbage cooked in fresh coconut milk with green chillies); *keel khatkhatem* (bamboo shoots with coconut and Goan spices); *val shaak* (cowpeas cooked with mustard seeds, asafoetida, green chillies and coconut); *varam* (curry of red lentils cooked with onion and garlic); *abreachim xacuti* (flavourful dish of mushrooms in gravy of roasted coconut and spices); and a fantastic spiced pineapple salad. Non-vegetarians too are well catered for with plenty of fish, seafood and meat dishes to choose from, including *tavele tal'le* (crisp-fried local whitebait); *hooman* (prawn curry with nutty local rice); *masa kodi* (beef cooked with ground coconut, tomatoes and curry leaves); and *harem maas* (salted pork on the bone, marinated with button chillies, ginger and garlic and cooked with kokum and onion). For dessert, try *manngannem*, a Goan Hindu sweet made from ground chana dal, coconut, cashew, rice flour, jaggery and cardamom.

**854 Martin Building, D.B. Street, Panjim–Miramar Road,
Near Magson's Supermarket
(M) 9822175559
11 a.m.–11 p.m. (7 days)
www.mumskitchengoa.com**

Panjim market on General Bernardo Guedes Road is very interesting to visit even if you don't have access to a kitchen to cook in. Among stalls selling commercial crops of apples and tomatoes grown in other parts of India are a number of kitchen-garden stalls where the proprietors sell small quantities of fruit, vegetables and spices grown in their own gardens. The produce on offer varies with the season, but when I visited there were several varieties of bananas, coconuts, papayas, various root vegetables and greens, pumpkins, gourds and beans. Another interesting culinary experience is a cooking class with **Branca** in her family home. Branca's family is of Portuguese descent and the emphasis is on preparing Goan Catholic dishes using pre-made spice pastes. In the class I attended, we made chicken cafreal, Goan sausage pulao and a dessert called *sheeru* made of sweetened milk, cardamom and semolina. We sampled these dishes at the family dining table, sharing a two-way cultural exchange in between mouthfuls.

**detroitinstitute@yahoo.com.au
(0832) 2435905, (M) 9822131835**

MARGAO

Margao or Madgaon is the capital of Salcete taluka (sub-district). It is the largest city of south Goa and the state's second largest. It is not on most tourist itineraries except as a pit stop on the way to nearby Colva and Benaulim beaches. To that end, it operates as a town devoted to serving the needs of the locals and is thus more interesting from a food perspective. It is worth spending a day in Margao, wandering through cafes and taking in the atmosphere and the old Portuguese mansions and churches. Margao is the trading centre for fish from the nearby coast, and rice and other produce from the fertile agricultural areas that surround it; you can see the local bounty of sea and land if you visit the huge market behind the municipal buildings. A visit to the market is always best early in the morning so head out for a Goan-style breakfast afterwards at **Café Bharat**. Start with a small plate of chickpeas cooked with coconut scooped up with soft pao, then order one of the harder bangle-shaped breads and break this up into pieces and dip these into a cup of tea.

Sunshine Building, NH17

The best-known restaurant in Margao, **Longuinhos**, with its 1950s' tiled floor, wood-framed mirrors and marble tabletops has a style that evokes colonial Havana. Locals and tourists watch the world go by over coffees in the morning, and beers, feni and arrack later in the day, accompanied by Goan sausages and other snacks. If you want something more solid, there are daily specials of Goan seafood dishes. In the evening, the road on which Longuinhos sits hosts a long line of men selling bread from baskets and carts. Once upon a time, the village baker would ride his bicycle every day and deliver bread directly to his customers. This practice still continues to some extent—I saw boys riding around Panaji in the evening with bread baskets on their bikes: they would ring a bell and people would come to their doors and flag them down; but picking up some bread on the way home from work is becoming more usual.

Margao Market Road, Dr Antonio Dias Building,
Opposite Municipal Building
(0832) 2739908
8 a.m.–10.30 p.m. (7 days)

Furtado's lies at the foot of the pedestrian bridge that crosses over the main railway line. It is open only in the evening and does brisk business as a bar, so it's a bit dark and dingy, but drinkers like to eat and the food here is authentic. I ordered a squid vindalho, which took some time to arrive because it was freshly prepared. What is on the menu depends on what is fresh in the market. On the day I visited, there was a choice of mackerel, kingfish and pomfret, as well as squid, all of which can be prepared in various Goan styles.

Margao Railway Overbridge
7 p.m. until late

Dom Pedro, a busy bakery and cafe in the town centre, is the place to sample sweets like doce, bebinca, bolinhas and dense, chewy *gons* made from wheat, jaggery and coconut. I wanted to try the prawn rissoles but the customer before me bought the whole lot. In the cafe upstairs, you can have pork vindalho, chicken xacuti or sorpotel with sanna.

Shop No. 2, Reliance Plaza, Behind Grace Church
(0832) 2713251

A short drive from Margao, through the lush countryside, is **Nostalgia**. The dining room and bar occupy the extensive veranda of this rural colonial villa. It was the custom in Goa for the wealthy to socialize on the verandas of their mansions so turning this same area over to entertaining patrons at Nostalgia is a natural extension. Part of the floor space is dedicated to a museum of household items including those used for food preparation, cooking and storage. The menu is dedicated to local cooking but ventures beyond the usual selection. You can enjoy dainty prawn rissoles and fish croquettes; *lulas recheadas* (stuffed squid); cucumber cooked in light coconut gravy; crisp ladies' fingers fresh from the garden cooked with onions, mustard seeds and tomato; and *kismet* (a Goan delicacy of prawns fried crisp mixed with tamarind, onion and coconut, eaten as a relish). In a show of true Goan hospitality, the patroness Margarida visits every table to ensure her guests are comfortable and enjoying their meal. The bar is well stocked with local liquors making Nostalgia a great place to take your time over some eats and drinks. A tour of the adjoining home can be taken, if prearranged.

608, Urzo Raia, Salcette
(0832) 2777054, (M) 9822103467
11 a.m.–3 p.m., 7–11.15 p.m. (7 days)
www.goacom.org/restaurants/fernando/restaurant.html

Near Margao at Betalbatim is **Martin's Corner**, which has earned a particular renown for its Goan seafood dishes such as crab *xec xec* (rich sauce of red chillies, coconut, coriander, garlic and tomatoes) but is famous for being popular with Indian cricketers on holiday. Because of its illustrious clientele everybody knows where it is.

(0832) 2880413
11 a.m.–11 p.m.

Somewhat further south on the NH17, a couple of kilometres ahead from the turn off to Palolem, at Nagarcem you can find the very simple **Goa Corner**. This little cafe and bar, with its Wild West–style saloon doors is a world away from the upmarket Martin's, but it serves fresh seafood and fish cooked in authentic Goan style. The menu changes with the daily catch; you choose your seafood or fish and elect to have it cooked in various styles such as *sukha* (sauce of coconut, chilli, onion and tomato). *Tizri* (clams), cooked with coconut, tomato and green chilli, are usually available and Goa Corner is renowned for its chilli fried lobster and crab—great with beer—but you have to order these in advance.

If you are lazing around Palolem, the beachside restaurant **Goyam & Goyam** serves a fabulous Goan iced tea made from feni, vodka, gin, rum and lime. It's a potent brew so take it with some Goan-style crab-stuffed papad.

MUMBAI

METRO FEEDS

Mumbai is said to be a city that never sleeps but making your way through the silent streets of Colaba towards the Sassoon Docks in the first creeping light of the morning would seem to put paid to that statement: that is until you arrive at the fish market and a riot of colour and noise confronts you. As your partially somnolent self draws into a fully alert state, and your eyes begin to focus, you will notice that the silvery blue scales of the displayed fish are interspersed with a pattern of yellow, red and green; then you will notice that this colour has form: a female form. What you see are Koli fisherwomen at work, hawking fish. The Koli are the original inhabitants of Mumbai. They have been fisherfolk for millennia and have maintained a distinct division of labour from that time: Koli men catch the fish and Koli women sell them. The waterfront around Sassoon Docks is where Koli fishing boats have always berthed and continue to do so. While Mumbai has grown into a mega city—the largest in India and one of the largest in the world—the Koli have managed to maintain, against significant challenges, their occupation and identity. They also play a role in feeding one of modern Mumbai's food habits, a passion for fish and seafood, but before we venture into the city's kitchens a little history will help orient us.

The almost impossibly densely inhabited area—21,000 or so humans per square kilometre—now known as Mumbai, was, prior to the seventeenth century, an archipelago of seven islands strung across the Arabian Sea. Some 2000-odd years ago, these were inhabited by the Koli. Over the millennia, the islands, and the Koli, came under the jurisdiction of various rulers. In the fourteenth century, the long arm of the Delhi Sultanate reached all the way to these islands; the local Sultan of Gujarat claimed them as part of his realm in the early fifteenth century, and then ceded them to the Portuguese in 1534. (In a culinary nose-thumbing to both the Muslim Sultan and local Hindus, the victorious Portuguese governor general, Nuno da Cunha, celebrated the victory over the islands by repairing to a local mosque and feasting on wine, boiled ham and beef.) Despite changes in leadership, and the foreigners this brought into the local populace, life on the archipelago went on much as it had. The local inhabitants such as the Koli kept on fishing, growing rice and farming coconuts. In addition to the abundant briny catch and the luxuriant crops, there was plenty of game to be had, and the Portuguese dubbed the islands *iha da vida*, 'the islands of the good life'. The main business they conducted there was the conversion of local souls to Catholicism: one imagines that the Franciscan friars sent to the islands probably partook of the 'good life' while fulfilling their divine mission.

Meanwhile, the British at Surat worried about the Dutch presence in the region; as part of their strategy to deal with this 'threat', they had the Portuguese include the archipelago in the dowry of the Portuguese princess, Catherine of Braganza, when she married Charles II of England in 1661. Not having much use for seven swampy islands, Charles agreed to lease them to the British East India Company for a proverbial 'peppercorn rent'. With a frontage on to the Arabian Sea that included a deep natural harbour, the British viewed the islands through an entirely commercial focus. All the converting they wanted to do was of local resources into hard currency by shipping these out of India.

Life was hardly good for the British though as they set about building a base for themselves on the main island. Malaria, cholera and a host of other tropical diseases and infections caused a disproportionate number of deaths amongst the British, who often succumbed to local conditions within weeks: it was said that you could make your fortune in Bombay,* if you could survive there for more than two years. Nonetheless, they persisted and by the early eighteenth century, Bombay had become the headquarters of East India Company operations. Prior to this, the British had only held the rights to set up trading posts but with Bombay they 'owned the land' and could shape it to their will—which they did.

Through a series of remarkable, and costly, land-reclamation projects, the British filled in the watery gaps between the islands and created the

* Bombay, the name that the British gave the region, was changed to Mumbai in 1996. In this chapter, I use Bombay in the historical sense and Mumbai for the present-day city.

promontory now officially known as Mumbai. To populate their new city, the British offered incentives to Indians to settle and work in Bombay. While most Indians bitterly resented European attempts to convert them to Christianity, they were most willing to assist them in converting Bombay into a commercial entrepôt. Hindus, Muslims, Jains, Sikhs, Jews, Buddhists, Christians and Parsis from across India came in, creating a polyglot population: one that still exists and represents India's diversity in a microcosm. All these communities contributed to Bombay's evolution and made it India's richest city.

Mumbai has no ancient monuments, palaces, forts. Its temples are those to mammon. Even its slums, such as the so-called 'mega slum' at Dharavi, are hives of commercial enterprise. But then, its richness lies in the diversity of its people. While this is no different from India's other major cities, it has bred a unique cosmopolitanism and tolerance. With respect to food, there is no distinct Mumbai cuisine but I would recommend it for its culinary diversity as you can eat authentic versions of regional food from all across India in this city. There are several communities though, such as the Parsis, that have a particularly significant presence in Mumbai and we will explore their distinct cuisine further on. First, let's take a look at the general food life of Mumbai and some of its unique features.

Every day, around 10 a.m., anywhere between 150,000 to 200,000 home-made lunches, prepared and packed by wives and mothers into cylindrical, multi-tiered lunch boxes called *dabba*s (tiffins), are picked up from across suburban Mumbai. Through a chain of men known as dabba-wallahs, these lunches are relayed to office workers in the city. There is a plethora of options there for buying lunch, but whether it is about taste, caste or economy, these 200,000 Mumbaikars prefer home-made food. Up to 5000 dabba-wallahs carry the dabbas on bicycle handlebars, on trains, on handcarts, on their heads, and on wooden trays that can weigh up to fifty kilograms. Many dabba-wallahs are illiterate and not a written word is used to get the lunches to their destinations. Instead, a complex code of coloured symbols on the dabbas tells the dabba-wallahs the exact destination of any particular lunch. Their accuracy rate in delivering these is 99.9 per cent: a feat so outstanding that international business leaders have studied the system and an American business magazine awarded Mumbai's dabba-wallahs their highest possible rating for correctness. The international accolades and attention does not make the dabba-wallahs' work any less onerous; it is hard physical labour performed under tight time pressures while navigating the crowded trains and streets of Mumbai, but they do earn a decent salary (compared to local standards). Not only do the lunches reach their destinations but they do so at the same time each day even though most dabba-wallahs do not wear a watch. After the lunches are eaten, the whole process is reversed with the dabba returning safely to the home from which it originated. On the rare occasion when a lunch does not reach its destination, it is usually because a 'dabba thief' has stolen it. It is believed that the idea for the dabba-wallah system was sparked in the nineteenth century when a British man arranged for a servant to bring his lunch from his home to the office.

Mumbai's dabba-wallahs largely hail from the same village near Pune and are related to one another. (How is that for 'keeping it in the family': 5000 related employees.) They are also all members of the Nutan Mumbai Tiffinbox Suppliers Charity Trust (NMTSCT). If you place yourself near an entrance to any of the downtown railway stations, such as Churchgate or Victoria, around noon on any working day you should be able to see the dabba-wallahs in action. They all wear white caps and loose pyjama trousers, but even if the uniform is not evident, you can't miss the pile of dabbas they are either sorting or carrying. My advice is to observe from a distance though and not get in the way as these men have a busy job to get on with and don't need to be waylaid by inquisitive tourists. If, like business tycoon Sir Richard Branson, you want to know more about dabba-wallahs, the NMTSCT can arrange for you to spend a day with a tiffin carrier on his rounds. (Make sure you are physically up to it though.)

The street-food scene in Mumbai is perhaps like nowhere else in India. Street stalls here provide millions of workers with breakfast, lunch, snacks and dinner every day. The offerings, particularly in downtown office areas, can be quite sophisticated, served off professional carts at very reasonable prices. Clustered on street corners under colourful umbrellas are stalls selling fresh seasonal fruit cut into chunks; thick, creamy lassi churned in earthenware pots; piping hot idlis and dosas; and full south Indian vegetarian meals. None of these dishes are unique to Mumbai but the city does have several indigenous street foods. The best known of these is bhelpuri, a mix of puffed rice (*bhel*), *sev* (thin, crisp noodles made of chickpea flour), crushed *papri*, roasted peanuts or chickpeas, finely diced onion and tomatoes and a few sprigs of fresh coriander dressed with thin tamarind chutney and a sprinkle of the vendor's own special spice blend. The bhelpuri-wallah is a master of mixing: he pulls the components together quickly into a bowl then deftly tosses them with a flick of the wrist that causes concurrent forward and upward motion not unlike that required to toss pancakes. The finished product is transferred into a small newspaper cone without spillage. Bhelpuri vendors are found at street corners everywhere, especially in the early evening, as this snack—light in substance yet blending textures and flavours that satisfy the palate—is perfect to hold oneself over until dinner. Dinner hour in Mumbai is a late one: many workers face a long commute home and it is just not done for wealthy Mumbaikars to eat before 10 p.m. Most upmarket restaurants do not even open for dinner before 7.30 p.m.; if you eat in them any time before 10 p.m., you will often find them fairly empty. A recent newspaper survey on Indian mealtimes found that midnight is a normal time for Mumbai families to eat dinner—so it's no wonder they need an early-evening bhelpuri.

While bhelpuri is the perfect light evening snack, Mumbai's famous *vada pav* is a more substantive treat of lightly spiced, battered potato patties served smothered with coriander, mint-and-green-chilli chutney and a sprinkle of spices squashed into a pav (soft bun). Mumbaikars say that the vada pav has a unique flavour when made in Mumbai that cannot be replicated outside of the city. Mumbaikars are certainly fond of soft white buns—possibly a Portuguese influence—as these are part of another indigenous Mumbai street snack called *pao bhaji*. The bhaji is a silken melange of mashed vegetables, red chilli and spices cooked in a very generous amount of butter. A substantial dollop of bhaji is served on a plate, dressed with chopped onions, with a toasted pao unstintingly spread with more butter. You will find pao bhaji vendors throughout the city and there are numerous stands dedicated to its production on the beaches at Chowpatty and Juhu.

I am not sure if it is politically correct to still call Bombay duck by that name or if the nativistically correct term is now Mumbai duck. This food in neither exclusive to Mumbai nor is it an avian species but, as it takes the city's name, we shall meet it here. Bombay duck is actually a fish, more correctly a dried fish. It is popular all along the Konkan coast where it is eaten as a fresh fish called *bombil*, and in its dried form during the monsoon months when fishing boats cannot go out to turbulent seas. Fresh bombil is slathered with a paste of asafoetida and hung up on lines to dry, emitting a fearsomely pungent odour. It was a smell that the British found hard to tolerate but they did enjoy Bombay duck fried until crisp and crumbled over food. They are also held responsible for christening this fish, and there are two different stories about it. The first holds that because the bombil swims close to the surface of the water, like a duck, the British named it after this bird. The second is that it was named after the Calcutta-to-Bombay mail train—the *dak*—which after travelling for three days across the breadth of the subcontinent in the monsoon arrived in Bombay covered in mould and reeking: just like drying fish. What these stories don't mention is that the bombil is a particularly ugly fish with a beak-like mouth: I wonder if the more pragmatic truth is that it was this feature which gave it its name.

Fish and seafood are incredibly popular with Mumbaikars. As India's richest city, the choicest fish and seafood caught anywhere along the country's coastline are packed on to planes and sent to Mumbai, as it is here these will realize the best price. Pomfret is perhaps the most popular fish in Mumbai: caught both locally and around India. The Koli community faces challenges from the import of fish—although it would be impossible for them to solely satisfy the city's gargantuan appetite for piscatorial sustenance—and concerns about possible contamination of the fish they harvest in the waters around Mumbai.

Amongst the communities that make up Mumbai's thirteen million denizens is one of some 80,000 Parsis. The maths on these numbers makes them weigh in at less than 1 per cent of the population, but this in no way reflects the vital contribution the Parsi community has made to the development of Mumbai, including its food culture. The Parsis are originally from Persia and are also known as Zoroastrians as they worship the god Zoroaster. They started to immigrate to India in the seventh century when the ruling dynasty in Persia converted to Islam and started to persecute non-Muslims, such as Zoroastrians. These immigrants were not the first Parsis to have visited India: there was an ancient trade between Persia and India in which Parsis were involved. Through this, they had gained some knowledge of India, which likely influenced their decision to seek haven here. Legend has it that the first boats of Parsi refugees were shipwrecked off the Gujarat coast. They sent a delegation to meet the local raja to plead their case for asylum, whereupon his highness presented them with a vessel filled to the brim with milk: apparently a polite way of saying 'sorry guys, no room at the inn, we are full up'. In response, the Parsi delegation stirred a spoonful of sugar into the milk to indicate that not only could they fit in without creating a spill, they would also sweeten things. Won over by this promise, the raja granted them permission to stay on and practise their religion, provided they bore no arms, caused no friction and adapted to various local customs such as the language and the practice of evening wedding ceremonies. Whether or not this is how things really happened, it is a good story for this book as it involves food and it faithfully represents the Parsi track record in India: they have never made trouble, they have fitted in and they have certainly contributed to making life 'sweet' wherever they have settled.

Having landed in Gujarat, the Parsis originally settled in the coastal cities of Bharuch, Navsari, Valsad and Surat where trade became the engine of their community: they ran shops, they ran ships. When the British began to offer incentives to Indians to settle in Mumbai, the Parsis were among the earliest to accept—Dorabji Nanabhoy is reputed to have been the first Parsi to arrive in Bombay in 1640—and Mumbai is now home to the world's largest Parsi community. In Persia, Parsis were stratified into priests, soldiers, civil servants, farmers, herdsmen, artisans and labourers, but in India their numbers were too small to support such a 'caste' system. They kept the priestly class, as this is a hereditary role, and collapsed all other social divisions to create a singular class. The result was that the Parsis were not bound by the caste rules that often made it very difficult for the British to work with the Hindus (and vice versa). The Parsis willingly learnt English and, with their diplomatic abilities and cultural knowledge honed from ten centuries of 'adapting' to India, they often acted as go-betweens for the British with other Indians. The British trusted and valued the Parsis and employed them—they liked having Parsi butlers and supported them in their pursuit of commercial opportunities in the burgeoning metropolis of Bombay. The Parsis became very successful, and very charitable. They gifted Bombay with many buildings and provided support for public institutions. The Parsi philosophy is described as a happy one—its motto: 'good words, good deeds, good thoughts'. Parsis are also very good eaters.

Mumbai cafe Britannia and Company is famed for its Parsi cuisine. Its motto is: 'There is no love greater than the love of eating.' Parsi interest in trying new foods and creating dishes that mix influences from across the country is arguably on par with that of the Mughals. They have few dietary restrictions, besides some prescribed days of fasting. If anything, Parsis are renowned for their 'non-vegetarianism' though beef and pork are not eaten out of deference to the communities they have lived with for 1300 years. In his book about life in Bombay in the late nineteenth century, Sir Dinshaw Wacha says that Parsis spoke both Gujarati and Persian: it can be said that their food did too. Dishes on offer in Parsi restaurants in Mumbai tend towards 'special dishes' of the community such as those served at weddings. A Parsi wedding feast, called *lagan nu bhonu*, follows a prescribed pattern. It starts with a pickle, traditionally made of carrots and dates, called *gajar nu achar*. Next comes a fish dish, perhaps *patra ni machchi*, fish fillets smothered with a finely ground paste of coconut, green coriander, mint, green chillies and lime, wrapped in banana leaf and steamed. This dish pays homage to the nearby Arabian Sea and the tropical blessings of coconut and banana enjoyed all along the western coastline of India. Coconut, fish and rice are considered symbols of plenty by the Parsis and are always included at festive occasions. Another fish dish customarily served at weddings is *lagan nu machchi nu saas* or fish fillets cooked in a flour-thickened sweet–sour sauce: the name of this dish and the style of sauce (*saas*) shows a British influence, while the flavouring is a Persian or Goan one. Many Parsis employed Goan cooks—as did the British—and their influence is evident in Parsi seafood such as patio-style prawns, cooked with spices, vinegar and chilli, not dissimilar to a Goan *vindalho*. Next in the wedding line-up comes a chicken- or meat-based stew such as *sali murghi* (chicken stew served with potato wafers—*sali*—which are matchsticks of crunchy fried potato). To prepare sali, potatoes are finely shredded, washed several times to remove the starch, soaked in ice water, thoroughly dried, then slowly fried to allow them to lose moisture to the oil until they are golden-brown and crunchy. The matching stew is a preparation of chicken cooked with dried fruit, cinnamon, cardamom, cloves and garlic: obvious Persian overtones there. At this point arrives a rice dish, typically a chicken/mutton pulao—another dish with origins in the Parsi homeland. European influence is evident in the traditional wedding dessert, *lagan nu custard*, a baked custard of eggs and cream flavoured with nutmeg and rose water. Ice cream, like kulfi, finishes the meal. While Parsi food rings with sweet and sour flavours, it is generally not 'chilli' hot, at least not when served at weddings, or in restaurants, as that has to suit a large number of people.

Perhaps the best-known dish of Parsi cuisine is the meat-and-lentil stew called *dhansak*. It is never served at weddings, because it is customarily served four days after a death and has associations that are not to be invited during a wedding. Apart from this stricture, dhansak is widely enjoyed and is another unfailing inclusion on Parsi restaurant menus. Parsi cooks are also masters at incorporating extensive numbers of ingredients into singular dishes. A simple dhansak might contain twenty individual ingredients while a more complex one almost twice that. To make dhansak, meat is cooked with various dals and spices; a dish of finely chopped vegetables and spices is cooked separately and various wet and dry spice blends are also prepared. These are then all blended with the final addition of some tamarind and jaggery. The resulting dish resembles a sludge but flavour is what it is about—a good dhansak has an incredibly complex taste. Dhansak is believed to have Persian origins and it may be partly for that reason that it is Parsi 'comfort' food. It is traditionally served with 'brown' rice—actually caramel-coloured, long-grained rice—meat kebabs and a mixed salad of onion, tomato, green chillies and coriander.

Another complex winter food is the sweet *vasanu*. This is fabricated from over thirty different ingredients including dried fruit, spices, nuts, sugar, ghee, *gond* (gum), dried water chestnuts and lotus roots. It is served in a thick paste that has a slightly gritty texture or rolled into laddoos. If you are in Mumbai in the winter, you can buy vasanu at the Ratan Tata Institute on Hughes Road, Chowpatty.

There can be no talk of Parsi food without mentioning the egg-based dishes. *Akuri* are eggs scrambled with various combinations of ingredients such as tomatoes, green chillies, fresh coriander, potatoes, ginger, garlic, dal, chicken, dried fruit and nuts. Another Parsi egg dish is *per eeda*—vegetables like spinach, ladies' fingers or bananas, or mincemeat, are cooked to a firm paste with onions and spices; this is spread out into a dish and hollows pressed in it with the back of a spoon; individual eggs are broken into these depressions and the dish is covered over and cooked in an oven or steamer.

The close working relationship between the British and the Parsis is reflected in the Parsi love of cutlets (patties) and crumbed chops (croquettes) made with meat and vegetables, as well as custards, pies, soufflés, cakes and biscuits. The best place to sample any of these is one of Mumbai's Irani cafes. In the latter part of the nineteenth century, a new wave of Zoroastrian immigrants came to India from Iran. Separated by more than a millennium, and living in different countries, these later 'Irani' Zoroastrians, as they are called, are quite distinct from the more established Parsi Zoroastrians, though the latter supported the Irani arrivals and helped them settle in, often employing them in their households. Apparently, a group of these Iranis met each evening to discuss the old country and their prospects in the new one; at one of these gatherings, one man brought along some tea and charged a small amount for it: this transaction among friends is cited as the seminal moment in the development of Mumbai's Irani cafes. A cup of tea vended to friends evolved into street-side stalls selling tea, biscuits, omelettes, fried eggs and small items such as combs, soap and headache tablets to the hordes of men who worked in the city's flourishing textile mills. A programme of road-widening in the city pushed Irani vendors off street corners into shops, which became known as 'Irani cafes'. Any article, whether historical or contemporary, on these now-famous cafes will comment on the utilitarian interior featuring classic wooden chairs, marble-topped tables, dark walls with a few strategically placed mirrors and fans whirring overhead. The Iranis who originally opened these cafes did not have a lot of money to spend on fancy fitments and their clients were predominantly working men who needed to eat cheaply, so any niceties beyond cleanliness and functionality were disregarded. The Irani restaurant owners were not concerned about the caste, religion or social status of their patrons; a neutral environment was welcoming and inoffensive to all. In their early days, Irani cafes did keep separate-coloured crockery and cutlery for the various communities that ate there, but this practice disappeared as people grew accustomed to the cosmopolitan and equitable nature of these cafes. To be truly inclusive, some Irani cafes installed private booths so that women and children could come and eat there as well.

Classic Irani cafe fare is *brun maska*, a soft, generously buttered bun dipped into a strong tea called *khari chai*, made with fresh and condensed milk flavoured with cardamom. There are also different biscuits, also for dipping into tea; cutlets and patties; egg dishes such as akuri and omelettes; and perhaps custard or other milky sweets. What is served in Irani cafes has evolved to satisfy customer needs: the limited menus of the early days suited factory workers with limited budgets; by the mid-twentieth century, more European-style baked goods, roast chicken, soups and confections were on offer as people had a little more money to spend on exotic dishes. Another relatively recent inclusion is a range of Parsi dishes. Bombay's textile industry collapsed in the 1980s and is now non-existent (with the former factories being progressively turned into fancy apartments, art galleries and shopping centres) and it is office workers who now take brun maska and tea or a meal in these cafes alongside businessmen, artists, labourers and students. Another distinct feature of Irani cafes, one that seems at odds with their generally convivial nature, is the presence of signs announcing a litany of behaviours prohibited within the cafe: no division of beverages; no talking loud; no beef; no bargaining; no spitting (I should hope so!); no combing (of hair, presumably); no leg on chair; no discussing gambling. I wanted to see one of these delightfully eccentric signboards for myself but despite visiting a number of Irani cafes I did not find one that extended beyond refusing credit and the bringing in of 'outside' food. It seems these signboards are disappearing, as are Irani cafes. In the 1950s, there were 350-odd Irani cafes in Mumbai; in 2010, only twenty-five remained. (The number may have dwindled further by the time you read this.) Some, such as the famous Leopold Cafe, have morphed into bars and more upscale casual restaurants; others have closed their doors, often because the owners have been so diligent in educating their children that they prefer professional work to taking over the family business. The possible extinction of Irani cafes has seen the remaining stalwarts acquire something of a cult status, such that there might even be a few well-educated Irani youth who decide that running a cult cafe beats commuting to the office in peak hour, sitting in a cubicle all day and having to account for one's time in fifteen-minute blocks. A note of interest here is that the *London Telegraph* reported in June 2013 that at least one Irani cafe was flourishing in that city.

Recommendations

Paradise on Colaba Causeway is run by a charming older Parsi couple who knows everyone who walks in through their doors (except visiting travellers). The waistcoated waiters exude an air of being well-looked-after, long-term employees, which gives this little restaurant what could be described as an 'old-fashioned' feel (in the nicest possible way). The menu features a permanent selection of Parsi dishes such as patra ni machchi, sali murghi, dhansak and lagan nu custard, and a daily special which might be *sali boti* (boneless mutton cooked with tomatoes and apricots, served with potato straws); *atheli murghi* (mildly spiced chicken stew) or *papeta ma gosht* (mutton cooked with potatoes). If you call in just for a snack, try the chicken-and-cheese patties.

Sind Chambers, Colaba Causeway, S.B. Singh Marg
(022) 22832874
9 a.m.–2 p.m., 3–9 p.m. (7 days)

Jimmy Boy is a popular modern Irani cafe with such an extensive menu of Parsi dishes that it is tough to choose. On offer are Bharuchi akuri (eggs cooked in Bharuch style with potatoes, onions, garlic and green chillies) and *bhendi per eedu* (eggs cooked on a bed of ladies' fingers and prawn patio). You can also have a complete lagan nu bhonu of sas ni machchi, sali murghi, mutton pulao, carrot pickle, Parsi roti (small wheat-flour flatbread), sago wafers and lagan nu custard.

Vikas Building, 1 Bank Street, Opposite State Bank of India, Off Horniman Circle, Fort
(022) 22700880, 22662503
11 a.m.–11 p.m. (7 days)

Ideal Corner is a long-standing Parsi cafe that sits, as the name suggests, on a corner in the Fort area. The menu includes daily 'Parsee' specials such as *railway gosht* (mildly spiced mutton cooked with cubes of potato). You can also enjoy a breakfast of akuri here.

12-F Hornby View, Gunbow Street, Fort
(022) 22621930
9 a.m.–4.30 p.m. (Monday to Friday)

Britannia and Company is Mumbai's most famous Irani cafe, the sort of place guidebooks list as a 'must visit'—but don't be turned off by that. Britannia's 'berry pulao' is superlative: basmati rice cooked in stock layered with a thick sauce of meat—chicken or mutton—tempered with cardamom, cloves and coriander; garnished with golden-fried onions, cashew nuts, a couple of kebabs and a generous sprinkling of barberries that the restaurant imports from Iran. (Britannia goes through some 500 kilograms of these in a year.) Eating a plate of this pulao under the whirring ceiling fans on a hot, sticky Saturday afternoon, surrounded by the hustle and bustle of the restaurant and the flirtatious banter of the indefatigable nonagenarian owner, probably adds to the flavour, and it deserves all the accolades it has received over the decades. Other dishes to try include dhansak, fried bombil (when in season) and caramel custard. Britannia is open only for lunch.

Wakefield House, 1 Sprott Road, 16 Ballard Estate, Opposite New Custom House
(022) 22615264, 30225264
Noon–4 p.m. (Sundays closed)

At 104 years **Kyani & Co.** is Mumbai's oldest operating Irani cafe. It is not fancy though it has an extensive offering of fancy cakes, biscuits and other sweet treats made in its own bakery. You could easily spend all day here, just watching the diverse mix of people coming in to have a snack, a cup of tea and a sweet titbit, a meal—or all of the above. As it was, I managed a lurid pink *falooda* (rose-flavoured milk-based drink), brun maska, a bowl of thick-set custard with a cherry on top, bread custard pudding and a pot of cardamom-spiced Irani chai. In true Irani fashion, the current owner mans the front counter, takes the money and keeps a close eye on operations. From the looks of it, the well-maintained decor and fittings have probably not altered much since the cafe first opened, and it is definitely 'Bombay' in here.

657, Jer Mahal Estate, Dhobi Talao
(022) 22011492
6.30 a.m.–9 p.m. (7 days)

I did not expect much when I pulled into **Palladium** for a quick lunch. It is a very plain Irani cafe—a lesson in why looks in this category are irrelevant. The vegetarian dhansak I gobbled down was excellent as was the crème caramel and bread custard. Palladium is so old-school I could not find a listing for it. It is on the western side of Churchgate Station at the top of the underpass.

Since it is the capital of Maharashtra, Mumbai's inhabitants are largely Maharashtrian. All come to the city from various parts of the state and bring in their subregional cuisines. The most popular is the coconut-infused seafood cuisine of the Konkan coastline. You can visit the highly recommended Mahesh Lunch Home in Fort, but I found it hard to get them to make me anything Maharashtrian style. (I ended up by giving in and having a tandoori ladyfish, as it was too late to go anywhere else.) If you want local seafood, it is well worth your while taking the train out to Dadar West: a bustling inner suburb that has a distinct Maharashtrian culture. The clean, friendly canteen at **Gomantak Boarding House** serves Konkan dishes such as fried bombil, spicy shellfish stew and a bread called *vadi*, made of rice, millet, wheat and chickpea flour, eaten with a very spicy, thick, coconut-based mutton or chicken stew. After this, you can soothe your palate and stimulate your digestion with a glass of *sol kadhi*, a drink prepared from dried kokum, coconut milk and garlic, and commonly taken after a meal in the Konkan region.

301 Mirinda Chawl, Near Shivaji Mandir, N.C. Kelkar Road, Dadar West
(022) 24311377
11.30 a.m.–3 p.m., 7.30–11 p.m. (Mondays closed)

Hotel Sindhudurg has a Konkan-style menu like Gomantak's, with speciality dishes like stuffed whole pomfret and a spiced crab stew.

Sita Building, R.K. Vadiya Road, Near Shivaji Park Police Station, Dadar West
(022) 24301610
11.30 a.m.–3.30 p.m., 7.30–10.30 p.m. (7 days)

Aswad Upahar specializes in Maharashtrian thali meals and snacks such as *misal pav*, and *bhakri* served with a slightly spicy, slightly sweet coconut gravy. (*See the Maharashtra chapter for more on these dishes.*) Their multilayered, saffron-infused *kesari falooda*, while not strictly a regional dish, was a wonderful treat on a hot afternoon.

252, Wavda Building, L.J. Road, Shivji Park (diagonally opposite Shiv Sena Bhavan), Gadkari Chowk, Dadar West
(022) 24451871
10 a.m.–10.30 p.m. (7 days)

The wooden benches at Prakash are rarely empty. As soon as one person vacates, another slides in. This simple cafe specializes in Maharashtrian snacks and light meals including *sabudana vada* (tennis-ball-sized crunchy sago fritters). I have a particular passion for sabudana vada and the ones at Prakash are the best I have eaten. (Pinned up on the restaurant wall is a copy of an ode that a journalist wrote to these same vadas in the *New York Times*.) Other regional items to try are *thalipeeth* (multigrain flatbread served with a chutney of curd and peanuts); *bhajani vada* (crisp fritters made from a batter of roasted ground rice and dal flavoured with cumin and coriander);

and the Marathi version of lassi called *piyush*, which is made with curd and saffron.

**19 Balkrishna Sadan, Shivaji Park, Gokhale Road, Dadar West
(022) 24304921
7.30 a.m.-10 p.m. (Fridays closed)**

Also visit **Panshikar & Company** for Marathi snacks and sweets such as piyush, *puran poli* (a thin pancake stuffed with coconut and sugar) and Maharashtra's most famous snack/light meal, *misal*—a many-faceted dish of sprouted dal, spiced coconut–garlic–onion gravy, fresh tomato and crunchy titbits (*see Pune for more on this dish*).

**18 Ganapath Chambers, S.B. Marg, Dadar West
(022) 24229526**

Culture Aangan offers several truly unique Mumbai food experiences. They can arrange for you to spend a day visiting local eating spots with a food-savvy Mumbaikar. Pay an early-morning/evening visit to a Koli home, where the women will prepare a fish or seafood dish in their own style for you. Or enjoy a home-cooking lesson and learn how to make Maharashtrian classics such as *pithla/pitla*, stuffed eggplant, spicy coconut fish stew and stir-fried greens. Any or all of these offerings are a great way to cut to the chase and get an 'insider' view.

**7B, G22, Sangeeta Apartments, Juhu Tara Road, Santacruz,
West Mumbai
(022) 26606448
www.cultureaangan.com**

Shree Krishna Boarding is a boarding house set up to cater to single Brahmin men who come to work in Mumbai from south India or elsewhere. Boarding houses have been very common in Mumbai, each catering to immigrant workers from various states or distinct communities. Shree Krishna is run by Konkani Saraswat Brahmins, but the food here bears closer resemblance to that which you would find in Tamil Nadu. The thali lunch is served on a banana leaf (laid out horizontally in southern style) and is pure vegetarian. The contents of the dishes change every day but the standard format is two vegetable dishes, dal, pickle, rasam, sambhar, roti, papad, rice, two sweet dishes and buttermilk. On the day I visited, my meal included an utterly delicious stew of pumpkin and yam: all in all, this was one of the best southern Indian–style meals I ate in India. Before you are allowed to sit at your allocated table, the dining room overseer insists that you wash your hands or your meal will not be served to you. If you have any concerns about cleanliness, this is the place to come to. At the time I dined at Shree Krishna, there had been a considerable spike in the price of some dal and there was a sign on the wall that informed patrons that they would be charged an extra five rupees if they asked for more dal-based rasam or sambhar and did not eat it all: I loved this concept of fining people for wasting food.

First Floor, L.B.S. Market Building, Near Matunga Central Railway Station
(022) 24142422
10.30 a.m.–2.30 p.m., 7–10 p.m.

If your time in Mumbai is to be spent visiting popular tourist spots, try **Chetana** in Fort for a Maharashtrian-style thali that includes *aamti* (a richly spiced sweet-and-sour dish of *toor* dal); *thecha* (a chutney of green chilli, curry leaves and turmeric); stuffed eggplant cooked with peanuts and coconut; spinach cooked Konkan style with dill (*subya*), onions, green chillies, moong dal and coconut; colocasia leaves cooked with peanuts and jaggery; and *khori roti*, crisp rice-flour roti crumbled into a spicy coconut gravy.

Kala Ghoda, Fort
(022) 22844968
12.30–3 p.m., 7.30–11 p.m. (7 days)

Gujarat and Mumbai were once part of the same state, Bombay Presidency, and Gujaratis are another distinct community to have played a vital role in Bombay's rise. They were among the first to come into Bombay when the British invited interested parties to set up shops in their new colony in the seventeenth century. Gujaratis are now the largest cultural group in Mumbai after Marathis. **Shree Thaker Bhojanalay** serves impeccable homely Gujarati food and is enthusiastically patronized by Mumbaikars of all backgrounds. It is very much a local eatery and tough to find, located as it is on the first floor of a boarding house, the entrance to which is a bit dingy, but don't be put off since it's worth the effort. I visited in early winter and my thali included *undhiyu*, a slow-cooked casserole of root vegetables, green bananas and fenugreek dumplings traditionally made in Gujarat in the cooler months; a tangy salad of shredded cabbage, tempered with cumin, mustard, curry leaves and a little green chilli; corn and millet roti; rice slow-cooked with milk, nutmeg and cardamom; and a sweet of ground rice and dal cooked with jaggery accompanied by rich, creamy curd and buttermilk.

31 Dadisheth Agyari Lane, Off Kalbadevi Road
(022) 22011232
11.30 a.m.–3 p.m., 7–10 p.m. (no evening service on Sundays)

The **Friends Union Joshi Club** (also referred to as **Joshi's Friends Club**) is a simple canteen that does busy trade in traditional vegetarian Gujarati thalis, regularly described as the 'best in town'. This place is also a little hard to find: use the Metro Cinema as a landmark, then cross over to Kalbadevi Road, head north and start asking people for Mahajan Wadi and you will eventually be pointed to it. Look for a sign in the window saying 'Bhojanalay'.

381A, First Floor, Narottamwadi, Kalbadevi Road
(022) 22058089
11 a.m.–3 p.m., 7–10 p.m. (Sundays closed)

Joshi's is a workingman's eatery: great fresh food, quick service, low-priced and very perfunctory decor. For somewhere more modern, where you can linger, **Soam** is very popular with the more fashion/status-conscious Mumbaikars for its contemporary experimental take on traditional Gujarati snacks and light meals.

3, Ground Floor, Sadguru Sadan, Girgaon Chowpatty
(022) 23698080
Noon–11 p.m. (7 days)

The upper part of Colaba Causeway is the tourist strip of Mumbai and many of the restaurants in this section cater to tourist tastes. But there is more to Colaba than this. If you don't have a lot of time in Mumbai, you can enjoy foods from a number of Mumbai communities in this part of town. There is Paradise for Parsi food (mentioned above). The Irani-style **Olympia Coffee House** has been open since 1918 and is well known for its breakfast of *kheema pao* (spiced mincemeat eaten with thick slices of soft white bread); the proper way to eat this is to squeeze lime juice over it, take a bite from a green chilli—both supplied—then take a mouthful of the kheema. Mumbai is home to many distinct Muslim communities, including Bohras from Gujarat; Khojas, Shia Muslims from Sind; and Konkani Muslims. The food at Olympia is that of the Chilla Muslim community who practise a forty-day period of prayer to progress towards losing the desire for this world. Other breakfast, or lunch, options are biryani or green-chilli-flecked omelette; a popular combination is omelette with kheema. Most customers take hot chai; opulent, chilled, rose-flavoured falooda is an alternative.

Rahim Mansion, No. 1 S.B. Road, Colaba Causeway
(022) 22021043, 22045220
11 a.m.–midnight (7 days)

The seventy-five-year-old **Kamat Sweets & Snacks*** serves south Indian tiffin items such as dosa, idli and *uttapam* as well as Mumbai street foods (if you prefer to take these sitting down). Kamat is well patronized by Colaba locals. I enjoyed eavesdropping on their conversation about the state of the world from a Mumbai perspective.

Colaba Causeway, S.B. Singh Road, Opposite Grand Bazaar
(022) 22848205
8 a.m.–10 p.m. (7 days)

Kailash Parbat is a Sindhi sweet-and-snack house—and a Mumbai 'institution'—that serves Sindhi-style dishes such as Sindhi curry, a thick stew of lotus stem and other vegetables flavoured with tamarind, cumin, fenugreek and asafoetida that is served at Sindhi weddings; a Sindhi version of stir-fried greens and the classic Mumbai street-food snack *ragda pattice* (patties of white beans and potato served with spiced chickpea stew and tamarind chutney).

Narayan Building, First Pasta Lane, Colaba Causeway
(022) 22841972
8.30 a.m.–11 p.m. (7 days)

....

* There is also a Kamat Restaurant on the 'tourist' side of the road but you don't want that one: it is full of tourists eating touristy food!

SOUL CURRY

Some citizens of Mumbai, capital of Maharashtra, seem to believe that their city is the centre of the universe—for which they may have good reason; it is so big it must be visible from deep space—but it's the far more sedate Maharashtrian city of Nagpur that has an actual claim to centrality, as it sits smack on the geographic centre of India. In the mid-eighteenth century, the region now known as Maharashtra was at the centre of a kingdom that covered most of the Indian subcontinent: the founder of this empire was the legendary Hindu leader, Chhatrapati Shivaji. Busy trade routes—running from the north of India to the ports of the west coast—traversed Maharashtra since at least the time of the Buddha, and major religious sites such as Ajanta and Ellora thrived there from the second century BC to the end of the first millennium AD. But it was the daring—or dastardly, depending on which side you were on—martial exploits of Shivaji, and his 'wild and unruly' Maratha army that propelled Maharashtra into prominence. One of the many legends about Shivaji has him cleverly escaping from the prison of his nemesis, the Mughal emperor Aurangzeb, by hiding in a basket of sweets. Shivaji died in 1680 but the Marathas kept up the momentum, capturing even more land and bringing the chilli into central and north India.

By 1535, the Portuguese had possession of a territory they called the Northern Provinces, which stretched for 100 kilometres along the coast and up to fifty kilometres inland, from Daman in Gujarat to just south of the future city of Bombay. This particular belt of land, between the Arabian Sea and the Western Ghats, was well watered and fecund. The Portuguese brought it under cultivation with various new-world plant species that they introduced to India (*see the Goa chapter*), including the chilli. The Marathas had been besieging the Portuguese, and anybody else stationed along this coast they saw as an enemy, since Shivaji's time finally driving them off in 1793. They annexed the region to their empire and inherited the established agriculture. (Shivaji himself led two successful sieges on the Mughal-held port of Surat, and it was partly because of these that the British moved to Bombay.) Some of the most distinctive dishes of Maratha cuisine feature new-world ingredients such as peanuts, cashew nuts and potatoes, suggesting that the Marathas continued to farm and eat the crops of the vanquished Portuguese. They also developed a particular proclivity for the chilli.

Shivaji's enthusiastic consumption of chillies is reputed to have imbued him with the strength to defeat the Mughals at Surat—although by this time the Mughals were considered to have gone 'soft' due to their consumption of rich food and preference for lying around watching dancing girls. Given that this event happened before the Marathas captured the greater region from the Portuguese, they had obviously had an earlier introduction to *Capsicum frutescens*. The greater body of Maratha soldiers were considered to be the finest Hindu warriors in India: they had a reputation as hot-tempered and ruthless fighters, and it is thought that they were responsible for the spread of the chilli across the lands they conquered. If their success was seen to be associated with their consumption of this hot pepper, many men throughout the Maratha confederacy would have been keen to eat a food that enhanced their manliness. This nexus between hot food and ultimate masculinity has not waned over time in Maharashtra, where a popular saying goes: 'If a man can't eat a [hot] *lavangi* chilli dipped in red chilli powder, he is not man enough!' Food of the Kolhapur region in the south-west of the state is reckoned to be amongst the hottest in India.

At its peak, the Maratha confederacy covered the greater part of India—except the deepest south, Goa and the south-eastern seaboard— and re-established Hindu rule after centuries of Islamic dominance: until a new enemy came along. The Marathas were a persistent menace to British ambition in India but these foreign interlopers finally quelled them in the early nineteenth century, and subsumed the Maratha home territory into the Bombay Presidency, which was divided after Independence into Gujarat and Maharashtra. With a girth that stretches from the Arabian Sea, across the tropical coastal plains, up the precipitous Western Ghats and over the Deccan plateau, Maharashtra has a variegated geography that supports the production of a wide variety of foods; this is reflected in the existence of several subregional cuisines within the state (*more later*).

Over its vertical axis, Maharashtra occupies a space between north India and south India and is often described as a 'crossover' state where the predominant foodgrain transitions from wheat in the north to rice in the south, with rice being slightly more predominant overall. (The Indian government actively subsidizes the price of rice, such that this grain is often cheaper than wheat and is now much more commonly eaten in regions where it was not traditionally grown.) Breakfast in Maharashtra is a good illustration of this grain duality; many people start the day with a rice-based dish such as idli or dal eaten with wheat roti. A distinct Maharashtrian dish also eaten at breakfast—but not exclusively since it is also had as a light lunch or snack—is *misal*. This name means 'mixture' and it is a layered dish built upon a base of sprouted *moth* dal cooked with onions and spices called *usal*; this is dressed with a well-spiced onion–garlic–coconut gravy called *kat*— key to the whole as it imparts most of the flavour—spiced potato pieces, crunchy fried titbits or rice puffs and finely chopped raw onion, tomato and coriander. This is the basic formula for misal but there are many versions: when dressed with curd, it is *dahi misal*; when eaten with soft white bread, it is *misal pav*. It is also made differently in different parts of Maharashtra: the kat of a Kolhapuri misal is rather well flavoured with chilli; the misal of Pune includes rice flakes called *poha*. This latter ingredient, reconstituted and quickly sautéed with chopped onion, mustard seeds, turmeric and green chilli is another breakfast dish—also called poha—eaten across Maharashtra (and much of north India).

For the bread eaters of Maharashtra, a basic meal includes wheat roti called *poli* or *bhakri*; thick rustic flatbreads made from grains such as pearl millet, jowar (sorghum) or rice, the latter usually eaten in rural and coastal areas; and a dal-based dish such as *aamti*, made from *toor* dal, garlic, tamarind, *goda masala* (*see below*) and jaggery. The sweet-and-sour flavour of this last dish is reminiscent of the food of neighbouring Gujarat, recalling that the two states share a history. A white dal called *val* or *varan* is another legume regularly used in Maharashtra, usually to make a less complex flavoured dal than aamti. A simple meal in interior Maharashtra is *pitla*, a smooth porridge made of *besan* (chickpea flour) cooked with buttermilk, onion, chillies, mustard seeds, turmeric and asafoetida, garnished with a chutney ground from raw onions and red chilli, and scooped up with bhakri. This rural dish has become somewhat fashionable in cities such as Pune and Mumbai where you can buy it from street stalls. Peanuts are an important crop in Maharashtra and are widely used in Maratha cooking, particularly to add substance and protein to vegetable dishes such as *batatyachi bhaji* (potatoes cooked with peanuts) and *bharli vangi* (eggplant stuffed with peanuts and coconut); peanut oil is the ordinary cooking medium in Maharashtra. *Rassa* is a thin—sometimes described as 'water gravy'—and well-spiced flavoured sauce/curry that accompanies meals. It is made in vegetarian as well as non-vegetarian versions.

Maratha cuisine derives one of its most distinctive tastes from the use of goda masala, a complex spice mix of coriander seeds, brown cardamom, cinnamon, cloves, bay leaf, star anise, cumin, asafoetida, turmeric, red chillies, sesame seeds, dried coconut (copra), sesame seeds and the unusual *dagad phool*, a dried lichen, the name of which literally means 'black stone flower'. The ingredients are individually roasted to a very dark colour and ground together. Goda masala has a strong flavour and needs a sour flavouring such as tamarind or kokum and a little jaggery to balance it out, such as in aamti. Every Maratha cook will have her, or his, own unique recipe for goda masala.

A popular snack in Maharashtra is *sabudana vada* or sago fritters, said to have originated in the interior Vidarbha region (of which Nagpur is the main city). The sago pearls that these are made from are constituted from the pith of various species of tropical palms that grow profusely in South East Asia. Sago is known to have been imported into India from Indonesia in the first millennium AD—Vidarbha is utterly landlocked but it had strong connections with various east-coast dynasties that traded with South East Asia during its long history as an independent kingdom. Most sabudana vada that you get in India nowadays is likely to have been made with so-called 'tapioca sago' produced in south India. In the early nineteenth century, tapioca (a native plant of South America) was introduced into India, most likely by the Portuguese. Tapioca is a completely different species from the sago palm. It is grown for its starchy potato-like root but the 'milk' extracted from it can be made into granules that are identical to those produced from sago pith, and can be used in the same way. Sabudana vada is made by soaking the sago granules overnight, making them swell and soften; mixing the swollen granules with mashed potato, peanuts, green chilli, mustard seeds and curry leaves; and shaped into balls or patties and deep-fried: the vadas have a crunchy exterior and a soft, somewhat sticky interior. Sabudana vadas are commonly eaten on Hindu religious fast days, particularly during the Navaratri festival, when cereals are not permitted. I find this interesting as the major components of this food item—sago, potato, peanuts, chilli—are all introduced species of plant food: perhaps this is why they can be eaten, as they were not known in ancient India when many of the food 'rules' of Hinduism were devised. You will find sabudana vada being sold at street stalls and in cafes throughout Maharashtra, and indeed all across India these days. (*See Mumbai recommendations for the best sabudana vada in India.*) Sago tapioca is made into a khichri—with very similar ingredients to those of the vada—also said to have originated in Vidarbha, and a sweet milky *kheer*. Both are eaten during fasts and are not widely available commercially though some restaurants put them on their menus during festivals.

Only one-third of the population of Maharashtra is vegetarian. Mutton is the most popular meat in the interiors, while fish and seafood are eaten in abundance along the coast. I found though that many of the restaurants serving Maratha-style food confine themselves to vegetarian offerings. This does not necessarily hold true in Kolhapur, which is famed for its blistering-hot meat dishes, though Kolhapuris say that their food is not 'hot', just very well spiced, and dishes prefixed with the name of the region anywhere outside of it are usually travesties of the real thing, overladen with chillies. However, most Kolhapuris probably have a well-developed tolerance for levels of chilli in food such that their measure of 'hot' is set higher than most. Distinct Kolhapur dishes are *loncha* (meat pickle); *tambada rassa* (thin 'red' meat gravy); and *pandhra rassa* ('white' meat gravy customarily eaten before the spicier tambada).

Puran poli is a Maratha sweet made from a soft, thin wheat bread stuffed with a paste of cooked chana dal, jaggery or sugar, cardamom, saffron and nutmeg; alternatively, it might be filled with a mixture of coconut and jaggery. Puran poli was once a food prepared and eaten only on auspicious occasions but it has become somewhat of a daily food item, often included as part of a Maratha meal in restaurants. *Anarsa* is a rice-based biscuit made in Maharashtra to celebrate Diwali. The process for making this confection begins some time before it is required: first rice is soaked, and the water changed regularly for several days; it is then drained, ground and mixed with jaggery to form a dough, which is covered and left for four to five days to mature; when the dough is ready, it is divided into pieces, rolled in white poppy seeds, pressed out into rounds and fried until golden and crisp. Given the complicated process required to made anarsa these do not often appear 'out of season', but if you are visiting Maharashtra around Diwali, look out for them in bakeries. Maharashtra is the largest producer of Alphonso mangoes, and in mango season, these are relished as fresh fruit. The flesh is also puréed to make *ambaacha ras*, which is eaten with poli. Marathas sustain the taste of the mangoes throughout the year by preserving the fruit as *ambaa pa barfi*, a sweetmeat made from mango juice cooked with sugar until it forms a thick paste, and mango cordial.

A traditional meal in Maharashtra is served on a *taat* (thali) that is laid out in a very particular order. Its centre-top is marked by a small mound of salt; proceeding counterclockwise are all the ingredients required to add additional flavour and texture to the mains: a piece of lemon; one or two fresh chutneys; various achars (oil-based pickles); raita; *koshimbar* (crisp salad of finely chopped vegetables); and two or three crunchy titbits such as vada and papad. The right side is reserved for the mains, one of which is always a sautéed preparation of leafy greens and the other a vegetable dish cooked in a sauce. The dry vegetable is always placed above the wet one so that the gravy from the latter does not run into the drier dish. Dal is served in a separate *katori* (small bowl) on the right along with the sweet items. Rice and bread are placed just below the centre of the taat within easy reach of the diner; a dal-based rassa is poured over the rice before the meal begins. If meat dishes are to be eaten, these are placed on the right. The first test a new Marathi bride must pass when she comes to live in the home of her husband's family is to serve a correctly laid-out taat: if she fails, her job of ingratiating herself with her in-laws will be made just that little bit harder. How many dishes and sundry other items are included on any Marathi taat depends on whether it is a celebratory or a regular family meal and the economic circumstances and preferences of any individual family. If the food is to be served on a banana leaf, it is laid out vertically following the same pattern. (Food is laid out horizontally on banana leaves in south India.) Now that you know the formula, you can assess whether any taat you might eat from while visiting Maharashtra would pass the daughter-in-law test.

The pace of life in the rest of Maharashtra is more sedate than that in Mumbai—modern Pune is 'fast' becoming an exception—and a large percentage of Marathis are engaged in agricultural work. Nagpur is at the centre of India's well-established orange farming industry while Nashik is at the centre of India's fledgling wine industry. Wine drinking is not usually associated with Indian food, nor wine production with India, yet modern Indian winemaking has developed exponentially over the past decade, with more Indian-made wine coming into the market every year. Wine drinking is not new to India though. Despite the prohibition on the consumption of alcohol in the Koran, the Delhi Sultans and Mughal emperors—except the pious Aurangzeb—were fond of wine. They kept extensive cellars, overseen by cellar masters, and wine was served by a high-ranking servant whose title was *saqi-i-khas* or 'one who serves the liquor'. The wine they drank had to be imported from Persia as attempts to grow wine grapes in India were not successful.

It is the use of chilli in Indian food that has contributed to the belief that wine does not pair well with it; for those used to eating Indian food in Indian restaurants outside of India, experience probably confirms this. If you are going to eat dishes that are 'hot', then you are better off drinking beer or very sweet wine, but if you eat moderately spiced—and more authentic—Indian cooking, then wine is eminently compatible with much of it.

Shiraz/Syrah grapes grow very well in India and wine produced from this variety is a particular favourite with Indian wine drinkers. Its characteristic berry and oak flavours stand up to a wide variety of Indian dishes and it pairs particularly well with rich Indo-Muslim meat dishes. Cabernet Sauvignon works well with Indian-style desserts and the somewhat sweet Gujarati vegetarian food. Chenin Blanc and Sauvignon Blanc pair well with mild coconut-based curries, seafood dishes and biryani. Recently, wine growers in India have been very successful at cultivating and making wine from varietal like Chardonnay, Gewürztraminer and Riesling too. Indian wine brands to look out for are Grover, Sula, Fratelli (especially their Sangiovese), Good Earth, Reveilo and Mandala.

The Maharashtra government does not levy an excise on wine, unlike many other Indian states that tax it with a cruel hand. And 90 per cent of the wine made in India is produced in Maharashtra, in the Nashik region from the grapes grown there: the remaining 10 per cent comes mainly from Karnataka. Indian wines are not going to knock your socks off—at least not yet—but some are eminently drinkable and there is a growing band of dedicated Indian winemakers, whose products are getting better over time. The wine region around Nashik is just beginning to open up for visitors with cellars, restaurants, winery tours and accommodation. Unfortunately, the focus of the Indian wine industry is on educating people to drink Indian wine with European-style food rather than Indian food. I find this lamentable but an Indian winemaker told me that it was partly because Indians, in the main, only drink wine when they eat in restaurants serving European food and therefore understand only that association. The practice in India is to take alcoholic drinks with titbits or snacks before a meal so there is no common cultural nexus between alcohol and food. Of course, this need not stop you from matching local wine with whatever Indian regional food you happen to be eating. Many of the more sophisticated restaurants in the major cities and popular tourist destinations offer a selection of Indian wines. I encourage you to sample these when you come across them. To visit wineries in Nashik, look up these websites:

www.sulawines.com
www.reveilo.com
www.vallee-de-vin.com

PUNE

Shivaji was not only an exceptional warrior, he was also a good leader; he knew his shortcomings and knew when to delegate. After crowning himself king of the Marathas, he installed a Peshwa, or prime minister, to govern his empire and the state finances. Shivaji had him work out of Pune, his hometown and capital of the sovereign Maratha state. By 1749, the Peshwa had evolved to become the hereditary ruler of the Maratha state and Pune the bastion of Maratha culture. Peshwa rule ended in 1817 when the British annexed Maratha territory.

Pune is the second-largest city in Maharashtra. It's a steep drive up from coastal Mumbai to where it sits perched atop the Western Ghats with the Deccan plateau stretched eastward behind it. This strategic location and the benevolent cool–dry climate saw the British use it as their alternative headquarters—they called it Poona—in the months when the monsoon turned Bombay into a humid hell. Central Pune, referred to as the Old City, is made up of seventeen *peth*s, or localities, established during the reign of the Peshwas: specific trade or artisan groups (guilds) would live in each peth. When the British came into Pune, they built a huge army cantonment south of the Old City and there was said to be a 'food line' that divided the Pune of taats and vegetarian food from the Poona of meat, beer and biscuits. Pune remains the cultural capital of the Marathas and, despite the popular historical image of them as mighty warriors fond of hearty chilli-infused meat dishes, Pune's traditional food is restrained and delicately vegetarian.

Recommendations

In the Old City is the Victorian-era Mahatma Phule Market where you can purchase, or just look at, excellent fish and seafood brought up from Mumbai and local fruit and vegetables including a range of freshly sprouted lentils used to make usal, the base of misal. **Bedekar Misal (also called Bedekar Tea Stall)** has been a favourite place for Puneris for this quintessential Marathi dish for more than fifty years.

418 Munjabacha Bol, Narayan Peth
(020) 24451270
8 a.m.–7 p.m. (Mondays closed)

After sampling Bedekar's mild misal pav, cross the Old City to **Ramnath**, and try their 'hotter' version made with authentic Kolhapuri rassa.

Tilak Road, Near Mahatriya Sahitya Parishad

Vadiya Upahar Gruha has been serving misal for a century and still keeps the same hours established by the current owner's grandmother, who opened the restaurant in between doing her domestic chores. In local parlance, Vadiya is a *gharghuti*, an eatery that serves a fixed number of items at strict timings, just like a home kitchen.

Phadke Haud Chowk, Raviwar Peth
7.30–11.30 a.m., 3–7 p.m.

Sherya's is a Pune institution for vegetarian taats. The food is laid out exactly as tradition dictates with items that change seasonally. An autumn taat might include green-mango pickle; peas cooked with coconut and a pea *tikki* (patty); spinach roti; *sol kadhi*; aamti; and *basundi* (a custard-like sweet made from reduced milk). There is a selection of Maratha sweets that you can order in addition, and these might include *amrakhand* (mango purée) and *modak* (steamed-rice dumpling stuffed with coconut and jaggery). Modak is the favourite sweet of the elephant-headed god Ganesha—he holds a modak in his hand in most representations—who is the Marathas' patron deity. During the annual ten-day

Ganesha Utsav (festival), modaks are made (or bought) in every Hindu home in Maharashtra.

242/B Apte Road, Deccan Gymkhana
(020) 25532023
11 a.m.–3 p.m., 7–11 p.m.

Hotel Atithi serves Maratha-style vegetarian taat and a much-talked-about *thalipeeth*, a pancake-like bread made from a mixture of ground whole grains, such as millet, sorghum, rice, corn and wheat, blended with besan, green chillies and spices.

Opposite Sambhaji Park, 1206 B/17 Junglee Maharaj Road,
Deccan Gymkhana
(020) 25532029
11 a.m.–3 p.m., 8–10.30 p.m.

Mathura is the place to try *pitla-bhakri* if you want to sit and enjoy it rather than eat it on the street.

Prestige Chambers, Opposite Sai Service Petrol Pump,
1262/A Junglee Maharaj Road, Deccan Gymkhana
(020) 25510565, 25531975
11 a.m.–11 p.m.

When the British set up camp in Pune and built their cantonment, this attracted new people to come in to take up the opportunities that arose from this development. These included Parsis from Mumbai. The Parsi-run **Dorabjee and Sons** is one of Pune's oldest eating establishments, indeed the place to come for a feast of meat. The venerable owner sits behind a large counter with pots of food lined up on shelves behind him—it's like a culinary Aladdin's cave. There are more than twenty mutton dishes on the menu including mutton *dhansak, patra ni machchi* (Parsi-style fish), omelette filled with *kheema* (spiced mincemeat) and dishes made from liver and trotters. Parsis are very fond of egg dishes and there are several on the menu, including *akuri* (soft scrambled eggs with tomato, coriander, green chilli and onion) served with the soft white bread called *pav*. (*See Mumbai chapter for more on Parsi cuisine.*)

Sharbatwala Chowk, 845 Dastur Meher Road, Dattawadi
(020) 26145955
11 a.m.–11 p.m.

Kings serves classic Parsi dishes such as dhansak, curry rice and
sali murghi and a selection of Irani-style dishes. Like the Parsis, the
Iranis are Zoroastrian immigrants from Iran but much more recently
arrived in India; they have a unique association with cafes (*more in
the Mumbai chapter*). The Irani dishes at Kings have a distinct Persian
flavour and style with a focus on rice and meats/vegetables cooked
on skewers. It is the sort of food the Mughals might have eaten if
they were having a very low-key meal at which they were not trying
to impress anybody, not even themselves!

Opposite Victory Cinema, Koyaji Marg, 7 East Street, Camp
(020) 26362667
11 a.m.–3 p.m., 7–11 p.m. (7 days)

The **Blue Nile** is a busy Irani restaurant that serves a variety of
kebabs such as mutton and *murg* (chicken) served with a generous
platter of rice delicately scented with cardamom and cinnamon. This
particular combination of meat and rice is called *chelo* (an everyday
dish in Iran). If you need a break from chilli and spices, then Irani
food will work well for you. Finish your meal with the excellent
caramel custard or *falooda* and enjoy the Indo-colonial atmosphere
of whirring fans, arched room dividers and tiled floors (especially
pleasant on a warm day).

4 Bund Garden Road, Camp
(020) 26125238
Noon–11 p.m. (7 days)

The most fashionable Irani joint in Pune is **Shisha Café**. The menu
includes a Persian-style roast-chicken platter that you can enjoy
while lounging around on divans, taking puffs on a scented hookah
listening to some very cool jazz. In the same complex as Shisha is
the ABC Farms shop where you can buy locally made cheeses such
as buffalo mozzarella and a range of local artisanal food products.

35/36, ABC Farms, Koregaon Park
(020) 65200390
10 a.m.–11.30 p.m. (7 days)

The Shrewsbury biscuit is a traditional British dessert named for the
town in Shropshire but Pune's **Kayani Bakery** is reputed to sell 200

kilograms of it every day. I was not able to find any statistics to back this up, but I would be surprised if the town of Shrewsbury sells that much of its named confection each day. The Kayani Shrewsbury is a lemony, shortbread-style biscuit, so delicious that devotees are said to drive up from Mumbai just to buy it in bulk. Kayani has been baking these biscuits in a wood-fired oven since the mid-1950s, in which they also bake their own sourdough. Kayani is equally renowned for its surly service—my experience was exactly that—which proves that their products are good since people keep coming back despite this.

6 East Street, Camp
(020) 26360517
7.30 a.m.–1 p.m., 3.30–8 p.m.

. . . .

KONKAN COAST

The 500-kilometre Maharashtra coastline forms part of what is called the Konkan coast, which runs from Raigad in Maharashtra (a region around Mumbai harbour) to Mangalore in Karnataka, and inland to the point where the Western Ghats begin to rise. The climate changes subtly along the coast from semi-tropical to tropical, getting wetter and more humid as it heads south. There is little variation in the geography but this long strip of land between coast and mountain is consistently lush and fertile. The foods grown in the Konkan do not vary greatly, and there are strong similarities in the cuisines of this region. There is, however, great diversity among the people collectively identified as Konkani. There are native Konkanis: a significant Christian population (*see Goa chapter and Mangalore section in Karnataka chapter*), Muslims and various Hindu communities. The Konkanis of Maharashtra are predominantly Hindu, though there is a sizeable Muslim population. Konkani Muslims are also referred to as Moplah, meaning 'brother-in-law' (*see Kerala chapter*). Muslims have a long history of living along the Konkan coast, having first come to the region from Arabia to set up as traders a millennia or so before the advent of Islam. The use of the word Moplah to describe them indicates that they married into local families. Konkani Muslims' distinct cultural identity is evident in their food practices, but like the gradual change in climate along the coast, the differences are often subtle.

Coconuts grow abundantly in the Konkan region and are used extensively in the cooking of all communities: the flesh is grated; ground into a paste or pressed for milk; and a common Konkani culinary practice is to cook dal or rice in coconut milk. The kokum tree grows prodigiously there. Its fruit is sun-dried and used in cooking to add a sour note, a smoky tang and some colour to dishes. It is also used to make one of the most distinctive food items of the Konkani region—*sol kadhi*, a thin sauce or drink, typically taken with each meal as a digestive. It is prepared by soaking dried kokum in water, straining off the liquid and blending with coconut milk, garlic and salt: you will know it when you encounter it first off from its pale-violet colour. Rice is the major cereal of the Konkan region; it is eaten plain as a regular accompaniment to meals and made into various breads, cakes, sweets and noodles (*see Recommendations for more*). It would seem from my explorations that the one-third of Maharashtrians that are vegetarians are mainly located in Pune and not many live in the Konkan region where fish is eaten at least once a day. Cashew nuts, bananas, jackfruit, ladies' fingers, eggplant and mangoes are used in the cooking of all Konkani communities. Commonly used spices are locally grown red chillies called *byadgi*, a variety that imparts a bright-red colour to food without adding too much heat, black pepper, coriander seeds, cumin, cardamom, ginger and garlic.

Recommendations

The Sindhudurg district occupies the southernmost area of the Konkan region of Maharashtra. It takes its name from Sindhudurg Fort, built by Shivaji in 1664, that sits in the sea, just off the coast, largely intact: apparently gur was among the materials used to construct this enduring edifice. The main town of Sindhudurg is Malvan; its people speak Malvan, a Konkani dialect, and their cuisine is called Malvani. This subregional cuisine shares all the general characteristics of Konkani food; its distinction derives largely from variations in the way these foods and flavourings are put together and is most evident in the taste of the food rather than in particular dishes or techniques. (All this means that you will have to go there to taste it.)

A Malvani of my acquaintance described Sindhudurg to me as 'nature's paradise'; a descriptor that might seem hyperbolic if written in a tourist brochure, but in this case it was expressed as a genuine pleasure at living in such a place. Despite its proximity to Goa, and an almost identical geography including long stretches of beach, Sindhudurg has been spared—so far—the type of character-eroding tourism development of coastal Goa. Undoubtedly, Malvanis would like to see more tourism dollars coming into their economy but they are not focused on this, and there is genuine welcome and hospitality to be enjoyed here, in addition to the physical attractions. One of the best ways to experience Sindhudurg, its people and the local cuisine is to stay at one, or more, of the several homestays developed in conjunction with the social enterprise **Culture Aangan**. I stayed at three different homes set up through this programme.

The first home I visited, actually a small farm, was in Sawantwadi, just over the border from Goa. Konkani cuisine is based on a 'what's in the backyard' philosophy and this lush 'backyard' housed coconut palms, guava, mango, kokum, jamun, papaya, plantains for cooking and finger bananas, ladies' fingers, green beans, black pepper, chillies and eggplant. On my arrival, I was greeted with a lunch that in large part was composed of food from the garden: pieces of green banana and fish coated with rice flour and fried golden crisp; fish cooked in a sauce of red chilli, coconut and black pepper; baby eggplant cooked with potato; aamti; wheat-flour roti and a large serve of rice. I whiled away the afternoon nibbling on home-made modak made to welcome me.

In the evening, my hostess Amrutha gave me a cooking lesson. I was taught how to make *vada kokombada*, which literally translates as 'bread chicken' but is actually a dry dish of chicken cooked with garlic, lime and coriander leaves and eaten with a soft, steamed bread made from rice flour, coriander seeds and cumin. We then made another type of local bread called *gharane*, from a batter of ground rice, coconut, chilli, coriander, ginger, salt and a little sugar, which is cooked in a flat cast-iron pan over charcoal to create a pancake. Dessert was a bowl of thin noodles called *shirvaralya* dressed with coconut milk, jaggery, cardamom and a little salt. These noodles are made from a mixture of ground rice cooked with water, ghee and salt to form a soft paste; this is rolled into balls that are cooked in boiling water until they float; once they have cooled slightly these are pushed through a special press to craft the noodles.

The hosts at my next homestay in Taluka, the Kadams, were so delighted at my interest in authentic local cuisine that they almost filled me to bursting with home-cooked delicacies. Upon my arrival I was greeted with *dhondes*, a cake made from grated deseeded cucumber, rice flour, semolina, jaggery, nutmeg, cardamom, cashews and sultanas, and baked in a tin lined with turmeric leaves in the coals of a dying fire. There was also *aloo wadi*, spinach leaves spread with a thick paste of ground rice and dal flavoured with cloves, pepper, coriander, cumin, cinnamon, gur, chilli powder and salt. To construct this dish, a layer of spinach is laid out and spread with the paste; another layer of leaves is laid atop, running in the opposite direction, and spread with the paste; the process is repeated again to create three layers. The whole lot is then folded to create a square and a final layer of paste applied after which it is cut into slices, steamed and fried: for a novice this would be a complicated process but Mrs Kadam made it in no time.

Dinner was served under the stars in the backyard. It began with a potato and cashew stew flavoured with coconut, onion and Malvani garam masala. Next came a dish of fish pieces slow-cooked with onion, coconut, coriander and turmeric in an earthen pot lined with turmeric leaves over a clay stove. The crisp accompaniment was a piece of fried fresh bombil (when dried this fish becomes 'Bombay duck': *see Mumbai chapter*) and a plate of local prawns coated in a paste of rice flour, red and green chilli, ginger, garlic and fresh coriander and fried. After this came a rich curry of prawns cooked in a sauce of coconut, coriander, tamarind, ginger and garlic, which I mopped up with freshly made rice *bhakra* (roti). I waddled off to sleep after this and woke up to a breakfast of another local bread made from fermented ground rice, *urad* dal and fenugreek—very similar to a dosa.

My next port of call was closer to the coast with the sea as its culinary backyard—not literally as the water was still some distance away. My meals included fresh local kingfish cooked in coconut sauce and fried bombil. From the literal backyard came a vegetable called *tondli*, somewhat like a gherkin, cooked with coconut and accompanied by rice, sol kadhi and sago cooked in coconut milk and jaggery.

Culture Aangan
7B, G22, Sangeeta Apartments, Juhu Tara Road, Santacruz,
West Mumbai
(022) 26606448
www.cultureaangan.com

SOUTH INDIA

SOUTH INDIA

ANDHRA PRADESH

EATING THE HEAT

Mahajanapada was the collective name for the sixteen most powerful states and kingdoms, mainly spread across the Indo-Gangetic plain, which existed in India between 600 and 300 BC. It was not a definitive list of sovereignty, as there were smaller fiefdoms on the subcontinent that did not merit a place on this list. The people of Andhra country in south India did not carry enough political and economic weight to warrant inclusion in the supreme sixteen, although they were mentioned and thereby came into historical record for the first time. In the third century BC, the Mauryan emperor Ashoka recorded that Andhra had come under his control. After his death, the Satavahana dynasty—likely of indigenous origin—took control of Andhra and ruled it until the third century AD. After this, the region came under the control of various rulers, in various configurations, including annexation to the great southern kingdoms of the Cholas and the Pallavas.

In the thirteenth century, Muslims from the north began to push into Andhra and eventually captured its north, featuring the famous Golconda mines and fort. The area was ruled as a province of the Delhi Sultans, but when that dynasty collapsed in the early sixteenth century, the Qutub Shahis took independent control and anointed themselves kings of Golconda. Despite sharing his religion with the Qutub Shahis, Emperor Aurangzeb wanted Golconda under direct Mughal control. He had his army persist in laying siege to the Golconda Fort for a year before its local rulers capitulated and a Mughal viceroy was installed to enforce imperial power. After Aurangzeb's death in 1707, and the ensuing collapse of his dynasty, the incumbent viceroy, Asaf Jah I, declared sovereignty and established the rule of the Nizams over Hyderabad state (formerly Golconda), which they retained, more or less, until 1949.

The Nizams exerted their own particular cultural influence over their dominion. The language of the court, and the city surrounding it, was Urdu. Yet the boundaries of Hyderabad state encompassed the older Telangana empire and most of the indigenous people spoke Telugu. These two languages have nothing in common nor did the respective cultures they represented, although over time each influenced the other, as is evident in the cuisine of modern Andhra Pradesh (*see below*). Telugu speakers were not confined to Telangana. The language was predominant along the coastal belt of Andhra and in Rayalaseema, the Deccan plateau region south of Telangana. In 1959, these three Telugu-speaking areas were merged to form Andhra Pradesh (AP) with Hyderabad as its capital.

Since this union, the cuisine of the Hyderabadi Nizams has become the dominant representation of the food of AP, yet each of the merged regions has a distinct culinary identity, affected as much by geography as by cultural events. AP is a vast state—the fourth largest in India—with 1200 kilometres of lush tropical coastline; a large area of the semi-arid Deccan plateau; and several major rivers. It borders Chhattisgarh and Odisha to its north and east, Maharashtra to the west and Tamil Nadu and Karnataka to the south. Let's first look at some common food habits of all the people of AP, then inspect the traditional cuisines of coastal Andhra, Telangana, Hyderabad and Rayalaseema more closely.

AP is home to two of the fastest-growing 'mega cities' in India, its capital Hyderabad and the coastal port town of Visakhapatnam, yet most of its eighty-four million people still live in rural areas, engaged in agriculture. Their major food crops are rice, chilli, mango, millet, banana and peanut. Rice is the dominant crop, accounting for over 70 per cent of agricultural output, and it is also the primary staple food in AP where a generous portion of rice is the centrepiece of a meal; everything else on the plate, or banana leaf, seems to exist to add flavour, and textural contrast, to this mild-tasting grain. Depending on whether the meal is a festive one or quotidian, the items provided to support the rice can be numerous. *Podi* is a mixture of various spices, red chillies, *urad* and/or chana dal roasted in oil and ground to a powder. *Pachchadi* is a tangy chutney of eggplant, cucumber, spinach and mango or fresh red chillies ground with roasted spices and dal, and tempered with whole spices sizzled in oil; curd or fresh coconut might also form the base. These two are usually served as condiments, but many Andhraites would be happy to make a simple meal of a podi (spice mix), a pachchadi (curd-based vegetable dish), rice and a small pot of melted ghee.

In addition to the rice and condiments, a typical meal would include a selection of more substantial dishes cooked in several prescribed styles to create a balanced meal. A *koora/kuru* dish is thick and dry, prepared from meat or vegetables; *pulusu* is a thick gravy made 'sour' by adding tamarind, tomato or curd; *vepudu* is a stir-fry, commonly of leafy greens, though it can also denote dishes in which some ingredients have been 'roasted' in more liberal amounts of oil; *pappu* is dal cooked with a vegetable; and *charu* is the Andhra version of the spiced broth called rasam that is taken at meals as a digestive throughout south India. Crisp items such as papad or green chillies soaked in curd and sun-dried, a pickle, and a little warm oil or ghee complete the meal. A meal would not be considered satisfactorily completed, though, without a dish of *perugu*, curd or buttermilk prepared with spices and vegetables or served plain and mixed with condiments as per the diner's preference. Sweets are usually only served with festive meals and eaten at the beginning, perhaps so as to not spoil the carefully considered balance.

AP has a reputation for having the 'hottest'—chilli-infused hot, that is—cuisine in India. This blanket statement is not without foundation but the levels of chilli Andhraites enjoy vary. It is mainly the pickles and condiments eaten with meals that are the real sources of 'heat'. Chillies are a major crop of AP. The state produces close to half of all the capsaicin-bearing fruit grown on the subcontinent, and one-third of that production comes solely from the coastal Guntur region, where a number of cultivars of *Capsicum annuum* have originated including *Guntur Sannam* (*Capsicum annuum var. Longum*). This long, thin, hot red chilli is called *koraivikaram*, or 'flaming stick', in Telugu. It is commonly ground with tamarind pulp and salt to prepare a chutney, which can be eaten with just plain rice and ghee. Warangal and Khammam districts in Telangana are also major chilli-producing areas, and the chilli-infused raw-mango pickle called *avakkai* is a speciality of this region. It is traditionally made with *reshampatti*, a small, round, dark-red chilli used extensively throughout south India.

The use of chillies in AP is certainly not confined to pickles and chutneys. Andhraites subscribe to the theory that you 'eat the heat to beat the heat'. As their state has a warm climate (with temperatures hovering around 40 °C in summer), there are few savoury dishes in which fresh or dried chillies, or both, are not included. For those unaccustomed to eating chilli regularly, it is understandable that they might find Andhra food consistently 'hot'. While Andhraites find the 'heat' of chilli useful in helping cool the body, they also manage the effect of these fiery fruits by balancing it off by cooking with spices and sour items such as tamarind, and on the plate with ghee and curd. I remember watching with mounting concern as a cook from Nellore—a coastal region of AP—kept adding more and more red chilli powder to the *chapa pulusu* (fish curry) that he was demo-cooking for me. When it was finished and he handed me a plate to try, I took a very sheepish spoonful expecting my mouth to be 'blown' apart by the heat of all the chilli but, to my relief, it was nowhere near as 'hot' as I had expected—he had balanced it out with sourness and spices.

Tamarind has been used to add tartness to prepared dishes throughout south India for aeons, but it is arguably employed most prolifically in kitchens in AP. Tamarind pulp is soaked in water and the liquid strained off and added to all types of dishes; it is also used to make a *sharbat* and a chutney called *chintapandu thokku*. In spring, the flowers (*chigur*) and tender new leaves of tamarind are collected and used to prepare seasonal dishes such as *chigur ka gosht* (mutton cooked with tamarind flowers, garlic, cumin, curry leaves, red chillies and mustard seeds) or *chinta chiguru pappu* (masoor dal cooked with tamarind leaves, red chillies and spices such as fenugreek and curry leaves). *Gongura*, leaves of a plant of the hibiscus family (*Hibiscus cannabinus*), are used throughout AP to impart a distinct tart flavour to dishes such as *gongura gosht* (mutton served in a spiced purée of gongura), *gongura pappu* and *gongura pachchadi*. The last dish is made by frying the leaves in oil until quite dry and grinding them to a paste with spices and chillies. Gongura leaves are also pickled. Tamarind and gongura are considered to help digest the rich 'spicy' food—which is why I think these work well to mitigate the heat of chilli—and cool the body. Green mango and tomato are also used for tartness.

An array of spices is used in cooking across AP. It is the preference for, and combinations of, these that differentiate the state's regional cuisines. The spices most commonly used are black mustard, fenugreek, sesame and coriander seeds, curry leaves, ginger, turmeric, star anise, clove, cardamom, cinnamon and clove. Asafoetida is widely used in vegetarian cooking; its presence usually signifies the absence of onion and garlic and the presence of legumes for it is believed to aid the digestion of pulses. Various dals are also used like spices: urad and chana dals are roasted and ground and added to dishes, particularly vegetarian ones, to impart a nutty flavour and act as thickeners, adhering liquid ingredients such as tamarind and coconut milk to the more substantial ones in the pot. Other spices in regular use are *nagakesara*, dried flower buds of the cassia tree that look similar to cloves and have a citrus/cinnamon flavour; *kallupachi*, a dried flower that I mistook for a lichen as it is black and crumbly in texture; and *maratimoggu*, a long, thin, dried pod of elusive origins suggested to be a member of the caper family, but I'm not sure of this as it has a more clove-like taste. These three particular spices are used throughout south India. I had often seen them in local markets and wondered what they were; it was an Andhra friend who was able to give me a little more understanding of them so I have placed them here.

Only about 10 per cent of people in AP are vegetarians. Those living in the coastal regions partake plentifully of the seafood bounty provided by the Bay of Bengal and those living near rivers enjoy fish caught from these. Fish is also dried for use when the season does not permit a fresh catch. Goat and chicken are the most widely eaten meats. This does not mean, however, that all Andhraites eat a lot of animal protein as economic factors often influence how much meat a family can enjoy. Meat dishes might be reserved for special occasions or, if they are eaten more regularly, served as a part of the meal—rather than the focus of it—along with a selection of vegetable preparations. Andhraites like to cook meat with greens, such as gongura and tamarind leaves, *amaranthus*, fresh fenugreek leaves and local varieties of spinach such as *thothikura* and *kadala*. Mutton and chicken are also cooked with rice in dishes such as the famous *kacchi biryani* of Hyderabad and Andhra *kodi pulao*, a fabulous dish of spiced rice layered with a thick rich sauce of chicken, coconut, curd, spices, tomato and nuts, baked over coals in a sealed pot. The Reddys are a large and successful merchant class who originate from coastal AP and largely reside there. *Kodi pulusu* (chicken cooked in coconut gravy flavoured with garlic, ginger, red chillies, cardamom, cinnamon, white poppy seeds and cloves) is a well-known dish of this community. The use of these particular spices indicates the wealth, and trading links, of the Reddys, as these were typically used in royal cooking and several were imported and therefore expensive.

AP is renowned for meat and fish dishes, and restaurants serving these are popular across south India. Another of its specialities, *baghare baingan*, comes from its vegetarian cuisine. It is a festive dish of fried eggplant in richly spiced sauce that employs similar spices to those used in elaborate meat preparations along with the addition of peanuts (a legume grown in the state). There are over 100 known indigenous varieties of eggplant throughout south India—though only a few are commercially grown—and this versatile vegetable is widely used in everyday cooking. Leafy greens are eaten every day in AP, typically cooked with dal or stir-fried with cumin, coriander and green chillies and tempered with mustard seeds and curry leaves.

Sweets served in AP are quite simple. The most common are *payasam* (milk cooked with gur or sugar and combinations of ingredients like rice, nuts, dal, coconut, saffron, cardamom and camphor) and laddoos (made with varied mixes of semolina, coconut, dal, ghee and sugar). Hyderabadi cuisine features a wider selection of Indo-Muslim-style desserts and sweet dishes.

Before we look at specific subregional dishes, let's wind up our general investigation of AP food habits at the start of the day. Rice is eaten at breakfast prepared as idli and dosa. Speciality rice dishes are also prepared such as *bisi bele huli*, *vangi bhaat* (rice cooked with eggplant), *pulihora* (tamarind rice) and curd rice. These can be served as 'one-pot' meals with a few sides—the AP version of 'comfort food'—or as sides in a more expansive meal. *Pesarattu*, a pancake made of a batter prepared from whole moong/urad dal ground with ginger, onion and green chillies, is a distinct breakfast, often served with a spiced semolina potage called *upma*. My favourite AP breakfast is *sabudana uttapam* (thick pancakes prepared from a batter of sago soaked in curd and mixed with rice flour, green chillies and fresh curry/coriander leaves), eaten dipped in soupy sambhar.

TELANGANA

Telangana is the north-central Deccan plateau region of AP and home to the state capital of Hyderabad. The soil is fairly shallow, the rainfall uncertain. This has traditionally restricted crop growth compared to dry-climate crops such as millet and wheat. Recently, irrigation has allowed rice and sugar cane to be productively cultivated, and rice has come to be more commonly eaten as government subsidies allow it to be sold cheaply. This intervention has disturbed the traditional food ways of Telangana in which meals were based around breads made from a variety of hardy indigenous millets and sorghum. The practice of eating millets has not disappeared though, and a basic village meal would still comprise jowar roti, or baked balls made of the same grain, eaten with a tamarind and red chilli–infused thick *pulusu*-style dish, or simply accompanied by a pickle or chutney. But because of the emphasis on rice as a commercial crop, millet cultivation has dropped away and some species are under threat of extinction (*see Recommendations for more*).

If you wish to encounter really 'hot' food in AP, then Telangana food is for you. This subregional cuisine is the most deeply infused with fieriness. There is a theory that this is because the region is economically poor—due to low agricultural yields caused by the shallow soil and low rainfall—and that eating really hot food dulls the appetite and/or makes it hard to eat very much else. Everyday food in Telangana is usually vegetarian, a habit that derives more from economic circumstance than philosophical conviction. (There are of course those who abstain from eating animal flesh out of moral/spiritual belief.) When meat is enjoyed, though, no part of the beast is wasted. *Dumpudu mamsumu* is a dish made from the liver and kidneys of a goat, slow-cooked over coals with chillies, garlic, curd, ginger, onion, coconut, cinnamon and cloves. The Telangana region came under Islamic occupation in the thirteenth century and, as a result, the region's cuisine has absorbed some Muslim influence as this dish demonstrates. (Conversely, the Muslim cuisine of AP has been shaped by Telangana influence, as we shall see in the Hyderabad section.) *Kodi kura munaki*, chicken cooked with drumsticks—seed pods of *Moringa oleifera* eaten as a vegetable throughout peninsular India—is a Telangana speciality generously enriched with various spices and a good slug of *sendi*, local toddy tapped from the inland growing species of the palm *Phoenix sylvestris*. Sesame seeds are another ingredient of kodi kura munaki and these seeds are widely used in Telangana cooking as is the oil pressed from them. *Ulva kuttu* is a sweet–sour vegetarian dish of horse gram (*ulva*) cooked to a purée and flavoured with tamarind, sesame seeds, gur, coconut and red chillies. *Sarva pindi*, a popular snack, is a crisp pancake made from rice flour, chana dal, peanuts, sesame seeds, green chillies, onions and *ajwain* (carom seeds).

Pickles are vital in traditional Telangana cuisine, both as a way to preserve seasonal foods and add zest to simple meals. Pickles made from green mango, ginger, lemon, tamarind, garlic and gongura leaves are prepared by pouring boiling oil over the ingredients to extract maximum flavour. *Allam bellam* is a fresh pickle (or chutney) prepared from ginger (*allam*) ground with gur (*bellam*), urad dal, tamarind and red chillies, tempered with mustard seeds.

Recommendations

Other than Hyderabad, Telangana does not have a lot of obvious attractions for visitors, but if you feel like taking a country drive, travel 100-odd kilometres north of the capital to Zaheerabad in Medak district for a meal at **Café Ethnic**, 'India's only organic millet restaurant'. This rural-style eatery was set up by the Deccan Development Society over a decade ago to promote the use of local millets and draw attention to their importance as highly nutritious crops, far more suited to dry-land agriculture than rice. All the dishes on the menu are prepared from organically grown, chemical-free grains. You can try millet roti, millet khichri, payasam made from millet and local gur and millet dosa. And buy a few laddoos made from sorghum or sesame seeds to sustain you on the return journey. The menu is full of information about the various millets used and they provide you with a free booklet of recipes for local millet dishes: well worth a drive to check out.

Zaheerabad Mandal, Medak District
(08451) 282271
10 a.m.–6 p.m.
www.ddsindia.com

HYDERABAD

The city of Hyderabad was founded on the bank of the Musi River in 1591 by Mohammed Quli Shah as an alternative capital to Golconda; the water supply of the older fortress city had begun to dry up and it remained the capital of Hyderabad state until 1948. After Independence, it became the capital of what was called Andhra state and then, in 1959, the capital of the expanded territory of Andhra Pradesh. As Hyderabad state, it was the largest semi-autonomous royal kingdom during British rule of India. The seventh Nizam of Hyderabad, Osman Ali Khan Asaf Jah VII, was the richest man in the world in the first half of the twentieth century, his fortune largely deriving from the diamond mines of his kingdom. His predecessors, stretching back seven generations to the first Nizam, Asaf Jah I, had all been super rich and were not shy of displaying their wealth—although Osman Ali was a notorious miser—via ostentatious palaces and the finest in clothing, the arts and, of course, cuisine.

The official flag of Hyderabad state included a symbolic representation of a kulcha, a round leavened wheat bread. (Kulchas can be square but the one on the flag was round.) It was there because, legend has it, the first Nizam consumed seven kulchas in the presence of a Muslim holy man who then prophesied that the Asaf Jahi dynasty would last for seven generations (which it did). Whether this story is true or not, it is fitting that the flag has bread on it—the Nizams certainly made Hyderabad famous for its food!

The Asaf Jahi food of Hyderabad is a hybrid of Indo-Muslim/Mughlai cooking with Telangana and Middle Eastern influences. The Nizams encouraged aristocrats of Persian, Afghan and Turkish descent to come to their courts. In fact, it was common practice for the Nizams to choose brides from the noble families of these countries. This meant that they kept taking new influences into the Indo-Muslim/Mughlai-style food around which their distinct cuisine was shaped. The Nizams had a reputation for indulging in absolute wanton luxury with their food: crushing pearls into dishes; distilling quail and venison into alcohol; and serving hundreds of dishes at banquets. (All in all, this was not actually much different from the culinary shenanigans of other Indo-Muslim rulers such as the nawabs of Lucknow.) Modern Hyderabad still has a significant Muslim population, and Urdu is spoken along with Telugu, but the Asaf Jahi style of food you will find these days is a little less exalted than that of the Nizams.

As is typical of Indo-Muslim cuisine, the traditional food of Hyderabad is heavily focused on meat preparations, with a supporting cast of breads, rice dishes and sweets. All the classic dishes of the Indo-Muslim repertoire are prepared: biryani, korma, *dopiaza* (meat cooked with onions), *keema* (spiced mince), *kofte* (meatballs), *nihari* (stew of sheep's trotters), *pasande* (thin slices of mutton), *raan mussallam* (spiced leg of mutton or lamb), *shab deg* (meat cooked with turnips), *seekh* and *shammi* kebab and *haleem* (slow-cooked meat and wheat porridge). The difference is that these gain a distinct regional flavour by the addition of tamarind, raw mango, lemon, coconut, lots of fresh mint and coriander leaves, a greater number of red chillies and spices like mustard seeds and nagakesara.

Modern Hyderabad's most famous dish is undoubtedly kacchi biryani. It is distinguished in its preparation as it has layers of uncooked meat (hence the name: kacchi means 'raw') and half-cooked rice, which cook together, whereas a regular biryani is typically prepared by layering cooked meat with rice. Meat for kacchi biryani is marinated in a mixture of curd, green and red chillies, ginger, garlic, onion paste, fresh mint, coriander and spices before it goes into the cooking pot with the parboiled rice. Another Hyderabad speciality to look out for is *dalcha* (meat cooked with chana dal, tamarind, mint, garlic and spices). The spices predominantly used in Hyderabad cooking are those of the 'royal' spice box: cinnamon, cloves, nutmeg, cardamom.

Indo-Muslim sweets such as halwa, jalebi, *falooda*, kulfi, *shahi tukra* and *zarda* (sweet rice) are part of Hyderabadi cuisine. A unique Hyderabadi sweet is *khubani ka meetha*, a purée of dried apricots and cream into which the ground, roasted apricot kernels are blended, giving the dish a particular texture and taste. *Anjeer ka roll*, a type of fig preserve encased in ice cream, is believed to have been introduced by a Turkish princess who married into the Asaf Jahi family a century ago—a time when ice cream would have been an expensive novelty worthy of place on the royal table. You can buy a version at any Hyderabad ice-cream parlour—a pleasant treat but no longer a status symbol.

Recommendations

Modern Hyderabad has gained the alternative moniker of 'Cyberabad' due to its significant role in India's information technology industry. This is a terrific economic boon for Hyderabadis, but it seems to have increased the pace of life and modernization (read office blocks, flyovers, fast-food joints) in equal measure. Given Hyderabad's reputation as a 'food' city, its inhabitants are passionate about this topic. There is a multitude of places in which to eat Hyderabadi food and many impassioned opinions on which are the 'best'. I've done my best to choose a good selection but this is a city that you could easily spend a week or more eating in.

You can still get a feeling, and taste, of a more unique Hyderabad in the old city. If you visit Charminar in the evening, just behind the arched monument is the bustling Lad Bazaar, which has been a place of commerce since the city was founded. Here you will find food stalls where you can sample street food such as meat kebabs served with kulcha or thin *roomali* roti, tamarind chutney and sliced onions.

Firdaus offers another taste of old Hyderabad, in more salubrious surroundings than Lad Bazaar. The charming dining room interprets the refined, but quirky, style of the Nizams. You can lounge on a bolster on the garden-facing window seats while enjoying a meal of classic Hyderabadi dishes. Try the slow-cooked *dum murghi biryani*, the slow-cooked meat–wheat porridge called haleem (*more below*) or sweet–sour *khatti dal*. If you order the delicate wheat-flour rotis called *phulki*, these will be cooked by your table on a portable stove to ensure that you eat them at their best—straight off the fire. Firdaus has a large menu and vegetarians are well catered for with dishes like *guthi vankay* (baby eggplant stuffed with spiced peanuts and cooked in a tomato sauce; like baghare baingan). Food at Firdaus is tasty and portions fairly generous so it might be a challenge to leave room for dessert but try and squeeze in a portion of *khubani ka meetha* or another Hyderabadi classic, *double ka meetha* (shahi tukra), a 'royal' version of bread pudding made of bread slices fried in ghee, dipped in sugar syrup, layered in a dish, drenched with cream, garnished with nuts and baked . . . followed by a walk in the garden!

Taj Krishna, Road 1, Banjara Hills
(040) 66293306
12.30–3 p.m., 7.30 p.m.–midnight (7 days)

Hyderabad House specializes in serving the dish the city has long been famed for but its hectic vibe, and focus on 'quick service', probably better represents modern Hyderabad—and I expect any Nizam would be shocked to eat from a plastic plate. Nonetheless, this is one of the most popular places for Hyderabadi biryani. Try the kacchi biryani in which the meat has been marinated twice—first with cinnamon, cardamom, cloves, mint and coriander, and then with curd, cardamom, fried onions, cream, saffron, ghee and a little milk. Once the marinating process has done its work, the meat is interwoven in three layers with parboiled rice, sprinkled with saffron-infused milk, and the pot sealed and placed over the fire to cook.

Plot #100, Road 3, Banjara Hills
(040) 23554747
Noon–11 p.m. (7 days)
www.hyderabadhouse.com

Paradise Food Court has become an institution for biryani. It reportedly serves up thousands of portions of this dish every day by offering several options: a parcel (takeout) service, a stand-up-and-eat-quickly eatery downstairs and a seated restaurant above, where you can sit out in a courtyard and enjoy a plate of chicken biryani and seekh kebabs while watching Hyderabad's streetscape. Paradise is actually located in the twin/new city of Secunderabad, but it's so popular that any taxi driver will know where to take you. In fact, the area surrounding this joint is colloquially known as 'paradise'.

38 Sarojini Devi, M.G. Road, Secunderabad
(040) 66313721
Noon–11 p.m. (7 days)
www.paradisefoodcourt.com

Paradise gets varied ratings from Hyderabadis as to the authenticity of its biryani, possibly because the place has become something of a tourist draw card—although it's not just visitors who are getting through all those serves of biryani. On the other hand, the unpretentious and inexpensive **Café Bahar** is very much an insider's pick. It's busy with locals, and the odd outsider in the know. Try the tangy fish biryani or a plate of haleem and linger over a cup or two of sweet Irani chai.

Basheerbagh, Near Police Commissioner's Office
(040) 23237605
11 a.m.–midnight (7 days)

Hyderabadi biryani is the city's most famous dish but Hyderabadi haleem quietly gained a Geographical Indicator (GI) in 2012. This means that the name 'Hyderabadi haleem' cannot be used outside the city, and that the product has been made in the traditional manner. Haleem is a potage of wholewheat and meat (mutton or chicken) flavoured with onions, garlic and spices such as cloves, cardamom, cinnamon, *shahi jeera* (*see Uttarakhand chapter*), nagakesara and chillies. It is eaten by Muslims throughout India during festivals such as Ramadan and Muharram. To justify its GI status, Hyderabadi haleem must have been cooked over a low wood fire for up to twelve hours in a large cauldron covered with a layer of mud (to protect the pot from the flames and keep the heat even), during which time it must be periodically stirred and mashed with a wooden paddle until it gains a smooth consistency. Haleem is served garnished with a generous drizzle of melted ghee, a sprinkle of crisp deep-fried onions, a few cashew nuts and a good squeeze of lemon. During the month of Ramadan, thousands of temporary outlets selling Hyderabadi haleem pop up across the city, only to disappear after Eid. Firdaus and Café

Bahar both serve haleem as a permanent menu fixture, in case you visit Hyderabad in one of the eleven months that are not Ramadan. The proprietor of **Pista House**, Mohammed Abdul Majeed, was instrumental in gaining GI status for Hyderabadi haleem and his restaurant was the first to use it for its product—which it sends around the world in tetrapacks. Pista House is also in the Charminar precinct so you can experience a traditional atmosphere when you visit here as well as authenticated haleem. All these places prepare their haleem using mutton (goat or lamb in the case of Firdaus). Those who do not eat beef, and end up eating elsewhere in Hyderabad, should check with the proprietor as to which type of meat has been used since beef or buffalo meat is sometimes used in festive dishes such as haleem.

Shahalibanda Road, Charminar
(M) 9396500786
11 a.m.–10.30 p.m. (7 days)

Hotel Shadab, also in the Charminar area, is also popular with the local citizenry for Hyderabadi haleem and biryani.

21 High Court Road, Charminar
(040) 24561648
Noon–midnight (7 days)

Once you have had your fill of Hyderabadi specialities, you might like to try some Telangana dishes in the major city of this region, though the commercial options for trying them are limited. **Narayana's Curry House Telangana Special** in the Secunderabad area comes recommended for *kodi vepudu* (chicken meat and liver sautéed with spinach) and *chepala pulusu* (dried fish in tamarind sauce).

Lane opposite Universal Store, Ramnagar Road
(M) 8106636665
8 a.m.–11.30 p.m. (7 days)

If you are not travelling to coastal AP, sample the fare of that region at the 'homely'—the restaurant is housed in a house—**Southern Spice** restaurant. Try dishes such as *royyalu iguru* (prawns cooked in a creamy, spiced sauce of coconut milk and tomato) or *bommidayalu*, made from the dried fish commonly known as Bombay duck cooked in a tamarind sauce (the flavour of this tangy fruit mellows the pungent 'duck'). *Ragi sangati* (*see below*) pairs well with these gravy-based dishes. Also try mutton cooked with gongura/tamarind leaves. The 'leeches with cream' listed on the dessert menu is a not a dish of bloodsucking creatures, merely a quirk of spelling for lychees. It's probably best to stick with the khubani ka meetha, though, if you want a sweet treat that is more authentic to the region.

Near Nagarjuna Circle, Road 3, Banjara Hills
(040) 66103434
Noon–3.30 p.m., 7–10.30 p.m. (7 days)

RAYALASEEMA

The area known as Rayalaseema is the Deccan plateau region, south of the Krishna River. It shares its geography and climate with Telangana and the food eaten in the two regions is likewise analogous. In Rayalaseema, *jona* (sorghum) and ragi (millet) rotis eaten with ghee are daily bread as is ragi sangati, a hearty and sustaining mixture of cooked rice and millet. It is served in a mound, with a little indent on top in which to pour melted ghee. It is typically paired with a gravy-like *naatu kodi pulusu* (country chicken or backyard-raised chicken cooked with onions, red chilli, curry leaves and spices such as nagakesara, cinnamon and cardamom). Regional vegetarian dishes include *methi pappu* (*toor* dal cooked with fenugreek seeds) and *ulava charu* (rasam made with horse gram). *Pakam undalu* (balls of rice, gur, coconut and cardamom fried in ghee) and *rava laddu* (balls of semolina, mixed with coconut, sugar and ghee) are the speciality sweets of Rayalaseema.

THE ANDHRA COAST

This region of the modern state of AP is traditionally referred to as Andhra and its people as Andhraites (though I have used this term earlier in the chapter to refer to all people from Andhra Pradesh). It's a fertile area watered by several major rivers that cut through it and includes the six-million-hectare delta lying between the Godavari and Krishna rivers. It is in this region that much of the rice of AP is produced. The 1200-kilometre coastline runs from the border with Odisha in the north-east to that shared with Tamil Nadu in the south. Given this geography, it is unsurprising that fish, seafood and rice dominate the cuisine. Freshly ground coconut flesh or milk is used prolifically (as it is all around the Indian coastline); tomato is preferred over tamarind as a souring agent (possibly because there is more water available to grow it); and the heat level of chillies is turned a notch or two lower than that in Telangana. This is not to say that chilli is not ubiquitous—it is. If you visit Visakhapatnam you must go to Porna market to see the huge variety of local chillies on sale there.

Sea and river fish are both eaten, although communities who live further away from the coast and get their catch from rivers and ponds prefer freshwater species to those caught in saltwater. Shark, snapper, seer fish, grouper, sea bass, prawns, whitebait, *bhetki* (*Lates calcarifer* or barramundi), sea murrel (a variety of snakehead fish common in the waters of peninsular India) and crab are just some of the fish and seafood caught. Sun-dried fish called *karuvadu* is added to dishes for additional flavour and is used to replace fresh fish during their breeding season. It is local practice to leave the fish undisturbed during that season so that they get on with replenishing their numbers. Fish and seafood dishes are commonly spiced with mustard, cumin, fennel and fenugreek seeds.

There are many different communities living in the coastal region of Andhra and each will eat a cuisine that is a variation on the basic patterns described in this chapter: there are those that are vegetarian and those that prefer mutton and chicken to fish if given the choice. Typical dishes to look out for are *royyalu pulusu* (prawns in a coconut and tamarind gravy); *Nellore chepala kura* (fish cooked in tamarind sauce); *chepala pulusu* (fish cooked in a sweet–sour gravy of onion, tomato, curry leaves, mustard seeds and coconut); *podichepala* (fried fish marinated in garlic, red chilli, coriander and lime); and *mamsam vepudu* or mutton fry (pieces of mutton stir-fried with curry leaves, garlic, ginger, red chillies, cumin and coriander).

TIFFIN TIME

Karnataka first appears in general books of Indian history in the fourth century BC as the place to which India's first emperor—Chandragupta, grandfather of the famed Ashoka—retired after renouncing his throne to spend his final days in austerity and religious devotion. Between the end of the Mauryan Empire in the second century BC and the sixteenth century AD, the region came under the control of a dizzying roll call of Hindu rulers. Arguably the most successful were those of the Vijayanagara Empire, which arose in the fourteenth century as a bulwark against Muslim incursion from the north. This powerful empire fell in 1562 to the Bahmani Sultans whose armies laid to waste the Vijayanagara capital—creating the ruins of Hampi that are among modern Karnataka's most popular tourist destinations. The northern section of Karnataka then came under the rule of a succession of Muslim rulers. The Hindu Wodeyar rajas governed southern Karnataka from Mysore until 1761 when a Muslim general, Haider Ali, supported by the French—who had come into India in the early seventeenth century—took control of the region and was later succeeded by his son, Tipu Sultan. Tipu continued his father's alliance with the French, which incensed the British—who had actively battled their Gallic enemies on Indian soil—as much as his military activities against them. The British formed an alliance with the deposed Mysore rajas to defeat Tipu. When this was done in 1799, the Wodeyars resumed their rule, until 1956 when the modern state of Karnataka was created by merging Mysore with parts of the Madras Presidency.

There are three distinct geographic regions of Karnataka: the lush tropical region between the Western Ghats and the Arabian Sea; the fertile, well-watered hills of the Ghats and a southern portion; and the dry, rocky plains of the Deccan plateau in the north and east. Each region has its distinct cuisine(s), which this chapter will explore after first looking at some commonalities. The varied geography of Karnataka supports major commercial crops of wheat, millet, rice, mangoes, coconuts, peanuts, sesame seeds, cashews, black pepper, cardamom, tea and coffee. Rice, millet and wheat are staple grains, consumed in roughly equal proportions. In northern Karnataka, breads made from millet, sorghum and wheat are eaten with food, while in the south, rice is the central grain of daily meals. In the coastal areas, fishing is an important industry; fish and seafood are important food sources.

As is common across south India, breakfast is usually a substantial meal in Karnataka. Popular breakfast foods are the pancake-like dosa (*more later*) and steamed rice cakes called idlis served with sambhar (spiced lentil and vegetable stew) and coconut chutney. Lunch and dinner tend to be similar, served on a banana leaf or thali. A typical meal would be rice served with *saaru* (soup-like dish of dal cooked with curry leaves, mustard seeds, asafoetida and a spice mix called *saarina pudi*); *koshimbar* (crisp, tangy salad of dal tempered with mustard seeds, red chilli, shreds of coconut and fresh green coriander); one or two cooked vegetable dishes; with curd and rice to finish. Chutney, pickles and papad accompany a meal, and perhaps a 'salad' of curd mixed with fruit, vegetables and spices called *pachchadi* or *rayatha* (raita) and some fresh fruit might be taken at the end. In the coastal region, a meal would generally include fish and/or seafood, except on a fasting day. A typical meal in northern Karnataka, where the population is still largely involved in agricultural work, would include unleavened bread, red chilli chutney and one or two substantial dishes such as eggplant stuffed with peanuts, sesame, ginger and garlic.

On festive occasions, the basic meal format is enhanced with items such as sweet *payasa* made from rice or semolina cooked with milk, jaggery/sugar and cardamom, a few mouthfuls of which are taken to begin the meal and it is then eaten throughout. There are many varieties of payasa prepared in Karnataka and these might include banana, coconut milk, dal, sweet potato, nuts and dried fruit. Other additions to a festive meal might be crisp *patrode* (colocasia leaves smeared with batter, rolled up and fried); *chitranna* (spiced rice); and *holige* (soft pancake-like bread stuffed with cooked chana dal, jaggery and coconut).

Karnataka's best-known dish is *bisi bele bhaat*. It's prepared with rice— bhaat—cooked with dal—bele; finely diced vegetables such as gourds, carrots and beans; a rich spice mix of nutmeg, asafoetida, coriander, coconut, white poppy seeds, cardamom and cloves; ground chana and *urad* dals; and garnished with fried curry leaves and cashew nuts. Many types of bhaat are served in Karnataka; the term ordinarily indicates that it is a savoury dish prepared from rice but the term can be more broadly used for dishes that have a similar soft texture such as *kesari bhaat*, made of semolina cooked with saffron. Bhaat, of any variety, is usually eaten as a light meal or snack called tiffin.

UDUPI

About a third of the population of Karnataka is vegetarian, quite a high percentage for a coastal state. The vegetarian ethos that likely influences this emanates most strongly from the town of Udupi. Bustling modern Udupi has grown around a medieval temple that houses a small stone idol said to contain the essence of the god Krishna as a child: because of his inquisitive juvenile nature, it is believed that he will wander away from this temple unless enticed with delicious food. Every day, the temple cooks have to come up with at least fourteen different delicious dishes to satisfy the young god and keep him secured in his place. After this food has been offered to Krishna it is served to devotees. The Udupi temple is one of the most important pilgrimage spots in India for Vaishnavites—followers of the god Vishnu, of whom Krishna is an incarnation—and the stream of pilgrims who come into the temple every day, and have done so since the thirteenth century, all head to the dining hall to eat after completing oblations to their child idol.

It is an ancient custom for pilgrims to be fed at the temples they visit, a practice that developed out of necessity. People would travel huge distances to visit particular temples, and in the days before restaurants and food stalls, the temple was obliged to feed them; tasty and well-prepared food was a reward for their devotion and ensured that what they ate supported the spiritual betterment that was the purpose of their journey. Because of the necessity to continually tempt Krishna with eatables, there is a particularly strong focus on nourishing pilgrims to Udupi. On the day I visited, the man who checked my bag into the storage area was far more interested in whether I had eaten in the temple dining room than whether I had seen Krishna or the actual temple. Inspired by his unsolicited advice—'eating is the most important thing as you can offer god as many prayers as you like but a human being still needs to eat'—I had a perfunctory look at Krishna and headed off to the dining area. The temple has several dining rooms: one is reserved for Brahmins, and is hidden from public view so I couldn't see what they were eating, but I was told that it was a much greater selection of the dishes made for Krishna, including several sweets, than that offered to the general devotee. Another dining room is where the temple benefactors eat in the company of the temple gurus and are publicly seen enjoying such an honour. Everybody else has to ascend a steep flight of stone stairs to the cavernous public dining hall. Pilgrims sit on the ground with a banana leaf in front: on this is served rice—dished up from a huge cauldron wheeled up and down the room—saaru, rasam and a vegetable stew of pumpkin and gourds. Bare-chested men serve the food so that pilgrims can see the sacred thread tied across their torso, which shows that they are Brahmins. This is important in the traditional Hindu environment of the temple as it means that people from all castes can accept the food being offered. People of any background are welcome to eat at the temple. Mealtimes are noon to 3 p.m. and 7 to 8 p.m.

Udupi is famed throughout India for its vegetarian cuisine, a reputation undoubtedly gained by pilgrims coming to the temple from all over India, eating there and returning home and talking about it. What they get to eat in the temple is only a fraction of a true Udupi feast—a six-course meal with multiple dishes and accompaniments. Only local foods are used in traditional Udupi cuisine and a huge array of dishes fashioned from pumpkin, gourd, cucumber, jackfruit—there is a whole repertoire made from the seeds and flesh of this versatile fruit—roots and leaves of colocasia, coconut (the food is also traditionally cooked in coconut oil), mango, *amla* (Indian gooseberry), banana, buttermilk, tamarind, sesame seeds and jaggery. Onion and garlic are not used nor are any 'English' vegetables such as tomato, carrot, potato, beans, cabbage or cauliflower: interestingly, however, other introduced species such as chillies and pineapple are included. Many foods employed in Udupi cuisine are used in cooking throughout coastal Karnataka—Udupi is unique in turning its back to the bounty of the nearby Arabian Sea—collectively called Tulu Nadu. The use of tropical fruit in savoury dishes is common in this region as the types of vegetables that grow well in the coastal climate are limited to tubers and yams, gourds, pumpkins, drumsticks, ladies' fingers and spinach.

There is a strong nexus between Udupi and dosa, the pancake-like item made from a batter of ground rice and urad dal that is left to ferment overnight: a process that happens naturally in the humid climate of south India. Dosa batter is poured on to a hot iron plate and spread out in a concentric movement to create a round crêpe. It is cooked only on one side and, when done, rolled up like a sheet of paper or folded over a filling; it's usually served with coconut chutney and sambhar. To eat, pieces are broken off and dipped into these items. There's no question that the dosa is indigenous to south India, but where exactly it originated is a matter of ongoing conjecture. In his seminal book *Indian Food: A Historical Companion*, food historian K.T. Achaya says that the first written mention of dosa appears in the literature of Tamil Nadu in the eighth century and that it does not appear in works in Kannada until over a century later. Despite this evidence, Udupi is popularly cited as the birthplace of the dosa, although another possible reason for this attribution might be traced to the proliferation of a particular style of restaurant.

Udupi also lends its name to a popular type of eatery originated by entrepreneurial men from the Shivalli community. The story goes that these men opened cafes in places such as Bengaluru (*see MTR*), serving Udupi-style food prepared by cooks trained in the kitchens of the Udupi temple and its associated *math*s (monasteries). Since Udupi cuisine was renowned, and 'safe' for Brahmins, Udupi cafes quickly found favour with the public: the fact that they were clean, inexpensive and served food promptly added to their popularity. Udupi restaurants are now so prolific that dosa has become a commonplace breakfast and snack item across India. My theory is that most Indians who are not from south India likely had their first encounter with a dosa in an Udupi restaurant resulting in the prevalent belief that dosa comes from Udupi. It is probably true to say that most Udupi cateries operating in India have no association whatsoever with this town, though restaurants with the names Kamat, Shanbhag or Pai affixed to them indicate that the owning family is originally from Udupi.

Recommendations

Aside from eating at the temple, try Udupi cuisine at **Mitra Samaj**. The same orthodox Brahmin family has run this restaurant since 1949. More than 1000 plates of *goli baje* (crisp, savoury balls of flour, curd, coriander, cumin and green chillies) served with freshly ground coconut chutney are sold here every day. Other local dishes to try include *kadubu olle* (a savoury semolina cake steamed in leaf cups); coconut holige and a sweet, gooey halwa made from pumpkin and jaggery. If you are in time for breakfast, you must have the *ksheera*, a sublime dish of pineapple paired with spicy semolina potage (*upma*).

Car Street
(0820) 2520502
6 a.m.–9 p.m. (7 days)

Shantisagar is popular with locals for dosa, and features a light and tasty millet/ragi dosa. You can eat goli baje or expend your daily budget of calories on one of the elaborate ice-cream sundaes on offer, for which I am surprised the sweet-loving Krishna has not abandoned the temple. And you can try *kashaya*, a class of drinks decocted from various spices and sweetened with jaggery, which are prescribed for a variety of ailments. (There is a strong health focus in Udupi cuisine.) I am not sure what my hot-spiced, milky kashaya is meant to be good for but it tasted great.

CPC Plaza, Opposite KRSTC Bus Stand
(0820) 2534853
Breakfast through dinner (7 days)

MANGALORE

Mangalore is only sixty kilometres from Udupi yet the food this coastal city is best known for is quite the opposite of that of its traditionally vegetarian neighbour. The abundant local produce of the surrounding region, called Tulu Nadu, such as ginger and black pepper, have been shipped out of Mangalore since at least the sixth century, and its excellent natural port has brought diverse influences into the town. Arab traders had settled in Mangalore by the eighth century and, in 1342, Ibn Battuta wrote that it had a population of more than 4000 Persian and Yemeni merchants. In the Middle Ages, Mangalore served as the main port of the Vijayanagara Empire; the Portuguese captured it in 1529; Haider Ali and Tipu Sultan controlled it while they held Mysore and then, when the British defeated Tipu in 1799, it came under their administration. Mangalore was subject to a particularly significant Christian influence since the arrival of St Thomas in nearby Kerala in AD 54, following which missionaries came into the region to convert people. The number of Christians grew after the arrival of the Portuguese, who were as active in converting souls as they were in trading goods. The Portuguese, unwittingly on this occasion, caused an additional increase in the Christian populace when the ferocity of their Inquisition in Goa caused many native converts to flee and seek asylum in Mangalore.

If there was one thing shared by the different peoples that converged in Mangalore, it was their enjoyment of the fish and seafood abundantly available to them. Fish curry and rice are eaten every day by Mangaloreans, whatever their religious persuasion or ethnic background. The local version of fish curry, *meen saaru*, has a distinct rich-red colour, which comes from the use of the mild and somewhat sweet *byadgi* chilli. This particular variety of *Capsicum annuum* imparts a bright hue to food as it has a high oleoresin content—an oil that is also extracted for colouring cosmetics such as lipstick. Byadgi is used throughout south India but originated in Karnataka and is named for a town in the north of the state. In 2011, byadgi was awarded Geographical Indicator (GI) status. Coconut, chillies and spices form the base of any fish or seafood curry made in Mangalore. A tamarind-based curry called *pulimunchi*, flavoured with mustard seeds, coriander, fenugreek and red chillies is another everyday preparation. Into either of these bases are added *teesria* (clams), *kane* (ladyfish), *bangude* (mackerel), kingfish, seer, prawns, pomfret or *cubbe* (cockles), depending on the season and what the fishing boats have brought in that day. A typical Mangalorean meal will include a piece of crisp fried fish as a textural counterbalance to the soft curry and rice. The term 'naked fry'—which you will encounter on menus in Mangalore—means that the fish in question has been cooked without any additions bar salt and pepper and a squeeze of lemon. Sweet-fleshed kane is popularly eaten this way.

The food of Mangalorean Catholics reflects their strong Goan ties. Pork dishes such as *dukra maas/bafat* (a slow-simmered stew of pork, garlic, tamarind, vinegar, cinnamon, cloves, ginger, green chillies and bafat masala—a mix of red chillies, cinnamon, peppercorns, cloves, cumin, coriander and star anise) and *sorpotel* (a heady stew of pig blood and innards slow-cooked with vinegar and red chillies) are distinct dishes of the Catholic community. The Goan/Portuguese influence is also evident in baked confections such as coconut macaroons and *kuswar*, a variety of sweets and biscuits made from nuts, dried fruits and sesame prepared for Christmas.

Mangalore is also known for its distinctive, spicy coconut-and-cardamom-enriched chicken curry eaten with thin, crisp rice flatbread called *kozhi kaaipu* or *kori roti* or *kori gasse*, depending on whether you are eating the Catholic version or the Bunt version. Hindu Bunts are an important community of Mangalore. The Bunts are traditional landowners; this high-caste community has martial ancestry and they are fond of non-vegetarian foods, but one of the dishes they are best known for is patrode. (Many versions of patrode are eaten throughout India.) *Neer dosa*, a tissue-soft dosa made from ground rice and water—*neer* means water in Tulu—is said to have originated in Bunt kitchens. This almost ethereal dosa is the perfect counterpoint to the rich coconut-based curries it is used to scoop up.

The popularity of meat and seafood does not mean that vegetables are ignored. Daily meals are supported by dishes of local fruit and vegetables and, of course, there are those whose diet is entirely vegetarian. Cashew nuts, peanuts, dal and vegetables are cooked into coconut-based curries such as *padange* (thick stew of moong dal and coconut milk) that is eaten for breakfast. Jackfruit is commonly used to provide substance in vegetarian dishes. This large fruit is one of the most ancient foods of the country and is indigenous to the south-western rainforests of India. It is eaten raw as a vegetable and as a sweet dish when ripe: when it is green, latex can be extruded from it and ground into a paste called *imba*, which makes a gum for chewing. *Meetmirsag* are delicious morsels made from breadfruit pieces coated in a paste of spices and vinegar and fried.

Recommendations

Operating since 1921, **Hotel Pereira** is the best place to sample Mangalorean Christian cuisine. Dark and sticky and rich sorpotel, properly aged for three days, is always available. There is a different pork special on the menu every day, or you can try chicken *sukka* (liver sautéed with coconut, spices and local peppercorns). Fresh local fish is cooked in a thick gravy of ginger, garlic, vinegar, tamarind, clove and cinnamon. Hotel Pereira is rudimentary in appearance but it is clean, inexpensive, friendly and always busy.

Opposite Government Law College, Hampankatta (town centre) 11 a.m.–10 p.m. (Sundays closed)

Just near Hotel Pereira is **Komal Sweets**, renowned for its unctuous banana–wheat halwa made with local bananas and chewy coconut-jaggery candies. Komal also makes jackfruit chips called *sante/sapne*. At **Ideal Ice-Cream** parlour in Hampankatta, try the famous sundae called *gudbud*, a 'confusion' of pistachio, strawberry and vanilla ice cream, jelly, dried fruit, nuts and fresh fruit. A modern 'regional dish', it originated at Ideal in the early 1970s. You needn't be shy about tucking into one of these for breakfast as Mangaloreans are not; as far as they are concerned, any time is a good time for ice cream. I saw adults happily eating gudbud at 10 a.m. Visit **City Bakery** in Gokul Market in Hampankatta to try Mangalorean macaroons.

If you feel like an upmarket meal, try **Gajalee**. Housed in the former British Circuit House, it has a panoramic view across Mangalore and a menu of Konkani-style seafood featuring the best of the day's catch. Local gourmets consider fresh fried *bombil* and crab in red chilli sauce the standout dishes here. The bombil is fried in a light batter and served with ginger and garlic chutney; eating this was somewhat incongruous at first as I associate bombil with its pungent dried version, Bombay duck, and the slightly sweet, tenderly fresh fish bears little resemblance to that. The crab in red chilli sauce was not as 'hot' as its intense colour might have suggested. It was made with mild byadgi chillies, the flavour of which enhanced the sweetness of the superlatively fresh crab rather than masking it. Clams, prawns, squid and a selection of fish are cooked in a variety of local preparations including pulimanchi, naked fry and pepper fry.

Circuit House Compound, Kadri Hills
(0824) 2221900
11 a.m.–3 p.m., 7 p.m.–midnight (7 days)
www.gajalee.com

Gad offers an elaborate lunchtime thali of Mangalorean specialities. I was regaled with a meal of fish curry with rice; a piece of fried seer fish coated in a chilli–turmeric paste and slowly cooked in oil until crisp; chicken curry made with coconut, curry leaves, garlic, cumin and local red chillies matched with Mangalorean fried chicken; baby octopus cooked with lemon, chilli, coconut, garlic, turmeric and finished with ghee; jackfruit cooked with tomato, pineapple, coconut, *kalonji* (*Nigella sativa* or nigella seeds), mustard seeds, cumin and red chilli. Accompaniments included a fresh, crunchy koshimbar of *toor* dal with coconut and mustard seeds and another of cucumber and coconut. Mangaloreans prefer locally grown, large-grained, unpolished rice, and there was plenty on offer. Despite being happily replete with all of this, I squeezed in a serve of the sweet payasa, made from moong dal, jaggery and cashew nuts.

The Gateway Hotel, Old Port Road
(0824) 6660420
www.thegatewayhotels.com

Just behind The Gateway Hotel, down a bylane, you find **Narayan's**. Walk along Old Port Road for a couple of hundred metres and turn right into the first road and ask a passer-by. This brightly painted cafe is very basic but sparkling clean and it is the place to come to for fish curry and rice if you are in the know (which you now are).

For traditional Mangalorean breakfast fare, **Hotel Ayodhya** has *sample moode* (idli batter steamed in jackfruit leaves) served with *gunda* (a salty sour pickle of whole mangoes) and *ragi manni* (a hot porridge of ground millet and jaggery). **Kulda Dasaprakash**, a friendly cafe directly opposite the bus stand, makes very good *rava dosa* and serves it with thick coconut chutney.

Hotel Ayodhya, Kodialbali
(0824) 2493681
7 a.m.–9 p.m. (Sundays closed)

For a luxurious experience of the food and ambience of coastal Karnataka, book yourself into **SwaSwara**. Guests are accommodated in chic villas built in traditional Konkani style and nourished with fresh produce grown on the twenty-six-acre property or sourced locally. Each day, fish and seafood are procured from local fishermen and transformed into fresh dishes reflective of the region's cuisine. The menu changes every day and at every meal: the selection is kept small to allow the chefs to concentrate on creating truly fresh and handcrafted dishes. During my stay, I ate crabs cooked in virgin coconut oil with mustard seeds, ginger, garlic, curry leaves, coriander, turmeric and kokum; squid cooked in a sauce of fennel, cumin, coriander, red chilli and roasted coconut; and kingfish cooked in freshly ground coconut curry. Local fruit and vegetables are given equal attention and cooked with spices, coconut, ginger, garlic, dal, chillies, peanuts, fresh coriander and curry leaves to create an infinite variety of tasty dishes. Lunch and dinner finish with a perfect portion of a sweet dish prepared with ingredients such as jaggery and honey, whole grains, home-made curd or cottage cheese, fresh fruit and coconut. Breakfasts are equally good and might include Konkani kokum roti (made with brown rice, coconut and kokum syrup) or ginger, cumin seeds and a little semolina ground to a paste and cooked inside a banana leaf on a grill to produce moreish 'bread'. The chefs welcome guests into the kitchen for hands-on lessons. A stay at SwaSwara is worth every rupee.

Om Beach Gokarna
(08386) 257131
www.swaswara.com

KODAGU

Inland from Mangalore, nestled in the lush forests of the Western Ghats, is the tiny (4000 square kilometres) district of Kodagu or Coorg. The people of Kodagu share the same love of rice and meat as their Mangalorean neighbours but they have their unique history and their cuisine is distinct. The Kodava people do not appear in historic records until the tenth century; their true origins remain a mystery. A popular theory posits that they descended from Alexander the Great—who entered the Punjab in 326 BC—and settled in the hills of Kodagu as the thick jungle and difficult terrain allowed them to remain isolated from other Indians and maintain their identity and culture. Another theory is that the Kodavas are descended from the indigenous people of the region. What is indisputable is that the Kodavas were a martial race, with a well-trained army, and successful agriculturists. Kodagu came under the purview of various rulers over the centuries and the Kodavas sometimes joined these armies as mercenary soldiers. When they found themselves under the rule of the aggressive Haider Ali, and later his son Tipu Sultan, they sided with their erstwhile Hindu king and the British against this repressive regime. The Kodavas suffered significant losses and hardship in the fight to rid themselves of Tipu and, after he was gone, they had to endure a succession of rajas ranging from mad to incompetent to immoral. The British relieved them of the last of this line, the despised Vira Raja, in 1834 and proclaimed the region a princely state, which it remained till 1956 when it was merged into Karnataka.

The British loved Kodagu with its highland forests, undulating tracts of lush jungle, open glades and misty vistas, bequeathing it the title of 'the Scotland of India' (a designation they also gave to Shillong, capital of the north-eastern state of Meghalaya): they were equally enamoured of the region's commercial potential, particularly for growing coffee. The coffee bush needs larger trees to shade it and with more than 200 species of shading trees, Kodagu was the perfect location. Muslims from the Konkan coast had introduced coffee into Kodagu in the eighteenth century but it was grown only for local use. In the nineteenth century, the British made extensive coffee plantations and developed coffee production into an industry. Today the region is the wealthiest in Karnataka largely due to coffee and the associated agricultural products such as black pepper—the vines of which grow around the trunks of the trees that shade the coffee—cardamom, vanilla and cocoa. Both *Coffea robusta* and *Coffea arabica* are grown and Kodagu coffee is ranked among the best mild coffees in the world; needless to say, it is the preferred hot beverage of the Kodavas.

The martial skills of the Kodavas were put to domestic use in hunting wild boar and venison in the forests and fishing in the rivers, streams and ponds for food. They also gathered a wide range of wild foods from the forests such as leafy greens, bamboo shoots, mushrooms, yams, mangoes, berries and honey. The produce that can be taken out of the forests of Kodagu is now strictly controlled—indigenous people are permitted to gather wild foods—but the cuisine of Kodagu continues to reflect a love of these. Rice was, and is, extensively grown—the Kodavas have a history of trading in large quantities of rice—and is the mainstay of meals. It is fashioned into items such as *akki roti* (flatbread made of a thick paste of ground rice and salt, rolled out between a damp cloth and cooked on a flat iron pan until crisp); akki roti has a dry texture so it is always eaten with a little butter or ghee A typical Kodagu breakfast is akki roti eaten with spiced pumpkin curry or sesame seed chutney. In the monsoon, akki roti is paired with a curry made from bamboo shoots. Another breakfast dish is *thaliaputtu*, a steamed pancake made from a batter of cooked rice, coconut and fenugreek leavened with bicarbonate soda. Steamed dishes are common in Kodava cooking and a special steamer called *chekala* is used.

One of the best-known dishes of Kodava cuisine is *pandi kari* (rich stew of pork cooked with kokum, pepper, ginger, garlic, green chilli, cinnamon, cloves, cumin) eaten with rice balls called *kadumbuttu*. The kokum used in Kodagu is indigenous to the Western Ghats. The variety is *Garcinia gummigutta*, locally known as *kachampuli*, which is also the name of a syrup made from this sour fruit. The hydroxycitric acid in kokum keeps the pork fat firm and chewy in pandi kari. This dish was customarily prepared on special occasions as its production relied on the capture of a wild boar, but it is now ordinarily made with farmed meat.

The Kodavas are decidedly non-vegetarian and all meals feature a meat/fish dish such as *koli kari* (chicken and coconut stew) eaten with neer dosa or steamed rice balls, or *pa puttoo* (mutton curry) served with broken rice. Each dish has a matching rice preparation but steamed rice can be served too, and is usually eaten with some ghee for flavour. The Kodavas do not neglect vegetables and each meal includes at least one preparation, varying with the season, prepared from mushrooms, jackfruit, yams, pumpkin, leafy greens or gourds. A thick gravy of moong beans cooked with tamarind, jaggery, coriander, turmeric, chilli, salt, mustard seeds, garlic and pepper is prepared all year round.

The wild honey collected in the Kodagu forests is in demand throughout India but the Kodavas do not seem to have much of a sweet tooth, preferring to finish a meal with fresh fruit. The sweet dishes they do prepare are simple and nutritious such as *thambuttu* (banana mashed with roasted rice, coconut, ghee and sesame seeds) or *puththari* (steamed yam served with jaggery syrup, grated coconut, sesame seeds and ghee).

Recommendations

Traditional Kodagu society is clan based and the ancestral family home, *ain mane*, plays a central part in the life of Kodavas. The house is considered sacred and always faces the rising sun. A family member can always return to the ancestral home in times of adversity, and they do so in any case for celebrations. The Kodavas are renowned for their warmth and hospitality, so it is only fitting that Kodagu food and culture is best experienced in a traditional home. One of the very best places for this is **The School Estate**, fifteen kilometres from the regional capital of Madikeri.

A scenic drive through forests, plantations and gently undulating fields of rice brings you to the turn off for The School Estate. The long driveway runs through coffee and cardamom plantations, eventually ending under the portico of a smart, contemporary home sitting in the centre of a lush tree-, bird- and flower-filled garden. Host Rani

Ayyappa is a Kodava woman who has lived all her life in Kodagu and Kodava hospitality is evident in the generosity with which she shares her home and culture with her guests. Rani is also an excellent cook and feeds her guests on traditional cuisine, much of which is prepared from produce grown on the estate. Rani also gives cooking lessons. You can take walks around the verdant property, through coffee plantation and cardamom jungle, and spot other food trees and plants such as jackfruit, although numbers of this particular tree are deliberately controlled as wild elephants are very fond of the luscious fruit and can cause significant damage in their quest to get to them.

(08274) 258358, (M) 9448647559
www.schoolestate.in

Gowri Nivas is a homestay in Madikeri, run by a young Kodagu couple who maintain the distinct cultural traditions of their community in their home while leading very modern lives. Meals are focused on traditional Kodava cuisine and I enjoyed a vegetarian version of pandi kari made with Mangalore cucumber instead of pork.

(08272) 228597, (M) 9448193822
www.gowrinivas.com

Traditional Kodagu cuisine can be hard to find outside of a homestay but **Coorg Cuisinette** in Madikeri specializes in local food. The menu features various pork dishes including pandi kari and *pandi beev barthadh* (a dry dish of spiced pork chops). In season, a curry of crisp bamboo shoots cooked with curry leaves, red chilli and black mustard seeds is available. You can pair your meal with a choice of akki roti, rice balls or rice with ghee and try local coffee (*kaapi*) sweetened with jaggery or ginger and cardamom.

First Floor, Yelakki Krupa Buildings, Opposite Head Post Office, Main Road, Madikeri
(M) 9845138649

Hotel bars in India are best avoided by lone women, or any women, and if I had known that **Capitol** was also the bar of Cauvery Hotel, I probably would not have entered. As it turned out, though, it was perfectly okay and served some very good Kodagu food. There is a nexus in India between consuming alcohol and eating meat, and the offerings here are decidedly meat-oriented so I was pleasantly surprised to find my lunch of spicy, dry-cooked pork barthad being served with an array of vegetable dishes including *kuru kari* (fresh pale-pink kidney beans cooked with mild spices), an eggplant preparation, rasam and a dish of coconut gravy, and a generous serving of rice balls. (These vegetable-based dishes come from the vegetarian cafe in front.)

School Road, Opposite Private Bus Stand
(08272) 225372

MYSORE

If Mysore were a person, he/she would be gentle, good-natured and inclined to wear ensembles suggestive of a carnival. The gentleness might derive from the fact that this city was ruled by Wodeyar rulers from 1399 to 1956—with a brief thirty-eight-year hiatus under Haider Ali and Tipu Sultan in the eighteenth century—a record quite miraculous in India where rulers and borders, as a rule, have changed with destabilizing regularity. Such stability must have effected the development of the good nature of Mysoreans. If our imagined personification of Mysore has a tendency to dress in outlandish attire, one need look no further than Amba Vilas Palace, the former home of the Wodeyars, to find inspiration. This Victorian-era royal residence is all turrets, domes and arches and every inch of the exterior is decorated with paintings, mirror work, carvings and stained glass in rich jewel hues highlighted with plenty of gold leaf. It is unsurprising then that Mysore's best-known contribution to Indian food is a confection that was invented in the kitchens of this palace, called *Mysore pak*. This fudge-like sweet is created from roasted *besan* (chickpea flour) cooked with sugar syrup and ghee until it forms a soft dough that is pressed into trays and served cut into squares: a little bicarbonate of soda is sometimes added to give it a flaky texture.

I arrived in Mysore for Diwali, during which it is tradition to give and eat sweets. In celebration, I decided to undertake a focused taste test of Mysore pak by gathering samples from recommended confectioners to taste and compare. Sampling a selection of Mysore pak was in no way a hardship, but buying it on Diwali proved almost as challenging as getting on to a suburban train in Mumbai at peak hour—such were the throngs. Anyway, I successfully collected all my samples and here are the results in descending order of preference.

1. **Shree Mahalakshmi Sweets** (Devaraj Urs Road / 2443553). Melts in the mouth, with a faint hint of cardamom and a delectable caramel endnote.
2. **Bombay Tiffany's** (498 Devaraj Market Building, Sayaji Rao Road / 2421087, 4250087). Dense, sticky with ghee but no distinct flavour, just sweet and rich.
3. **New Bombay Tiffany's** (33 Devaraja Market Building, Sayaji Rao Road). Rich and dense with a caramel undertone.
4. **Guru Sweet Mart** (KR Circle, Sayaji Rao Road / 2443495). I tried their special Mysore pak—nice flavour and aroma but too rich with ghee for my liking although my rickshaw-driver and the hotel staff had all recommended it to me as the best in town, probably because they like ghee.

Mysore has it own dosa, the Mysore dosa, which is thicker than usual and comes anointed with a generous coating of home-made butter. Apart from this distinctive dosa and the pak, the cuisine in Mysore largely resembles that found throughout southern India albeit in a somewhat milder form with respect to the use of chillies—a reflection of the mild disposition of its citizens perhaps? Rice forms the basis for most meals and vegetarian food is strongly influenced by Udupi cuisine. Dosa and idli are ordinarily eaten for breakfast and again in the afternoon as snacks. Coffee is the preferred beverage.

Recommendations
....

Hotel Original Mylari is a very popular, no-frills, spotlessly clean cafe with people spilling out on to the footpath, tucking into the food. Only Mysore dosa is served here—thick, soft and deliciously silky with butter, paired with rough-textured coconut chutney. A 'legendary' biryani can be had when the hotel opens for its evening service.

79 Nazarbad Main Road
7.30–11 a.m., 4–7.30 p.m. (Wednesdays closed)

Hotel Dasaprakash is one of the oldest restaurants in Mysore, a spacious cavern constantly filled with people taking meals or a snack. The Mysore dosa served here is rated as one of the best by Mysoreans. There is also a 'special idli' stuffed with cashews, mustard seeds and grated carrot that spill out from its top causing it to resemble a flower (pretty and decorative, just like Mysore). *Guliappa* are fried rice balls served with tamarind and coconut chutney for dipping.

Gandhi Square
(0821) 2442444
7 a.m.–10.30 p.m. (7 days)
www.mysoredasaprakashgroup.com

If you want to get a real taste of Mysorean life, then you might enjoy a homestay at **Rooftop Retreat**. Located off the tourist trail in a tranquil neighbourhood, a short autorickshaw ride from the town centre, this modest family home has two simple and scrupulously clean rooms (one with a rooftop balcony) with good, home-style meals served at the family dining table. Pre-booking is essential, so contact Divya at divyanivya@rediffmail.com or (0821) 2450483.

BENGALURU

Modern Bengaluru (earlier known as Bangalore) has metamorphosed over the past decade from the laid-back and verdant 'Garden City' of public parks and tree-lined avenues popular with retirees to a booming metropolis of high-tech industries—the Silicon Valley of Asia—beloved of a younger generation. It is not altogether surprising that Bengaluru has been able to alter so rapidly: on the Indian scale of things, it is a relatively recent city so it had less history to hold it back. In 1537, a mud fort was erected in the area by a local Hindu chieftain. In the mid-eighteenth century, the territory fell to Haider Ali who expanded upon the existing fort and laid the foundations for the city to come. When the British defeated Haider's son Tipu in 1799, they established a permanent military station and the city grew around it as people came in to take up employment and business opportunities servicing the troops. The British handed the administration of the city over to the maharaja of Mysore in the late nineteenth century but they remained a significant presence in Bengaluru until Independence.

Bengaluru is often described as the 'most westernized' in India, and its well-paid professional denizens are proud of its plethora of restaurants, cafes and bars serving food and drink in various global styles. The recent personality-erasing changes wrought on their once-charming and distinctive city do not sit well with many established Bangaloreans, however. Fortunately for them, and for the visitor, the city still has an authentic heart south of the city centre, where you can find some good local-style eats.

Recommendations

....

Mavalli Tiffin Rooms, or MTR as it is popularly known, is a Bangalore institution, enthusiastically patronized by native and nouveau Bangaloreans. Two brothers from the Udupi district who immigrated to Bangalore started MTR more than eighty years ago. Depending on who you are talking to, MTR is said to serve 'Karnataka Brahmin cuisine' or Udupi cuisine: whichever descriptor is used, the food at MTR is distinctly Udupi-influenced although coconut oil is no longer used as the cooking medium. The Brahmin aspect is also indisputable: the decor is decidedly utilitarian and spotlessly clean. At one time, customers entered the restaurant by walking through the kitchen to see for themselves how clean it was and that Brahmins were cooking. If you take a peek into the kitchens now, you will still see shirtless Brahmin men, their torsos strung with their sacred threads, stirring large pots or supervising the grinding of idli or dosa batter.

Service begins at MTR at 6.30 a.m. and early risers can have idli and dosa. As the morning progresses, other items such as rava idli become available: this item is said to have been invented at MTR during the Second World War when rice was in short supply and rava (semolina) was substituted in the idli mix. Even when rice supply was reinstated, rava idli was kept on the menu as customers had grown to like it. At 12.30 p.m., lunch is served. The menu is written on a blackboard in the foyer: it is a set meal that follows a set pattern but the content changes daily and reflects seasonal availability. It starts with fresh fruit juice; then a crunchy *kosambari* (a finely chopped 'salad' of cucumber, coriander leaves, green chillies, coconut and cooked moong dal dressed with lemon juice); two vegetable dishes; a small dosa; a bhaat; *gojju* (a seasonal vegetable such as ladies' fingers in a thick sweet–sour gravy); rasam and plain white rice—a waiter comes around and announces this as 'rice for rasam' and you take as much as you consider you'll need to eat with your rasam. It is also acceptable to drink your rasam rather than mix it with rice and scoop it up with your hand. Next comes pongal, a dish of rice sweetened with jaggery. A dish of sweet payasa is placed on the thali during the meal and you can choose to alternate this with savoury foods; then there is curd rice paired with a pickle; and just when you think you can't take any more, a bowl of fresh fruit salad and ice cream is placed before you.

The late afternoon/early evening service is dedicated to a menu of tiffin items including bisi bele bhaat; stuffed rava idli accompanied by spiced potato stew; and rava dosa, smeared inside with a cooked paste of dried green peas and wrapped around a ball of spiced potato. If you order tea or coffee, the waiter brings it to the table and pours it from one tumbler to another to create froth and cool it slightly. He then pours a little into a cup for you to help yourself to the rest as you desire. A charming and old-fashioned practice you will not experience in any of the city's modern coffee bars. There is a story, possibly apocryphal, of how the brothers who founded MTR would issue their staff (most from Udupi) a small living allowance and bank the rest of their wages into individual bank accounts. When enough money was accumulated, and presumably enough experience gained working at MTR, they would send the employee out into the world to start his own restaurant, thus beginning the spread of Udupi restaurants across India.

14 Lalbagh Road
(080) 2220022
6.30–11 a.m., 3.30–7.30 p.m. (breakfast, tiffin)
12.30–2.45 p.m., 8–9 p.m. (meals)

The best masala dosa I have eaten (so far) was at **Vidyarthi Bhavan**, another iconic eatery. The menu, the decor—and some of the customers—haven't changed in the sixty-odd years that Vidyarthi has been operating. It's a large space with black-and-white-tiled floors, hard bench seating and the slightly institutional feel favoured by traditional Udupi places. In the early morning, uniformed waiters serve the mainly male clientele coffee and dosa; these are made in traditional Karnataka style and are much thicker and smaller than the large, thin versions more often served commercially. They are also liberally dressed with butter and come wrapped around a filling of spiced potato. A selection of other tiffin items is also available.

32 Gandhi Bazaar, Basavanagudi (near Gandhi Bazaar circle)
Monday to Thursday: 6.30–11.30 a.m., 2–8 p.m.
Saturday and Sunday: 6.30 a.m.–noon, 2.30–8 p.m.

New Krishna Bhavan is another Bengaluru 'Brahmin' restaurant that differs in having a whimsical 1950s chocolate-box-coloured decor and a menu that extends beyond the usual dosa–idli fare of an Udupi joint. Interior Karnataka is reflected in dosas made of millet (ragi), wheat (*mandya*) and sorghum (jowar); 'green masala idli' is a plate of coin-sized idlis dressed with a green chilli and coriander chutney; and Udupi bun is a soft, sweet bread served with coconut chutney, perfect with a cup of tea. The menu changes across the day with tiffin items served in the morning, afternoon and early evening and set meals for lunch and dinner. NKB attracts a broad cross-section of people but many of its loyal customers are stately, older Bangalorean men dressed in traditional white pyjama or dhoti, long vest and a 'Congress' cap.

33/39 Sampige Road, Malleswaram
(080) 23561251
7 a.m.–10 p.m. (7 days)

For those looking for a quick snack and a coffee, there are two hole-in-the-wall places to visit. Veena Stores serves some of the best idlis in Bengaluru along with *vada*, kesari bhaat, *khara bhaat* (made with semolina, not rice), sweet pongal and coffee.

15th Cross, Opposite Telephone Exchange, Malleswaram
Monday to Saturday: 6 a.m.–noon, 3.30–8 p.m.
Sunday: 6 a.m.–noon

Brahmin's Coffee Bar sticks to the classic five-item menu—idli, vada, khara bhaat, kesari bhaat, coffee—that it has been serving for thirty years. Be prepared for queues at both places, though these move very quickly.

Ranga Rao Road, B.H.S. Main Cross, Sankarapuram
(M) 9845030234
6.30 a.m.–noon, 3–7 p.m. (Sundays closed)

For leisurely lingering over a coffee, or two, **Koshy's** is the preferred haunt for Bangaloreans. The filter-style coffee—sourced as green beans from Coorg and Chikmagalur and roasted and ground on the premises—is reputed to be the best in the city. Spend some time in this convivial cafe and you will see a changing cross-section of society: mid-morning is for legal types and politicians taking their coffee with 'bread roast' (toast); lunch is for local office people; in the afternoon, locals and tourists come in for a drink; and local creative and intellectual types take the evening slot. Look out for people doing what is called 'buy two, buy three' whereby two coffees are bought and split between three people. This is not an act driven by parsimony but from the belief that sharing is socially important—the same three customers are likely to then order another two coffees and so on until they have had sufficient.

Koshy's began operating in 1940 as a bakery supplying bread and pastries to personnel stationed in the cantonment, and grew into a restaurant specializing in serving British-style food to the British army personnel who were its main clients. To ensure that an authentic taste was captured the chefs were taught by army wives. When the British left, Bangaloreans still wanted to eat Koshy's British-style food. Today its 'roast' chicken (fried in a huge pot, not cooked in front of a fire or in an oven), fish and chips, plum pudding with brandy butter and excellent spiced sausages—made from pigs raised specially for the restaurant—are in high demand. Koshy's is one of the few restaurants in India that still serves food of the Raj, and does it well. If you are in Bengaluru during Christmas and feel the need for a full-scale festive meal you can enjoy the works at Koshy's.

39 St Marks Road
(080) 22213793, 22915840
9 a.m.–11.30 p.m. (7 days)

You can't miss **Hallimane**: its street frontage replicates a traditional and elegant mud-walled village house (a *hallimane*), and they specialize in traditional vegetarian fare of rural northern Karnataka. Try village lunch staples of *ragi mudde* (millet balls served with vegetable sambhar) and ragi roti (tasty flatbread of fresh ground millet, onions, coriander, ginger and curd): both dishes that sustain many a farmer. Other regional items are *sukkina unde* (balls of moong dal and chickpea flour coated with coconut, sesame and jaggery); *othu shyavige* (rice noodles dressed with peanuts, coconut, curry leaves, fried dal and mustard seeds); and *gasagase* (a sweet of ground poppy seeds and sugar), so popular that even a recent steep rise in the price of poppy seeds has not quelled the demand for it. During festivals such as Pongal (celebrated in January) special meals of regional delicacies are offered.

Third Cross, Sampige Road, Malleswaram
(080) 65611222, (M) 9611211222
6.30 a.m.–10.30 p.m. (7 days)
www.hallimane.com

Coastal Karnataka comes to the city via **Kanua**, an airy, modern restaurant named for a lost variety of Konkan rice. It is a bit of a trek out to Kanua but it is definitely worth the drive. The menu, a work of art in itself, focuses on seafood and vegetables. Starters include snake gourd stuffed with spiced potato served with a tamarind sauce; slices of jackfruit coated in spices and fried and *bolanjeer* (semolina-encrusted, fresh fried whitebait). More substantial dishes include *soorna pachi* (diced yam sautéed with black chickpeas); a pulao of sprouted moong dal, rice and spices; *thuakache randhei* (a light buttermilk stew of long beans, gourd, potato, sweet potato, drumsticks, coconut and cashews); and *mottè saar* (sliced, hard-boiled eggs in a coconut-based gravy flavoured with sesame seeds, poppy seeds and star anise). As a side, there is a *kismuri* of fried banana, lime, onion and coconut. A dish of musk melon sauced with cardamom-infused coconut milk and finished with a sprinkle of crunchy rice flakes is a simple but perfect finish to an excellent meal.

6/2 Kaikondrahalli Village, Sarjapur Road
(080) 65374471, 65374472
Noon–3 p.m., 7–11 p.m. (7 days)

ALL THAT TASTES NICE

Thou art the rulers of the minds of all people
Dispenser of India's destiny
Thy name rouses the hearts of Punjab, Sind, Gujarat and Maratha,
Of Dravida and Orissa and Bengal

These are the opening lines of India's national anthem, *Jan gana mana*. Among the regions referred to, 'Dravida' corresponds with the modern states of Karnataka, Tamil Nadu, Kerala and Andhra Pradesh—collectively called 'south India'. For many Indians, though, the state that most represents Dravida, and 'the south', is Tamil Nadu. Ethnic Tamils share a Cambrian-era genetic heritage with indigenous Australians and Africans—a legacy of the time, 500-odd million years ago, when these two continents were joined with India to form the supercontinent of Gondwanaland. Tamil, the local language, belongs to the Dravidian family of languages, which includes those spoken in Kerala, Karnataka and Andhra Pradesh. Among the world's oldest living languages, it has no relationship to the Indo-Aryan languages of the north. It is believed that Dravidian speakers were once spread out across India but were pushed exclusively into the south by later waves of immigrants who came in from the north. Speculations over who the earliest Dravidians might have been are complex and unresolved, but no one disputes that Dravidian culture is a very ancient one indeed, and that Tamil Nadu is the Dravidian 'heartland' of modern India.

It is not until the emergence of several dynasties in south India circa second century BC that Tamil Nadu becomes noteworthy in India's history. By this time, the region was engaged in a busy maritime trade with Sri Lanka and South East Asia, and it was through this connection that cloves, nutmeg, mace and cinnamon came to south India. A couple of hundred years later, the Tamils had built up active trade in these spices with the Roman Empire: the Romans believed that India was the indigenous source of these, an understanding that wily Indian traders did not dispel. Trading remained a consistent occupation in Tamil Nadu even though its rulers changed regularly, as did its borders. The south's most important ruling dynasties—Cholas, Cheras, Pandyas, Pallavas—were constantly at war, claiming rule over various configurations of south India. At one time, Tamil Nadu included Kerala in its domain and, in the fourteenth century, it was subsumed into the Vijayanagara Empire. This mega kingdom—which ruled over most of the south—protected Tamil Nadu from Muslim incursions but, after its collapse, the south fractured into many smaller domains. The various rulers reverted to the earlier model of feudal warfare, making it relatively easy for the British to assume control over the region and bring it under their auspices into the Madras Presidency along with much of south India. In 1969, the modern state of Tamil Nadu came into existence, after being separated from its Dravidian siblings.

Tamil Nadu occupies the southernmost part of the Indian peninsula: it has a long coastline bordered by a tropical coastal belt and an interior that runs from a verdant river delta to dry, dusty plains to lush mountain jungles. The overall rainfall averages only 1000 mm—although the humidity levels and gushing monsoonal rains give the impression that it is a much wetter place—and the temperature hovers between 35 and 40 °C for much of the year. It is not an easy climate, and while this limits the type of foods that can be grown, the region has long yielded an abundant and diverse supply of food. Tamil Nadu is one of India's leading producers of agricultural products. Rice is one of its richest crops—the Cauvery delta is alternatively called the 'rice bowl of India'—and rice plays an integral part in the Tamil diet. It is eaten at every meal in Tamil Nadu and often in several forms: plain boiled or steamed rice is basic; rice flavoured with tamarind or coconut might be a separate course; ground rice is used to coat fried items or as an ingredient within dishes; a sweet dish might be rice cooked in milk; and no matter how much rice has already been eaten, most Tamilians will finish their meal with plain rice mixed with curd. I was astounded at their ability to eat this at the end of a meal when I could barely take in air—but then they believe this combination to be an effective digestive. A variation of this is *thayirsadam*, a delicious blend of rice and curd tempered with chillies, ginger and curry leaves.

At breakfast, rice appears as idli or dosa. Both are made from a batter of rice, hulled *urad* dal and salt ground to a fine paste and left to ferment overnight—a process made easy by the humid climate. Fenugreek seeds are often added to the batter to control the level of fermentation. If the batter is intended to make dosa, it is traditionally ground a little finer than that for idli. To turn this batter into idli, it is spooned into special indented trays, lined with damp muslin cloth, and steamed in a lidded vessel. To make dosa, the batter is cooked on an iron griddle. The combination of rice and dal is essential to catalyse the fermentation. It is thought that the concept of mixing and grinding rice to create an effervescent reaction came into south India in the thirteenth century via trade and cultural connections—several Hindu kings ruled kingdoms in South East Asia in the medieval era—with Indonesia as that country has a long history of fermentation of food.

The ingredients that go into idli and dosa are simple enough, but to turn these into a soft batter requires, in addition to the natural magic of fermentation, a lot of grinding. Traditionally, the batter was prepared at home, rice and dal manually pounded in a stone mortar and pestle, or between two stones with the top stone rotated backwards and forwards by a rope. Women of the household did all the grinding and while the domestic realm was their sole responsibility, there was time to do this. Now, particularly in urban areas, people tend to go out to eat idli and dosa in restaurants where mechanized grinders do all the work. The tradition of making idli and dosa has not disappeared from homes though: my friend Kavita Chessety, a busy woman who publishes the Chennai-based food magazine *Malli*, blends the best of both worlds by using a domestic electronic grinder to made idli and dosa every morning for her family without the manual labour.

Idli and dosa reappear as afternoon snacks called tiffin in south India. The term 'tiffin' is derived from the old English slang 'tiffing', which meant to take a small amount of drink and, by extension, implied a small or light meal. The British in India employed the word tiffin to describe their afternoon meal, despite the fact that this was usually a substantial one. The use of the word tiffin throughout south India to denote a snack or light meal more accurately reflects the sense of smallness inherent in its parent word. (In Mumbai, tiffin is still used to describe the lunch meal.) The offerings at tiffin time extend beyond idli and dosa to include flavoured rice dishes; *uttapam* (a thick rice pancake spread with a topping of tomato, onion, chilli and coconut); *upma* (savoury spiced semolina); and *vada*. This last item is made from a batter of ground dal, green chillies, ginger and curry leaves, slid by hand into hot oil to form a doughnut shape. If vada is eaten at breakfast, it is usually as a side with idli/dosa; if taken as a stand-alone item at tiffin time, it is often dressed with spiced curd. Pongal is the most important festival in Tamil Nadu, and is celebrated on the solar equinox in January. It has roots in the ancient nature-worship practised in Tamil Nadu before Hinduism came along. Pongal is also the name of a savoury porridge of rice and lentils customarily made during its namesake festival, though it has become a regular item on tiffin menus. *Chakkari pongal* is a sweet version made with jaggery.

The preference for rice is often used as a culinary marker between south and north India, where wheat-based breads are predominant. What is interesting is that rice originated in north India and took about 1000 years to make its way to the south. In those distant days, rice was very widely eaten in north India while millets were the major cereal food in the south. In light of this, there is some poetic justice in the widespread misconception—outside of India—that basmati, a north Indian variety of rice, is the only one grown and used in India. Over 1000 types of rice have been grown in India: many have now disappeared, or are on the verge of extinction due to the introduction of more commercial strains. A visit to any standard provisions store in Tamil Nadu will reveal a selection of different varieties and processed forms of rice: puffed, husked, parboiled, broken, beaten, ground and pressed.

Whether idli and dosa are eaten for breakfast or tiffin, these are served with freshly ground coconut chutney and a soupy lentil–vegetable stew called sambhar (*more later*). The spongy, slightly sour idli soaks up the tangy, chilli-infused sambhar to form one of the world's best food matches. Alternatively, idli might be eaten sprinkled with ghee and dipped into a spice mix called *podi*, ground from dried red chillies, chana dal, coriander seeds, coconut, asafoetida and salt. The proper accompaniment to breakfast or tiffin is a cup of sweet, milky south Indian coffee. The introduction of coffee into India is attributed to a fifteenth-century Muslim holy man who smuggled seven green coffee seeds out of Arabia—an illegal act at the time—and brought these to India where he cultivated them in Karnataka. Coffee was a fashionable drink amongst the Muslim aristocracy in India in the Middle Ages—they obtained their roasted beans largely from Arab sources—but its use did not extend beyond this niche of Indian society. It was the British who introduced Tamilians to coffee when they established coffee plantations in the hilly tracts of Tamil Nadu in the nineteenth century: today the state is a major producer of shade-grown coffee.

As a beverage, coffee is prepared in Tamil Nadu—and throughout south India—in a distinctive metal filter that looks like a small canister, and this is universally referred to as a south Indian coffee filter. This filter has two interlocking pieces: the top half has a finely perforated bottom and finely ground coffee is packed into this and tamped down; this section is slotted on to the hollow bottom half and boiling water poured over the ground beans. It takes about an hour for the coffee decoction to filter through and is quite cool by the time the process is completed. The coffee is not reheated, as this turns it bitter, so boiling milk is added to it to heat it instead. Given that south Indian coffee is largely milk, this certainly does the trick. In fact, it makes it so hot that people order 'metre coffee', whereby a waiter decants the steaming coffee back and forth between two cups to cool it and create froth: people order 'one metre' or 'two metre' coffee depending on how cool they want it. 'Degree coffee' is coffee made with milk that has been measured by a lactometer to ensure its purity. In places where the waiters might not be up to the performance of metre coffee, it is served in a *dhabra*, a steel tumbler that sits inside a small steel bowl; coffee is poured into this bowl to cool.

Tamil Nadu is a major producer of a vegetable called drumstick, the long-ridged pod of *Moringa oleifera*. The whole pod is cooked until it is tender and it is eaten by scraping a piece along one's teeth and sucking out the soft seeds inside it, then discarding the stringy shell. Drumstick is regularly used in sambhar. Tamilians believe that eating chilli-hot food helps beat the heat: my own experience bears out the validity of this piece of culinary wisdom. If you eat a chilli-laden dish in humid south India, it causes you to break out into a cooling sweat, an effect that is not as pronounced in a dry climate. A dish of sambhar usually has a bite to it imparted from the use of a small round chilli that is popularly referred to as sambhar chilli. To counteract its effect, but not undermine its sweat-inducing properties, a sour ingredient like tamarind is added. Sambhar is served at every meal in Tamil Nadu: at breakfast, it accompanies idli and dosa; at lunch or dinner, it is served with plain rice as a second course. Despite its ubiquitous presence, it seems that sambhar, in its current form, might be a relatively recent addition to Tamilian cuisine. For a brief moment in the eighteenth century, a Maratha king ruled Tamil Nadu; one of his favourite dishes was *aamti*, a spiced lentil stew with sour kokum as a key flavouring (*see Maharashtra chapter*). Apparently, he asked his cook to prepare aamti but finding no kokum available, the cook substituted tamarind and thus created sambhar. Even if this story is true, it is unlikely that a spiced vegetable–lentil stew was a new dish to Tamilians.

Rasam is a thin, clear extract of *toor* dal and tamarind spiced with curry leaves, asafoetida, mustard seeds, red chillies, coriander seeds, ground masoor dal and turmeric: it is sour, spicy, sharp and served with rice as the first course to stimulate appetite. Rasam is said to be the parent dish of the Anglo-Indian soup mulligatawny: a dish that is said to have been created when a British army officer stationed in Madras asked his Indian cook to prepare soup for dinner; the cook, with no cultural concept of 'soup', prepared the closest thing he knew and that was rasam; to this, he added some chicken—because he knew that sahib did not consider anything a meal unless it included meat—and rice. His version of 'soup' must have included freshly ground black pepper: when this spice is added to rasam, it is properly called *molagu rasam* and the word 'mulligatawny' is believed to derive from this.

Tamil Nadu produces India's largest crop of bananas, of many varieties. Large green bananas, *kaccha kela* or plantain, are used extensively in cooking. This starchy fruit is used like a vegetable: stir-fried with various spice combinations; cooked in gravies of coconut and tamarind; mashed and spiced into chutneys; and sliced finely and deep-fried to create chips eaten as snacks or crunchy sides to meals. Ripe bananas are used in sweet dishes or served as simple desserts. The leaf of the banana tree is customarily used as a plate in Tamil Nadu—it has now been superseded by stainless steel thalis in many households for everyday use but a festive meal is always served on banana leaf—and there is an established etiquette for its use. The leaf is laid horizontally with the tip pointing left. The top half of the leaf holds the condiments; the top-right corner the spicy items; rice and rice dishes are placed centre-bottom; crisp items such as banana chips and papad are placed in the middle. If non-vegetarian items are served, these might be served on a second leaf. A guest is always given the top of the leaf that has less 'spine' as this allows it to sit completely flat and is easiest to eat off; if there is no guest at dinner, the head of the household gets this choice part. When finished, the diner can fold the leaf towards himself (if the meal was enjoyable) or away (if not). A variation of this is practised in Chettinad—folding the leaf towards you indicates that the meal celebrated a happy occasion, folding it away means it was a sad one.

Like the rest of India, various dals are fashioned into an array of dishes. Tamilians also roast dal in oil as a seasoning that imparts a subtle nutty flavour to dishes. The spices most commonly used in Tamil cuisine are ginger, turmeric, dried red chillies, coriander seeds, cardamom, fenugreek, mustard seeds and curry leaves. The latter are the fresh leaves of a tropical tree, *Murraya koenigii*, which grows profusely in south India and are used pervasively in Tamil Nadu, paired frequently with mustard seeds: a combination that imparts one of the most distinct flavours of the region's cuisine. Coconut is another everyday seasoning, and ingredient, and Tamilians prefer to use grated coconut in cooking rather than coconut milk. (*See Kerala chapter for more on the coconut.*) Other fruit and vegetables that happily thrive in the tropical climate include beans, pumpkin, gourds, leafy greens, yams, jackfruit, onions, eggplant and ladies' fingers. These are made into many vegetable dishes such as *kottu* (stew of finely chopped vegetables tempered with mustard seeds and urad dal); *avial* (diced vegetables cooked with coconut and curd); *pachchadi* (cooked or raw vegetables in tempered curd); *masiyal* (vegetable mash tempered with dal, mustard seeds, chilli and curry leaves); *poriyal* (finely shredded or sliced vegetables such as beetroot or colocasia leaves sautéed with mustard seeds, dal and red chilli); and *kari* (well-spiced preparation of vegetables or meat).

The lush lands of Tamil Nadu produce India's highest yield of sugar cane but Tamilians do not seem to have quite the same passion for sweets as some of their countrymen. If a sweet dish is served at a meal it will typically be a semi-liquid *payasam*, perhaps of dal cooked with coconut milk and jaggery, or tapioca sago cooked with milk, sugar and saffron; a payasam is always included at a festive repast and it is ordinary practice to start the meal with this and continue to take tastes of it throughout. A regular family meal is more likely to conclude with a piece of fruit such as a banana. While rice-based tiffin items or crunchy savouries are largely preferred as snacks by Tamilians, there is certainly a market for sweet confections. Barfi, halwa, *Mysore pak* and *jangiri/jalebi* are popular sweets but not indigenous: there are localized versions such as coconut barfi and jangiri made from a batter of ground rice and urad dal rather than wheat flour. A distinctive sweet is *adhirasam*, a doughnut-like confection made from a cooked paste of rice flour and jaggery pressed into rounds and deep-fried. The finished product has a soft, dense texture and is a little sticky: it reminds me of gingerbread though it is flavoured with cardamom not ginger. Adhirasam has been eaten in Tamil Nadu since the fifteenth century and is popularly offered to the gods, so you should be able to find it in any sweet shop near a temple.

Popular perception is that the food of Tamil Nadu is vegetarian when, in fact, less than one-third among Tamilians abstain from eating meat or fish. My theory is that this belief originates in the temples of Tamil Nadu. Before they adopted Hinduism, Tamilians worshipped a deity called Murugan, and the focus of daily life was the village temple dedicated to this god of war and fertility. As Hinduism made its way into peninsular India, it was taken up by various southern rulers who influenced their subjects to accept it and it soon became the primary religion. Murugan was reconsigned to the Hindu pantheon as an avatar of Shiva and the Vedic social system was adopted, albeit in a distinct variant that conferred exceptional significant status, and thereby power, on the Brahmin (priestly) caste. They controlled Tamilian society from the village temples that retained their primacy, even if the god who had originally occupied these had changed his name. This change in socio-religious orientation resulted in the construction of lavish temple complexes throughout Tamil Nadu to demonstrate where power, and a whole new pantheon, resided. When the armies of the northern Islamic rulers began to aggressively press into the south in the Middle Ages, Tamil Nadu was largely spared any serious incursion. As a result, the culture absorbed little Muslim influence and perhaps, most significantly, its magnificent temples were left untouched— unlike those in other parts of the country that the Muslim armies desecrated—and Tamil Nadu became an important site of pilgrimage for Hindus, their travels facilitated by the network of trade routes that joined north to south. For centuries, most outsiders visiting Tamil Nadu would have been on a pilgrimage. It is tradition that only vegetarian food is served in temples and this is usually mimicked in the surrounding towns. A pilgrim would likely only be exposed to vegetarian food and thus gain the impression that the local food was exclusively vegetarian. Written records serve to enhance this understanding since Brahmins act as both priests and scholars and were often the only literate people in a community—it was not unusual in India for a king to be illiterate—and were the keepers of tradition and the source of most written material.

Inevitably, they reinforced their position in society by promulgating their own traditions; and since Tamil Brahmins were vegetarian, and wrote much of the historic information about food in Tamil Nadu, you can see how this idea gained sway. As modern visitors to Tamil Nadu typically continue to make the state's temples the focus of their travel—whether spiritual or cultural—they also largely encounter local vegetarian food. Even in tourist locations not associated with a temple—admittedly there are few of these—commercial eateries tend to serve vegetarian cuisine. The distinct upside is that Tamil Nadu has a sophisticated vegetarian cuisine, commonly referred to as 'Tam Bram' (Tamil Brahmin) cuisine. Because orthodox Tam Brams are strict vegetarians, and shun foods such as onion and garlic, there is a misconception that their food is austere when it is actually refined, diverse and flavourful. Perhaps what is forbidding about traditional Tam Bram food is that its preparation and service is subject to rigorous rituals to ensure that the food is 'pure' and will not expose the consumer to caste pollution. (*See Recommendations, in particular Chettinad and Chennai.*) The crucial thing is that it is all about the rice: everything else on the plate, or banana leaf, exists to support and flavour this.

CHENNAI

In 1997, Madras was renamed Chennai in an attempt to expunge its colonial identity. This act might have helped reassert Chennai as an Indian metropolis but the city itself was a British creation. Admittedly, when the British arrived here in the seventeenth century, the thriving trading port at Mylapore (now a suburb south of the centre) had already been in operation since the second century, and the Portuguese had set up a fortified trading post close by. (The port was named Santhome for Thomas the Apostle who is believed to have been martyred in the area in AD 72 and buried at Mylapore.) The British built their own fort a little north of Mylapore and gradually brought more of the area under their auspices. The French captured the city from the British in the eighteenth century and held it for three years, after which the British won it back and governed the Madras Presidency from Madras until Independence. Despite the name change, it is the material relics of colonial Madras that are Chennai's most popular tourist attractions: the less charitable might suggest that these are the only draws the city has but for the culinary explorer this is irrelevant. Chennai is a great place to eat at.

Recommendations

....

Mylapore is the Brahmin centre of Chennai, well known for its 'mess', small, simple, inexpensive, vegetarian eateries where people come to take an everyday meal. The main clients of any mess are office workers, students, labourers and travellers: people who cannot go home for lunch or dinner. If the food is good—and it often is—the clientele can be very diverse. For an authentic Mylapore mess experience, visit **Myali Karpagambal Mess**. There is no menu here; the waiters reel off what is available that day. If your Tamil is not up to much, just point to what someone else is eating: the food is all local style and freshly cooked so you can't go wrong. There are always tiffin items such as podi dosa; *keerai vada* (made with leafy green amaranth); pongal and *kasi halwa* (grated white pumpkin cooked with jaggery). What is available will change over the course of the day. You can always get a cup of good aromatic filter coffee in a mess.

20 East Mada Street, Opposite Bharathiya Vidya Bhavan, Mylapore
(044) 24642902
7 a.m.–10 p.m. (7 days)

Rayar Mess is a tiny eatery—only four tables—but serves some of the best idli and pongal in Chennai.

31 Arundale Street, Near Kapaleshvara Temple, Mylapore
(044) 24670519
7–10.30 a.m., 3–6.30 p.m. (7 days)

At the centre of Mylapore is the Kapaleshvara Temple. The narrow streets that cosset it hold visual and aromatic feasts of flowers, fruit and twinkling bowerbird stalls hawking the paraphernalia and unguents needed to carry out religious rituals. There are also interesting options to satisfy more worldly needs, such as hunger. In the perimeter wall of the temple is a small window from which meals and other foods, cooked in the temple kitchen, are dispensed; this might be a leaf bowl filled with flavoured rice, an idli or coconut-based sweet depending on the time of day. In a side street adjacent to this literal hole-in-the-wall is **Miami Tiffin Stall**. This eatery cooks up twenty varieties of flavoured rice every day including tamarind, curd, sambhar, lime and coriander:

each serve comes with crunchy titbits to create textural diversity. On the south side of the temple is a small shop called **Kabali Kadai** that sells rose-flavoured milk and has a cult following in Chennai. To the north is a branch of **Saravana Bhavan** where you can have a full meal of Tam Bram cuisine or singular tiffin dishes such as curd rice, dahi vada and rava idli. If any chilli lingers in your mouth after your meal, the home-made tender-coconut ice cream will alleviate it very nicely.

70 North Mada Street, Mylapore
(044) 24611177
www.saravanabhavan.com

Grand Sweets & Snacks is good for adhirasam and other local sweets like coconut barfi, *sonasi* (coconut-stuffed pastry) and mango halwa. Of the large selection of snacks, try crunchy, pinwheel-shaped *murukku* made from ground rice, cumin and asafoetida and a plate of small fritters of tempered dosa batter called *kuzhi paniyaram*. You order your items and are issued a bill that you take to a separate counter to pay. While you wait for your items to be packed you can avail yourself of *donnai*, an item offered to customers to tide them over while they wait. A donnai might be a sweet or a leaf cone of savoury rice: apparently there are customers who come and order an item off the menu just to have the donnai.

24 Second Main Road, Gandhi Nagar, Adyar
(044) 24914213
www.grandsweets.com/index.html

Annalakshmi specializes in recreating forgotten recipes: the sort of dishes people ate in their grandmothers' kitchens but don't remember how to make. The food is all vegetarian and a typical selection includes *paruppu thogayal* (thick, spicy dal) served with dry-roasted papad; rice cooked with fenugreek greens; *azhakki podi* (raw banana powder); ginger rasam and burnt buttermilk curry. Female volunteers do all the cooking and all proceeds are donated to charity.

18/3 Rukmani Lakshmipathy Road (Marshall Road), Sigapi Achi
Building, First Floor, Egmore
(044) 28525109
Noon–2.30 p.m., 7.30–9.30 p.m. (Mondays closed)
www.annalakshmichennai.co.in/index.htm

Chennai boasts one of the longest beaches in the world and a local fishing community that hauls in fresh catch every day. If you head for the central stretch of Marina Beach in the early evening, you can have a simple meal of fresh fish or seafood cooked to order from one of the shacks perched on the sand. If you want a dining experience that is the polar opposite of eating simple fried fish on the beach, visit **Dakshin**. The menu incorporates dishes and influences from across south India but owes its primary culinary and cultural allegiance to Tamil Nadu. As you cross into the restaurant from the impersonal marble hotel hallway via heavy wooden doors, you are enveloped in an interior of rich colour, and the warm hum of people at work, enjoying a superlative feast. The meal begins with a small, sweet dosa made with a batter enriched with banana and ground cashew nuts, smeared with freshly churned white butter, ginger chutney and jaggery, followed by a small dish of dal fried with green chillies, onion, ginger and curry leaves to stimulate the appetite. After these starters, take a deep breath, relax and get ready for: masala fried prawns; crab cooked with chilli, tomato, curry leaves and black pepper; *kodikova* (chicken cooked in curd, milk and butter with green chillies and black pepper); potatoes cooked in coconut milk, cumin, dal and curry leaves; *nandu puttu* (crabmeat tossed with onions, ginger and green chillies); and lamb cooked with onion, tomato, red chilli, black pepper and curry leaves. The meal is accompanied by all manner of chutneys and crunchy titbits, and of course there is curd rice at the end.

ITC Park & Sheraton Towers, 132 TTK Road
(044) 24994101
www.itcwelcomegroup.in

A feast of Tamilian cuisine at **Coromandel Fig** begins with a small bowl of thick, sweet, condensed milk called *basundi*—an appetizer. You will understand the sense of this as you are regaled with a selection of regional lamb, chicken and prawn specialities accompanied by *appam*, a lacy rice pancake. A light dessert prepared from tender-coconut water, coconut flesh and sweetened coconut milk finishes the meal. In between courses, you can have your fortune divined by a tame parrot.

Taj Connemara, Binny Road
(044) 55000000
www.tajhotels.com

The most popular non-vegetarian cuisine in Chennai is that of the Chettiar community (*see below*). If you cannot travel to Chettinad to sample it, visit **Ponnusamy** instead. This busy restaurant has a diverse menu but you should only concern yourself with the Chettinad section. Dishes to try are *mutton kola curry* (spiced meatballs in gravy); rabbit fry; meat sautéed with various spices and flavouring ingredients (ditto chicken pepper fry and brain fry); and *viral* (deep-fried whitebait).

55 Gowdia Mutt Road, Royapettah
(044) 28130986
Noon–4 p.m., 7–11 p.m. (7 days)
www.ponnusamyhotels.com

Respite from Chennai's hectic streets is found at **Café Amethyst**, in an old Chennai mansion. Sit under a fan in the veranda or in the lush garden and relax with tender-coconut water, sugar-cane juice or a cup of tea from the Nilgiris, the tea/coffee-growing region of Tamil Nadu. (The menu of Western-style food is not for you, dear culinary adventurer; save your stomach space for authentic local food.)

14 Padmavathi Road, Jeypore Colony, Gopalapuram
(044) 28353581, 28353582
10 a.m.–10 p.m. (7 days)

CHETTINAD

Chettinad is the ancestral home of one of Tamil Nadu's most influential communities, the Chettiars, whose distinct cuisine is renowned. They played a key role in the Chola kingdom (circa 300 BC–AD 1279) as traders in salt, gems and equipment for ships: from this, they moved into shipping itself and traded directly with South East Asia. At this time, they lived on the Tamil Nadu coast. When a Chola king abducted a Chettiar girl, the law-abiding Chettiars were so distressed and shamed by the king's action that the community committed mass suicide, leaving only the young men behind. Understandably, these men were unhappy to live and work in Chola territory, so when the rival Pandyas made them an offer to move inland, to what is now the Chettiar region, and work for them, they took it. Another tale says that the Chettiars were driven inland after a tidal wave destroyed their coastal home and they wanted to protect their families from future risk.

The move away from the coast did not stop the Chettiars from trading with South East Asia. While they spent long periods absent from home on business, few Chettiars settled away from their community, and poured much of their wealth into creating huge family mansions in the Chettinad region. The Chettiar community suffered huge financial losses after the Second World War, particularly in the wake of Burma's (now Myanmar) independence, as they had significant assets tied up there. This caused the Chettiars to move away from Chettinad into other parts of Tamil Nadu (and India), seeking new opportunities. Many of their splendid mansions were locked up and left: some were returned to on special family occasions, others slowly decayed through neglect. It is these mansions that have brought new prosperity to the Chettiars as they have become significant tourist attractions. Many are being dusted off and reopened as hotels.

Only Chettiar men travelled; the women remained in the confines of the home. The men brought all sorts of goods back from their travels as well as new foods and recipes, which were subsequently incorporated by the women into Chettiar cuisine. I like to think that the men wanted to share their experience of the world at large by presenting their families with the tastes they experienced. The Chettiars have a strong religious orientation but it is not one that precludes many foods; non-vegetarian dishes predominate in traditional Chettinad cuisine. The variety of spices is similar to that used throughout Tamil Nadu, but these are employed very generously and Chettiar dishes tend to be more aromatic than those eaten by other Tamilian communities. This is a culinary distinction indicative of the community's collective wealth in that they could afford to eat meat and use plenty of spices. Arguably the most famous dish of the Chettiar community is chicken pepper fry aka 'Chettiar chicken'—essentially, chicken pieces sautéed with black pepper, aniseed, chillies, tomatoes, onions and garlic. There is a dish called 'Chicken 65' that is served in restaurants throughout India: it is purported that this is the original 'Chettiar chicken', and that it was prepared such that it stayed edible for sixty-five days thus providing a decent stock of food to Chettiar men on long sea journeys.

Evidence of the Chettiars' coastal roots is found in their ample use of coconut, in fish and seafood dishes such as *sora puttu* (shark 'scrambled' with spices); *prawn vaural* (prawns stir-fried with garlic, cumin, fennel, black pepper, coriander and chilli); and *nandu masala* (crab cooked in a

348   The Penguin Food Guide to India

gravy of freshly ground coconut, tomato, cinnamon, cloves, fennel, cumin and curry leaves). Many Chettiars are vegetarians but their non-vegetarian food gets all the attention. Chettiar food is often described as being 'hot' with chillies and pepper. There is some truth in this, which stems from the 'eat the heat to beat the heat' philosophy, but authentic Chettiar cooks adeptly balance the bite of chilli in a way that is not often demonstrated in restaurant versions of 'Chicken 65'.

Recommendations

The luxurious yet restrained style of one particular Chettinad family is available to you to experience at the lovingly restored art deco mansion **Visalam** that was originally built by a father for his daughter and now operates as a boutique hotel. It took five years of work to return this building to its original state. The effort put into creating an authentic Chettiar aesthetic and atmosphere extends to the food at Visalam. The kitchen is staffed by a team of local cooks and professional chefs who learn from each other. The elegantly simple kitchen has a large communal table where guests can enjoy a lunch of traditional Chettiar specialties served on a banana leaf; later in the afternoon, you can return to the kitchen for a cooking class and learn to make local dishes such as *wadai vallapoo* (banana-flower fritters); *kathirika piratal* (eggplant cooked in a rich paste of coconut, cinnamon, cloves, cardamom, fennel and garlic); and *mutton uppu* (meat cooked with coconut and spices including *kaalpasi*, a dried lichen that grows on the cinnamon tree). In the evening, a selection of Chettiar dishes is served in European-style courses: crisp appetizer; light soup of local vegetables such as the leaves of the lettuce shrub (*Pisonia alba*) that grows in the hotel garden; pepper chicken fry; mutton uppu paired with onion dosa; ladies' fingers cooked with curry leaves; and a sticky pudding of red Burmese rice cooked with jaggery and cashew nuts. The ethos of Visalam is to preserve and promote local culture. The kitchen staffers enthusiastically share and show all they can about local food, and a visit can be arranged to a local snack factory where you can see traditional rice-based sweet and savoury snacks being prepared.

Kanadukathan, Karaikudi
(04565) 273301
www.cghearth.com
visalam@cghearth.com

Along with their wonderful homes and cooking, Chettiars are renowned for their generous hospitality. You can experience all three at **Chettinadu Mansion**. This sprawling nineteenth-century home spans an entire block and has an in-house museum featuring many local kitchen items. The garrulous owner will happily regale you with stories about the food life of a traditional Chettiar home over a meal of Chettiar dishes (requires an advance order).

SARM House, Behind Raja's Palace, Kanadukathan
(04565) 273080
www.chettinadumansion.com

The Bangala is a heritage hotel specializing in home-style Chettinad food. My banana-leaf lunch included *puli mandi* (chickpeas cooked in tamarind and rice water); mango pachchadi, tempered with mustard seeds, chilli and curry leaves; masiyal of local spinach cooked with moong dal, garlic and green chillies; pepper chicken and *meen varuval* (kingfish marinated in a paste of garlic, cumin, fennel, chilli and coriander and deep-fried). It probably goes without saying by now, but just so you can picture the meal fully, there were crunchy fried items served throughout the meal and plenty of pickles and papad to mix up with the main dishes. If you are not staying in one of The Bangala's craft-filled rooms you might need to avail yourself of a comfortable armchair in the sitting room for a little rest after eating your lunch.

Devakottai Road, Senjai, Karaikudi
(044) 24934851
www.thebangala.com

If you want to eat local food with the locals in Karaikudi—the main town of Chettinad—visit **Priya Mess**. This very simple eatery is renowned for its non-vegetarian meals and serves lunch to 250 people every day. On the day I visited, a dish of spicy quail was amongst the offerings.

31 Ara Street, Karaikudi
12.30–3.30 p.m.

MADURAI

Madurai is one of the world's oldest cities, famous for the mighty Meenakshi–Sundareswarar Temple. Greek ambassador Megasthenes visited Madurai in 302 BC and wrote effusively of its splendour. He did not go there to worship Hindu gods, nor would he have found the temple as it appears today, for it was not built until the sixteenth century AD. He was there to trade. The magnificence he describes was temporal, as well as sacred, as the city was an astoundingly wealthy trading centre: the coffers of imperial Rome were said to have been drained to buy silks, spices and pearls from Madurai. It was the wealth generated from trade in goods that provided the funds to ultimately build the city's defining temple. Modern Madurai is not quite the place of civic and commercial majesty it was in Megasthenes' time but it remains one of India's most celebrated pilgrimage centres, and the Meenakshi Temple is enduringly brilliant with the sound and colour of people enacting ancient rituals that have not altered over millennia.

The streets around the temple are laid out in a concentric pattern that forms a magical diagram symbolizing the cosmos. Circumambulating the central temple anticlockwise is said to activate the magic of the diagram: this might account then for Madurai's vibrant street food culture. If you want to get an authentic taste of the local region the streets are a good place to start. Each morning, outside the mission hospital on East Veli Street, you can find a vendor famed for his *idiyappam*, or string hoppers (thin, handmade rice noodles), universally eaten for breakfast in south India. These can be enjoyed in various ways but in this case they are served in a mound dressed with sugar and freshly grated coconut. In the evening the streets of the old city come alive with food vendors. All you need to do is walk around and make culinary discoveries. Among the items I ate on my explorations were *thanka boli* (a crêpe-thin roti stuffed with fresh grated coconut and jaggery); coin-sized fried bread (puri) flavoured with *kewra* (screw-pine essence) and sprinkled with ginger powder; steamed colocasia root (taro) cut into cubes and dressed with a subtle spice mix; slices of fresh, sweet-banana stem, reputed to aid digestion; and a drink called *paruthi paal*, made from the milk extracted from the seeds of cotton—an important local crop—rice flour, coconut, ginger and jaggery. This thick concoction is served hot and the vendor decants it back and forth between two brass cups to cool it a little before handing it over to a customer. Paruthi paal is found only in the Madurai region.

Recommendations

For a city defined by a Hindu temple, it is curious that three of the foods recommended to me as most distinctive of Madurai show strong Muslim influence. *Jil jil jigarthanda* ('cool cool heart') is a cross between a drink and an ice-cream sundae. It is prepared from sweetened reduced milk mixed in a glass with small pieces of agar-agar, *nannaari* (sarsaparilla syrup) and vanilla ice cream. Other versions include rose water and almonds and provide a more immediately recognizable taste of the Muslim influence on this drink and its similarity to *falooda*. The most 'famous' place in Madurai for jigarthanda is the aptly named **Famous Jigarthanda** on the corner of East Marret and South Masi streets. The sign is in Tamil and if you can't read this just look out for crowds standing around and digging spoons into glasses. Madurai *parotta* is a fried wheat bread, essentially the same as a paratha except that the dough is kneaded and folded in a way that creates a much flakier texture than the north Indian version. These are eaten in a distinctly southern way: several parottas are piled on a plate accompanied by coconut gravy, chilli gravy, coconut relish and sliced onion; the parotta is then 'mashed' with the hand into these sauces just as it is done with rice. A variation is *kothu parotta*, where the parotta is chopped very finely on the grill and cooked with tomato, green chilli, coconut leaves and fresh coriander. Madurai's parotta stalls are as celebrated for the distinct sounds that come from them as the food. Parottas are cooked at roadside stalls on iron-grill plates perched atop forty-gallon drums in which fires burn; some stall holders beat out a rhythm on this drum to attract customers; there is the sound of the dough being vigorously slapped on the bench top during its preparation; and the sound of the knife hitting the grill plate as the parotta is deftly chopped and minced—a task carried out with quite a flourish of showmanship. Madurai is renowned for the high quality of its milk; legend has it that this stems from an ancient injustice done to a woman from the cow-herding caste by the local king; when his highness discovered his miscarriage of justice, he ordered all the inhabitants of Madurai to be slain, leaving just the cow herders! The third distinctive Madurai food recommended to me was milk halwa—a sweet of Muslim parentage—at **Prema Vilas** (84, Town Hall Road).

Modern Restaurant is recommended as serving lunchtime meals that are the 'type of food you would get in a Brahmin home'.

No. 161/1B Nethaji Road, Near Raja Opticals
(0452) 2344487
www.modernrestaurant.in

Murugan Idli Shop serves the freshest snowy idlis with unusual, and very tasty, chutneys.

196 West Masi Street
(0452) 2341379
www.muruganidlishop.com

For the best south Indian filter coffee jostle with the crowds at **Sri Sabaree's** on the corner of West Perimal Maistry and Town Hall Road. If you want to try local non-vegetarian food, hire an autorickshaw and head out on Alagar Kovil Road to **Mudaliar Idli Kadai** for dishes such as chicken in red chilli gravy and quail in coconut gravy.

PUDUCHERRY

Puducherry, on the coast of Tamil Nadu, was a French territory till 1954 (the French called it Pondicherry and this name remained in official use until 2006 when it was changed to Puducherry). The French arrived in 1617 and obtained permission from the local raja to set up a trading post. The following year the Thirty Years' War broke out in Europe and the opportunity was forgotten. In the meantime, the Dutch opened a trading post in the same area. They had received a royal decree to do so but their arrogance grated on the sensibilities of the local nobility who purposefully invited the French to reconsider establishing a trading post there, which they did in 1675. The British and the French then fought various territorial battles over the region during which the French-built town at Puducherry was razed to the ground. In 1742, the French governor Joseph Dupleix rebuilt the town and many of the civic works he initiated still exist in the French quarter of modern Puducherry.

The French were not as squeamish about intermingling with the locals as the British—they were not without prejudice though: Madame Dupleix, the governor's wife, was so determined to remove a Hindu temple from the French part of town that she ordered lumps of meat to be thrown on it to defile it in the eyes of Hindu worshippers. There was considerable intermarriage between the French and the Tamils. Given the sexual politics of the era the intermingling was confined to French men taking wives of Tamil parentage, but this meant that local foods and cooking techniques made their way into the kitchens of Puducherry and resulted in a style of cooking variously called Franco-Tamil, Puducherry Dubash or Creole. Green and red chillies, cumin, turmeric, fennel and pepper found their way into French-style dishes—although chilli was applied sparingly—and coconut milk replaced cream. In dishes that were Tamil in origin, much more garlic was used and new foods such as green beans were added. Franco-Tamil cooking is milder than Tamil cooking and uses a distinctive flavour base fabricated from red onion, crushed garlic, curry leaves, masoor dal, urad dal, fenugreek and mustard seeds.

Recommendations

While the French heritage of Puducherry is evident on the streets, it is not so obvious in the food. Only about sixty homes in Puducherry still cook Franco-Tamilian food and prefer to keep it to themselves. There are, at the time of writing, two places where you can try Creole cuisine—unless you have access to one of those sixty homes. I do predict that more Franco-Tamil-style food will appear on menus in Puducherry soon. **Salle A Manger** is located in the Tamil quarter in a building that was originally the mansion of a wealthy Chettiar trading family. The Franco-Tamil dishes on offer demonstrate that the influence of the one cuisine on the other can be subtle yet the dishes have a distinct character that is not like either cuisine. When I ate here, I enjoyed a soup of local leafy greens, coconut and ginger prepared with a stock base—a French touch as stock is rarely used in Indian cooking; a composed salad of green beans, potato and red onion dressed with coconut milk sauce; shrimps cooked in a sauce of spices, coconut cream and egg; a croquette of spiced fish paired with home-made mayonnaise; and chicken cooked with mint and coconut milk. The spicing across all the dishes is milder than encountered in Tamil cooking but much more pronounced than you would ever encounter in classic French cuisine.

La Maison Tamoule, 36 Vysial Street
(0413) 2223738
www.neemranahotels.com

In the French quarter the restaurant at **Hotel L'Orient** has a small selection of Franco-Tamil dishes, all prefixed on the menu with 'Creole'. You can try curry Creole *aux petites legumes* (spiced dal); Creole rice with curry leaves, ladies' fingers, capsicum, onion and small eggplant; curry Creole *au pullet resettle traditionelle* (chicken cooked with coconut and cashews); and Creole-style squid cooked with fennel, tomato, garlic, red chilli and curry leaves.

17 Rue Romain Rolland
(0413) 2343067
www.neemranahotels.com

Café Lune on Rue Suffren has a French name and French flag on its signage but that's about as Gallic as it gets. This quirky little cafe serves excellent south Indian filter coffee, which the proprietor swirls so high and so fast between two brass tumblers that you would swear he makes it do a loop. Simple, inexpensive meals of flavoured rice and tiffin items are as good as the coffee. **Cherish Family Restaurant** is another place for idli, dosa, uttapam and idiyappam. Timing is everything here: the later in the day you come in the less choice you have as this place has a dedicated following and items sell out quickly. I sauntered in at about 10 a.m. and had to suffice with a plate of savoury pongal served with sambhar and coconut chutney; fortunately it was an elegant sufficiency.

31 Sri Aurobindo Street, Near H.K. Kassim Salai
(0413) 2222321

GOD'S OWN KITCHEN

In legend, the verdant land of Kerala emerges from the ocean when the god Parashurama hurls his axe into the waves of the ocean and demands that the waters recede to the point where his blade has embedded itself in the seabed. (Since the same divine act is said to have created Goa, Parashurama can perhaps take credit for creating much of India's lush west coast.) Kerala emerges in recorded history in the third century BC as the land of the Chera dynasty. They ruled over a kingdom that was engaged in cross-border commerce with Sumer and Greece. By the dawn of the Christian era, the Romans were sailing to Kerala in ships laden with gold to be exchanged for pepper.

After the collapse of the Roman Empire—which must have left a hole in the Kerala economy for a while—the region built up a vigorous trade relationship with China and Arabia. Traders came to Kerala for teak, ivory, silk and spices; of the latter, the locally grown ones were pepper, ginger, turmeric and cardamom. Nutmeg, cloves, mace and cinnamon came into Kerala from Sri Lanka and South East Asia via the east-coast ports of Tamil Nadu from where they were carried overland to spice depots on the south-west coast. Buyers were often unaware that the origin of these various dried seeds, fruit, roots and bark was other than the place they bought them from, and Kerala became renowned as the 'land of spices'. As such, it became the focus of European efforts to gain a greater share of the highly profitable spice trade. Christopher Columbus is purported to have been heading for Kerala when he set out on his famous voyage in 1492. He well missed his intended mark—though his discovery of the West Indies and the Americas ultimately gave India the chilli—and the first Europeans to find their way to Kerala were the Portuguese. In 1498, they landed near Kozhikode in north Kerala and later established themselves at Kochi from where they mercilessly pursued domination of the spice trade. The Dutch ousted the Portuguese from Kerala in 1663; in 1792, the British moved out the Dutch, and took control of the region until 1947. In 1956, what is now Kerala was created by merging parts of Mysore state (Karnataka) and Madras state (Tamil Nadu) with the princely states of Kochi and Travancore. The official language of modern Kerala is Malayalam and its people are referred to either as Malayalis or Keralites.

Kerala is one of India's smallest states, and the most densely populated one, yet this particular demographic reality does not play out on the ground as you might expect it to. When Ibn Battuta visited north Kerala in the fourteenth century he said that 'every man has his own separate palm-grove with his house in the middle' and that 'not a patch of ground, be it as small as a span in breadth, is left uncultivated'. Kerala's population has grown considerably since Battuta's time but the landscape still appears as one luxuriant garden shaded by an endless canopy of trees. Since ancient times Kerala has been blessed with rulers acutely attuned to the importance of the natural environment, and they have led their people to live in harmony with nature. This does not mean that land has not been brought under cultivation—after all, food needs to be grown—just that it has been done in a way that has allowed Kerala to remain home to more than 4000 different plants. That is nearly a quarter of all the flora species found on the subcontinent—considering that Kerala is only a narrow slip of land, 120 kilometres at its widest, undulating from the Western Ghats down to the sea, and that its famed 'backwaters' region is more water than terra firma, this is a proud achievement. There are also forty-four rivers running through the state with numerous rivulets and waterholes further stemming off from these. All this water provides an abundance of salt and freshwater fish and fish cooked in coconut milk and eaten with rice is the typical daily meal in Kerala. Only 6 per cent of Keralites are vegetarian, largely due to this fish-eating habit; even in inland areas, where fresh fish is not easily accessible, dried fish has traditionally been used. Prawns (*chemmeen*), sardines (*mathi*), mussels (*kallummekkaya*), clams (*kakka**) and crab (*njandu*) are also widely eaten. The fish called *karimeen*, or pearl spot, is unique to Kerala's backwaters.

All that water also makes it easy to grow rice, which is the staple grain of Kerala. A meal without rice is as unthinkable for a Malayali as it is for

---

* I have found that the word kakka can also be used in Kerala for mussels.

a Tamilian. The common rice is fat-grained and purplish, typically called 'red rice'. Traditionally, the harvested paddy—unhusked rice—is parboiled and dried before storage; this hardens the kernel, making it relatively unassailable by insects, and thus preserves it in the humid climate. Red rice is lightly milled just before cooking and it has a wholesome substance and nutty flavour. Plain boiled rice is the usual accompaniment to meals in Kerala but it is prepared in other ways. It is ground and mixed with coconut milk to form a batter that is leavened with toddy and cooked in an *appachatti* (iron and terracotta pot shaped like a wok with upright handles) to make a pancake called *appam*. Appam batter is poured into the hot appachatti and the cook rotates the pan by holding the handles, causing the batter to swirl up the pan where some of it sticks to the sides and cooks to a crisp filigree. The remaining batter falls to the bottom of the pan and cooks to crumpet-like consistency giving the cooked appam two contrasting textures. Appams are commonly eaten for breakfast paired with gravy-based dishes such as *moilee* (fish or seafood stew; see Christian cuisine further on for this dish and more on appams) or *ishtoo* (a delicately spiced stew of potatoes and coconut milk) or dipped into sweetened coconut milk. *Puttu* is another Kerala breakfast dish made from broken rice and coconut that are layered into a hollow piece of bamboo or a slim metal cylinder—*puttukutti*—and steamed. Puttu is eaten with small, sweet, ripe bananas or spiced chickpeas. Muslims in Kerala (*see Moplah cuisine*) eat a version of puttu called *irachiputti* in which the rice is layered with spiced mincemeat. Rice-based idli, dosa and *idiyappam* are other commonplace breakfast dishes in Kerala.

Coconuts have always grown profusely in Kerala and it is arguable whether this fruit permeates Malayali cuisine more than that of any other southern state. The coconut is called the 'blessed fruit' in India as this palm can grow in soil and climatic conditions that few other trees can withstand and it provides a multitude of edible and useful products: to cut down a coconut palm is considered a sin. When young, the coconut is full of slightly sweetish water rich in potassium, a mineral that helps in rehydration; thus, coconut water is the perfect drink in the hot, sticky climate of Kerala, where one sweats profusely. You cannot fail to notice coconut-water vendors in Kerala with their coconuts piled high on carts or kerbsides. The vendor wields a machete to lop the top off the coconut and, for a small sum of ten rupees or so, a deliciously refreshing—and hygienic—drink is yours. Tender green coconuts are used for this water as they contain only a little of the so-called 'flesh' that lines the shell; the flesh is quite jelly-like at this stage and some vendors provide a small spoon to scrape it out. As a coconut ages the flesh absorbs the water inside the shell and thickens. A mature coconut has little liquid left in it and is lined with firm white meat that is scraped out, ground, mixed with hot water and crushed to produce coconut milk. The 'first extract' is rich and thick and is added to dishes at the end of the cooking process to prevent it from curdling. More hot water is added to the coconut pulp and it is pressed again to get a thinner 'second extract' used to cook food in. Fresh coconut flesh is also grated and added to many preparations. Dried coconut is called copra and thin or finely shredded slices of this can be used in cooking or it can be boiled to obtain oil. Coconut oil was traditionally used extensively in Kerala but the erroneous modern belief that coconut, particularly the oil, is 'bad for you' has seen it fall somewhat out of favour. The bad press the coconut received emanated largely from places like the US where tests to determine whether it had 'good' or 'bad' fat were carried out on hydrogenated coconut oil, yielding the result that it was 'fattening' and 'unhealthy'. This idea has recently been rectified as it has been discovered that fresh-pressed virgin coconut oil and coconut flesh are rich sources of lauric acid, a substance that has proven antiviral, antibacterial and antifungal properties. It also triggers the mechanics of satiation in humans and has a thermogenic effect, that is, its consumption increases metabolism, so, ironically, eating coconut might actually help you stabilize weight, or even lose it, rather than gain it. In Kerala's coastal lowlands, coconut is used in almost every dish, either as freshly grated flesh or fresh-pressed milk. In the interiors, where the palm is not as prolific, copra is often used in cooking instead of fresh coconut meat, though not quite as generously since its flavour can be quite strong.

Toddy is a mildly alcoholic beverage made by 'tapping' the sap of the unopened flower of the coconut palm. The flower stem is cut and scraped to stimulate sap production; a clay pot is tied below to collect the drip; some clay is rubbed around the incision to control the flow. Professional toddy tappers scale the palms in the morning, and again in the evening, to collect the sap, by which time it has begun to ferment due to the interaction of its sugars and naturally occurring yeasts, catalysed by the humidity. At collection time toddy typically has about 4 per cent alcohol content. If left longer, it will continue to ferment and become more alcoholic; if left long enough, it will eventually turn into coconut vinegar. One coconut palm can ooze up to thirty litres of sap per day and will do so for about four months at a stretch. Fresh toddy is cloudy and somewhat sweet with a distinct undertone of coconut. Once the toddy is collected it is sold in simple bars called toddy shops, which also dish out food. The exemplar dish of 'toddy shop cuisine' is karimeen cooked in coconut-milk curry and served with red rice and *kappa*. Kappa is made of boiled or steamed tapioca cooked in a paste of coconut, onions and red chillies and tempered with mustard seeds and curry leaves. The combination of karimeen and kappa has become somewhat of an iconic Kerala meal. Toddy-shop cuisine is typically well seasoned with red chillies to stimulate patrons to drink more. Toddy shops have traditionally been male domains, darkish dens with the interior divided into private booths, but toddy-shop cuisine has recently become fashionable and there are now family-friendly eateries, particularly in the Kottayam area, to which families travel from the suburbs of Kochi for Sunday lunch outings. Along with rice, coconut and tapioca, the other important crops grown in Kerala are pepper, banana, sugar cane, cashew, cardamom, tea and coffee.

The fact that most Malayalis are non-vegetarian does not mean that animal foods dominate meals. A typical day or evening meal consists of rice; two or three vegetable dishes; curd or curd-based *pachchadi*; a fish stew or meat dish; and pickles, chutneys and crunchy papad, banana chips or fried fish. A sweet dish or fresh fruit finish the meal. There are several distinct styles of vegetable dishes prepared in Kerala: a *thoran* is made from vegetables like gourd, bean, banana flower or jackfruit seeds (mild-flavoured and textured like chestnuts), cooked with ground coconut; *avial* is a potage of mixed vegetables in a coconut and spice paste; pachchadi is prepared from fruit or vegetables mixed with curd and ground coconut, tempered with mustard seeds and curry leaves; *mezhukkupuratti* is an everyday stir-fry of vegetables minus coconut. Traditional Malayali vegetable dishes are lightly spiced with combinations of black pepper, ginger, cumin, turmeric, cardamom, chilli, curry leaves and mustard seeds. A dish suffixed with the word *kari* indicates that it is more highly spiced and is influenced by, or belongs to, the cooking of Kerala's Christian or Muslim communities. These richer vegetarian dishes are often adaptations of the fragrant meat/fish dishes of these communities and employ cinnamon, clove, nutmeg, coriander and aniseed alongside more commonly used spices.

The repertoire of traditional vegetable dishes eaten in Kerala comes primarily from Hindu Namboothiri–Nair cuisine. The Namboothiris are Brahmins and their diet is vegetarian: they are also only 6 per cent of the population and there you have your statistical representation of vegetarians. The Nairs were traditionally warriors and nobles and, as such, ate meat. On fasting and festival days, however, they would eat vegetarian food similar to that of the Namboothiris.

Namboothiri–Nair cuisine has evolved with particular concern for health based on Ayurvedic principles (discussed further on in this chapter). Ayurveda is the traditional medicine system of India; the first writings on it appeared in the first millennium BC but the practices it describes are older. Food and eating habits are given particular attention in Ayurveda as what one eats is considered to have a significant effect on physical and spiritual well-being. Many of the 'foreign foods', such as chilli, that came into India many years after the system of Ayurveda was recorded, were not included in its dietary canon, or were assimilated only as medicine (modern Ayurveda practitioners do include more 'recent' foods in their dietary prescriptions). The Namboothiris traditionally led a lifestyle closely guided by the principles of Ayurveda and, as a result, stuck to using local spices. The fact that spices were valuable trading items might also have limited their use in cooking; even traditional Kerala papad is made without spices.

A traditional Malayali Hindu feast is laid out on a banana leaf in a particular order. The items are to be eaten from left to right, progressing from mild, smooth dishes to those with a more determined texture and stronger flavour. The meal starts with a mouthful of rice mixed with dal to clear the palate; sambhar with rice is next; then come various vegetables, chosen to ensure a balance of tastes and textures; a second course of rice is served with rasam followed by *payasam*—often served with a side dish of pickle to clear the palate of its desired, but cloying, sweetness—the meal ending with curd and rice. It is the vegetarian feast food of Namboothiris that you will likely be served in restaurants in Kerala because it is 'special' and more crafted than everyday food. The southern part of Kerala, from Alappuzha to Thiruvananthapuram, is considered to be the most distinctly Hindu region of Kerala.

While Kerala played its first historical role as a BC-era international entrepôt, its social constructs had evolved in an even more ancient era when the population was largely agrarian. In this world the need to designate people to function as traders would not have been apparent, and the Kerala form of the caste system does not have an exclusive trading caste. This must have seemed like a serious oversight in the light of later developments; one solution was to encourage people from other parts of

India, and the world, to settle in Kerala and fill this functional gap. At different times people from the various countries with which it traded set up shop in Kerala, most significantly Christians and Arabs. Because these outsiders fulfilled a need, and did not arrive in marauding armies, their absorption into Kerala society was a relatively peaceful process, though not a homogenizing one. These communities developed their own identities in the context and conditions of Kerala and one way their differences found concrete expression was in cooking. Today, the food of Kerala is categorized as Hindu, Muslim (Moplah) and Christian.

CHRISTIAN CUISINE

In AD 52, St Thomas the Apostle arrived in Kerala where he made the first Christian conversions in India by placing himself in front of a group of Brahmins, tossing some water into the air and making it stay there. On witnessing this miracle several of the Brahmins immediately converted. It was a strategic move—whether intended or not—on the part of St Thomas to fix his sights on bringing Brahmins into Christianity as their acceptance of this new religion ensured it a wider appeal than would have occurred had he first converted fishermen. The Keralites he converted and their descendants are called Syrian Christians because the liturgy of their worship is in the Syriac language. Various other Christian influences have come into Kerala over the ensuing millennia and the Christian community of modern Kerala is a complex one, but we shall focus on the cuisine of the Syrian Christians, also called Nazaranis or 'followers of Jesus'.

It is not known how long it took for St Thomas's Brahmin converts to give up their vegetarian ways but Kerala Christians are famed for not being able to eat a meatless meal. They have even broken the greatest food taboo in India and eat beef, something they are freely able to do as Kerala is the only state in India where this meat is sold legally. One of the best-known dishes of Syrian Christian cuisine is *erachi ularthiyatu*, pieces of beef cooked in a gravy of coconut, vinegar, fennel, cinnamon, coriander, pepper and chilli and then fried with mustard seeds, onions and curry leaves to create a 'dry' dish. Nazaranis are also very fond of eating *tharavu* (duck). *Meen moilee*, a fish stew made with coconut milk, ginger, curry leaves, garlic and coconut vinegar, is a signature Syrian Christian dish as is *kozhi mappas*, a special-occasion dish of chicken in coconut milk and spices. Both these stews are customarily served with appams. This soft rice bread is considered to have its origins in the Syrian Christian kitchen and Nazaranis prepare several different types including *kallappam* (made with palm toddy), *vattyappam* (steamed) and INRI appam (an unfermented version flavoured with onion, garlic and cumin), which is eaten to commemorate the Last Supper and as part of the Passover meal. The fact that a Christian community celebrates a Jewish festival might seem somewhat incongruous but it is believed that St Thomas specifically came to Kerala to convert the Jews living there (*see Kochi*). The dual function of the INRI appam is possibly evidence that he succeeded and that Jewish converts brought some of their traditions into the Syrian Christian community. INRI appam represents the body of Christ and is served with *pesha pal* (custard-like sauce of coconut, cumin, cardamom, and ground rice) that represents his blood.

Kerala's Syrian Christians worked as traders and commercial cultivators of pepper, cardamom, tea, coffee and rubber and they are most closely associated with the midland region of Kerala where the land is most amenable to plantation growing of these products. There are also Nazaranis living in the coastal area and their cooking varies with location; those living close to the coast traditionally use more aquatic foods, coconut and chilli, and fresh fish and seafood and rice form the basis of daily meals; Syrian Christians living inland use much less coconut and more meat, such as duck, beef and mutton. When a fish dish is prepared, it is traditionally made with dried fish, though advances in transport have made fresh fish more readily available inland nowadays.

Recommendations

The bustling midland town of Pala is the municipal centre of a wealthy region of rubber plantations, mostly owned and run by Syrian Christians. It is also where you can enjoy a unique homestay at **Nazarani Tharavad**, the ancestral mansion of a prominent Syrian Christian family. Hostess Thressi John Kottukapally is an accomplished cook who takes great pleasure in preserving the culinary and cultural traditions of her community by sharing these with her guests. The refined and generous hospitality that Syrian Christians pride themselves in is evident in the elaborate Nazarani *sadhya* (festive meal) served to guests at the expansive family dining table. A banana leaf dotted with salt, banana chips, ginger chutney and lime pickle is laid out for each diner. The first course is *neyyappam*, small and mildly sweet dumplings of rice, banana and coconut, after which comes moong dal lightly fried with spices, dried prawns cooked with coconut, *meen pollichatu* (fish cooked in banana leaf with onions, garlic, tomato and vinegar), *beef ularthiyatu* and a pachchadi of bitter gourd. At this point, a range of small dishes are served as 'palate cleansers', including an *olan* of beans and ash gourd cooked in coconut milk; banana in spiced curd; carrot and mango pickle; banana fried with sugar; and a crumbed fillet of fish. I could hardly believe it when, after this, out came the 'second course': mutton stewed in coconut milk with appam and spiced roasted quail with potato straws. Somehow, I managed to fit it all in—it would have been ungracious to refuse.

(M) 9846212438
www.nazaranitharavad.com

MOPLAH CUISINE

Traders from Arabia had settled in Kerala before the Romans found their way there. Their religious and cultural affiliations were diverse; among them, there would have been Jewish Arabs and, later, Christian Arabs. With the advent of Islam in Arabia in the seventh century it was a natural progression for this religion to travel to places with Arab populations. It is unlikely that all those of Arab descent in Kerala converted to Islam but the community essentially became a Muslim one. Kerala Muslims are now referred to as Moplah (meaning 'brother-in-law') or Malabar Muslims. The word Malabar was once used to denote India's entire south-west coastal region; in its modern usage, it refers to Kerala's northern coast, home to most of Kerala's Muslims.

Moplah cooking shares many of the hallmarks of Indo-Muslim cuisine: preference for non-vegetarian dishes, fondness for richly spiced food and very sweet sweets, and a reverence for rice preparations such as biryani. Malabar Muslim cuisine, though, is arguably the most distinctive variant of the Indo-Muslim culinary repertoire as it is a product of the local environment as much as it is of cultural and religious influences. Malabar Muslims share the general Malayali habit of eating rice and fish every day; *meen varutharacha charu* (fish cooked with coconut, onion, garlic, chilli, ginger, curry leaves and tamarind) is their daily fish stew. Moplahs have a particular passion for mussels, which they prepare in various styles such as *kallummaki porichathu* (fried with chilli, mustard seeds and curry leaves); *varutharacha kallummaki kari* (cooked in a coconut-and-tamarind gravy); and *kallummaki achar* (sweet-and-sour pickle made with kokum, green chilli, garlic, jaggery, ginger and the heady Moplah version of garam masala ground from aniseed, mace, star anise, cardamom seeds, pepper, cinnamon and nutmeg). This blend is a historical legacy of Moplah involvement in the spice trade as several of these spices were 'imports' and would have been expensive flavouring items; only those trading in them could afford to use them in cooking.

Appams are not part of traditional Moplah cuisine as these are leavened with alcoholic toddy. Instead, flatbread called *pathiri* is used to scoop up rich gravies. Pathiri is most commonly made of rice flour and coconut milk and its preparation is considered an art form by Moplah cooks. There are said be around fifty types of pathiri including *nei pathiri* (made of boiled rice mixed with coconut, aniseed and shallot that is fried and eaten for breakfast); wheat pathiri stuffed with spiced meat or fish filling; *adukku pathiri* (made with egg and cardamom); and sweet *chattippathiri* (a baked dessert created by layering wheat flour pathiri with nuts, raisins and rose-flavoured sugar syrup). Unique Moplah sweets are *unnakkai* (a banana fritter stuffed with cashew nuts and raisins); coconut halwa; and *muttamala* and *pinnanathappam*. Muttamala is made by dripping beaten egg yolks through a hole in the bottom of an empty coconut shell into hot sugar syrup to create bright yellow strings or garlands (*mala*). The egg whites are beaten up with the leftover sugar syrup and cardamom powder and steamed to create a custard-like pudding that is served garlanded with the muttamala.

The Moplah version of biryani is referred to as 'Malabar biryani'; the use of fish or prawns, coconut, curry leaves, fresh lime juice and Moplah garam masala gives it a distinct local flavour. It is baked in layers, which are taken apart after it has cooked and the rice and filling are served separately. It is paired with a pungent, sweet–sour date chutney; Suleimani chai, a hot black tea flavoured with fresh lime juice and sugar, is customarily served after it. Moplah biryani is a complex and refined dish; it requires a long list of ingredients and several hours of chopping, grinding and cooking. It has become very popular in restaurants in modern Kerala.

Recommendations

In 1498, the first Europeans to sail to India, Vasco da Gama and his crew, set down at Kappad beach just near the northern coastal city of Kozhikode. Two years later, the Portuguese destroyed Kozhikode in a pique after the local ruler, the zamorin, made it clear that they were not welcome. It was not that he had any issues with foreigners; Kozhikode was a prosperous trading city that had been engaged in international commerce for close to two millennia before the Portuguese arrived, and a cosmopolitan population had settled there from various partner trading countries. The city hosted so many different nationalities that it had developed its own unique 'finger' system for trading whereby a buyer and a seller, who did not speak the same language, would clasp each other's fingers under a towel to transact the deal, each finger having a predetermined price. What the zamorin would not tolerate was the aggressive attitude of the Portuguese when everybody else under his dominion went about their business peacefully. Amongst the population of Kozhikode was a community of Moplahs descended from Arab traders, who ran the zamorin's navy and trade. It took some centuries for Kozhikode to recover from the bombardment inflicted upon it by the sulking Portuguese, and its modern prosperity is largely due to remittance money sent home from workers in the Gulf states.

The modest appearance of **Zains Hotel**—a simple pink-fronted house on a quiet residential street—belies its reputation as being the 'holy grail of Moplah cuisine', but the constant stream of people attest to the truth of it. A central cabinet displays Moplah classics such as stuffed fried mussels called *arikkadukki*; beef pathiri; unnakkai; muttamala–pinnanathappam; and chattippathiri. You can order chicken biryani with a bowl of freshly grated coconut, onion raita and lime pickle or masala fish served with a pile of pathiri.

Convent Cross Road, Behind Tagore Centenary Hall
(0495) 2366311
Noon–11 p.m. (7 days)

Paragon is celebrated for its local seafood preparations including crab steamed in a spicy sauce; fish stir-fried with thick coconut

crescents, curry leaves and chilli paste; various mussel preparations
and a superb fish biryani. There are also local meat preparations such
as *naduvannar* (chicken and banana cooked in richly spiced coconut
gravy) served with pathiri.

Kannur Road, Under C.H. Flyover
(0495) 2767020, (M) 9846497611
6 a.m.–midnight (7 days)
www.paragonrestaurant.net

In mussel season—October to December—Kozhikode's streets host
a plethora of street stalls selling crisp deep-fried mussels. Kozhikode
is also renowned for its banana chips and 'Kozhikode halwa' made
of rice and coconut milk. Mithai Theruvu ('Sweet Market' or 'SM
Street') is the place to go for this (any auto- or rickshaw-wallah will
know where this street is). There is a conglomerate of sweet shops
around the street junction of SM Street and Palayam Road and each
store is packed with large jewel-coloured blocks of halwa. At **Pulari
Sweets** the shop assistant generously provided me with samples
which he daintily sliced off with a large, inelegant, machete-like
knife. Among the many flavours on offer those with a more local
touch include tender coconut, jaggery, roasted rice and pineapple
as well as the eponymous Kozhikode variety.

Palayam Road
(0495) 2701408

The best pepper in the world comes from north Kerala. It is grown
inland but as the coastal town of Tellicherry was the port from
which the British shipped it out to the rest of the world it came to
be commonly referred to as 'Tellicherry pepper'. It seems a little
incongruous then that very little pepper is used in the kitchen at
Ayisha Manzil, a majestic colonial Malabari bungalow perched on
a hillock overlooking the Arabian Sea in Tellicherry that welcomes
homestay guests. Hosts Moosa and Faiza are a complementary act:
Moosa is the garrulous and charming host and Faiza is a renowned
Moplah cook and a self-contained commander of the kitchen. The
food is purposefully that of the 'high end' of Moplah cooking,
intended to demonstrate the wealth of influence that has come into
the community through its success, particularly in spice trading.

The reason pepper is not used here is that it tends to dominate the flavour of the food and, after all, it was people on the other side of the world who were crazy about its taste, not necessarily the locals. Moosa takes guests on early-morning trips to the local fish market to see the astounding variety of fish and seafood that comes in every morning. When I visited, there was mackerel, sardines, whitebait, anchovies, prawns, barracuda, snapper, crabs, Dover sole, pomfret, seer fish, kingfish, mussels, a hammerhead shark and a dissected sting ray complete with its fat. This market is part of the social fabric of the town and there is a buzz of conversation as well as shopping activity; Moosa says it serves the same social function as 'the pubs of the west'. The bustle will give you a hearty appetite for breakfast, served in the garden, back at the house. A morning repast might comprise a hot dish of local bananas mashed and tumbled with eggs, sugar, cashew nuts, raisins, coconut and cardamom served with nei pathiri or appam—with baking powder used as a raising agent instead of toddy—or fresh bananas dressed with a coconut-milk-and-cardamom sauce. Fish and seafood, purchased from the market, is cooked for lunch and dinner in dishes such as tamarind prawns, stuffed mussels, and fish coated with a spice paste, wrapped in a banana leaf and pan-fried with a little oil. A rich beef curry is served with *mutta sirka* (fried bread made of cooked rice and eggs). Guests can take a hands-on cooking class with Faiza in the afternoon, and relish their handiwork at dinner. The Englishman who built Ayisha Manzil in 1862 is said to have introduced the concept of 'teatime cake' to India and instigated the first commercial baking of a cake in India, in Tellicherry. The city still trades in industrial quantities of spices and you can visit a local spice trader to see, smell and buy high-quality spices.

Court Road
(0490) 2341590, (M) 9847002340
cpmoosa@rediffmail.com

KOCHI

Kodungallar, fifty-odd kilometres north of Kochi, was the major trading city on the Malabar coast but a huge storm in 1341 silted up its port and simultaneously opened up an inlet into a fine natural harbour at Kochi, turning what was a fishing village into a port city at the centre of the spice trade. The harbour at Kochi connected it to the Arabian Sea and the outward world, but behind it was a labyrinth of 'backwaters' that connected it to the inland areas from where came spices and other trade commodities. This meant that goods could be loaded on to boats and transported relatively easily into Kochi for distribution. In an era where the only other option to move goods was by bullock carts along rough roads—an excruciatingly slow process—this made Kochi a particularly attractive hub.

After laying siege to Kozhikode the Portuguese sailed 200-odd kilometres south to Kochi. On their arrival they built themselves a fort on the thumb-shaped peninsula that comprises the modern districts of Fort Kochi and Mattancherry. The Portuguese were determined to gain control of the Indian spice trade by any means and their violent tactics did not endear them to the local populace in Kochi either. The local rulers assisted the Dutch to take control of the spice trade out of Kochi from the Portuguese in 1663; the British relieved the Dutch of the responsibility in 1795. These European interlopers intermingled with a cosmopolitan mix of people of varied races and ethnicities in Kochi, most of whom had established themselves there before da Gama was even born. Modern Kochi is still home to over thirty communities and the local cuisine has absorbed influences from many of them.

Recommendations

Jewish traders first travelled to Kerala from the court of King Solomon circa 900 BC. If it is true that St Thomas converted the Jews in Kerala to Christianity, then they must have been established there early in the Christian era. It was not until the destruction of the Temple of Jerusalem in AD 70 that a significant number of Jews migrated to India, where they settled at Kodungallar and worked as traders. When the storm of 1341 hit this city the local Jewish traders headed down to Kochi. The Jews in Kochi won particular favour with the local rulers and they were a very successful merchant community; the beautiful synagogue in Mattancherry with its famous interior with blue-and-white tiles from China is an enduring testament to their worldly success. They also had their own cuisine, which observed orthodox

Jewish food rules (such as avoiding shellfish and not cooking or eating meat and milk together) and incorporated Middle Eastern, European and Indian influences.

The three-storeyed **Koder House**, built in 1808 as the home of a wealthy Jewish family, was a landmark building then. It now operates a luxury boutique hotel and the Indo-Jewish culinary heritage of its original owners is enshrined in a small selection of well-crafted dishes on its restaurant menu. These include a light stock-based fish soup gently flavoured with ginger; a Jewish salad of pineapple, green capsicum and carrot dressed with a vinaigrette of cumin, red chilli, cinnamon, nutmeg and pepper; and a sweet chocolate and coconut jelly prepared from a household recipe.

Tower Road
(0484) 2218485
www.koderhouse.com

The menu of **The History & Terrace Grill** is a labour of love for presiding chef, Ajeeth Janardanan. He has dedicated himself to learning about the cuisines of the different ethnic communities of Fort Kochi, often by visiting family homes to hear their food stories and learn their cooking traditions. He brings this knowledge back to the restaurant to share with his team and they set about creating high-quality dishes to capture these histories. Each dish on the menu has a story and a meal here is an education in local cuisine. Ajeeth's culinary detective work will ensure that the menu is constantly evolving. At the time of my visit, it represented the Arab, Persian, Syrian Christian, Portuguese, Jewish, Dutch, British, Tamil, Gujarati, Chinese, Konkan, Kutchi, Namboothiri and Nair communities that have lived, or are still living, in Fort Kochi. A fine mud crab and ginger soup spiced with star anise is redolent of the Chinese who have left a permanent mark of their presence in the distinctive fishing nets still used in Kochi harbour. First-class railway lamb curry reflects the British presence; this enduringly popular colonial dish is created by slow-cooking mutton with various spices and chillies for six to seven hours in a brass vessel, after which the tender and intensely flavoured meat is tempered with coconut milk to make it less assertive yet exciting to the palate. Another initiative of the kitchen brigade is their work to eliminate the use of any processed foods in the food and to prepare everything from scratch: just as all the different Kochi communities would have done for most of their history.

Brunton Boatyard Hotel
7.30 a.m–10.30 p.m. (7 days)
(0484) 2215461, 2215462

A cooking class with Leelu Roy at **Leelu Homestay** is an opportunity to experience authentic local domestic cooking. The dishes prepared in the class are those typically eaten every day in Malayali homes with a focus on fish, rice and vegetables. After the cooking is completed, the group sits down at the family dining table to enjoy a meal together, a particularly pleasant experience for the traveller who has been eating hotel meals—albeit very good ones—for some time.

Quiros Street, Behind Head Post Office
(0484) 2215377
Cooking classes: 11 a.m.–1 p.m., 6–8 p.m. (book in advance)
www.leeluhomestay.com

Shala is a chic eatery with a neat menu of classic Kerala dishes of fish, prawn and chicken in coconut-milk curries and a mild 'colonial beef curry'. Shala is unashamedly touristy but the food does not suffer for that. It is light, healthy, tasty—typical of domestic cuisine in Kerala.

Burgher Street
(0484) 2215769
5.30–10 p.m. (Sundays closed)

Hotel New Ananda Bhavan, a homely vegetarian joint on Mehabool Road at Aspinall Junction, is well patronized by locals. The meals served here are vegetarian and a typical lunch comprises several seasonal vegetable dishes, pickles, payasam and red rice. Directly behind Ananda Bhavan you will find a clean, simple eatery called **Classic Hotel** that serves non-vegetarian meals. On the day I ate there, my lunch included curried sardines, roasted banana, beans and ash gourd cooked in coconut milk, a glass of buttermilk and rice.

Kayees Biryani has been serving biryani for more than fifty years; this longevity, and the patronage of the uber-famous Indian artist M.F. Husain, has bestowed legendary status on this modest hotel. Around 500 people eat here every day, most of them choosing to enjoy a plate of the renowned biryani served with tangy date pickle. My pick is the prawn biryani but chicken, fish and mutton versions are available. I advise you to get in early as the biryani often runs out by 2 p.m.

Rahmattullah Hotel, New Road, Mattancherry
(0484) 2354321
Noon–6.30 p.m. (7 days)

Pai Brothers Fast Food in Ernakulam serves sixty-six types of dosa—the variety is in the filling rather than the type of dosa—and this place is a local institution. In twenty years, it has evolved from a street cart to a large shop standing on a lane named for it.

Pai Brothers Lane, Off M.G. Road
(0484) 2374879
5.30 p.m.–2 a.m. (7 days)

BACKWATERS

The Kuttanad region stretches for ninety-five kilometres from Kollam in the south to the north of Kochi and inland to where the hills begin to rise. Popularly referred to as the 'backwaters', the region is made up of a network of lakes, canals, rivers and creeks and is, as is evident, more water than land. The backwaters historically functioned as an aquatic thoroughfare joining the inland to coastal ports as well as providing food for local consumption and export. Much of the rice grown in Kerala comes from this region—earning it the alternative name of 'the rice bowl of Kerala'—and lobster, karimeen, clams and huge freshwater prawns are all harvested from these waters. Kuttanad is also renowned for its toddy shops so look out for them along the waterways and roadsides. Take a chance on one to see what they have cooking. In a toddy shop I visited just outside Marari Beach Resort, I ate delicious *muthi kari* (fresh sardines cooked with lots of red chillies, black pepper, garlic, *gambodge*—also known as Malabar tamarind or *Garcinia gummi-gutta*, coriander and fenugreek).

Recommendations

With the advent of the railways, vastly improved roads and air travel, the need to transport goods by boat across the backwaters declined, leaving a lot of redundant rice boats. Someone had the idea of renovating these boats and operating them as houseboats for tourists. The idea was an immediate success and an industry was born. Today, there are 500-odd houseboats, called *kettu vallam*, on the backwaters. Many of these moor on the south-western edge of Vembanad Lake at the old port town of Alappuzha. This is where many visitors go to negotiate a houseboat adventure that includes meals. If you let your cook know that you are interested in eating local dishes, you should receive good fresh meals based on the Malayali trinity of fish–rice–coconut. If you do find yourself in Alappuzha and require some sustenance to enter into houseboat negotiations, **Unis Restaurant** on YMCA Road serves a banana-leaf lunch of fresh local fish such as mackerel or sardines as the feature dish.

If you can afford to pamper yourself, the ultimate backwaters cruise can be enjoyed aboard the ultra-luxurious **Oberoi Motor Vessel Vrinda**. This mobile five-star hotel provides guests with commanding views across the lakes and surrounding countryside. Every morning, as breakfast is served, life along the backwaters becomes the backdrop as the cruiser travels to a particular spot where guests are transferred to a kettu vallam to undertake explorations with a local guide. Back on board, cooking lessons can be had in the compact and pristine kitchen. I tried my hand at Kerala parotta, a flaky bread that requires a lot of tricky twisting and slapping to create; the chefs made it look very easy but I certainly did not master it in one lesson. Somewhat easier to prepare were appams; a coconut-milk-based vegetable stew; and a dish of kakka (clams)—hauled from the lake by local fishermen in a purpose-designed basket—cooked with ginger, coriander, cumin, fennel, black pepper and freshly grated coconut. The menu changes for every meal on board the *Vrinda* but there is always a selection of Malayali dishes available with a particular focus on seafood and fish.

(011) 23890606
www.oberoihotels.com/oberoi_vrinda/itineraries.asp

A stay at **Coconut Lagoon** on the eastern edge of Vembanad Lake is enchanting from the start. You can only reach the resort by boat, which picks you up at a designated spot and delivers you to the reception area via one of the canals that run through the property. The focus is on preserving the magnificent natural environment and the local social culture, while providing guests with an experience that is enriching and relaxing. All the buildings on the property are in traditional Kerala architectural style; some purpose-built and others rescued from neglect and even relocated from other parts of the state. This preservation and promotion of local heritage is also incorporated into the way food is procured, prepared and proffered. Huge, sweet-fleshed freshwater prawns (some the size of a small lobster) and fish from the backwaters such as karimeen (also bred in the property's fish sanctuary), carp and seabral, or 'lake tuna', are cooked in various regional preparations such as *chemmeen olathu* (prawns stir-fried with green chillies, ginger, curry leaves and gambodge) and *meen pattichatu* (fish cooked in a light gravy flavoured with red chilli, fenugreek, black pepper, garlic, mustard seeds and curry leaves). Duck farmed on the backwaters is 'free range' and features regularly on the menu in a Syrian Christian–style mildly spiced coconut-milk stew. As the name suggests, *Cocos nucifera* are significant at Coconut Lagoon; upon arrival you are given a young green coconut to drink the water from; high-quality coconut oil is the cooking medium and milk made from coconuts grown on the property enriches the food. The organic red rice served at each meal is grown on the property. Seasonal vegetables are cooked in several traditional styles such as a vegetable stew infused with star anise; kappa; beetroot thoran; and green mango pachchadi. For the sweet tooth, there is always a payasam-style dish such as *ada pradhaman* (rice flakes cooked in coconut milk and jaggery), which you should eat with plain papad and small bananas in true local style.

Kumarakom, Kottayam
(0481) 2524491
coconutlagoon@cghearth.com
www.cghearth.com

As you travel away from the coast and the backwaters, the land gently rises lifting you out of the salty stickiness of the lowland climate into the dense, moist greenery of Kerala's high ranges, the area called

Cardamom Hills. As the name suggests, cardamom grows profusely in this region as do tea, coffee, pepper, ginger and turmeric. The town of Kumily is still a busy spice-trading centre and its bazaar has many stores selling local spices and chocolate made from local cocoa. Near the bus stand, I made an afternoon tea of sweet treats sold off tea and coffee stalls. These included a popular rural snack called *chakka kumbla* (jackfruit blended with rice flour, cumin, cardamom, salt and jaggery, wrapped in cinnamon leaf cones and steamed). The large cinnamon leaves used for this are often called 'bay leaves' but they are from *Cinnamomum tamala*, not the *Laurus nobilis* of European cooking.

....

AYURVEDA

Ayurveda is an ancient system of medicine that has been practised in India for 3000 years. It is often called the 'science as life' as it is a holistic system that considers that mind, body and spirit are inseparable in achieving optimum well-being. Ayurveda is practised throughout India, but it has a particularly strong association with Kerala because the popular Ayurvedic treatment called *panchakarma*—rigorous fasting and elimination procedures practised over a number of days—originated here. Ayurveda is all about balance; to achieve good health, in mind and body, a person needs to keep three key elements, or *dosha*s (*vatta, pita, kappa*), in equilibrium. Ayurveda works on the premise that individuals ail when their doshas are unbalanced due to unsuitable eating habits, emotional stress, anxiety, climatic conditions and poor posture, among other things, and that healing and vitality is achieved by resetting the natural balance of the doshas. Food plays a vital role in Ayurveda—what is eaten, how it is prepared, the vessels used in cooking and the various combinations of produce, spices and herbs are all considered. For instance, if you are of the vatta type—that is, you have more vatta than pita or kappa—it would be recommended that you avoid dry, salty foods and eat sweet, wet carbohydrate-rich food to realign your doshas and alleviate any physical or psychological problems you might be experiencing. The construction of a meal based on Ayurvedic principles requires that a balance be sought between sweet, salty, bitter, pungent and astringent tastes—a principle that underlies the inclusion of the side dishes of pickles, chutneys and crunchy items served at most Indian meals.

Recommendations

If you want a first-hand experience of genuine Ayurveda practice, you might like to stay at **Kalari Kovilakom**. While it is housed in a beautifully restored palace surrounded by green lawns and luxuriant garden beds, this is no frivolous holiday resort. Guests undergo a thorough Ayurvedic examination after which they are prescribed a course of treatments and an individual diet based on body type. Each guest is served food designed to ease diagnosed imbalances in his or her system. All the food is vegetarian and cooked in traditional stone or bell-metal pots over low heat. There is no roasting or deep-frying, and very little oil, salt and chilli are used. This might sound quite restrictive but the food prepared and served at Kalari is the haute cuisine of Ayurvedic cooking. What is used in abundance are seasonal vegetables and organic whole grains, nuts, local spices and tropical fruit. All eating and drinking utensils are fashioned from bell metal as its 'purity' is believed to confer health benefits. A meal is artistically laid out on a thali with a variety of vegetable dishes—perhaps cucumber lightly cooked with chana dal; beans cooked with freshly grated coconut; thin slices of white pumpkin poached in coconut milk and moong dal; and lemon soup served with red rice and delicate wholewheat rotis. You have to make a commitment to stay for a few days at Kalari during which time you cannot have meat, tea, coffee or alcohol so it's not for the faint-hearted. From my own experience I can say that if you do stay you will come away feeling lighter, physically and mentally, and a stay at Kalari might just be the perfect way to end your culinary exploration of India.

Kollengode, Palakkad
(04923) 263737
www.kalarikovilakom.com

SELECTED READING

COOKBOOKS

Here is a list of regional Indian cookbooks that I enjoy cooking from and which I recommend to you here.

Abdulla, U. *Malabar Muslim Cookery*. New Delhi: Orient Black Swan, 2009.

Ammal, S.M. *The Best of Samaithu Paar: The Classic Guide to Tamil Cuisine*. New Delhi: Viking, 2001.

Bhatnagar, S., and R.K. Saxena. *Dastarkhwan-e-Awadh*. New Delhi: HarperCollins, 2006.

Das Gupta, M., B. Gupta and J. Chaliha. *The Calcutta Cookbook*. New Delhi: Penguin Books, 1995.

Das, J. *Ambrosia . . . From the Assamese Kitchen*. New Delhi: Rupa & Co., 2008.

Gill, P. *Panjabi Cooking*. New Delhi: Sterling, 1998.

Giri, J., and P. Jain. *Cooking at Home with Pedatha: Vegetarian Recipes from a Traditional Andhra Kitchen*. Chennai: Pritya, 2005.

Hauzel, H. *The Essential North-East Cookbook*. New Delhi: Penguin Books, 2003.

Husain, S. *The Emperor's Table*. New Delhi: Roli Books, 2008.

Kannampilly, V. *The Essential Kerala Cookbook*. New Delhi: Penguin Books, 2003.

Kottukappally, T.J. *Syrian Christian Favourites*. Kerala: Dee Bee INFO Publications.

Kuttaiah, R.J. *Cuisine from Coorg*. New Delhi: Sterling, 2000.

Latif, B. *The Essential Andhra Cookbook*. New Delhi: Penguin Books, 1999.

Mahale, P. *Ishtann: The Best of Goan Saraswat Cuisine*. Goa: Printers Devil, 2009.

Manekshaw, B.J. *Parsi Food and Customs*. New Delhi: Penguin Books, 1996.

Mangaldas, A. *Bhojan no Anand* (series on traditional Gujarati food) available at www.houseofmg.com/cookbooks

Menezes, M.T. *The Essential Goa Cookbook*. New Delhi: Penguin Books, 2000.

Narain, P. *The Essential Delhi Cookbook*, New Delhi: Penguin Books, 2000.

Natarajan, P., and V. Varadarajan. *Classic Tamil Brahmin Cuisine*. Chennai: Orient Enterprise, 2009.

O'Brien, C. *Recipes from an Urban Village: A Cookbook from Basti Hazrat Nizamuddin*. Delhi: The Hope Project, 2003.

Singh, D. *Cooking Delights of the Maharajas*. Mumbai: Vakils, Feffer & Simons Pvt. Ltd, 2002.

Rajalakshmi, U.B. *Udupi Cuisine*. Bengaluru: Prism Books, 2010.

Rai, R. *Tandoor: The Great Indian Barbeque*. New Delhi: Viking, 2006.

Rasheed, Khader R., R. Joseph and S. Pushpanath. *Malabar Cuisine*, Kerala: Dee Bee INFO Publications.

GENERAL READING

The list below includes more general reading on Indian food, culture and history.

Achaya, K.T. *Indian Food: A Historical Companion*. Delhi: Oxford University Press, 1994.

Albinia, A. *Empires of the Indus*. Great Britain: John Murray, 2009.

Banerji, C. *Life and Food in Bengal*. New Delhi: Rupa & Co., 1993.

Collingham, L. *Curry: A Biography*. London: Chatto & Windus, 2005.

Dumont, L. *Homo Hierarchicus: The Caste System and Its Implications*. Chicago: The University of Chicago Press, 1980.

Glancey, J. *Nagaland: A Journey to India's Forgotten Frontier*. London: Faber and Faber, 2011.

Keay, J. *India: A History*. London: HarperCollins, 2001.

Keay, J. *The Spice Route*. Great Britain: John Murray, 2005.

Kosambi, D.D. *The Culture & Civilisation of Ancient India in Historical Outline*. London: Routledge and Kegan Paul, 1965.

Lewis, N. *A Goddess in the Stones*. London: Picador, 1999.

Narayan, S. *Monsoon Diary: Reveries and Recipes from South India*. London: Bantam, 2004.

O'Brien, C. *Flavours of Delhi: A Food Lover's Guide*. New Delhi: Penguin Books, 2010.

Roy, N. (ed.) *A Matter of Taste: The Penguin Book of Indian Writing on Food*. New Delhi: Penguin Books, 2004.

Sanjeev, S. *Land of the Seven Rivers: A Brief History of India's Geography*. New Delhi: Viking, 2012.

Subramanian, S. *Following Fish*. New Delhi: Penguin Books, 2010.

BROAD INGREDIENT CATEGORIES

algae/fungus/lichen: *dagad phool*, *kaalpasi*, mushrooms

aquatic life: anchovies, barracuda, *bhetki*, Bombay duck (*bombil*), carp, catfish, clams, crab, crustaceans, *cubbe* (cockles), Dover sole, eels, fish, frogs, grouper, *ilish* (*hilsa*), *kane* (ladyfish), *karimeen* (pearl spot), *koi* (perch), lobsters, mackerel, mussels, octopus, oyster, *parshey*, pomfret, prawns, *rui*, salmon, sardines, sea bass, sea murrel, seer fish, shark, shellfish, shrimps, snapper fish, squid, trout, whitebait

dried fruits: dates, elephant apple, plums, raisins, sultanas

fish: *See* aquatic life

flour: *besan* (chickpea flour), rice flour

flower: *amaltas*, banana, cockscomb, coral jasmine, flame of the forest, *kallupachi*, lotus, mahua, *nagakesara*, rhododendron, rose, roselle, water lily

fruits: *amla* (Indian gooseberry), apple, apricots, banana, barberries, berries, cherries, *chikoo* (sapodilla), coconut, custard apple, figs, *galgal*, grapes, guava, jackfruit, jamun, *kachri*, *ker*, kingfish, kokum, lemon, lychee, mango, melons, musk melon, *omora* (hog plum), oranges, papaya, passion fruit, peach, pears, pineapple, plums, pomegranate, pomelos, pumpkin, quinces, *sangri*, star fruit, stone fruit, sugar cane, sweet lime, tamarind, water melon

grains: barley (*jau*), buckwheat, corn, horse gram, maize, millet (ragi), rice, semolina, sorghum (jowar), wheat

insects/worms: dragonfly larvae, hornets' larvae, insects, leech, red ants, silkworms, snails

leaves: banana, *bathua*, betel, canna plant, colocasia, coriander, curry leaves, fenugreek, *gongura*, *jhakya*, lettuce, *lomba*, mint, mustard, oak, onion, *pabri*, pumpkin, radish, spinach, sugar beet, turmeric, *xaak*

legumes: black-eyed beans, chickpeas, dal, lentils, red kidney beans (*rajma*), soybean

meat: beef, buffalo, chicken, dog, duck, goat, ham, junglefowl, lamb, mice, monkey, mutton, partridge, pigeon, pigs, pork, quail, rabbit, rats, wild boar milk products: butter, buttermilk (*chhachh*), cheese, *chhena*, cream, curd, ghee, *khoya*, paneer, whey

nuts: almonds, betel, cashews, chestnuts, peanuts, pistachios, walnuts

oil: canola, coconut, linseed, mustard, olive, sandalwood, sesame, sunflower

plants/shrubs/trees: *amaranthus*, *anthur*, arrowroot, basil, cassava, *ching*, ferns, herbs, lemongrass, *lengmaster*, neem, oak, palm, paw-paw, sago palm, sea buckthorn, stink bean, tapioca

roots/shoots/tubers: bamboo shoots, beetroot, carrot, colocasia (taro), ginger, lotus, potato, radish, sweet potato, yams

seeds: amaranth, bamboo rice, canola, coffee, cotton, fox nuts (*makhana*s), hemp, pomegranate (*anardana*), sesame, poppy

spices: *ajwain* (carom seeds), *amchoor* (dried green-mango powder), aniseed, asafoetida, bay leaf, caraway, cardamom, chillies, cinnamon, cloves, coriander, cumin, fennel, fenugreek, *gandherian*, *jamboo*, mace, mustard, nigella (*kalonji* or *kala jeera*), nutmeg, pepper, rock salt (*kala namak*), saffron, salt, star anise, *tej patta*, turmeric

stem: banana, drumstick, lotus, rhizome

vegetables: beans, cabbage, capsicum, cauliflower, Chinese cabbage, cucumber, eggplant, garlic, gourds, kohlrabi, ladies' fingers, *maratimoggu*, onion, peas, shallot, tamarillo, tomato, *tondli*, turnip

INDEX

380